Gathering

*A Theology and Spirituality of Worship
in Free Church Tradition*

Christopher J. Ellis

scm press

For Marilyn,
with love,
and to the members of Cemetery Road Baptist Church, Sheffield,
with gratitude

© Christopher J. Ellis 2004

British Library Cataloguing in Publication data

A catalogue record for this book is available
from the British Library

0 334 02967 8

First published in 2004 by SCM Press
9–17 St Albans Place, London N1 0NX

www.scm-canterburypress.co.uk

SCM Press is a division of
SCM-Canterbury Press Ltd

Printed and bound in Great Britain by
Biddles Ltd, www.biddles.co.uk

Contents

Part 4 Liturgical Theology   223

Foreword

In the historical study of Christian worship, ecclesial communities that do not rely on ritual texts for the structure and content of their services often get short shrift from liturgical scholars who are accustomed to basing their research in the more permanent and easily accessible materials of missals, sacramentaries, breviaries or Books of Common Prayer. Ecumenically also, such churches tend to receive less attention than they might: when, for instance, Brother Max Thurian and I were compiling a handbook to illustrate 'ecumenical convergence in celebration' in connection with Faith and Order's Lima text on *Baptism, Eucharist and Ministry*, we were at a loss as to how best to represent the free-church traditions. Now Christopher Ellis has remedied this situation, particularly in the case of English Baptists.

From multifarious sources Ellis traces the complexities hidden in the simple statement of the eminent Baptist historian and ecumenist Ernest Payne in 1952: 'The general pattern of church services has remained the same from the seventeenth century to the present: scripture, prayer and sermon, interspersed with hymns.' The story begins with the Separatist exiles under John Smyth and Thomas Helwys in Amsterdam in 1609, whose worship is described in a letter home from a married couple in the congregation, Hughe and Ann Bromhead. The tale passes through the Broadmead Church in Bristol and the Paul's Alley Church in London later in the century. Eighteenth-century patterns are reflected in the Independent Bury Street Church in London, where Isaac Watts was pastor for the first decade, and subsequently in descriptions of baptisms and the Lord's Supper from the 'Church Book' of the Stone Yard Meeting, Cambridge, in the 1760s. William Brock (1807–75), pastor of St Mary's Baptist Church in Norwich and then of the Bloomsbury Chapel in central London, provides evidence for the nineteenth century, followed by the biblical expositions and sermons of C. H. Spurgeon at the Metropolitan Tabernacle. In the mid twentieth century, influences from the Liturgical and Ecumenical Movements were mediated by such as Stephen Winward and Neville Clark, whereas towards the century's end, charismatic styles and technological innovations changed the feel of worship in many Baptist churches.

Ellis's thesis is that the story of Baptist worship reveals what might be called the Baptist soul. He demonstrates an 'embodied spirituality' as he unfolds across the centuries both the continuities and the nuances in the practices and understandings of free prayer, scriptural preaching, congregational song, the dominical meal and the baptismal pool.

Thus the author's historical accounts are set within a theological framework. In his own tradition, he discerns a Baptist theology of worship in terms of heartfelt devotion, attention to the Word of God, the fellowship of believers, and concern for the coming Kingdom. Then, in return, he suggests how a free-church practice and understanding of worship may contribute to the broader ecumenical exercises of allowing worship to inform all Christian theology as well as bringing constructive theological critique to particular patterns and acts of worship. The key category for Ellis, in all instances, is that of a 'community of disciples', gathered under the Lordship of Christ, and dispatched to share in the mission of the Triune God to the world.

On account of both its careful retrieval of the Baptist past in a cultural context and its searching exploration of contemporary questions in the theory and practice of Christian worship, this engagingly written book has much to offer to historians, liturgists, ecumenists and theologians, and I commend it warmly to them all.

Geoffrey Wainwright
Duke University
Easter 2004

Preface

Christian worship is God-ward in focus and communal in nature. It is here that the church faces its nature and its destiny, its pettiness and its glory. Here, culture, as revered tradition and missionary engagement, is called upon to express both the longings of the worshippers and the call of God. Here is challenge and promise, relevance and subculture, human agenda and the Spirit's promptings.

I cannot imagine a richer field of study or a more fertile context for theological reflection. And it is theology which has prompted and sustained the long preparation of this book. Worship provides not only a way of approaching God through the experience of the worshippers, but also a way of knowing God and expressing that knowledge in forms which are at least as valid as the critical methods of what is usually called 'theology'.

Corporate worship is naturally communal, even though it may sometimes be corrupted by individualism, passivity or dysfunctional leadership. Therefore liturgical theology invites collaboration, just as worship invites the various ministries of the body of Christ. Shared worship and intriguing conversations lie behind most of what is here – even though the final flaws are mine. I hope the loose ends, historical gaps and unanswered questions will stimulate others to share in the task of doing theology in the context of free church worship. The form of the study is an exploration of the faith practices and shared values of particular Christian communities, but the enterprise is itself nothing less than a journey into God.

There are many thanks to be gladly offered. Foremost is my gratitude to those local churches which over the years have entrusted me with leading their worship. This trust began when I was a teenager and I now look back in awe at the radical daring of churches inviting an eighteen year old to lead their worship of Almighty God. Special thanks are due to Central Church, Swindon, for the years of ecumenical partnership and mutual enrichment and to Cemetery Road, Sheffield, for the largeness of heart which encompassed different spiritualities and cultures within its evangelical worship and witness. Both churches risked experiment and sought God.

It was Cemetery Road which enabled me to undertake doctoral research at the University of Leeds where I was ably guided and stimulated by my supervisors, Professor Haddon Willmer and Professor Nigel Biggar. During this time, the Baptist Union of Great Britain made it possible for the survey of current worship practices to be undertaken, a project which informs many of the interpretative judgements that lie behind this book. During that time generous grants from the Baptist Union and the Particular Baptist Fund also played their part in making research possible.

Unlike my main dialogue partner, Fr Alexander Schmemann, I believe that worship needs to be continually reformed, though such work must be shaped by a theological vision which arises from within worship itself. I am a practitioner and these reflections are work in progress and reflections on worship in progress.

Many individuals have engaged with the questions with which I have persevered. Revd Dr Roger Hayden stimulated my exploration of Baptist history and Revd David Staple was the pastor who opened my eyes, as a teenager, to liturgical questions. Revd Dr Ruth Gouldbourne, a colleague at Bristol Baptist College, listened and questioned as I was formulating the arguments which shape this book. Professor Paul Fiddes has been a life-long friend and theological inspiration. Revd Myra Blyth, Revd Dr Paul Sheppy, and the various members of the Joint Liturgical Group of Great Britain and of the Baptist Union's Doctrine and Worship Committee have all been stimulating companions in discussions which have been more akin to play than work.

Contacts and conversations with friends around the world have helped me to see British Baptist worship in context and to begin to understand Baptist worship elsewhere. In particular, I am grateful to Revd Nathan Nettleton in Australia and to those who acted as guides and conversation partners during a sabbatical visit to North America, namely Professor Gordon Lathrop, Professor Horace Russell, Professor Barry Morrison, Revd Brad Berglund and Sally Morgenthaler.

Christopher J. Ellis
Pentecost 2004

I

In Search of Faith

An Introduction

Prayer must precede our attendance at the house of God: but little good is to be expected without this. The benefit to be derived from public ordinances depends not so much on intellectual capacity, as on the spirituality of our minds; and nothing tends so effectually to promote this as drawing near to God. There is an intimate connexion between the duties of the closet and those of the family, and between these and those of the house of God. The one pre-pares for the other, and infuses a savour into all that are to follow. If we can but go as hungering and thirsting after righteousness, we shall be filled; but if as rich and needing nothing, we shall be sent empty away . . .

Let your attendance be *regular* and *constant*. Appear not as strangers or as a guest, but like a child at home. Dwell in the house of the Lord all the days of thy life, to behold the beauty of the Lord, and enquire in his temple.

J. W. Morris, June 1805
on behalf of the Northamptonshire Baptist Churches[1]

How do we find out what Christians believe? Should we turn to a pro-fessional theologian, someone who spends their life researching, reflect-ing, analysing and explaining what various Christians down the ages have thought and said about what they believe? Should we approach a minister or priest, someone responsible for helping others understand the truths of the Christian faith? Perhaps we should interview an ordinary Christian, in the hope of a more practical and down-to-earth answer. A scouring of library shelves or the displays of a religious bookshop might help. A study of the creeds will provide us with certain information. Each of these paths is likely to offer some help in understanding what Christians believe. But there is yet another way, the exploration of Christian worship, which can lead us towards a rich appreciation of Christian faith. Worship will not only inform us about the content of Christian believing, but will demonstrate faith's embodiment in prayer, proclamation and the patterns of community life.

The gathering for Christian worship is where Christians express what they believe in a forthright and explicit way. In worship, Christians articulate what they believe, and express it in ways which are often memorable. They use their own words and they use the words of others, often passed down from previous generations. They use actions and gestures to express what cannot easily be put into words. Most importantly, they bring themselves: their hopes and fears, their guilty feelings and their concerns, their gratitude and their longings, their self-examination and their seeking for that which is beyond them. In short, they come to worship God, to seek some kind of communication with divine reality and to ask for help, both for themselves and for a desperately needy world.

In this event of worship we find exposed what the Christian community is concerned about – what it values, what it takes for granted, what it regrets and where it wants to go. In this mixture of lofty thoughts and down-to-earth regrets, the Church states more clearly than anywhere else what, as a community, it stands for. Worship is embodied theology.

This book does not explore Christian worship as an end in itself – because the end of worship should always be God. Rather, it goes in search of God, or at least what Christians believe about God, through an exploration of worship. It is written in search of faith, seeking to discover the heart of Christian believing.

All human experience is marked by a tension between how things might be, or should be, and how things really are. Worship is no exception. It is supposed to be about what God wants, but often it is about what the worshippers want. The focus should be the divine will, yet often consumers gather, ready yet again to assert their requirements and express their choices. How can we learn from this messiness? How can we explore not only worship as it is, but the possibilities for transcendence, the possibilities of recognizing the glory of God amidst human striving and wilfulness? And what of that believing? How can we test the beliefs and values which are expressed in worship in such a way that we can agree about who God is and what God is like? How can we agree about what it means to be a Christian, about how we should act and what we should pray for?

This is the work of theology. We need to clarify and examine, but we also need to celebrate and explore. Because worship is embodied theology, we need some anatomy lessons before we can undertake a physical examination. Our aim is to understand the living reality of worship, and as in any medical examination we will require both honesty and a respect for the subject. We will also need to ensure that the examination does not develop into a post-mortem!

In John Updike's novel *Couples*, a biochemist explains his work to a fellow guest at a dinner party. 'I used to slice up starfish extremely thin, to study their metabolism.' He is asked, 'And then do they survive in two dimensions?' but he laughs and replies, 'No, they die. That's the trouble with my field. Life hates being analysed.'[2]

Life needs to be celebrated more than it needs to be examined. Yet there is also a place for examination: study can lead not only to greater understanding but also to a greater sense of wonder.

This book offers a study of Christian worship as a way of learning more about God and our experience of God. But this is what worship is really about. It is the celebrating of God, a journey into the mystery of divine love.

Gathering for Worship

Worship stands at the heart of the Christian community. This is doubly true because the word 'worship' has a double meaning. First, the word refers to that attitude of heart and mind which is the only appropriate attitude of a creature toward its creator. In this sense 'worship' implies wonder and humility, attention and obedience, confession and self-offering. Such worship is not contained within the walls of a church building and is not restricted to what happens within a worship 'service'. Indeed this root meaning of 'worship' is an attitude of life and a way of being Christian:

> I appeal to you therefore, brothers and sisters, by the mercies of God, to present your bodies as a living sacrifice, holy and acceptable to God, which is your spiritual worship. (Romans 12.1)

This mixture of praise and submission will obviously undergird all that follows. To believe in God is to open ourselves to a relationship of dependence and awe, and if those sentiments are sincere and deep they will impinge on every part of living. However, that is how things *ought* to be, when we are being logical or healthy. In reality, we get side-tracked, deflected and self-absorbed and need specific opportunities to focus on God in a worshipful and 'awestruck' way. This is where worship as a particular event, at an agreed time and in an agreed place, becomes so important. This is the second, and most common, use of the word 'worship' – an occasion when what should be true *all* the time becomes true for a short time. So in gathering for worship, we offer God praise and gratitude, we confess our sins and express our longings, we pray for the world and dedicate ourselves to God's service. These things are the very stuff of Christian living and need to be true all the time, but they are not. In gathering for worship we face up to who we really are and who God really is.

Prayer will be a *part* of this worship event, but prayer also offers us an illustration of the link between these two dimensions of worship. We always live in the presence of God, yet in prayer we give our attention to that presence in a focused and persistent way. We think about what God is like. We may also talk to God and, in our better moments, listen to God. When the prayer is over, we may be changed and the world may be changed. Something has happened: we have acted out our relationship with God in a way that is truthful. In some small way we have aligned ourselves to God's will and we have attempted to influence others by our praying for them.

These things are also true about worship, but there is a significant difference. Worship is a communal event. It is something which Christians do together. In fact, it is the central activity of the Christian Church. There are, of course, other things which the Church is called to do, such as share the good news of Jesus Christ in word and action – what is usually called 'mission'. But worship is the *central* activity of the Church because it is here that what it believes is most clearly expressed and it is here that it regularly encounters God and is confronted with what God has done in the past and what God has promised for the future.

Worship is the primary event for which the community gathers and is the activity in which its beliefs are most comprehensively and consistently expressed. While groups will gather for study or mutual support, while teams will gather to share in service to the world, it is in worship that the largest gatherings occur. Size isn't everything, but the largest gathering of people will tell us something about where that community puts its priorities. And rightly so. The Reformed theologian Jean-Jacques von Allmen explains:

> by its worship the Church becomes itself, becomes conscious of itself, and confesses itself as a distinct entity. Worship thus allows the Church to emerge in its true nature.[3]

We can only understand the true nature of the Church in terms of its relationship to God because it is God's community. Von Allmen argues that the Greek word *ekklesia*, which is translated in the English New Testament as 'church', was used by the earliest Christian writers because it had been used in the Septuagint to translate the Hebrew *qâhâl* which refers to the 'assembly' of Israel.[4] This assembly, he suggests, was primarily an assembly for worship, whether before the tabernacle in the wilderness or in the temple in Jerusalem. Not only does the Church gather to worship God, but that very gathering for worship gives the Church its name!

But there is even more in the name, because *ekklesia* literally means 'called out'. The Church gathers for worship, and indeed exists in the first place, because it is called by God – gathered by God. When we talk about 'gathering for worship' we should think not only in terms of people deciding to gather, though that is important, but of God inviting and gathering people in order to be the people of God, his *ekklesia*. As the author of 1 Peter affirms:

> You are a chosen race, a royal priesthood, a holy nation, God's own people, in order that you may proclaim the mighty acts of him who called you out of darkness into his marvellous light. (1 Peter 2.9)

Worship is the place where the Church is gathered by God and becomes *ekklesia*; the place where God's Word is encountered communally and where the Church is confronted by its divine vocation.

Face to Face

Worship is a gathering with a purpose. It is a meeting in which people encounter one another and plan to encounter God. Here relationships will be expressed and nurtured, and it is hoped that the gathering will 'make a difference'. Consequently, worship is best seen as an event, a 'happening' in which encounters take place and in which transactions occur. Worshippers have an effect on one another, for good or ill. More importantly, they hope to encounter God and when this happens they are likely to be changed by the experience.

How can human beings dare to expect the divine presence to be available on demand each Sunday morning? There is something very presumptuous in this. Yet this is not quite as daring as it might seem, so long as we see the gathering as a gathering *by* God of worshippers who truly seek to worship.

Of course, 'truly' is a qualitative word. It assumes not only the action of gathering, or the uttering of praise, but an integrity of behaviour in which heart and action are one. Sincerity will be a theme to which we shall return more than once. Here, it is a reminder that our exploration of what worship might mean must take account of human frailty and sin, because little from the human side can be taken for granted. However, a great deal can be taken for granted with God because God does the inviting and has promised to turn up and meet the worshippers! As the psalmist summoned Israel not only to worship God but to share in an encounter, so Christians have continued to use these words as a reminder of God's invitation to meet in worship:

> O come, let us sing to the Lord;
> let us make a joyful noise to the rock of our salvation!
> Let us come into his presence with thanksgiving;
> let us make a joyful noise to him with songs of praise!
> . . .
> O come, let us worship and bow down,
> let us kneel before the Lord our Maker!
> For he is our God,
> and we are the people of his pasture,
> and the sheep of his hand. (Psalm 95.1–2, 6–7)

Similarly, Matthew reports the promise of Jesus Christ which has often been interpreted as a promise related to worship: 'For where two or three are gathered in my name, I am there among them' (Matthew 18.20). Whatever the original context of this saying, its continuing interpretation as a promise about worship ensures that this expectation – that when believers gather for worship Jesus will be present through the work of the Spirit – is based on a belief in the goodness of God rather than an assumption about the worthiness of the worshippers.

In addition, gathering 'in the name of Jesus' provides a profound character to the proceedings which goes far deeper than the headline claim might suggest. To gather 'in the name of Jesus' means the worshippers aligning with the will of Jesus revealed in Scripture; it means that the proceedings and the relationships should somehow carry Christ-like characteristics. To gather in this way will inevitably result in some kind of change, as worshippers pattern themselves after the Jesus in whose name they gather.

But to see worship as a meeting between God and the worshippers is to make a very bold claim. 'The presence of God' can be a rather woolly idea and can sometimes mean little more than an awareness of some kind of 'divine ethos'. To speak of worship as a meeting with God, an encounter with the creator of the universe, is to be much more ambitious. Yet this is what we mean by Christian worship: *an encounter in which*

God and humanity are active participants and in which 'something' happens. In other words, worship is an event in which there is a different state of affairs afterwards than there was before. How this might happen remains to be seen, and our study of worship will need to grapple with this question as we explore not only what Christians believe about *worship*, but what that worship tells us of what Christians believe about God.

Thinking about God through Thinking about Worship

What follows is an example of 'liturgical theology'. We shall explore the beliefs of the Christian community through a study of its worship practices. As a distinct discipline, liturgical theology is relatively recent, though arguably we can find examples of it in the early Church.[5] Chapter 2 tackles the question of method: how are we to study worship in such a way as to uncover its theological meaning?

Chapter 3 introduces the particular church tradition which will provide the case study for our reflections. If worship embodies theology, then we have to recognize that it is particular, concrete examples of worship which need to be examined. The specific practices we shall study are those of the Baptist denomination, and some explanation is needed as to why these in particular. While a relatively small group in Britain, Baptists are a significant part of the world Church, with an assessed community roll of over 100 million.[6] However, their story began in England and the community developed many of its present characteristics while taking root in the soil of English history. They also have a significance beyond their size, as they bridge two streams of the world Church. On the one hand, in Britain and many parts of the world, they are active, though sometimes awkward, participants in the mainstream ecumenical movement. On the other hand, they are avowedly evangelical in theology and practice and maintain many links with Christian groups who have little to do with such ecumenical concerns.

Baptists are also one of the denominations which may be seen as representing what has been called 'the Free Church Tradition'. In the study of Christian worship this is significant for two reasons. First, their worship may be described as 'free worship' in the sense that no prayer book will be used, other than as an occasional resource for the worship leader. We shall see that this creates complications for its study and so will need to develop a method which can take account of this challenge. Second, attempts to reflect on the theology of Free Church worship are distinctly thin on the ground. Indeed, it has been argued that liturgical studies have been dominated by those Christian traditions which are sometimes called 'liturgical' rather than 'free' and that there is a need to develop ways of understanding the free worship of the Free Churches.[7]

The ecumenical significance of this should not be overlooked. It is important to understand any community within that community's own terms of reference, and this applies to worship as much as to anything else. Through exploring this example of Free Church and evangelical worship, we shall be exploring ways of studying and understanding similar worship in other Free Church and evangelical communities. Baptist history is intertwined with Congregationalists and Methodists, with independent evangelicals and revivalists, as well as with charismatic Christians of various denominations. Baptists have known persecution, growth and decline and have responded to changing circumstances in ways both similar and dissimilar to the response of other Christians. This book will engage with voices and insights from across the Christian Church and will attempt both to interpret this free worship and to engage in dialogue with worship traditions which are very different.

Part 2 tells the story of free worship through the ups and downs of the Baptists' history and explores the distinct spirituality of free worship as expressed in this particular community. Part 3 examines the building-blocks of worship and unpacks the spirituality which is expressed through prayer, preaching, singing and sacraments. Part 4 reflects on the living faith which has been expressed in this free worship and assesses its theological and ecumenical significance. It also reflects on the nature of worship and begins to ask how theology might guide its practice and renewal.

To Whom it May Concern

Such a broad agenda runs the risk of offering too little to too many. However, if worship is indeed the central event in the life of the Church, then it will reflect and influence many aspects of the Church's life. To place worship in a box and study it in a narrow and detailed way is even more risky than our broad approach and may kill the subject in order to study it under the microscope. This book sees worship as something which is alive – a moving target which can only be studied in motion, a living reality which can only be truly presented when its living relation-ships within the community are taken seriously. This is bold talk, but a bold attempt may be more interesting than a safe, but narrow, study.

Consequently, various groups will find some, or all, of this book of interest. Those interested in Christian worship, both liturgists and practitioners, will find discussions of theology, history and method. Baptists and members of the Free Churches will find much material on the spirituality of free worship, as well as an introduction to some spiritual giants of previous ages who deserve to be rediscovered. Those concerned to develop an evangelical theology of worship will also find resources in these pages, as will those concerned that the ecumenical forum be enriched by such voices as those of John Bunyan and John Fawcett, Isaac Watts and William Brock, Charles Haddon Spurgeon and Henry Wheeler Robinson. But we will also hear Orthodox, Catholic and Anglican voices, as this study of Free Church worship is undertaken in partnership with the whole community of God's people.

Part 1

Worship as Theology

2

The Invitation of Liturgical Theology

Come Thou fount of every blessing,
    Tune my heart to sing Thy grace;
Streams of mercy never ceasing
    Call for songs of loudest praise.
Teach me some melodious measure,
    Sung by flaming tongues above.
O the vast, the boundless treasure,
    Of my Lord's unchanging love!

Here I raise my Ebenezer,
    Hither by Thy help I come,
And I hope, by Thy good pleasure,
    Safely to arrive at home.
Jesus sought me when a stranger,
    Wandering from the fold of God;
He, to rescue me from danger,
    Interposed His precious blood.

O to grace how great a debtor
    Daily I'm constrained to be!
Let that grace, Lord, like a fetter
    Bind my wandering heart to Thee.
Prone to wander – Lord, I feel it –
    Prone to leave the God I love:
Here's my heart, O take and seal it,
    Seal it from Thy courts above.

Robert Robinson, 1735–90[1]

There is more than one way of doing theology, and liturgical theology shares with a number of other disciplines a way of working which is distinct from what many would see as the traditional methods of theology. In the 'traditional' approach, although it is arguably not as traditional as some might suppose, theology is seen as a set of beliefs, a creed which is explained and then applied in Christian living.

There is, of course, much truth in this approach, but it is not the only way to do theology. To begin with theological truth and to move to its application, is to use a thought process called 'deduction'. It moves from truth to consequence, from belief to implementation. By contrast, liturgical theology works, at least partly, by the reverse thought process known as 'induction', where we begin with a situation and from our observation draw out its meaning. In science, deduction is the thought process of the mathematician proving a theorem, beginning with axioms and moving through logical argument to proof. Conversely, induction is the thought process through which scientists develop a theory to make sense of some happening in nature which they have observed. In liturgical theology we observe the worship practices of a community and then draw from them what we perceive to be their theological meaning. Worship is embodied theology. We can observe what is done and listen to what is said and build a picture of what a particular worshipping community believes. This is not as strange as it may seem and two examples from other areas of theology will show similar examples of inductive thinking.

First, the word 'spirituality' is slippery and is used in various ways and in a variety of settings. It is not, of course, a specifically Christian word and can refer to the spirituality of any religion or, indeed, of no religion at all. Sometimes it seems to suggest a vague idea of self-improvement or, at least, self-discovery. By contrast, in some Christian circles it can be defined very tightly, only referring to the devotional life of prayer. The browser in a Christian bookshop can reasonably expect the spirituality section to yield manuals on prayer, books on Ignatian spirituality, guides to meditation or journalling and other activities of the personal, devotional life. However, they may be surprised if, in that same section, they encounter books on theology or reflections on how to behave in the workplace!

Yet prayer alone offers us too narrow an understanding of spirituality and I believe that Philip Sheldrake offers us a more healthy and inclusive definition:

> Spirituality is understood to include not merely the techniques of prayer but, more broadly, a conscious relationship with God, in Jesus Christ, through the indwelling of the Spirit and in the context of the community of believers. Spirituality is, therefore, concerned with the conjunction of theology, prayer and practical Christianity.[2]

Here is a holistic understanding of spirituality which embraces far more than just prayer. The interaction of theology, prayer and practical Christianity – what Christians think in respect of God, how and what they pray, and how they act *as Christians*. From a Christian perspective, what is being referred to is 'life in the Spirit' or 'life in relationship with God', an affirmation that the whole of life is affected by being a Christian and that God cannot be placed in a prayer compartment, separate from the actions and thoughts of the believer. In this sense, spirituality is embodied – it has an historical actuality in the world. Sheldrake comments that particular traditions of spirituality 'are initially embodied in people rather than doctrine and grow out of life rather than from abstract ideas'.[3] Consequently, the way in which contemporary students of spirituality set about their task is by doing history. In other words, they work inductively, discovering spiritual traditions by examining the life of communities which embody and pass on those traditions.

This is quite similar to the way in which we shall explore worship as embodied theology. In worship, we find a bringing together of what Christians believe, examples of their praying and various liturgical actions. These thoughts, prayers and actions interact so that we can even say that the gathering for worship is itself an expression of communal spirituality.

Second, we can see a parallel in the discipline of 'practical theology'. This area of theology is concerned with the interaction between theology and life. In recent years, exponents have developed a method of reflecting on situations which is sometimes called 'the pastoral cycle', in which the facts are established and examined before theological reflection takes place and future action is ascertained.[4] Again, this uses an inductive thought process from experience to reflection.

Yet, as we shall see, inductive reflection will also need critical and deductive scrutiny. The results of reflection will need to be tested against existing criteria – what we might call 'orthodoxy' – just as a spiritual tradition will need to be tested for its compliance with what the wider Christian community believes. Later in this chapter, we shall see how the reflection on worship practices also requires critical scrutiny and theological analysis. But first, we shall examine the methods of liturgical theology and try to establish how, and to what extent, the inductive flow from worship to theology can take place.

What is Liturgical Theology?

The recent development of liturgical theology is one of the fruits of the Liturgical Movement. Although this renewal movement has had a focus in worship, it has been far more than simply a movement to reform worship[5] and has gathered and encouraged a number of concerns which find expression in worship: both a concern for community in the life of the churches and a commitment to the use of accessible language, from a rediscovery of the Bible by some to a rediscovery of the Eucharist by most.[6] With these themes has come a renewed interest in history and the study of liturgical developments. Historical study has played an important part in all this, as people have sought to uncover the liturgical life of seemingly authoritative earlier ages.[7] Liturgical studies are far wider than simply the study of early liturgies, but this historical work has focused and supported the wider work of liturgical revision, the renewal of congregational life and, especially, the development of theological reflection on worship and the Church. This reflection is important because there needs to be a way of determining *how* worship might be revised. A way needs to be found to avoid either a slavish copying of the past or an inappropriate submission to the spirit of the present age.[8] Liturgical theology attempts to guide us through this dilemma.

However, the term 'liturgical theology' is used in a variety of ways. Sometimes it has been used interchangeably with the term 'theology of worship', but in what follows the two terms are going to be contrasted rather than equated. As early as 1955, the French liturgist Louis Bouyer distinguished between the two. He complained of those authors who interpret the liturgy by imposing 'ready-made explanations which pay little or no attention to what the liturgy says about itself'.[9] Alexander Schmemann soon built on this insight and continued to develop it throughout his life, becoming its foremost exponent until his death in 1983.[10] He argued that liturgical theology is an independent discipline, with its own methods, and that it is to be distinguished from what he called 'the theology of the liturgy'. An extended extract from an essay written not long before his death states his views most clearly:

> I designate by 'theology of the liturgy' all study of the church's cult in which this cult is analyzed, understood and defined in its 'essence' as well as in its 'forms' with the help of and in terms of theological categories and concepts which are exterior to the cult itself, that is, to its liturgical *specificity*. In this case, in other words, the liturgy is 'subordinated' to, if not subject to, theology because it receives from theology its 'meaning' as well as the definition of its place and function within the church.
>
> . . . Liturgical theology, on the other hand, is based upon the recognition that the liturgy in its totality is not only an 'object' of theology, but above all its source, and this by virtue of the liturgy's essential ecclesial function: i.e., that of revealing by the means which are proper to it (and which belong only to it) the faith of the church; in other words, of being that *lex orandi* in which the *lex credendi* finds its principal criterion and standard.[11]

He has two distinct complaints about what he calls 'theology of the liturgy', or what I shall call 'a theology of worship'. First, it uses theological principles which have been developed away from worship, such as in a systematic theology, and uses this alien material to interpret worship. Second, he complains that in this process, worship is subordinated to the judgements and analysis of this theology.

Schmemann is critical of critical theology. He believes that the theology embodied in worship carries an authority which needs to be recognized and which is in fact a source of the whole theological enterprise. As we shall see, these views are very consistent with his being an Orthodox theologian, a Christian tradition which not only gives a high place to the authority of Tradition, but sees the Liturgy as the main vehicle through which that Tradition is passed on. He is critical of what he calls 'Scholasticism' both within Orthodoxy and within the Roman Catholic Church. By this he means the use of theology as rational analysis which deals irreverently with the mystery of God's revelation. It is true that up to the time when Bouyer and Schmemann were first writing, Roman Catholic theology tended to deal with the theology of the sacraments as an aspect of systematic theology rather than as a subject which grew out of a study of the liturgy itself. While sympathetic to Schmemann's concerns, there are challenges and modifications which will need to be registered. For now, we may note with approval his concern that worship should gain its own theological voice.

Schmemann claims that historically, as well as theologically, worship comes before theology. He quotes the old Latin tag *lex orandi lex credendi* in support of this. But even here his Orthodox position is clear. The phrase derives from the Anti-Pellagian writings of Prosper of Aquitaine, and much recent debate has centred around what is a correct reading of Prosper's argument. In fact, little is proved by establishing what Prosper actually wrote, illuminating though it is. For our purposes, the way in which people quote Prosper illustrates both their denominational allegiances and their respective views on the relationship between theology and worship. Schmemann actually paraphrases Prosper by adding an *est* – the rule of prayer *is* the rule of believing. In other words, what is expressed in worship becomes the basis and norm for what the Church is to believe – theology flows *from* worship. The Roman Catholic liturgist Aidan Kavanagh, greatly influenced by Schmemann, also asserts this through an exact quotation of Prosper, though arguably without full attention to his wider argument: *ut legem credendi lex statuat supplicandi*. 'The law of worshipping founds the law of believing . . . The old maxim means what it says.'[12] In contrast, the Methodist Geoffrey

Wainwright observes that the *lex orandi* has played a more normative role in the Roman Catholic, and we might add Orthodox, traditions than it has within Protestantism where the *lex credendi* has exercised 'almost absolute control' over liturgical life. He argues that Protestantism has largely held that theology should control worship and what is expressed in it.[13]

The appeal by Schmemann and others to the Latin tag alerts us to the fact that there is a long tradition of recognizing a flow of thought between worship and theology. It does not, however, settle the matter of where authority is to lie between them.[14] Using Baptist worship as a case study for doing liturgical theology in a Free Church context will enable us to see some of the difficulties of giving uncritical authority to the theology embodied in worship. The free nature of that worship requires that there be norms and guidelines which will ensure that the worship indeed expresses what the Christian community believes. However, the relationship of theology to worship is more complex, or richer, than a simple either/or argument can sustain, and this encourages us to explore the ways in which theology can be an expression of faith.

What Kind of Theology is Liturgical Theology?

What is being claimed for liturgical theology can be illustrated by the distinction which some wish to make between what they call *primary theology* and *secondary theology*.[15] The argument here is not so much about the priority of theology, within or outside worship, but the subject of theological reflection and the mode in which that theology operates. In Schmemann's view, Western rationalism led to the construction of 'an *objective* or *scientific* theology' in which faith was identified with propositions rather than experience.

> Yet it is precisely faith *as experience*, the total and living experience of the Church, that constitutes the source and the context of theology in the East ... It is 'description' more than 'definition' ... Its criteria lie not in formal and, therefore, autonomous 'authorities,' but in its adequacy to and consistency with the inner life and experience of the Church ... For the faith which founds the Church and by which she lives is not a mere assent to a 'doctrine,' but her living relationship to certain events.[16]

These events are the incarnation, the death, resurrection and exaltation of Jesus Christ and the gift of the Spirit at Pentecost. Schmemann argues that the Church is 'a constant "witness" and "participant" of these events', and that this experience of God is mediated through the Church's liturgy in her *lex orandi*. The task of theology is therefore to describe this experience of God, this 'epiphany' in worship. This raises two important questions.

First, what is the main focus of liturgical theology? David Fagerberg argues that its subject matter is God, humanity and the world, and their interrelationship, rather than liturgy. He states the argument clearly and robustly in the striking statement, 'Liturgy is theological precisely because here is where God's revelation occurs steadfastly.'[17] In this, he follows Schmemann who insists that liturgical theology is primarily about *God*, rather than about worship. Such claims suggest a further distinction, already hinted at in our introduction, between liturgical theology and a theology of worship – while the focus of a theology of worship will be worship itself, the focus of liturgical theology will be the Church's faith in God which has been manifested in worship.

Second, what kind of theological activity is liturgical theology? As a form of communal spirituality, worship both expresses the faith of the believing community and provides a place of encounter with God and the challenges of the Kingdom. In this view, liturgical theology is seen as the exposition of the faith of the Church which is embodied in the event of worship and, as an exposition, is described by some liturgical theologians as 'primary theology'. This is distinguished from 'secondary theology' which, they argue, scientifically analyses and tends to reify that which it studies. We may fruitfully compare this to the relatively recent concern among some theologians that theology be undertaken in the context of prayer.[18]

While there is a very strong bias towards *theologia prima* in Schmemann's writings, some theologians have seen both modes as potentially valuable. Sally McFague, in her examination of the use of models in theology, equates primary and secondary language with 'metaphorical language' and 'conceptual language' respectively and argues for their interdependence.[19] In this both/and view, secondary language, with its critical distance from the object of its reflection, is seen as the language of *explanation*. Primary language is seen as more evocative, using metaphors in its exploration of reality and its expression of faith.[20] David Power comments on the distinction between what he calls the 'theoretical' and the 'symbolic':

> the Christian community needs a language through use of which it can express
> an objective study and understanding of revelation, and also a language which

can incite it to respond intersubjectively to God's call and to dispose of itself to God. It is this latter which ought to be the language of liturgy. The value of the liturgical is its capacity to transmit that Christian experience, deeply felt and demanding, in which God makes his claims upon us.[21]

Such a distinction assumes a valid role for both primary and secondary theology. As well as the need for 'communicating intersubjective experience', Power remarks that there is the task of 'explaining what that experience is all about'.[22] Such an inclusive approach will value both the things which are affirmed in worship, with their exposition in liturgical theology, and their critical analysis and explanation.

Schmemann is not without his critics when he argues that liturgy should not be subordinate to dogmatic theology.[23] For example, Maxwell Johnson suggests that Schmemann's apparent equating of liturgical theology with catechesis implies a theological model which 'is much closer to preaching than it is to lecturing'.[24] Similarly, Kevin Irwin criticizes Aidan Kavanagh for what he argues is a 'liturgical fundamentalism' in which he claims that 'Kavanagh betrays an approach to liturgy that is so concerned to theologize from the Church's euchology that he avoids offering any critique of the present liturgical rites.'[25] The relationship between critical theology and worship will have to remain an area for negotiation as worship is studied in a tradition very different from Orthodoxy, with different understandings of the relative authority of Scripture and Tradition. Schmemann was also concerned that a 'theology of the liturgy' is usually based on principles established in systematic theology away from worship. However, a more interactive relationship between liturgical theology and its critical evaluation might go some way towards addressing this concern. We shall keep these questions in mind as we develop a method for studying Free Church worship and when we come to review our progress at the end of this work.

All worship, to some extent, is influenced by secondary theology. This is especially true within Protestantism in general, and the Free Churches in particular. Whether through ecclesiastical canons, the education and training of ministers, or simply the theological framework of the worship leaders of a congregation, secondary reflection and analysis is always going to affect what is done and said in worship. Indeed, the Anglican liturgist Paul Bradshaw observes that 'both in the past and in the present liturgical texts and rubrics are often themselves the products of *theologia secunda*, compositions deliberately intended to reflect some previously articulated doctrinal position'.[26]

This should not lead to a rejection of the categories of primary and secondary theology in themselves, so much as a recognition of the subtle modes within which theology is called to operate. Even Schmemann engaged in secondary theology, or the theology of liturgy, in the very act of arguing for liturgical theology. His claims that worship is an expression of the Church and that it has an eschatological nature, appear to be examples of a theology of worship.

Schmemann's preference for what others call 'primary theology' reflects, as we have seen, his Orthodox belief that worship is a manifestation of Tradition and as such has an authority for the Church's believing. He is reluctant to give analytical theology an authority over that Tradition. There is an illuminating parallel between this attitude to Tradition manifested in worship and the attitude of some Evangelicals in their approach to the Bible. An earlier generation of Evangelical scholars were more inclined to engage in 'lower criticism' which clarified the text of Scripture than they were to engage in 'higher criticism' which seemed to submit Scripture to the authority of the critic. It is interesting to reflect on this parallel in the light of Schmemann's own use of biblical theology as an analogy for the function of liturgical theology.[27] The emphatic statement of his views may well in part be the result of his attempting to swim against what he considered to be the very strong tide of Western rationalism. Nonetheless, his insistence that worship reveals what the Church believes can encourage us to explore worship in order to uncover and understand these beliefs. As Kevin Irwin explains, 'In essence, liturgy is an *act of theology*, an act whereby the believing Church addresses God, enters into a dialogue with God, makes statements about its belief in God and symbolizes this belief through a variety of means . . . '[28]

Beginning with Worship

How are we to begin to understand the theology implicit in Christian worship? If a theological explanation is not to be developed apart from worship, as Schmemann feared it often is, then we must begin with worship itself.

What does this mean? We will not begin with a generalized, or abstract, statement about worship but with descriptions of actual worship. In most cases this will be the worship of particular denominational groups because this is how worship is usually celebrated and experienced – it will be Orthodox worship, Roman Catholic, Anglican, Pentecostal or Baptist worship. Even to speak of 'Free Church worship' has its dangers, as we shall see in the next chapter. Liturgical theology needs to concern itself with the explication of particular acts of worship and not general statements drawn from a theology which has been developed in a non-liturgical setting. But before we examine what such a strategy will mean in practice, two further observations on Schmemann's approach might be helpful.

First, particular acts of worship do not seem to mean for Schmemann particular occasions, with all the variables which will characterize any specific worship event.[29] Even though he is keen to recognize that worship is more than the text printed and read aloud, he seems to draw on celebrations of the Divine Liturgy in general as being specific enough, rather than attempting to analyse each distinct occasion. While the theological interpretation of specific worship occasions is an important task, especially for worship leaders reflecting on their practice and their pastoral responsibilities, there is also value in the examination of the general worship of a specific tradition. Schmemann does not make this clear, probably because his Orthodox views meant that he did not see Orthodox worship as 'denominational' but as the normative expression of Christianity. But for others, Orthodoxy will be seen as a denomination, and its Divine Liturgy as one expression among others of Christian worship. From this inference we may develop a method for liturgical theology which works with the general worship practices of particular denominations, yet remains within the spirit of Schmemann's concern that we give due respect to actual worship.

Second, Schmemann's commitment to deal with specific worship is closely allied to his concern that liturgical theology should begin with the historical study of worship.[30] For him, historical work is not an end in itself, but the means through which a theory of worship may be developed. Historical study is needed because the theology in worship has from the beginning expressed itself in facts, it has 'become concrete in facts and has been revealed in facts'. However, this theology has sometimes been obscured and distorted by developing worship practices which have not had an appropriate theological basis. The work of the historian and the liturgical theologian must include the task of clarifying the tradition in order to eliminate these accretions. This historical perspective will be evident in what follows below.

After the historical investigation, Schmemann argues that there should be a theological synthesis which will be an exposition of the *lex orandi*, because 'the Church sees in the tradition of sacraments and sacred rites an inviolable element of Tradition'. Again, this insistence that worship provides a source for theology needs to be understood within the context of his Orthodox tradition, where the Divine Liturgy is believed to be the primary place of encounter with God. But this insight cannot be applied to the study of Free Church worship without qualification or amendment. We have already noted Geoffrey Wainwright's observation that Protestantism will give an authoritative priority to doctrine. Indeed, the exposition of the theology embodied in worship may be seen as primarily *descriptive* in nature. For theology to have a *normative* authority, we need to find a means of evaluation which will take account of the wider counsels of the Church. Consequently, we shall add a stage to Schmemann's method for liturgical theology which will enable this transition from the descriptive exposition of worship as it is, towards normative claims about how it should be.

Developing a Method

How do we set about doing liturgical theology? What are the steps by which we can study Christian worship in order to discover what it affirms about God and the Church and in order to achieve an authoritative view about the nature of that worship? The approach taken to what follows uses a method which is based on Schmemann's writings but which takes account of our discussion of the relationship of theology to worship.

In the notes of an address he was due to give to a conference towards the end of his life, Schmemann gave the clearest outline of the three practical steps which he believed should constitute a method for liturgical theology.[31]

The first stage is to establish the liturgical facts. Here is work for liturgical historians and phenomenologists, as the facts of evolving practices are established. This is the step which takes worship seriously by respecting its specific and concrete reality, both in its historical development and in the contemporary life of the Church. To enquire about what happens, and happened, in worship is an important first step.

Second, there comes the theological analysis of those liturgical facts. Here is a theme evident in all his writings about liturgical theology, namely, that no text or liturgical action should be interpreted in isolation. Worship, he argues, is undergirded by an *ordo*, or pattern, and this *ordo* is manifested through the way in which the individual components interact. He calls this their 'theological "content" or "coefficient"' and these components need to be understood in their theological context if they are to be understood aright. For example, an item in worship, though outwardly unchanged, may have a different theological meaning when placed at different points in a service.

Finally, the most important step for Schmemann is that of synthesis, 'the release of the inherent theological meaning from the witness of the liturgical *epiphany* itself'. This exposition is not in itself critical, but enables the theology implicit in worship to have a voice.

These three steps offer a practical approach which has much to commend it and which will form the basic method for what follows. However, I believe we need to add a fourth stage to this process, a stage in which we place the exposition of the faith of the worshipping community under a broader theological scrutiny. The exposition of the third stage is, as we have seen, essentially descriptive. But if we are to arrive at a point where it can have an authoritative status for guiding the Church in its believing and in its worship, then it will be necessary to engage with other theological expressions of faith within the Christian community, such as creeds, confessions of faith, analytical theology and, especially, Scripture. While worship embodies a theology which we will attempt to identify, clarify and expound, that theology also needs to bear the same scrutiny which any other theological endeavours may properly face.

Here is a four-stage approach to the theological study of worship. While it is based upon the work and insights of Alexander Schmemann, it moves beyond his judgments to take account of ecumenical realities in relation to both the nature of the Church and the nature of theology. Because liturgical theology must work with specific expressions of worship, our study focuses on the worship of a particular community. Thus our exploration of Christian worship and Christian believing will be approached through the lens of Free Church worship and, within that, the specifics of Baptist worship. In this we shall need to recognize the particular challenges with which any study of this free worship is confronted.

3

An Invitation to Free Church Worship

Our modern Protestants usually define the Church thus, *Where the Word of God is sincerely taught, and the Sacraments rightly administered, there is the true Church*. Dr. Wollebius gives it thus, *The visible Church is a visible society of Men, called to the state of Grace, by the Word and Sacraments.*

Again, The definition of Christ's Church may be taken out of the word *Kahal, Ekklesia, evocare,* to call, or *Evocatus per Evangelium,* to call, or called out by the Gospel, and then the Church is defin'd, *A company of Men called out of the World, by the voice of Doctrine of Christ, to worship one true God according to his will.*

Thomas Grantham
Christianismus Primitivus, 1678[1]

What kind of church is a 'Free Church'? To what does 'Free' refer and how are these churches different from other Christian churches? Who are their members and what do they stand for? What is their history and what form does their worship take?

Who are the Free Churches?

It is easier to describe the Free Churches than it is to offer a precise definition because the term refers to a stream of disparate groups and not to a single organization. Sometimes the term has been seen as synonymous with 'Nonconformist', though that term has itself changed in meaning over the years.[2] In some ecumenical discussions the term has referred to what was once called 'the old dissent', meaning Baptists, Congregationalists, Presbyterians and Quakers, with the later addition of Methodists.[3] To this list we need to add many others – Churches of Christ, Brethren, Independent Methodists, Pentecostals, Independent Evangelical Churches and those newer groups which emerged out of the Charismatic and Restoration movements of the 1970s and 1980s.

These denominations will differ from each other in various ways. They will organize themselves and make decisions in different ways. Some will have strong links between local congregations, complete with regional and national structures, others will not. Some will have a professional, paid ministry and others will not. There will be differences of theology and differences of culture. Many of these denominations will have a clear Evangelical identity, though we cannot describe the whole group that way. Not all would wish to describe themselves as 'Evangelical' and there will be many within the Anglican Communion, for example, who would wish to apply the term 'Evangelical' to themselves but would not necessarily espouse the freedoms listed by Ernest Payne:

> Freedom from State connection and control, freedom from essential depend-
> ence of a priestly succession, freedom from fixed liturgical forms, freedom of
> conscience and inquiry: these are still most vital freedoms.[4]

This catalogue of freedoms may seem rather negative to some readers, but freedom is often expressed in negative terms. What this statement offers is a list of concerns which have been historically important for those denominations regarding themselves as 'Free Churches' – a statement which hints at what kind of church they are. While there will be many differences between the various Free Church denominations, this list of freedoms clearly distinguishes this strand of the world Church from other stands, such as the Orthodox, Roman Catholic, Anglican and Lutheran traditions.

To speak of freedom *from* various authorities will often suggest a history in which freedom has been achieved as a result of suffering and perseverance. It does not in itself identify what that freedom is *for*. Payne's list of freedoms needs to be expanded if we are to identify the core of this freedom language. Fundamental to it is a belief that the spiritual realm is under the authority of God and that no civil authority has the right to control or restrict a church's expression of its faith.[5] In addition, the church must be free to choose its own ministers, to plan and conduct its own worship and to witness to its convictions. If this seems a benign list which any church might support, we must recognize that it has not always been so and that Christians have often found their free-doms restricted by fellow Christians. Most recently, however, trends in Western society have led to a widespread suspicion of authority. In this climate, most of the denominations have had shifts in the way in which authority has been understood and decisions have been made. For example, the Church of England is again the subject of debate concern-ing its place within the national establishment, though whether change will result is far from clear.

But what do the Free Churches stand for? Why is freedom so central to their self-understanding? If liturgical theology can present us with a portrait of what Christian communities believe, then a study of Free Church worship should present us with at least a partial answer to these questions. What are the values which they espouse? To build a comprehensive picture would require our studying the worship of each of the Free Church denominations. Instead, we shall focus on the Baptists, a case study which will have the advantage of being specific and relatively detailed. As a case study it cannot be regarded as representative of all Free Church worship, but it can suggest ways in which the worship of these others groups might be studied in turn.

Free Worship

Payne's concern for 'freedom from fixed liturgical forms' is a good example of how the negative statement concerning freedom *from* certain restrictions needs to be supplemented by a presentation of what in fact that freedom is *for*. This freedom is the freedom of local congregations to order their own gatherings for worship; it is the freedom of spontaneity which is open to the extempore guidance of the Holy Spirit; and it is the freedom of a particular worshipping community to respond to the reading and preaching of Scripture addressed to them as God's living Word. We shall explore what this means in practice.

Such worship offers particular challenges to any who would study it, and this free worship has certainly suffered from neglect. Most liturgical studies have not originated in Free Church circles[6] and have tended to exemplify an agenda which is not always relevant for Free Church worship. In his study of Protestant worship, the American Methodist James F. White claims:

> The study of Protestant worship has usually been conducted by methods derived from the study of Roman Catholic worship. In practice, this has meant that the chief concerns addressed have been liturgical texts, and most of those were for the Eucharist . . . I contend that this gives a distorted image and is totally irrelevant to the worship of most Protestants . . .[7]

There may be all kinds of reasons for this situation. Certainly, the majority of academic publications reflecting on the meaning of worship do so within the broad context of the Liturgical Movement of the nineteenth and twentieth centuries.

Within this movement, there has been much liturgical convergence between those churches in which Tradition is valued and in which worship is structured. This convergence expresses itself in a number of ways, but the most significant is in a shared commitment to the centrality and common pattern of the Eucharist. There is an increasingly widespread belief that the Eucharist is the central event of Christian worship, that it is the norm for Sunday assemblies and that all other worship is truncated or secondary. Commenting on the maxim, 'the Lord's people round the Lord's Table on the Lord's Day', Fenwick and Spinks assert, 'It is now widely recognized as an ideal even in those Churches that have not achieved it (e.g. Methodism).'[8] In practice, this has led to the Eucharist becoming more central in the worship of many churches. For Anglicans, the weekly Parish Communion has become the central event for most worshippers, replacing the earlier pattern of an early morning Eucharist for a few, followed by Morning Prayer for most, worshippers. In the Free Churches, a separate communion service following the main worship service has been replaced by the Eucharist as an integral part of worship, albeit on a monthly or even less frequent basis. However, it is one thing to regard the Eucharist as important and to feed on its rich sacramental life. It is quite another to see the Eucharist as central to all Christian worship. While this is patently true for Orthodox and Catholic Christians, it is not true in the same way for Sunday worship for many Protestants.[9]

Although White has acute pastoral and theological observations to make, he is primarily a liturgical historian. He is concerned to map the developments within Protestant worship since the Reformation. He evaluates those developments as a historian rather than interacting with them as a theologian:

> The role of the historian of worship is to record what practices actually persist and to be descriptive about them. Our function is not to make normative judgements . . . The historian, then, must be descriptive, not normative. In that way, others are helped to function as liturgical theologians so they may elucidate what the Christian faith is on the basis of what Christians do when they worship.[10]

The liturgical agenda, however, is broader than a debate as to whether eucharistic worship is the normative expression of Christian worship. There is the question of the forms and words for worship and the assumption that worship will be conveyed, and even controlled, by the use of agreed texts. White correctly observes that many Protestant groups do not worship using such texts and that liturgical theorizing which reflects text-based worship is not necessarily going to be helpful in the understanding of such oral worship services.

Free Church worship is indeed different from the text-based worship of most of the liturgical theologians, and when books are used, they will be a resource for those leading worship rather than a centrally authorized set of words in the hands of the congregation. Each service will be different, using an infinitely variable mixture of hymns and extempore or specially written prayers.[11] So as there is no written liturgy to form the basis of our analysis, how are we to determine the worship data which will provide the basis for our study? The primary subject matter of most services will be expressed in the words of the one leading worship and only rarely, apart from hymns, in patterns of expression and words borrowed from others. This form of worship, in which each service is composed by the worship leader, presents particular difficulties for the liturgical historian and theologian. What is the liturgical data upon which we can reflect? What is the worship, not in its abstract intent, but in its concrete particularity? What experience of God is encountered in this worship and how is it to be understood when its expression is so varied?

One possible solution is to look for recurring patterns in worship which might provide the basis for the theological exposition of that worship. However, the study of the developing shape of Baptist worship in Chapter 4 will offer only limited assistance in such an enterprise. While Schmemann could talk of the significance of the 'liturgical co-efficients',[12] the components of Free Church worship may not interact in such a way as to tell us much beyond the intentions of the particular worship leader. The very fluidity of free worship means it will not be easy to determine how this tradition might best be allowed to speak, and in what way what is heard should be interpreted.

The student of such worship need not, however, gaze enviously at more liturgical traditions, as though the task there were wholly straight-forward. For those traditions which use centrally agreed texts, the current situation is one of revision, change and contextualization. Kevin Irwin, a Roman Catholic, demonstrates this when he discusses how the liturgist is to determine precisely what worship is to be used in the formulation of a liturgical theology – the very question facing us here in relation to Free Church worship. Commenting that many earlier liturgical theologians worked in a worship situation dominated by the fixed post-Tridentine rites, he suggests that new methods are now required, with a particular emphasis on *liturgy as event*.[13]

While contemporary Roman Catholic worship is still very different from Baptist worship, the recognition that worship is *event*, not simply *text*, means that even when the same liturgical script is employed in different churches, each performance of that script, and therefore each event, will be different. Irwin urges that liturgical theology should not simply examine the revised liturgical books, but their *use* in actual services. He proposes a process of *dynamic dialectic* in which tradition, theology and spirituality provide the text, the raw materials for liturgical theology, and in which the resulting reflection informs and affects that theology and spirituality and therefore the worship tradition.[14] This is similar to the extra step which, in the previous chapter, we proposed adding to Schmemann's method, a stage in which the exposition of the theology embodied in worship would be open to theological critique. What Irwin rightly proposes is that such a critique will be interactive – the theological reflection will be influenced by the exposition of the worship it is studying. His wider definition of what constitutes the worship 'text' is also helpful, and the basis of our case study in the following chapters will be wider than simply the reported speech of worship services. The worship 'text' will include commentaries and reflections on worship in the Baptist community, as well as descriptions of that worship where they are available.

Who are the Baptists?

Baptists world-wide form one of the largest Protestant denominations, representing over 45 million baptized members, and an estimated community total in the region of 110 million. While Baptists are found in every continent, with a particular concentration in North America, our case study will be restricted in its scope to the churches in membership of the Baptist Union of Great Britain, representing some 145,000 church members.[15]

Baptists emerged at the beginning of the seventeenth century and, in Britain, consisted of two main groups until their final merger at the end of the nineteenth century. Both streams of Baptist life began from among the Separatists who believed that the Church of England was not sufficiently reformed. Those who separated themselves from the Church of England, and gathered for rather different worship, were concerned both about prayer book worship, which they regarded as Papist, and the very notion of a state church in which all the citizens were seen to belong.

The first group, the General Baptists, were Arminian in theology[16] and began with a congregation of English exiles in Amsterdam under the leadership of John Smyth and Thomas Helwys. The first Baptist church on English soil was established by Helwys in London with some of the returning exiles in 1612. Because of the period in Amsterdam, and subsequent contacts between the emerging General Baptist congregations and the Dutch Mennonites, there have been those historians who have argued for important links between the continental Anabaptist tradition and Baptist life in England. However, a strong case has also been made for the General Baptists emerging from the English Separatist and Puritan groups at the end of the sixteenth century,[17] and their worship seems to have developed from the worship of other radical groups such as the Barrowists and Brownists.[18]

The other, and soon to be larger, stream of Baptist life was made up of the Particular, or Calvinistic, Baptists. Whereas the General Baptists believed in a 'general salvation' in which Christ had died for all, the Calvinists believed in a 'particular salvation' in which Christ had died for those who belonged to the elect of God. Recent historians have begun to recognize that these two groups were more distinct from one another than had previously been thought. While there was some contact and cross-over between them, there were probably closer links between the Particular Baptists and the Calvinistic Independents (later to be known as Congregationalists) than between the Particular and the General Baptists.

The Particular Baptists developed as a group when they began to break away from the Calvinistic Separatists in the 1630s. This parting of the ways seems to have been fairly amicable and it was a characteristic of the Particular Baptists that they retained close links with other Calvinistic groups during the subsequent centuries and especially with the Calvinistic Independents. Their confessions of faith were at pains to indicate their agreement with other Calvinists on most points of doctrine and, from the eighteenth century onwards, they often shared worship, with a common theological corpus and hymnody, as well as occasional ministers' meetings. The separation from the Independents was originally over the question of baptism and, while this Baptist emphasis on the recipients and mode of baptism eventually led to a distinctive ethos, there remained close affinities between Baptists and Congregationalists which were reflected in their respective worship.

There were clear differences between the ethos of the Particular and the General Baptists in their worship, although both sprang from the Puritan Separatist tradition which in turn had represented a spectrum of opinions. As part of the Radical Reformation they were concerned for the authority of Scripture, not only in the formulation of theology, but in the governing of church practice, and this had implications both for the role of Scripture in worship and the way in which Scripture was used to validate particular worship practices. In reaction to the worship of mediaeval Christendom and what they perceived to be the compromises of the Anglican settlement, Separatist worship focused on the preaching of the Word and extempore prayer. As we shall see, the General Baptists were very reticent in the use of singing and only permitted the solo singing of psalms. On the other hand, the Particular Baptists sang psalms and psalm paraphrases in unison, and were a group within which congregational hymn singing developed, as it did among Independents. Indeed, the leading Independent minister, Isaac Watts, provided the core hymn material for both Particular Baptists and Independents for much of the eighteenth century.

In understanding this worship, it is important to recognize the covenantal nature of the Separatists' ecclesiology. The Church was understood to be the gathered fellowship of believers and this communal dimension was the setting in which leaders were entrusted to preach, and various individuals led prayer. In addition, there was a concern for 'spiritual worship' expressed through extempore prayer and a resistance to written forms of prayer. Following 1662, this led to considerable persecution through the refusal of these groups to recognize the validity of the *Book of Common Prayer* and their persistence in assembling for what they believed to be a scriptural form of worship.

Circumstances and a number of prevailing trends influenced the development of Baptist worship. For example, the Puritan worship of the early Baptists found its simplicity refined during the period of persecution between 1660 and 1688. Secret worship inevitably meant that only those elements regarded as essential were usually undertaken.

In the early eighteenth century, the growing rationalism of British intellectual society led to a period of greater formality, until the Evangelical Revival left its mark on the theology and worship of Baptist churches. In fact, the situation was rather more complex than this. There is considerable evidence for a warm evangelical spirituality in the Particular Baptist churches and association life of the West Country, the Midlands and the North throughout the century. In contrast, London Baptist life seems to have been more dominated by High Calvinism, as seen in the teaching and ministry of John Gill. With this came a deep suspicion of the religious affections.[19] After various struggles with unorthodox theologies throughout the eighteenth century, many General Baptist churches became Unitarian or ceased to exist. Meanwhile the New Connexion of General Baptist churches emerged in mid-century, much influenced by Methodism, and continued the Arminian tradition, though in a form modified by the Evangelical Revival. The use of hymns in the Wesleyan movement inevitably influenced hymnody among Particular Baptists and the New Connexion, though its impact was gradual. The development of evangelistic preaching also affected Baptist worship, an effect which has lasted until the present day.

The nineteenth-century concern for individual responsibility, with the consequent undervaluing of corporate categories, had its impact on the Free Churches generally, in their understanding of the Church, conversion and personal Christianity. Theological trends also reconfigured the profile of Calvinism among Particular Baptists, making it more inclusive, as the growing links with the Evangelical General Baptists of the New Connexion illustrate. Similarly, the Free Church reaction to the resurgence of Roman Catholicism and the Tractarian Movement influenced their worship through a self-conscious resistance to any use of liturgies or visual images in worship, as well as through distinctively 'low' views on ministry and the sacraments.[20] Through the century a gradual process of convergence led to the New Connexion General Baptists and Particular Baptists being united in a single denomination by the 1890s. The Baptist Union, which began as a Calvinistic Body, became more inclusive and its Declaration of Principle re-formed around an Evangelical identity which enabled the General Baptist churches to join.

In the twentieth century, ecumenical contacts, the Liturgical Movement and charismatic renewal have all played their part in influencing, in various ways, the development of Baptist worship. However, the pre-eminent place given to preaching, the tradition of extempore prayer and, more recently, an enjoyment of congregational singing have all been features which may be said to characterize the worship of the Free Churches.

The Interpretation of Baptist Worship

Why do Baptists worship the way they do? What does Baptist worship mean, both in terms of the intrinsic meaning of what takes place and in terms of its significance for our understanding of the wider life of Baptist churches? What principles determine its shape and content, and is there a theological integrity and coherence to them? While these questions cannot all be answered here, they will emerge at various points. It is often claimed that Baptist, and indeed Free Church, worship has no theology.[21] However, this probably reflects an assumption that by 'a theology of worship' is meant an *explicit*, pre-existent theology which moulds and informs the worship of Baptists in a self-conscious and deliberate way. But is there an *implicit* theology embodied in Baptist worship, in its patterns, actions and words, in the expectations of the congregation and the leading of its ministers?

A number of British Baptists have written about worship in the last half-century, of which the two leading representatives are Neville Clark and Stephen Winward.[22] Both stood within the mainstream of the Liturgical Movement and were strong advocates of reform.[23] However, there are two particular ways in which this present study will differ from their work. The primary concern here is to understand the worship of the Baptist community through a process of historical enquiry and theological reflection. The renewal of worship is an important matter, but it should follow the logically prior task of seeking to understand that which is to be reformed. Therefore, the central focus of this study is located in a different place from the work of Clark and Winward.

The very title of Stephen Winward's book, *The Reformation of our Worship*, indicates that his agenda was a reforming one. As the pastor of a congregation, he addressed others who were responsible for leading worship in Baptist churches and sought to provide a basis for change. The themes which he developed provide a rich resource for reflecting on worship in a Free Church context, but they are based upon a reasoning found elsewhere, in the theological mainstream of the Liturgical Movement and not in the study of Baptist worship. Indeed, they focus around a number of definitional statements about the nature of Christian worship in general – worship as dialogue, offering, sacrament, embodiment and community. Our present study will also identify a number of key themes, some of which overlap with those of Winward, but these themes will be approached through the study of Baptist worship itself. Alternatively, we can say that this book is a study of *Christian* worship, approached through the experience of a particular confessional community, Baptists and the Free Churches.

The application of general principles of Christian worship to the reformation of Baptist and Free Church worship is even more clearly displayed in the work of Neville Clark. Writing at a particular point in the assimilation of liturgical principles in the British churches, he recognized that the Free Church community had been less influenced by the Liturgical Movement than other parts of the Church and therefore set out to present principles and proposals for the reform of Free Church worship. Clark's overwhelming emphasis is that theology is the driving force which governs the reformation of worship, but the question of the *origin* of that theology remains. To some extent the principles which

Clark utilized from the Liturgical Movement had originated in the study of worship in Scripture and in the history of the Church. It could therefore be argued that the theological principles arose out of a theological reflection on worship. However, this was primarily worship in general – abstract worship – the distilled wisdom of the Liturgical Movement in the 1950s, a wisdom which also argued for a dialogical ordering of worship. For example, it is one thing to claim that all worship should have a coherent structure, because we are rational beings and need order and meaning. It is another matter to offer, as Clark does, one particular structural principle, the dialogical principle of Word and response, as the foundational principle of 'liturgy'.[24]

Both Clark and Winward stressed the importance of structure and pattern. They were writing within a few years of one another, at a time when liturgical studies seemed to offer a confidence in historical reconstruction[25] and ecumenical encounters were still at the stage of early discovery and appropriation. A decade later, another Baptist writer, Michael Taylor, subtitled his book on worship, 'Some guidelines for everyday Christians who want to reform the Liturgy'.[26] The use of the word 'liturgy', rather than 'worship', was significant and his principles were clearly described as the fruit of the Liturgical Movement. Here was another example of a reforming agenda in which a confidence in an ecumenical liturgical consensus provided the principles by which Free Church worship was to be ordered and renewed.

In our historical survey of Baptist worship in the following chapters we will find little concern over the ordering of worship in the sense of sequencing.[27] What we will find, however, is a recognition that certain components should be present in worship and, most importantly, a concern about the intent and disposition of the worshippers. Clark and Winward's programme for the reform of Baptist worship was based upon a number of assumptions that come more from a contemporary liturgical orthodoxy than from an exposition of Free Church worship. In contrast, we shall attempt to construct an explanation of worship which begins with the experience and distinctive emphases of Free Church worship as displayed in the Baptist community.

So our approach will not concentrate on the reforming of Baptist or Free Church worship but on its interpretation. The theological reflection will be based on the actuality of that worship rather than on principles developed away from it and then applied to it. Here the influence of Schmemann should be apparent, though his method has been modified to include an interactive role for critical theological reflection.

The Scope of this Study

The span of four hundred years is a very long time. Furthermore, is it possible to talk about *Baptist* worship at all? Like most denominations, Baptists display considerable diversity of thought and practice, both in their contemporary life and in the various historical stages of their developing worship. The danger of inappropriate selectivity is considerable. Nonetheless, this study is based on the conviction that it is meaningful to talk about Baptists in a collective way, as well as seeing them in the broader context of Free Church worship.[28]

This is a broad canvas, but meaning is to be found in pattern as well as in detail. As the Free Churches cannot turn to specific liturgies,[29] it is largely through generalization that we will need to approach their worship with the questions which we have chosen to ask. This broad approach will illuminate Free Church and Baptist life and worship, as well as contributing towards ecumenical discussions about the nature of Christian worship. Another way of viewing our case study is to see it as an approach to Christian worship through the lens of Baptist liturgical activity and experience. Consequently, values and principles which will be identified here should not be regarded as distinctives exclusive to the Baptist community so much as characteristics of Christian worship which will also be found in other traditions, though in different forms.

Part 2

Story and Soul

4

The Story of Baptist Worship

London, 22 May 1695

The Agreement of the Brethren appointed by, and respectively representing the two Baptized Congregations meeting at Barbican and Turners Hall, London, who agreed to unite and join together, and make one intire Church . . .
That the publick Worship in the Congregation on the Lord's Day be thus performed, viz. In the morning about half an hour after nine, some Brother be appointed to begin the Exercise in reading a Psalm, & then to spend some time in Prayer; & after y^t to read some other Portion of H. Scripture, till the Minister comes into the Pulpit; and after Preaching & Prayer to conclude wth singing a Psalm. The afternoon exercise to begin abt half an hour after One, & to be carried on & concluded as in the forenoon.

Paul's Alley Church Book[1]

What do Baptists believe about worship and what does that worship tell us about what they believe? To answer these questions we must first explore what their worship looks like. How has it evolved over the years and what does it look like today? The telling of any story is inevitably selective, as the narrator chooses which details, among the infinite details of daily life, are relevant to the story being told. Which pieces of information illustrate a time and place, which events lead to others and flow from others? Despite the risk of selectivity, an attempt must be made to tell the story, before we can reflect on its meaning.

Apart from the occasional study of particular areas of worship, such as the emergence of hymnody,[2] or the spirituality of preaching,[3] there is no comprehensive account of the development of worship among English Baptists.[4] In so far as the story has previously been pieced together, the fullest account is that which becomes available when the various sections relevant to Baptists in Horton Davies' *Worship and Theology in England* are connected.[5] But once those sections are read sequentially, clear gaps emerge. The continuous story which Davies relates is the broader narrative of the English churches as a whole, rather than the story of a single confessional strand. His Baptist material offers a beginning, but much remains to be done to fill in the gaps, and to appreciate the texture and integrity of the Baptist tradition. This chapter can only offer a beginning, a series of snapshots of worship in different periods and among different groups. Nonetheless, the picture which will emerge will offer us some of the raw materials from which we can attempt a liturgical theology.

As Alexander Schmemann has put it: 'First establish the liturgical facts.' So the primary concern of this chapter is not 'What *ought* Baptist worship to be?' but 'What *is* Baptist worship and what has it been?' Historical enquiry will run through much of our case study; this chapter will begin by examining the overall shape of worship among Baptists and will offer an outline narrative of the development of that worship. It will also suggest ways in which Baptist worship, or the Free Church tradition of which it is a part, differs from more liturgical traditions. But first, what can the patterns mean?

Patterns, Order and Meaning

As we examine the shape of worship services and their evolution over the centuries, what significance are we to give to the connections between the component parts, the proportion of time given to those parts, and the order in which those parts occur? Can the structure of Free Church worship services tell us anything of significance about the meaning of that worship?

A number of words are used to talk about the structuring of worship, and clarity requires that we use these different terms with consistency. In what follows, *order* will refer to the principle of there being order, rather than disorder, while *pattern* will indicate the shape of a particular ordering of worship. *Sequence* will refer to the sequential order in which things follow one another, and *ordo* will contain some of the ambiguity it currently reflects in ecumenical discussions.[6] In recent years, this word *ordo* has been given a range of meanings, similar to the variety of interpretations available to the English word 'order'. It can refer to a timetable of events, such as a calendar of readings and festivals, the mediaeval collections of *ordines* with their directives on how to perform a service,[7] descriptions of specific liturgies,[8] or more generally it can operate as a synonym for the English term 'order of service'.

Schmemann used the word *ordo* to suggest those principles which lie behind the worship of the Church and which yield meaning as the *lex orandi*. In his Orthodox context, the word indicates the regulations which order that worship, such as the rubrics that relate the changing aspects of the Divine Liturgy to the continual changes of the calendar. He recognized that the Slavonic *ordo* and the *ordo* of the Greek Church are each the exposition of local rules and therefore the codifying of pre-existent liturgical practices. As such, they are the carriers of tradition and a communication of the *lex orandi*,[9] though it is important to understand the way in which this takes place. The rubrics establish the sequence in which events occur within the liturgy, as well as the way in which they are performed, and as such fix their relationships to one another. These relationships are the 'liturgical co-efficients' and we have already seen how Schmemann argued that an explication of their meaning will provide theological content for liturgical theology.[10] However, he also uses the term *ordo* to refer to those fundamental principles which undergird Christian worship.[11]

Schmemann's concern to identify the liturgical co-efficients as yielders of meaning provides us with an important question to place before the historical material: do the patterns of Baptist and Free Church worship, in the sense of the sequence of its constituent parts, carry any liturgical meaning, or is that worship simply a collection of units which occur in no significant order? In addition to this question about the relative position of liturgical units in Baptist and Free Church worship, there is another more general question about the overall patterning of the worship life of the Free Churches.

Both these questions arise out of a study of Schmemann, but they will also arise in any attempt to locate Free Church worship within an ecumenical context, clarifying its meaning by distinguishing its character from that of other traditions. Here, as elsewhere, Baptists may be out of step with other denominations, though their contribution to the discussion of an ecumenical *ordo* will resonate with other Free Churches and Evangelical groups.

For example, in 1994 the Faith and Order Commission of the World Council of Churches held a consultation on worship which, in its report, spoke about the *ordo* of Christian worship as

> the undergirding structure which is to be perceived in the ordering and scheduling of the most primary elements of Christian worship. This *ordo*, which is always marked by pairing and by mutually re-interpretative juxtapositions, roots in word and sacrament held together. It is scripture readings and preaching together, yielding intercessions; and, with these, it is

eucharistia and eating and drinking together, yielding a collection for the poor and mission in the world. It is formation in faith and baptizing in water together, leading to participation in the life of the community. It is ministers and people, enacting these things, together.[12]

The consultation seems to have been influenced by the contribution of one of its participants, Gordon Lathrop.[13] A more detailed exposition of his argument, that the *ordo* may be seen in a series of juxtapositions, may be found in his book *Holy Things: A Liturgical Theology*,[14] where he develops from Schmemann's notion of 'liturgical dualism' the idea of pairings in creative tension. Schmemann was referring to the newness of the primitive Christian cult alongside the continuing worship of Judaism,[15] but Lathrop sees the tension in his pairings as the place where meaning is to be found.

That these component parts are to be found, in a variety of forms, in the various churches is not in dispute. Further, to describe Christian worship dialectically as various components in tension with one another can be both creative and illuminating as a theological method.[16] However, to assert that the heart of Christian worship is to be found in the *ordo* of juxtaposed pairings, and to claim that 'such is the inheritance of all the churches', is to claim for this observation too high a level of dogmatic authority.[17]

Lathrop argues that 'meaning occurs through structure'.[18] But does the pattern of a Baptist service matter, and, if it does matter, what level of importance is it to be given to the sequence of the various component parts? This question will be asked as we reflect on the developing patterns of worship among Baptists, but our other *ordo* question, concerning the overall pattern of the worshipping life of congregations, will also need to be addressed.

Schmemann identified the relationship of Eucharist to calendar, or eschatology to history, as a way of describing a fundamental aspect of Christian worship. In doing this, he portrayed the relationship between word and sacrament as a central dimension of the *ordo* and of the *lex orandi*.[19] In his view there is meaning not only in the reading and preaching of the Word and in the celebration of the Eucharist, but in the relationship between them. Following Schmemann, Lathrop identifies this relationship in his discussion of Justin's account of the Sunday assembly in the middle of the second century, and suggests, 'For Justin the *ordo* for the meeting . . . is word and meal in apposition.'[20] As a Lutheran, he is keen to emphasize the unity of word and table. The Liturgical Movement, as we have seen, has also encouraged not only a higher profile for the Eucharist, but a central place for it in Sunday worship.

By way of contrast, James White notes that much Protestant worship is not eucharistic and that it needs to be understood on its own terms.[21] There is certainly a theological debate to be rehearsed about the relationship of word and sacrament, but in our study of Baptist and Free Church worship the main emphasis will be on non-eucharistic worship.[22] The most frequent experience of Sunday worship does not include the Eucharist and this pattern needs to be taken seriously if we are to understand the meaning of such worship. Even to use such a designation as 'non-eucharistic worship' is to denote that worship in negative terms. We shall see that the Lord's Supper has an important place within the overall worship of a local Baptist congregation, but it will distort our understanding of that congregation's worship if we forget that most Sunday assemblies do not gather around the Lord's table for the sharing of bread and wine.

So to repeat, the notion of a Baptist or Free Church *ordo* needs to be understood and examined in two senses. On the one hand, it may refer to the pattern of worship services and the meaning implicit in their ordering. On the other hand, it may refer to the overall shape of worship practices and the dynamic interaction between various concerns in the life and witness of a congregation. It is with both these senses of *ordo* that we begin our survey of Baptist and Free Church worship.

Basic Ingredients and Evolving Patterns

The leading Baptist historian and ecumenical statesman Ernest Payne wrote in 1952:

> The general pattern of church services has remained the same from the 17th century to the present day: scripture, prayer and sermon, interspersed with hymns.[23]

This generalization provides both an anchor and a landmark for our survey. It is a fair representation of most Baptist, and indeed Free Church, worship up to the mid-twentieth century, though two qualifications need to be added. First, we should recognize that there has never been a period without change and development. It is tempting to see the Free Church worship of the 1950s as somehow 'traditional' in the sense that it has existed in that form for a long time. Free Church worship evolved from the late sixteenth century to the time of Payne's statement. The components he identifies were present in most worship for most of that time, though their shape and interaction was subject to considerable change. Second, the date of Payne's summary is significant because it marks a transition between an age of gradual development and a period of more rapid change for many churches, of all denominations. At the time when Payne was writing, there is at least anecdotal evidence that worship among British Baptists was similar in most places and that Payne's summary would be true for most, if not all, churches.[24] However, with the influence of the Liturgical and Charismatic Movements, as well as other late twentieth century cultural influences, two trends have manifested themselves. On the one hand, many local congregations have reordered their worship on the basis of Charismatic, Evangelistic or Liturgical principles. On the other hand, some churches have remained fairly traditional and a situation of considerable variety has replaced the relatively uniform scene of the first half of the century.

Some of this contemporary variety has been mapped in two surveys of Baptist churches in the late 1990s and the results published in my *Baptist Worship Today*.[25] In conjunction with the Baptist Union of Great Britain and its Doctrine and Worship Committee, a questionnaire on current worship practices was sent to every member church.[26] Over 85 per cent of forms were returned, providing significant information both about actual practices and the patterns of worship across the denomination, and informing much of what is written here about late twentieth-century Baptist worship. Alongside this snapshot of worship practices, a second survey was undertaken which sought to discover the attitude of worship leaders and congregants to various issues. A second attitude survey was undertaken which sampled types of congregation and provided qualitative data about the attitudes of both leaders and members of the congregation in relation to worship.[27]

The results of these surveys make it possible to plot the trends in worship since Payne was writing. Part 3 will examine the components of worship which Payne mentions, while our next chapter will look at various attitudes to worship and their theological interpretation. But now we shall examine the development of worship practices and, in particular, the pattern or order which services have taken.

Early Separatist Worship

Not all British Christians were able to participate in the Elizabethan Church of England with a clear conscience. There were a number of groups who believed that the state church was not sufficiently reformed. Partly this was a reflection of the fact that the Elizabethan Settlement was not as radical as the reforms had been during the brief reign of Edward VI. Partly the dissidents had been radicalized by the Catholic reign of Mary and their years of exile, which for some were spent in Geneva under the influence of John Calvin. Of these dissidents, the Puritans wanted to reform the Church on the basis of what they saw as scriptural principles, though they decided to remain within the Church of England. Others were not able to remain within the national church with a clear conscience and so separated themselves, gathering in secret for worship, fellowship and instruction.

This latter group were the Separatists. Those who were to become Baptists were from among their number, but before they emerged as a distinct community, there were two earlier groups which are relevant to our survey of early Free Church worship. The Brownists, who left Norwich for Holland under the leadership of Robert Brown in 1581, had worship that consisted of prayer for about half an hour, followed by an hour-long sermon and a further exposition by another person on the same Scripture text. The Barrowists, led by another Separatist, Henry Barrow, in the last years of the sixteenth century, developed worship that included extempore prayer, the exposition of Scripture, a meal together and the collection of money for the support of those in prison. This was secret worship and the rendezvous was changed from week to week. The Barrowist leaders were martyred, and in their examination, each gave arguments against the use of set prayers in church, including the Lord's Prayer.[28]

Early General Baptist Worship

In the town of Gainsborough, Lincolnshire, there gathered around 1606 a growing group of Separatists. With the threat of persecution, the group decided it had become too large to meet as one group and amicably divided. One group was led by John Smyth, a Puritan clergyman, and Thomas Helwys, a layman. Smyth had been a fellow of Christ's College, Cambridge, and the city lecturer at Lincoln, until his dismissal for radical views and forthright preaching. The other group included William

Brewster, William Bradford and John Robinson, and some of their group were to travel on the *Mayflower* in 1619 and help form the nucleus of the Congregational Church in New England. The threat of persecution continued for Separatists, for James I had promised to 'harrie them out of the land', and both groups migrated to Amsterdam in about 1607 in order to meet freely for worship.

Before they left for Holland, Smyth drew up a covenant which Bradford paraphrased:

> They shooke of this yoake of antichristian bondage, and as ye Lords free people, joined them selves (by a covenant of the Lord) into a church estate, in ye fellowship of ye gospel, to walke in all his wayes, made known, or to be made known unto them, according to their best endeavours, whatsoever it should cost them, the Lord assisting them.[29]

The story of Baptists, as a distinct group, begins with the group of exiles who met in Amsterdam under the leadership of Smyth and Helwys. Their worship is described in a letter of 1609 sent home to England by a married couple in the congregation.

Exile Worship in Amsterdam 1609

Prayer
Reading *one or two chapters of Scripture*
Give the sense *and discuss*
(*lay aside books*)
Solemne Prayer *by one who then offers*
Exposition of a text *and propheseying out of the same for one hour or three quarters*
Prophesying from the same text *for a similar length of time by a second speaker*
Propheseying *by third, fourth and fifth speakers, as time allows*
Prayer *by the first speaker* and
Exhortation to contribute to the poor
Collection
Prayer[30]

The proceedings, outlined above, began with prayer, and then one or two chapters of the Bible were read. Discussion ensued to establish the meaning of the Bible passage. Then we are told that all books, including the Bible, were laid aside as though this was in fact the beginning of worship and there followed prayer led by a person who preached on the agreed text for the best part of an hour. After this a second, third, fourth and sometimes even fifth speaker preached on the same passage, none of them using the Bible other than by their quoting from memory verses which supported their exposition. At the end, the first speaker prayed again and there was an exhortation to contribute to the needs of the poor before the service ended with a collection and prayer. This worship lasted about four hours and happened twice each Sunday.

Here is charismatic worship in which most of the time is spent by different members of the congregation expounding and applying Scripture. A distinction seems to be made between the early part of proceedings, which were seen as preparation for worship and which mainly consisted of Bible study, and the worship proper. At the point of transition, even the Bible is laid aside so as to enable what is perceived to be a true, spiritual worship which flows from the heart. There seems to be an assumption that true worship is inspired by God and that its mode of operation is through spontaneous inspiration rather than through written media, even Scripture. So Helwys wrote in a letter of 1608:

> All bookes even the originalles themselves must be layed aside in the tyme of spirituall worshipp, yet still retayninge the readinge & interpretinge of the Scriptures in the Churche for the preparinge to worshipp, Iudginge of doctrine, decidinge of Controversies as the grounde of o^r^ faithe & of o^r^ whole profession.[31]

This group was in fellowship with the Mennonite community in Amsterdam and, after General Baptist churches developed in England, some maintained intermittent contact with the Mennonites.

The avoidance of books in worship, even the Bible, continued some way through the century, though in some General Baptist churches Scripture reading became established before the end of the century.[32] The concern for spontaneity and 'openness to the Spirit' remained a significant feature of General Baptist worship and it is not surprising that some of their number were to become Quakers in the early years of that movement.[33] Only the solo singing of psalms was permitted,[34] usually in an improvisatory way, and only ministers were allowed to preside at the Lord's Supper.[35] In addition, they developed a method of running exposition of the Bible, or interpolated comment during the public reading of Scripture, as well as discussion by the congregation of the various expositions, though at the beginning this was seen as preparatory to worship rather than an integral part of it. It was the method used by the New England Puritans and seems to have had a wide influence in Puritan and Separatist circles.[36]

Separatist Worship before the Civil War

There is a considerable gap in our knowledge of Baptist worship in the middle of the seventeenth century. However, a fragment of a description of Separatist worship in London around 1640 has come to us through a hostile witness, an informer whose report was published in a polemical attack on the Separatists and their worship.[37] This secret worship required a doorkeeper to act as look-out. The person leading prayed for 'about half an hour' and then preached for an hour, after which another stood up 'to make the text more plain':

Secret Separatist Worship in London circa 1640

Prayer   *(half hour)*
Sermon   *(one hour)*
Sermon   *(by another)*

Another hostile witness was Thomas Edwards, who published his *Gangraena: or a Catalogue of Many of the Errours, Heresies and Pernicious Practices of the sectaries of this Time* in 1646. It provided an account of worship at Thomas Lambe's General Baptist Church in Bell Alley, London, which drew crowds with its lively services. Like the Amsterdam congregation, several men preached in succession and when there was a disagreement about who should preach next, it was sometimes decided by vote of the congregation. General debates often followed, and on occasion the speakers were interrupted in these proceedings, which were popular, with curious visitors from other churches and 'especially young youths and wenches'.[38] Edwards also recorded the account of quite different General Baptist worship in Edward Barber's congregation. This took place in November 1645 in a substantial house in Bishopsgate Street and involved the laying on of hands with prayer for the reception of the Holy Spirit, as well as a meal 'dressed for them by a cook' followed by the Lord's Supper before the tablecloth had been removed. The laying on of hands suggests a democratic ecclesiology in which the congregation waits to see who will be gifted by the divine Spirit in order that they may be commissioned for evangelistic activity. This account also indicates the growing practice among General Baptists of celebrating the Lord's Supper immediately after a love feast. So the Warboys congregation was to agree, in 1655, 'The order of love-feast agreed upon, to be before the Lord's Supper; because the ancient churches did practise it, and for unity with other churches near to us.'[39]

There seem to be no full accounts of Particular Baptist worship for much of the seventeenth century. Horton Davies argues that it closely resembled the worship of the Independents, and this seems to fit what we know of the continuing close relations between the two groups.[40] Indeed, the exclusion of nonconforming Presbyterians from the Church of England after 1662 resulted in their aligning themselves with Independents and Particular Baptists. Davies also claims that the involvement of the Independents in the Westminster Assembly suggests that their worship was close to the Presbyterians and probably influenced by Genevan patterns.[41] We have to admit that we are in the realm of speculation, though indirect evidence seems to point to the worship of the Particular Baptists being closer to the other Calvinistic groups, the Independents and the Presbyterians, than to the more radical worship of the General Baptists.

With these cautionary words in mind, it is interesting to look at the order of service proposed by the Westminster Assembly in the *Directory* of 1645.

Service for the Lord's Day proposed in the Westminster 'Directory'

Prayer
Old Testament Reading
New Testament Reading
Psalm
Prayer before the Sermon
Sermon
Intercessory Prayer
Lord's Prayer
Psalm
Blessing

The Assembly replaced the *Book of Common Prayer* with a *Directory* of worship which offered guidance with regard to content and approach, rather than set forms and prayers, for use in parish churches in England during the Presbyterian years prior to 1660.[42] This was the fruit of a compromise reached between Presbyterian and Independent members of the Assembly, so we cannot be sure as to how far, if at all, Particular Baptist worship diverged from this. Baxter's solo writing of the *Reformed Liturgy* is interesting, but its rejection by the conference and the exclusion of Presbyterians in 1662 led Presbyterians to a more basic and free form of worship during the years of secret gatherings.[43]

Worship under Persecution

The Broadmead Church in Bristol represented that strand of Calvinistic life which straddled the boundary between Independent and Particular Baptist during much of the seventeenth century, though it had moved to a Baptist position by the close of the century. One of the elders, Edward Terrill, kept a detailed account of the congregation's life during the Restoration period and offers some glimpses of worship, though there is not a complete account of a service there.

The worship of the church was open to the public and contained readings, expositions of Scripture, lengthy prayers by various members and occasional psalm singing.[44] Unlike most churches, the Broadmead congregation used psalm books, with continuous unison singing, rather than 'lining out', and there is a moving account of their continuing to sing even when interrupted by the Mayor and his sergeants. With three other Separatist congregations in Bristol, they agreed in 1675 'concerning ye ordering of ourselves in our Meetings in this day of Trouble, *that none Stirr* from ye Meeting when ye Informers or any officers come whatsoever'.[45]

Perhaps inevitably, descriptions of Nonconformist worship during this period are few and far between. The description of worship by an informer in Great Yarmouth in 1674 is still far from complete:[46]

Nonconformist Worship in Great Yarmouth 1674

'Teacher' enters the pulpit
Long extempore prayer
Congregation sings metricated psalm, seated
Sermon

Here is worship reduced to the essentials. The simplicity which they believe resulted from a faithfulness to Scripture has been refined by the practical considerations of a congregation meeting in secret under threat from the law. The informer comments that, 'They never read a chapter in the Old or New Testament, nor so much as a verse, except it be for a proof in their teaching.' This suggests the more radical approach of the General Baptists, though we do not know the precise denomination which was being reported.

Persecution not only brought Baptists, Independents and Presbyterians closer together, it also heightened the divide between 'chapel and church'. There were other, more positive consequences such as an intensifying of personal religion and a close binding of fellowship within the congregations. But much of the details of their worship remains hidden to us. With 1688 there came a considerable change in fortune for the Free Churches. Worship no longer needed to be held in secret, meeting houses could be built and the longer-term challenges, such as the training of ministers, could begin to be addressed.

A Baptist Congregation in London in 1695

In 1695 two Baptist congregations in London merged to form the Paul's Alley, Barbican, Baptist Meeting.[47] The Paul's Alley church had a Calvinistic history, though it had not associated with other Particular Baptist churches, and the congregation which joined it from the Turner's Hall was General Baptist.[48] Both churches were clearly not typical, for the minister of Turner's Hall became the pastor of the united congregation and was apparently in favour of congregational singing.[49] He was, for a while, assisted by Joseph Stennett, a Seventh Day Calvinistic Baptist who had been serving the Paul's Alley congregation on a part-time basis. The united congregation tended towards a General Baptist position, though it steered a course between the controversies of the early eighteenth century. We cannot draw inferences with regard to more widespread General or Particular Baptist worship practices, but we are given a glimpse of some Baptist worship at the turn of the century by the uniting compact which included a policy statement concerning the form of their worship together. In particular, the Scripture reading and the final psalm may be evidence of this denominational mingling, with Whitley suggesting that this psalm was metricated and sung in unison, something most unusual for a straightforward General Baptist Church.

A London Baptist Congregation 1695

9.30 *and* 1.30
Psalm
Prayer
Scripture Reading
Sermon
Prayer
Psalm

Sunday worship was to begin with a psalm read by 'some brother . . . appointed' who would then lead in prayer and 'read some other portion of Holy Scripture'.[50] The minister would then enter the pulpit to preach the sermon, afterwards offering prayer. Finally there would be a sung psalm. The General Baptists did not normally allow congregational singing even of psalms, as it might result in 'promiscuous singing' in which unbelievers sang hypocritically and defiled the praises of the covenant people. However, the mixed nature of this particular congregation suggests that this psalm may well have been sung congregationally. Whitley is of the view that, although General Baptist churches permitted solo singing, most of the church services contained no singing at all.[51] On those, probably monthly, occasions when the Lord's Supper was celebrated, it was incorporated into the afternoon service: 'On Breaking-Bread-Days the Psalm to be omitted in the afternoon till the conclusion of the Lord's Supper.'[52]

Early Eighteenth-Century Independent and Particular Baptist Worship as reflected in the Worship of Bury Street Church, London

We have already noted the absence of any descriptions of the sequencing of Particular Baptist worship in this period, and the strong case for a similarity between their services and the worship of the Independents. We shall therefore need to rely on an account of worship at the Independent church where Isaac Watts was pastor in the early years of the eighteenth century.[53] The following is an outline of worship at Bury Street.[54]

Particular Baptist and Independent Worship 1723

Morning Service:

Psalm
Short prayer
Exposition of Scripture
[Psalm or hymn]
Prayer
Sermon
Psalm or Hymn
Short Prayer
Benediction

Afternoon Service:

Psalm
Long Prayer
Sermon
Psalm or Hymn
Short Prayer
Benediction

Watts had a wide influence among eighteenth-century dissenting circles, both through his hymns and his *Guide to Prayer*. The first Particular Baptist group had broken away from an Independent congregation during the 1630s over the issue of baptism. However, it is generally assumed that in most other aspects of church life, such as worship, there were few differences between the two communities. The assumption here that the worship at Bury Street would give us an indication of Particular Baptist worship seems a reasonable one, though we must nonetheless remember that this was a city church led by a learned scholar of national repute.

The opening psalm would have been metricated and sung by the whole congregation, normally by the method of lining out, though Watts's own congregation may have used books, thus enabling continuous congregational singing. In an 'Advertisement to the Reader' accompanying the preface to his *Psalms of David* in 1719, Watts had written, 'It were to be wished that all Congregations and private Families would sing as they do in foreign Protestant Countries, without reading Line by Line.'[55] The prayer would have been an invocation 'asking for the Divine presence in all the following parts of worship'. There followed an exposition of Scripture which lasted about half an hour and was in addition to the later sermon, perhaps being a development of the earlier 'propheseyings'.

The metricated psalm or hymn would have been sung after the sermon in most congregations, but was placed after the exposition in the morning service at Bury Street because of the nervous disposition of Isaac Watts, who asked that the hymn be sung before he entered the pulpit to preach. The shorter afternoon service was led by a colleague, and the hymn was then placed in the normal position after the sermon. It may well have been one of Watts's own paraphrases or compositions.

The 'long prayer' consisted of requests for various blessings, spiritual and temporal, for the whole congregation, confession of sins, thanksgiving for mercies, petitions for the whole world, for 'the churches of Christ', for the nation, for all rulers and governors, together with any particular cases represented. In some Free Churches, requests of the congregation were usually written on pieces of paper and passed to the minister.[56] The usual place for the second item of praise was after the sermon and, as the practice of hymn singing, and therefore hymn writing, increased, those local ministers, such as Benjamin Beddome of Bourton-on-the-Water, who set about writing hymn texts, did so in order to provide a response to the sermon of that week.

At Bury Street the Lord's Supper was observed after the afternoon sermon on the first Sunday of the month,[57] and on the third Sunday there was a collection at the door for the needs of the poor and for defraying some of the church expenses. The main running costs of the church were met by members' subscriptions. After the sermon, the Lord's Supper continued with the words of institution, 'that it may ever be kept in mind to regulate every part of the practice',[58] and 'a short prayer of eight or ten minutes'[59] of blessing for each of the bread and cup. While this eucharistic event was usually incorporated into the afternoon service, we ought not to see this as a conjoining of word and sacrament in any primary sense. Here the word precedes the sacrament because the sacrament requires it, not because the two are juxtaposed in a fundamental *ordo*. The Lord's Supper is certainly central to the worshipping life of the congregation and it is the place where new members are received. But the dominant worship experience is of weekly preaching services, as it has remained for most Free Churches.[60]

Again, we may note the general assumption that worship at this time was fairly similar among Calvinistic Nonconformists, and Ernest Payne comments:

> Baptist worship in the eighteenth century was similar to that of the Nonconformist body. Two or three paraphrases or hymns were sung, the latter being often original compositions of the pastor, given out line by line with the right note for the tune sounded on a pitch pipe. The Scriptures were read. Lengthy extempore prayers were offered, often by deacons or elders as well as by the minister. Sermons of the pastor were long and dealt with doctrinal themes.[61]

Apart from an increase in congregational singing and the demise of the exposition, this pattern seems to have remained substantially the same until the middle of the twentieth century.

Nineteenth-Century Baptist Worship in Norfolk

This can be illustrated by an example from the mid-1840s. William Brock (1807–75) was minister of St Mary's Baptist Church, Norwich, 1833–48, after which he became the first pastor of Bloomsbury Baptist Church in central London. He exerted a wide influence in denominational affairs and was often in the forefront of new developments. In 1845 he wrote the Norfolk Baptist Association's Circular Letter on 'The Behaviour becoming the House of God':

> That in every thing which constitutes the essentials of public worship, we [Baptists] are evangelically consistent and scripturally right, we quite believe . . . among the churches of Jesus Christ, we are favoured to occupy a pre-eminent position in respect to sound doctrine and genuine devotion. In preaching we keep a firm hold of the glorious gospel of the blessed God; and in prayer, we are unfettered by those liturgies whose boundaries must not be passed: in whose precise words men must express themselves, whether suitable or unsuitable to their state of mind.[62]

We shall return to the main concerns of his address in the next chapter but, in the course of urging a reverent 'deliberateness of action', Brock describes the pattern of a typical Sunday morning service,[63] implying that this was the normal pattern in Norfolk Baptist churches in the 1840s (see the outline below).

The worship looked beyond the bounds of the liturgical event itself. The opening prayer of invocation was for all the events of the day, which may well go on to include fellowship at lunchtime and other meetings of the church. The long prayer was inclusive in another way, for it was offered 'for all men, especially the household of faith'. In so far as the discourse expounded Scripture 'to the people, that they may become wise unto salvation by faith in Jesus Christ', it was also addressed to those who were not yet committed members of the community of faith.

Norfolk 1845

Prayer for the Holy Spirit
Song of Praise
Scripture Reading
Prayer: supplications and intercessions, with thanksgiving
Song of Praise
Exposition
[Hymn?]

This pattern is clearly focused on prayer and praise, with the reading and preaching of Scripture. Indeed, Brock elsewhere responded to his friend the Bishop of Norwich's assertion, that churches were houses of prayer but the dissenting meeting houses were for preaching, by claiming that each Sunday, Baptist congregations would spend at least two hours in prayer.[64] There are still only two hymns and the service appears to end with the sermon and the benediction. It is not clear why the practice in Norfolk did not include a final hymn, though Brock's practice in Bloomsbury was similar, with a third hymn before the sermon and the occasional use of the doxology afterwards.[65] Yet, as we have noted already, there was a widespread practice of singing a hymn after the sermon, often as a means of response to the preaching.

Bloomsbury, at its foundation meeting, had decided to celebrate the Lord's Supper weekly, at 3.00 pm on the first Sunday of each month and otherwise after the morning service. In 1862, one celebration was moved to the evening, and Brock wrote, 'Our weekly observance of the Lord's Supper greatly facilitates such attendance; especially as in the course of the month it is observed at different times.'[66] He goes on to explain that different people found different times helpful. This offers a picture of a large central London church catering to different congregations at each Sunday service so, although there was weekly eucharistic provision, as with most Baptist churches, many people only participated in the Lord's Supper once or twice a month.

While Brock, in the Norfolk letter, expounds the meaning of the component parts of the service, and in doing so implies some logic in the placing of those components, he is primarily concerned with the integrity of the individual parts, rather than the flow of the service. Indeed, he advocates gaps for reflection between the parts of the service in order that people might engage fully in them. Thus, for Brock, worship is important for the various activities it contains, and the worshippers' engagement in those parts, rather than as a liturgical event which is in some way greater than its component parts.

The Early Twentieth Century

By the twentieth century, worship in most Free Churches had developed into what is often called 'the hymn sandwich' (see below). Indeed, it is often assumed that this is a traditional Baptist or Free Church form which has long existed, whereas, in its four-hymn version, it is probably a late nineteenth-century development. The hymns are interspersed through the service, providing the congregation with regular opportunities for active participation. However, there does not seem to be much of a rationale to this pattern, other than a moving towards the climax of the sermon. There was often little attempt to provide thematic cohesion between different parts of the service and it was not uncommon for the hymns to be chosen by the organist rather than the preacher.[67]

Early Twentieth-Century Worship

Invitation to worship
Hymn
Bible reading
Hymn
Prayer
Notices
Offering
Hymn
Sermon
Hymn
Benediction

Charles Booth's account of religious life in London at the turn of the century includes a description of Baptist worship very similar to that described here.[68] He comments that the worship of the Baptists is very similar to that of the Congregationalists, but describes Baptist life as 'virile' with an emphasis on doctrine and piety. He also observes that members of the congregation are more likely to contribute through reading or prayer than would be the case among the other churches. The worship he describes includes a short prayer after the opening hymn, and sometimes a second reading after the long prayer; the offering is taken during the third hymn and the notices precede the sermon. In addition, he reports that some churches include a 'sermonette' and hymn directed at the children in the congregation and the giving of Scripture verses to be committed to memory. Booth observes that 'the family side of religious feeling' is strong among the Baptists – intriguing for a denomination which does not baptize infants. We can speculate that perhaps the Evangelical concern for personal commitment leads to a concern for the nurture of children so that they might come to faith in due course, and a sense of the Church as a fellowship will also lead to a family ethos. Here is little attempt to produce a flow of worship in which the sequence carries much significance. Rather, we have the context within which

Payne offered his description of Baptist worship: 'scripture, prayer and sermon, interspersed with hymns'.

By the middle of the twentieth century, the Lord's Supper was still a separate service which followed a main service. A common pattern was for the service to be held after the evening service on the first Sunday of a month and after the morning service on the third Sunday. The service would usually include an offering for the poor of the fellowship.

From about the beginning of the century, the common cup began to be replaced with individual glasses. As a result of the Temperance Movement, non-alcoholic 'wine' had been introduced during the nineteenth century and the introduction of individual glasses was a result of growing concerns over hygiene. Many churches tried to counteract the loss of symbolism which came with the loss of the common cup by inviting the members of their congregation to drink simultaneously. In the latter part of the twentieth century, this loss of symbolism has been addressed by a few churches returning to a common cup, probably as a result of increased ecumenical engagement. It was not until late in the century that communion services were normally integrated into the main worship service. Initially, this was a result of influence from the Liturgical Movement, but the convenience of eliding the two services was probably also a factor. Thus the Lord's Supper became part of public worship and had a higher profile in congregational life. Another consequence of the change was a relaxing of restrictions on who could communicate and the practice of an open table became increasingly widespread.[69]

The Late Twentieth Century and its Movements

The period since 1950 has seen the greatest and most rapid developments in Baptist worship, with a considerable increase in the level of diversity. While the early part of the century saw a number of city churches developing liturgical forms of worship, with the use of litanies and responses, robed clergy and even sometimes robed choirs and chanted psalms, most churches seem to have had some version of the four-hymn service. However, the Liturgical Movement, increasing ecumenical contact and Charismatic Renewal have all interacted to provide a number of alternatives.

The Traditional Pattern

Many churches continue to worship with interspersed hymns. Often these will be small churches, limited in resources, usually traditional in outlook, and often dependent on visiting worship leaders. Despite the general ferment in worship, nearly 44 per cent of churches claimed at the end of 1996 to use only interspersed hymns.[70] It is difficult to tell whether this is a static figure or whether the proportion of traditional congregations will decrease further. We should note, however, that these congregations now represent a minority of churches in the Union, though admittedly a substantial one, and probably represent an even smaller proportion of church members.

Liturgical Worship

A second, though much smaller, group of churches are those which worship with liturgically structured forms. Some are led by ministers self-consciously motivated by liturgical principles, while others have been enriched by ecumenical contacts and have grasped the opportunity for more structured services resourced by the wider Church. Thus the influence of the Liturgical Movement is evident in some Baptist churches. For example, a concern for the overall shape and flow of the service has led to a restructuring of the components in worship. An increased emphasis on the church as the people of God, and the congregation as active participants in worship, has led to the use of more written material to be said by the congregation as well as a series of manuals for the use of ministers and others leading worship.[71]

Mid- and Late Twentieth-Century Liturgical Worship

Approach to Worship	Call to Worship
	Hymn of Praise
	Prayer: Confession
	Lord's Prayer
The Word of God	Scripture: Old Testament
	Psalm or Hymn
	Scripture: New Testament
	Sermon
	Hymn
	Prayer: Intercession
	Te Deum

The Offertory   Offering of Alms
                                   Offering of Elements
                                   Offering of Penitence
                                   Words of Invitation

The Consecration   Eucharistic Prayer
                                   Thanksgiving
                                   Anamnesis and Oblation
                                   Invocation

The Communion   Words of Institution
                                   Fraction
                                   Delivery and Reception
                                   Lord's Prayer
                                   Nunc Dimittis
                                   Gloria in Excelsis
                                   Hymn
                                   Dismissal and Blessing

An example of a liturgical Free Church service can be found in Neville Clark's *Call to Worship* and is reproduced above.[72] This is an ideal type and, while Clark implemented it fully in the congregations where he served, few others are likely to have done so in this precise form. However, the shape of a Service of the Word as ante-communion – Approach, Word and Response – gained some ground, not least through the influence of Clark's book and the writings of Stephen Winward.[73]

It is a service of Word and Sacrament. Clark advocated a weekly celebration of the Eucharist, though when he was writing in 1960 he recognized that this may not be welcomed widely or rapidly. Indeed, the most common pattern has been for churches to celebrate the Lord's Supper on a monthly basis, though often this will mean monthly Eucharists during morning and evening worship respectively. In 1996, only 5 per cent of Baptist churches celebrated the Lord's Supper every week and some of those were Local Ecumenical Partnerships where their united status might have required a weekly Eucharist. In addition, if use of a lectionary can be any kind of indicator of liturgical ethos, then less than 8 per cent of churches make up this strand of the denomination.[74]

Clark was committed to the notion of structure, and the architecture of the service is an important consideration: 'The Liturgy exists to be the vehicle of worship. For its effectual discharge, its structure, meaning, and purpose must be understood.'[75] This is a concern for an *ordo* as well as order and a desire to see the events of worship interacting and contributing to a greater whole. The influence of the Liturgical Movement is evident, not only in the use of liturgical prayers and responses which have been drawn from other traditions, but in this concern for a structure, replicating an ecumenical consensus which claims biblical and historical precedent, as well as theological integrity.

A variant on this liturgical worship might be described as 'experimental' or 'niche worship', with the construction of special orders of service, using creative media or resources from such places as Iona or Taizé. The worship resources and styles of both Iona and Taizé enjoy considerable support, far wider even than the many thousands who visit each centre every year. The repetitive chants of Taizé and the songs and liturgical prayers of Iona, with their strong emphasis on prayer for justice and peace, are often inserted as units of song within worship of varying styles. Sometimes, however, whole services are prepared using the ethos of Taizé or Iona, and this is what is meant by a 'niche' service, for it is likely to appeal to a particular part of the congregation or draw supporters from across various local congregations. The 1991 denominational hymnbook *Baptist Praise and Worship* included a small amount of material from these two communities, and the annual *Spring Harvest Songbook* has more recently included such material alongside its primary diet of Charismatic worship songs.

These influences illustrate a not uncommon feature of liturgical development, namely, the principle of borrowing or appropriation. Features seen to be good ideas are taken from one cultural context and used in another. This was already happening with compilers of ministers' manuals, such as Stephen Winward and Ernest Payne utilizing in 1960 material from the *Book of Common Prayer* and elsewhere. Now a multitude of books provide resource material for worship, and African songs are sung alongside Celtic prayers and Orthodox chants. What experimental worship can in fact demonstrate is not only the use of resources from another Christian tradition or national culture, but the desire to construct whole services around a coherent theme and sequences in which the actions of the service contribute to a developmental experience for the worshippers. This again suggests an interest in the use of an *ordo*, though it will be one which is customized or constructed locally for thematic or pastoral purposes.

Charismatic Worship

The Charismatic Renewal has also had its impact on Baptist congregations, usually in different churches from those influenced by ecumenical
and liturgical developments. It has led to extended periods of singing and
prayer, a concern for the engaging of the religious affections, together
with the opportunity for the exercising of 'spiritual gifts' by members of
the congregation.

The classic Charismatic service has a tripartite structure as demonstrated in the outline below. It begins with a period of praise, which may
include penitence and devotional intimacy. There is then a clear transition and change of mood to the sermon, usually, though not always, preceded by a reading. This, in turn, is followed by a period of 'engagement'
which may take the form of a 'ministry time' in which people come
forward for prayer, or an open time of worship which is sometimes preceded by the epicletic 'Come Holy Spirit', and in which it is anticipated
that various charismata will be exercised. Often this time will provide an
opportunity for response on the part of the congregation, but with an
expectation that the Holy Spirit will prompt people to repent, come to
faith or make an act of rededication.

Charismatic Worship

Worship Time	*Usually as a sequence of songs, with prayers*
Sermon	*Usually, but not always, preceded by Scripture reading*
Ministry Time	*Prayers for healing and help (often for individuals who come forward), active response to sermon and the exercising of charismata*

This tripartite structure is interesting in a number of ways. It has a strong
similarity to the structure of a liturgical service of word and sacrament
where the opening praise corresponds to the approach and the sermon
corresponds to the service of the word, albeit with less emphasis on reading and more emphasis on explaining. But the parallel continues once
we see the third stage as a time of engagement between the worshippers
and the Holy Spirit. The epicletic nature of eucharistic worship enables
us to see communion as a place of rendezvous in which the worshipper
is open to communion with God through the eucharistic sacrament. A
similar expectation leads a Charismatic worshipper to pray 'Come Holy

Spirit' and expect both the inspiration of spontaneous worship gifts for some and the opportunity for devotional communion for most worshippers.

Such parallel understandings of a sacramental nature ought not to be surprising once we have recognized the likely history of this tripartite Charismatic worship. It flows from two main streams – what James White has called 'the Frontier Tradition'[76] of American Evangelicalism, and Pentecostal worship, itself influenced by the Frontier Tradition.[77] This tradition had its origins in the camp meetings of Kentucky in the years immediately following 1800. What were originally large gatherings of rural worshippers met to prepare for the Lord's Supper[78] through worship and evangelistic preaching – gatherings which lasted several days and which usually ended with the baptism of converts and the Lord's Supper. This Frontier Tradition received influences from various sources – the camp meeting itself sprang from Presbyterianism, while Separatism contributed a biblicism and a commitment to local autonomy, and Methodism encouraged an emphasis on congregational song and a passion for making converts through evangelistic preaching.

This was the genesis of revivalism and what White has called 'the Americanization of Protestant worship'.[79] Worship was specially designed to make converts – choruses, often from hymns by Isaac Watts, were sung repetitively and a mourners' bench was available for those seeking prayer for conversion. Long before the frontier disappeared, this form of worship had spread widely, but it was Charles G. Finney who promoted and systematized the frontier practices into a programme for revival, both in his own ministry and in his *Lectures on Revival*. Theologically Arminian, his methods were essentially pragmatic and his 'new measures' were the methods which had proved evangelistically effective on the frontier. Finney represented an important departure in Free Church worship, not only in America but wherever Evangelicalism has travelled, claiming that 'a revival is the result of the *right* use of the appropriate means'.[80] He argued that the only scriptural prescription with regard to worship was that 'there should be decency and order'[81] and that the primary concern for worship was its effectiveness in producing converts. The tripartite structure reflects this pragmatic concern with its technique of warming up the congregation that it might be open to the call to conversion and given practical opportunities of responding during the worship service.

This revivalism came to dominate Evangelical worship in the USA and, while its influence in Britain has had many channels, some of the obvious connections are through the meetings of Moody and Sankey in the closing decades of the nineteenth century and the crusades of Billy Graham.

Eclectic Worship

The previous section has described 'traditional', 'liturgical' and 'charismatic' as distinct forms of worship, but there are, of course, many examples of these traditions mingling and interacting. For example, the dissemination of a praise and worship culture is probably far wider than the Charismatic Renewal from which it has partly sprung. The widening influence of Charismatic Renewal has inevitably meant its partial assimilation into mainstream church life with a concern for the renewal of devotion, a focus on praise and the assimilation of worship songs without necessarily embracing their implicit theology. This 'culture of renewal', or even the devotional warmth of renewal, may well have travelled far further than a concern for the charismata or the epicletic expectations of the ministry time.[82] The influence of such conference holidays as *Spring Harvest* and the widespread commercial popular music culture of Evangelicalism will have provided songs and forms of worship which have been assimilated without their implicit theologies necessarily being espoused. Some would see this as an example of consumerism or post-modernism in the Church, but, whatever its cause, we need to note that blocks of worship songs have increasingly become a part of Baptist worship and that this will inevitably affect the structure of that worship. There is, of course, nothing new in hymns being transplanted from one tradition to another. However, the *use* of the 'charismatic' worship songs will have an effect on the host liturgical structure through their spirituality as well as their musical style.

Another variant form is that of 'the seeker service', an attempt to provide a worship event aimed at the interested enquirer. It has a clear ancestry back to Finney and his pragmatism,[83] not least because of its use of various media and the vehicle of entertainment in order to challenge those present with the claims of the gospel. While distinct from Charismatic worship, it shares a hope that God will move among the worshippers in the latter part of the service and lead to a response.[84]

This survey of Baptist patterns of worship has been primarily descriptive, with some attempt at tracing the influences and cross-currents. But what of its meaning? Can any general statements be made, supported by this evidence, which indicate a theology implicit in the structures of Baptist worship?

The Patterning of Worship

Early in this chapter, a dual meaning was proposed for the term *ordo*. On the one hand it can refer to the pattern of worship in its relation to life and faith, the linkages between cultic activity and the larger horizon of the life of the world and the Kingdom of God. On the other hand, and more particularly, it can refer to the patterning of worship services and their internal dynamics.

Arguably, all worship should have a point of reference beyond itself, not only in relation to God, but in relation to the world beyond the Church. We shall see later, for example, how preaching can apply the Word of God to the life of the worshippers and the life of the world, or how intercessory prayer or the co-ordinated mission of the local congregation can bridge the two worlds of cultic activity and daily life.

But what of the relationship between the Lord's Supper and the wider worshipping life of a congregation? We have already seen that there is a considerable ecumenical consensus which regards eucharistic worship as the normative worship of the Lord's Day. Sunday, as the day of resurrection, is seen as the day in which the Paschal Mystery is rehearsed through word and sacrament, and so liturgical theology has primarily been an exposition of eucharistic worship. The juxtaposition of word and sacrament which Lathrop identifies usually takes place within a single worship event.[85]

Schmemann's understanding of liturgical dualism in the primitive Christian community portrayed the early Christians as *both* worshipping in the Jewish temple and synagogue *and* breaking bread, that is, celebrating the Eucharist, in their homes. In this continuing relationship with the old and the simultaneous celebration of the new, he saw an expression of God's new creation where, as in resurrection, the new does not replace the old but transforms it. He argued that this was later to find expression in the linking of the *synaxis* and the Eucharist and in the relating of the Eucharist to the Liturgy of Time, where again he saw a witness to the relationship between creation and new creation.[86] However, the polarity of temple and eucharistic domestic table could also be seen as offering a model in which different events, such as separate services of the word and services of the table, provide a polarity which overarches the life of a congregation but which is not elided into a single act of worship.

In Baptist worship, newness of life is to be found elsewhere – in the desire for conversion and in the need for continuing dependence upon God. A tendency to spiritualize and avoid the materialist dimensions of worship has meant that the Lord's Supper, while important, has not been regarded as the primary channel of divine grace which it is in some other traditions. This spiritualizing is one aspect of the Radical Reformation's reaction to what it perceived to be mediaeval excesses and an expression of that rationalism which is a continuing feature of Free Church perspectives. Attitudes to the Eucharist are probably also affected by the Reformation conviction that each person can enjoy direct access to the Father through Christ and the Spirit, a conviction which contributed to the breaking down of some of the distinctions between sacramental and non-sacramental worship.

Alongside other Christian traditions, Baptists give a priority to the rehearsing of the Paschal Mystery in worship, but it is not only achieved at the Lord's table. The death and resurrection of Christ are proclaimed in evangelistic and other preaching, as well as in song, testimony and prayer. A monthly communion service does not indicate a less Christo-centric faith so much as a different cultural and liturgical approach to the mystery of divine grace. The patterns of Baptist worshipping life are configured differently from those traditions with a weekly eucharistic celebration.[87] A challenge, therefore, for the liturgical interpreter is to enquire how such 'non-eucharistic' worship functions in ways which are analogous to the eucharistic rites of others.

Patterns and Meaning

Schmemann argued that within the Orthodox tradition it is possible to find meaning in the liturgical co-efficients, the intricate relationships between the varied components of a service. Our survey of Baptist services and their evolution does not suggest a concern for detailed sequence, though there are some regular patterns in the various services. Do these patterns have any *theological* meaning? This question does not require evidence of conscious theological ordering, indeed the relationship between worship and theology is more subtle than simply the conscious theological ordering of worship. In the next chapter, an examination of writings on worship by various Baptists will not provide evidence for a theological rationale influencing the shape of services, yet it is difficult to believe that the shape of those services was never questioned. It is possible, however, to identify a number of principles which may be regarded as implicit in the patterning of the services we have examined.

First, the very notion of order underlies the worship surveyed. There is a concern that there should be a structure, even though there may sometimes be an apparent indifference as to what that structure should be. This may even be true in relatively free worship, although the structure may be provided by the guidance of a leader and the shared expectations of the congregation, rather than by a predetermined order of service. For example, in his ethnographic observation of the free worship of an independent Charismatic congregation, Martin Stringer noticed that there was order, both through the leadership of the elders and through the thematic linking of ideas. Because preparation was not acceptable, spontaneous contributions, such as the suggesting of a song or the leading of an extempore prayer, tended to follow the theme of what had preceded them in open worship. Thus liturgical units were ordered sequentially by association.[88]

Second, the very developments observed in our historical survey suggest a readiness to change whatever the current practice might be in the interests of some high ideal such as faithfulness to Scripture or 'more relevant' worship. Tradition does not carry for the Free Churches the burden of authority which it would within the Roman Catholic or Orthodox churches. Authority is found elsewhere – in Scripture, the missionary imperative, pastoral need and common sense rationalism. Thus the *ordo*, or underlying principles, of evolving worship cannot carry the *lex credendi* in the way that Schmemann claims for the Orthodox, because the patterning of worship is subservient to other theological authorities. Interpreting the notion of 'Tradition' in the Orthodox Church, Vladimir Lossky argues for a nuanced understanding of the relationship between Scripture and Tradition in which both are understood to be within the operation of the Holy Spirit.[89] This is different from the looser meaning of tradition within the Baptist community, in the sense of inherited patterns of behaviour or shared community values. A study of Baptist worship can help to answer the question 'What do *Baptists* believe?' but in doing so will not provide information which can be identified as the *lex credendi* of the Christian Church without further scrutiny, especially with regard to its congruence with Scripture. This is quite distinct from Schmemann's Orthodox perspective and is the basis for our suggesting the need for a fourth stage of theological critique in the way in which liturgical theology is attempted.

The high value which Baptists place on Scripture offers them a place from which to critique Tradition, including those values which are carried within worship. For the Separatists, including Baptists and Independents, the task of reformation 'without tarrying for any' meant a stark simplicity in worship in which Scripture was the only arbiter of what was permitted. Until at least the middle of the nineteenth century, great authority was given to what were called 'scriptural ordinances' in the ordering of worship, and this term did not only refer to baptism and the Lord's Supper, but denoted a scriptural mandate in which all aspects of worship had to be justified through either the command or example of Scripture. More recently, a certain pragmatism has come to bear on the question of what should or should not be included in worship. Although this utilitarian perspective is often submerged below scriptural language, it probably reflects the cultural and theological changes of the last century and a half.[90]

Third, there is a concern for simplicity and freedom. This simplicity is evident in the lack of ceremonial activity and in the valuing of spontaneity, while the concern for free worship is found both in a willingness to change an order of service and in the use of free prayer. The use of free prayer in public worship is particularly significant in our understanding of Free Church worship as it exemplifies a spirituality which expresses not only freedom from central control, but dependence upon divine guidance and help.

The scriptural principle had inevitably led to worship services which were stripped of anything which might be regarded as 'ritual'. In addition, the decades of persecution which followed the restoration of the Stuart monarchy in 1660 were largely focused on worship – both the absence of dissenters from parish worship and the convening of dissenting conventicles – and that worship was itself refined by the difficult circumstances under which congregations met. Inevitably, the awareness that violent interruption might happen at any moment, as well as the reconvening of the worshipping assembly in remote rural places, further stripped worship to what were seen as its essentials.

Fourth, while reflecting on the principle of change and development, we ought not to ignore the transformation that has come through the gradual increase in the proportion of congregational singing. Significantly, it was Particular Baptists, that strand of denominational life which was to survive and bear fruit, which first pioneered congregational singing. As a vehicle of active congregational participation, its increase should be seen not only as a reflection of cultural changes but as a shift in the nature of congregational worship. This is particularly evident in Charismatic culture, but is also true for other strands of Baptist life. An increase in active congregational participation both reflects and influences the way in which worship and its leadership is viewed. James White makes a helpful distinction between 'passive' participation in worship, in which members of the congregation hear or see someone else do something, and 'active' participation, which means 'people doing things themselves: praying, singing, shouting, dancing'.[91] It is interesting that the nineteenth-century pioneer of the Liturgical Movement, Abbé Guéranger, saw plainsong as a way of increasing congregational participation. He saw this participation as a vital aspect of Christian worship and, in due course, it became a core value of the Liturgical Movement.

Fifth, while a concern for detailed structure may not have been significant until the attempts at reordering in the twentieth century, there does seem to be a concern for the main movements of worship, what we might term the 'deep structures' of worship.[92] These movements below the surface seem to be very simple. There is an early need to address God, and the service moves towards the proclaiming of the divine Word. Similarly, there has often been a concern to provide a vehicle for responding to that address. The regularity of the sequencing of these sections of the services suggests a logic, but it is far from clear that such a logic carries theological weight. It is more likely that there is a diachronic ordering in which the various parts take their 'logical' place in the service with, for example, the act of approach at the beginning and response to the Word near the close.

Finally, a survey of Baptist services down the years will suggest that preaching has usually taken a relatively large proportion of the time allotted for each service. The dominance of the sermon will be seen by some[93] as an example of Protestant didacticism, though it is better seen as an expectation that God will address the congregation through the preacher. In eighteenth-century London, Benjamin Wallin admonished worshippers for sometimes arriving late, as though the preceding worship was unimportant,[94] and, over a century later, Spurgeon encouraged his students to give adequate attention to worship and not allow the sermon to unduly dominate.[95]

It could be argued that the importance of the sermon has been reduced in both the Liturgical and Charismatic Movements. While there may be other factors at work in this, such as the erosion of religious certainty, a 'liturgical' approach to preaching has placed the sermon as the servant of the read Word and subservient to the celebration of the Eucharist. In Charismatic worship, the place of preaching remains, though often as an explanation of, or preparation for, the experience of the Holy Spirit in prayer and 'ministry'. There are often complaints about the lack of Scripture reading in such worship, though this was not borne out by the survey of Baptist churches in 1996, and one is reminded of the Quaker–Baptist disputes of the mid-seventeenth century, circling around issues of experience or objectivity, freedom from, or subservience to, the Word. If we were to ask where congregations saw the primary focus of their encounter with God in worship, we would probably receive different answers which might well correspond to what they saw as the climax of the service. Thus the congregations' expectations in relation to 'experience' are another way of discerning meaning alongside the theological explanations which might be given about the meaning of that worship. To anticipate meeting God in preaching will reflect a different understanding of worship to one in which the worshipper expects to meet God in the felt 'blessing' of a ministry time, or the communion of a eucharistic celebration.

We have seen a number of themes emerge in our survey of Baptist worship which loosely relate to Payne's statement about the main features of that worship. There is the communal nature of worship, demonstrated by the increasing place given to congregational singing; the central place given to Scripture and preaching; the role of extempore prayer and a readiness to engage in varying levels of spontaneity. In addition, there is a concern for a proclamation of the gospel which leads to response, especially in personal faith and commitment, and we shall see that this missionary concern is nurtured and expressed in the practice of believers' baptism. These themes will provide the focus for the next stage of our study which will explore the *spirituality* of Baptist worship. Here we shall enquire further into the Baptist *ordo* in the second sense in which Schmemann uses the term, namely, the spirituality which undergirds the whole pattern of Baptist worship both in its cultic expression in gathered worship and in the relationship of that worship to the life of the Church and the world.

5

The Soul of Baptist Worship

You remember the language of Jesus, John iv.24. 'God is a *spirit*, and they that worship him, must worship him in *spirit* and in truth.' Our obligation to worship God in *spirit*, or in a *spiritual* manner, arises from the *spirituality* of his nature. Was God a corporeal being, mere bodily acts might serve; but seeing he is a *spirit, his worship must be agreeable to his nature.* Not that bodily worship is to be discarded: Jesus Christ worshipped his divine Father with his body as well as soul. But, with this, never rest satisfied. God demands the whole man, but looks principally at the heart. Consider this as the mark by which you are to distinguish between sincerity and hypocrisy in religious acts. 'As an holy priesthood, offer up *spiritual* sacrifices.' 1 Pet. ii.5. Be earnest with God for the gift of his HOLY SPIRIT, in an abundant measure. Seek his divine influences, to furnish you with *spiritual* ability, in order that you may be found in the discharge of that which is your indispensable duty. Highly prize his sacred operations. These are the real excellency of all religious duties. Brilliant parts and abilities, natural or acquired, can never supply their place.

John Sutcliffe, June 1786
on behalf of the Northamptonshire Baptist Churches[1]

What does this worship *mean*? What matters to this congregation? What do they believe and what do they value? As our study of free worship continues we shall begin to respond to these questions. So far, we have identified a number of themes which characterize Baptist worship, and in this chapter we shall examine what various commentators have had to say about them. The importance of Scripture with much of the service dedicated to its explanation and application; the freedom and devotional intensity of extempore prayer; extended singing which enables the congregation to offer praise and prayer with one voice; evangelistic preaching and prayers which ask God to act in the world and in the lives of the congregation – here are the beginnings of a Free Church *ordo*, a presentation of the patterning of Baptist worship, the DNA of the worshipping community. Put more traditionally, we shall explore the soul of Baptist worship – a soul which will not only tell us things about worship itself, but which will characterize the essence of the Baptist community and the wider Church of which it is a part.

Patterns, Themes and Values

We shall do this by looking at what various people in that community have said about worship and the themes we have found. It is tempting to see the use of writings *about* worship in developing a liturgical theology as precisely the sort of secondary theology which Schmemann and others eschew. However, two observations may show how this judgement would be a mistake.

First, the primary concern of the writers to be studied in this and the following chapters is devotional, an expression of faith often close to the language of worship. Most are Baptists, but not all, for the story of this community has been part of a larger story and sometimes its faith has been best expressed in borrowed, or adopted, words. Though Baptists have often claimed him in the past, John Bunyan would probably not now be regarded as a Baptist, though he stood astride an ambiguous boundary between Baptists and Independents in the second half of the seventeenth century.[2] Isaac Watts was quite definitely not a Baptist but an Independent; however, the reception of both his and Bunyan's writings among Calvinistic Baptists demonstrates that they represent many of the ideas of that community, even though their own membership lay elsewhere. The writings range across nearly four centuries. The Confessions of Faith, John Bunyan, Benjamin Keach and Hercules Collins represent the seventeenth century, while Isaac Watts and Benjamin Wallin were writing in the early and mid-eighteenth century. The Northamptonshire circular letters date from the latter part of that century until the middle of the next, a period which encompassed at its beginning the ministry of John Fawcett and at its end the ministry of William Brock. Charles Haddon Spurgeon and Alexander Maclaren were active in the second half of the nineteenth century and Henry Wheeler Robinson was writing in the first half of the twentieth.

These writings provide important information about what Baptists, and those they respected, believed about worship. In addition, *what* they write about worship has a devotional intent. They are more concerned with what we might call 'spirituality' than the details of liturgical ordering. Even when concerned with what is and is not permissible in worship, their reliance upon Scripture demonstrates an important strand in this Free Church spirituality. The Confessions are, in part, explaining Baptist beliefs to other Christians, the circular letters are providing pastoral advice to the churches of a county association, and the concern of most of the individual writers was to improve the worship practices of their respective readers as well as their original audiences. Much of this writing, therefore, is in some sense *primary* theology.[3]

Further, Schmemann distilled his *ordo* not only from the liturgy itself, but from the Orthodox typica, the books of ceremonies and rites which contain detailed instructions for the conduct of worship. He explained that these books reflect and preserve the tradition of worship and apply it to particular circumstances, with their instructions for celebrating the liturgy through the Christian year. Historically, the worship existed prior to the typica:

> To find the Ordo behind the 'rubrics', regulations and rules – to find the unchanging principle, the living norm or 'logos' of worship as a whole, within what is accidental and temporary: this is the primary task which faces those who regard liturgical theology not as a collecting of accidental and arbitrary explanations of services but as the systematic study of the *lex orandi* of the Church.[4]

Using various Baptist and other writers on worship, we shall examine instructions about the conduct and meaning of worship. However, instead of providing rubrics for the detailed ordering and conduct of worship, we shall find that these writers want to order worship through the application of a number of values, an *ordo* which patterns worship from the perspective of spirituality.

Here are the first two stages of our Free Church method for liturgical theology. The first stage has established the liturgical facts and stage two seeks to find meaning through various relationships. For Free Church worship, those relationships are not primarily the 'liturgical co-efficients' within a service, the relationships between the various components in an 'order of service', but the interaction of the values which shape the worship and provide it with theological coherence.

Four themes will be proposed as the primary concerns of the selected writers with regard to worship, themes which have already emerged in our historical survey. As theological themes, they represent something of the faith of the Baptist community, but they also express the values which inform and shape Baptist worship. These are convictions which are embodied in the worship of the community.[5] The spirituality which underpins and is expressed in Baptist worship is presented here as a group of core values, beliefs which are *so* important that they affect the practices of the community. An exploration of these denominational values will both help to explain why Baptist worship has developed in the way it has, and make a contribution to the ecumenical debate about the nature of Christian worship.

Baptist Liturgical Values

Baptists and many in the Free Churches tend to be more concerned about the content of worship than about the structure or sequence of the various parts. Manuals of worship have attempted to correct what their editors perceived to be a fault and, in so doing, they provide evidence for the widespread disregard of liturgical structures. For example, Stephen Winward, in the introduction to *Orders and Prayers for Church Worship* in 1960, argued that, 'we must avoid that "squalid sluttery" and un-inspired disorder which comes from disregarding the traditional pattern and forms of Christian worship'.[6] However, we have noted in our survey that there has been a concern for order, though we also saw that there was no great concern about the particular sequencing of the component parts. To understand Free Church worship within in its own liturgical terms of reference, it will not be sufficient to examine the sequences and structures of worship. We need also to examine its spirituality, and, in what follows, this examination will be undertaken through the study of those values which shape and are implicit in the worship of the Baptists' community.

There are two primary values for Baptists – attention to Scripture and the importance of devotion. This latter theme is actually a cluster of concerns, including a concern for personal faith, a devotional openness to the Holy Spirit, a valuing of sincerity and religious experience. These values – Scripture and devotion – stand in a polar relationship to one another, a relationship in which there is both tension and dialogue. Each separately provides an important interpretative key for understanding Baptist worship, and both together offer a field of activity in which the values, and the theology which shapes and energizes them, come alive in the event of worship.

In addition to these, there are two further values which, in a different way, contribute to the interaction that results in Baptist approaches to worship. First, the nature of worship as the gathering of the church community provides a communal *context* within which worship takes place. Finally, eschatology, an orientation towards God's future, which includes a concern for mission, offers a *horizon* for the worship event.

Before examining these values in more detail, it is interesting to compare the observations of a recent Roman Catholic liturgical theologian, Kevin Irwin. He argues that the 'theology of liturgy' contains three strands, the *epicletic*, the *anamnetic* and the *ecclesiological*.[7] Worship is *anamnetic*, bridging the past, present and future, not only in the anamnesis of the eucharistic 'Do this in memory of me', but in all the proclamation and remembering that goes on in worship. Similarly, worship is *epicletic* in all its actions, not only in prayers which explicitly invoke the presence and power of the Spirit, such as at the Eucharist. All of worship is derived from and dependent upon the action and power of the Holy Spirit. And because worship is a gathering of the community of God's people, it is *ecclesiological*, as 'it is always an act of the Church's self-understanding and self-expression'. The parallels between Irwin's typology and the four values identified in this study will illuminate the discussion of Baptist worship and its spirituality at several points. The worship of which Irwin speaks is, of course, *eucharistic*, though these principles do represent fundamental aspects of Christian worship in general.[8] We may compare his *anamnesis* with the Baptist attention to Scripture, *epiclesis* with the concern for devotion and the Spirit, and *ecclesiology* with the Baptist understanding of the Church as primarily manifested in the local congregation.

In Spirit and in Truth: The Polarity of Faith

A self-conscious concern for *simplicity* has often marked Baptist worship. As heirs of the Radical Reformation,[9] early Baptists, like the wider Separatist stream of which they were a part, began by wanting a worship which was stripped to essentials. Reaction to what were perceived to be mediaeval ecclesiastical abuses expressed itself in England in the Separatists' rejection of the newly formed state church which, though Protestant in theology, was regarded as 'Papist' in worship.[10] Affirming a believer-church ecclesiology, these Separatists attempted to reconstruct 'scriptural' worship by rejecting those human innovations which could not be substantiated by a direct recourse to the Bible.

Attention to Scripture

Like other radical groups, early Baptists separated from the state church in their search for the purity of the Church, and their ordering of worship was based on the Genevan premise of including only that which was ordered or modelled in Scripture.[11]

The purpose of the *Second London Confession* (1677 and 1689) was in part to show how much common ground the Particular Baptists had with the Congregationalists and the Presbyterians, during and after the time of persecution. B. R. White points out that the confession is an explicit revision of the *Savoy Confession*, which, in turn, was closely based on the *Westminster Confession*.[12] The *Second London Confession* founds its understanding of worship on the sovereignty of God:

> The light of Nature shews that there is a God, who hath Lordship, and Sovereigntye over all; is just, good, and doth good unto all; and is therefore to be feared, loved, praised, called upon, trusted in, and served, with all the Heart, and all the Soul, and with all the Might.[13]

It also articulates the common Puritan theme that God may only be worshipped in ways that he has appointed:

> But the acceptable way of Worshipping the true God, is instituted by himself; and so limited by his own revealed will, that he may not be worshipped according to the imaginations, and devices of Men, or the suggestions of Satan, under any visible representations, or any other way, not prescribed in the Holy Scriptures.[14]

Worship is placed under the authority of the notion of *divine ordinance*, a phrase which is frequently used in Baptist writings to indicate far more than simply the dominical sacraments of baptism and the Lord's Supper.[15] The root meaning of *ordinance* refers to something which is ordained or commanded and has often been used in a wide and inclusive sense in Baptist and other Free Church writings. For example, prayer is an ordinance because, as the confession puts it, 'Prayer with thanksgiving, being one special part of natural worship, is by *God* required of all men.'[16] Similarly, the reading and preaching of the Scriptures, the singing of psalms, hymns and spiritual songs and the administration of baptism and the Lord's Supper, must all be 'performed in obedience to him, with understanding, faith, reverence and godly fear'. In fact, some of the Separatists believed that even Calvin had been enticed away from a rigorous use of Scripture as the *only* basis for worship practices.[17]

While this approach inevitably encouraged a use of proof texts,[18] it did provide a framework within which Baptists and others had confidence that their worship was not simply their human offering to God, but a divinely appointed means of grace. At the beginning of the nineteenth century, John Fawcett argued that holiness is related to obedience:

No acts of worship can properly be called holy, but such as the Almighty has enjoined. No man, nor any body of men have any authority to invent rites and ceremonies of worship; to change the ordinances which he has established; or to invent new ones . . . The divine word is the only safe directory in what relates to his own immediate service. The question is not what we may think becoming, decent or proper, but what our gracious Master has authorised as such. In matters of religion, nothing bears the stamp of holiness but what God has ordained.[19]

This ordinance paradigm is important in the developing history of Free Church worship, but as we explore the spirituality of that worship we will need to recognize the tension between the two perspectives of outward obedience and inward sincerity. This concern is not, of course, restricted to the Free Churches, as the collect for the Fourth Sunday after Easter in the *Book of Common Prayer* demonstrates:

Almighty God, who alone canst order the unruly wills and affections of sinful men; *Grant unto thy people, that they may love the thing which thou commandest, and desire that which thou dost promise*; that so, among the sundry and manifold changes of the world, our hearts may surely there be fixed, where true joys are to be found; through Jesus Christ our Lord. *Amen*[20]

Here is a key intersection in Christian spirituality, the relationship between outward practice and inward disposition, and is a constant theme in Baptist writings about worship. For example, disputes over hymn singing in the seventeenth and eighteenth centuries were largely concerned with arguing whether or not such singing was, in fact, an ordinance, and how the biblical material which mentioned singing was to be interpreted. Indeed, the title of Benjamin Keach's famous defence of the congregational singing of hymns, which he had introduced to the weekly worship of his Horsleydown congregation, includes the words, 'Singing of Psalms, Songs and Spiritual Songs, proved to be an Holy Ordinance of Jesus Christ'. His chief critic, a member of his congregation called Samuel Marlow, had argued that the references to singing spiritual songs referred to an interior singing which does not result in audible sound. Keach argued that this supposed inner activity of 'heart singing' is similar to the worship of the Quakers:

Thus the Quakers have cast off the Holy Ordinances of Baptism and the Lord's Supper, and have gotten spiritual ones (in the blind imaginations of their hearts) in their room; as you would have a heart singing of psalms without the voice, so they have got a heart baptism without water, and a heart breaking of bread without bread and wine.[21]

The argument is no passing allusion, but reflects some of the robust debate in the second half of the seventeenth century between Baptists and Quakers. The inwardness of worship is seen to be vital to the integrity of worship – yet for Baptists and other Christians, the inwardness must be the fount from which will flow the outward expression of worship, an expression which must be in obedience to the divine ordinances. This interiority does not replace outward expression, but is a vital condition of the action's integrity and the worshipper's sincerity.

This concern for integrity and sincerity in worship should encourage us to see that an ordinance was not regarded as an external imposition likely to command mere obedience rather than heart-felt worship. The logic of a command is that it is obeyed and we might think that such obedience will often be grudging, or at least subservient. However, we might detect a number of reasons why ordinances were generally regarded as upholding, rather than undermining, true worship.

First, while democratic structures were developing in society, particularly from the seventeenth century onwards, there were still broadly unchallenged hierarchies. These provided a mental framework within which commands were not rejected outright, but judged on the basis of the benevolence or otherwise of the one who issued the command. So commands were received within the context of a relationship and on the basis of what was known about the one who issued the command. Divine ordinances were seen to be the commands of a just God who was worthy of obedience. John Fawcett, for example, quoted the letter to the Hebrews:

> Wherefore we receiving a kingdom which cannot be moved, let us have grace, whereby we may serve God acceptably with reverence and godly fear. (Heb. 12.28 AV)

Second, this God was known as the Saviour of the world and his commands were seen as being for the benefit of humanity. Divine ordinances were seen as 'means of grace', God-appointed ways through which, in his grace, God would meet human beings in their need. Worship was not a human invention, as tradition was perceived to be, nor a ladder of human effort attempting to scale heaven. It was divinely appointed as the means by which God might reach humanity with a fullness of grace that resulted in blessing for the worshippers. This view of ordinances which sees them not as onerous and heteronomous commands, but as instructions full of promise and invitation, reflects faith in a gracious God. It also reflects doctrines of creation and incarnation which undergird a view of the material world in which divine agency and spiritual benefit have a place.[22]

Finally, Baptists, and other radical groups, did not have an *ex opere operato* view of these ordinances. Although it was regarded as important for true worshippers to worship in the manner believed to be appointed by God, the outward observance of such ways was never regarded as sufficient. To view the outward observance as efficacious, irrespective of the attitude of the worshipper, was regarded as magic and ritual and to be rejected.[23] The efficacy of the worship practice, it was believed, depended on the integrity of the worshippers. Outward obedience and conformity were not sufficient, and, if not accompanied by an inward grace, were seen as 'lip worship' and a contravention of the teaching of Jesus.[24] This will become evident when we examine some of the instructions for the conduct of public worship. The *way* in which worship is undertaken is not in order to fulfil external instructions, thus ensuring validity, but so that the inner attitude of the worshippers might be at one with the outward expression. But this is to anticipate. This principle of divine ordinance is a clear example of doctrine controlling worship and substantiates the claim that at some point the theology implicit in Baptist and Free Church worship will need to be critiqued, if the method of liturgical theology is to be consistent with the Free Church tradition. We also need to recognize, however, that since Fawcett's time, the ordinance principle has for many mutated into a wider concern for a biblical undergirding of life and practice.

Scripture is not only a guide to the practice of worship through the search for divine commands and scriptural precedents, but also an influence on the shape and content of worship. These influences are clear and explicit. For example, we have already observed that a significant proportion of each service is dedicated to preaching. We shall examine this in more detail in Chapter 7, but here we may note that Scripture is central to this worship because it provides the *raison d'être* for the sermon which should be an exposition of Scripture, albeit in a variety of forms. The core value of attention to Scripture is demonstrated in this expository preaching in the Baptist and Free Church community. Exposition involves not only interpretation but the applying of scriptural truth to the lives and beliefs of the congregation. Scripture is authoritative in the life and faith of the Church: it guides disciples, it nourishes and enables growth in faith, it witnesses to God's revelation in Jesus Christ and it invites worship and a trust in God's promises.

In contemporary Baptist life, as in some other evangelical Free Church groups, there is some concern that the reading of Scripture is subsumed into the preaching.[25] Again, reflection on this is best dealt with in our chapter dedicated to preaching. For now, we may note that the very concern that the omission of Scripture readings leads to a deficiency in worship, confirms that the norm *is* the reading of Scripture. This judgement is not only a liturgical one, for the authority of Scripture does not only refer to its priority in matters of doctrinal or ecclesiastical rule-making. The Bible is viewed as 'the book of life', relevant and authoritative for daily living and the nourishing of personal faith, which is partly why preaching provides a bridge between the gathering for worship and daily living.

As well as providing the authority for the ordering of worship and the authority for preaching itself, Scripture impinges on worship in many ways. A detailed exploration of this complex relationship is beyond the scope of this study,[26] but it would be illuminating to recognize just how pervasive the influence can be. Writing more widely in the Reformed and Lutheran traditions respectively, J.-J. von Allmen and Peter Brunner identify six loci of influence: 'the reading of Scripture, preaching, the absolution, the greeting and the blessing, the psalmody of the Church, and those indirect forms of the Word such as hymns, confessions of faith, doxologies and the collects'.[27] In contemporary Baptist worship, we might list

- the call to worship through Scripture sentences,
- the reading of Scripture,
- the quotation of Scripture in prayers, both directly and through 'the language of Zion', and the use of biblical phrases and images,
- the occasional use of psalms and other responsive readings as prayers or affirmations,
- the singing of hymns and the offering of prayers which employ extensive biblical quotations and allusions, including occasional metricated psalmody and worship songs which primarily comprise paraphrased scriptural texts,
- the reading of Scripture as a narrative framework for such liturgical actions as baptism, the Lord's Supper, infant presentation or the imposition of hands for ordination or commissioning.

This list demonstrates just how pervasive the influence of Scripture is in Baptist worship, though its anamnetic influence is widespread in most forms of Christian worship. However, the Separatist origins and a continuing Evangelical identity place Scripture in a position of authority which is different from that afforded it in denominations which define the relationship of Church, Tradition and Scripture differently.

Attention to Scripture need not imply a fundamentalist approach to the Bible, though for some Baptists such a designation would be accurate. Rather, it displays a readiness to order the faith and practice of the Church, as well as the daily living of the believer, in the light of what are perceived to be scriptural principles. So a recent statement by the Study and Research Division of the Baptist World Alliance explained:

> Baptists believe that the Bible is both the true record of God's revelation to our world and the supreme written guide for our faith and practice today. Because it leads us to Jesus Christ the living Word, we speak of the Bible as 'the Word of God,' and believe it was inspired by God's Spirit. Baptists reflect different views about the mode of the Bible's inspiration, but all regard it as totally sufficient; that is, all teaching must be in harmony with the Scriptures, and all teaching must be tested by the Scriptures alone.[28]

However, Scripture should not be separated from the testimony of personal experience, what Wheeler Robinson identifies as 'the Reformation principle of the *Testimonium Spiritus Sancti Internum*',[29] and it is to this second theme of personal faith that we now turn for the other aspect of the polarity of spirit and truth.

Devotion and Openness to the Spirit

Like other radical groups, early Baptists separated from the state church in their search for the purity of the Church, but their reading of the Bible extended beyond the search for detailed instructions about the components of worship to include a radical piety which centred on the believer's relationship with God. A concern for personal salvation, and for the individual Christian's growth in grace, will be central features in any account of Baptist beliefs and have imposed their authority on the writings about worship as much as in other areas of thinking.

An example of this is the way in which the response of Jesus to the Samaritan woman's question, concerning the competing claims of Mount Gerizim and the Jerusalem temple, has been used as a biblical basis for various statements about Christian worship:

> But the hour cometh, and now is, when the true worshippers shall worship the Father in spirit and in truth: for the Father seeketh such to worship him. God is a Spirit: and they that worship him must worship him in spirit and in truth. (John 4.23–4 AV)

This passage suggests that the basis for worship after the coming of the

Messiah is quite different from the worship which preceded it. Free Church writers have at times seen this text as a reason for rejecting the ritual practices of more liturgical traditions. For example, in 1845 Thomas Gough wrote the circular letter of the Northamptonshire Baptist Association, at a time when the ripples of the Oxford Movement were beginning to lap into Free Church consciousness with a fear that the Reformation was about to unravel. He likened the ceremonial of Roman Catholic and Anglican worship to the ritual of the Jewish temple and founded his rejection of such worship on the theology of a new dispensation:

> We object to the organisation of the Christian Church, on the model of the Jewish. A national church we hold to be contrary to the precepts and opposed to the genius of christianity. If referred to the ancient pattern therefore, we urge that 'if any man be in Christ, he is a new creature;' . . . Nor is there any reason to suppose the arrangements of the Jewish church were designed to afford a general idea of the manner in which divine worship should be conducted in subsequent ages.[30]

True Christian worship, he argued, was to be understood in the light of what he believed to be the heart of Christianity – personal religion; and he quoted the words of Jesus:

> 'The hour cometh and now is when the true worshippers shall worship the Father in spirit and in truth,' &c. 'True worshippers' here seems to intend real worshippers; those who are not the types of a worshipping Church, but that church itself. There are, now, no accepted worshippers of any other description. It is necessary, therefore, that all acts of worship, whether they consist of prayer, praise, or ceremonial observances, should be performed in spirit and in truth. Unless this be the case, our worship is more than vain, and worse than useless.[31]

Arguments about worship which have been based on John 4.23–4 have primarily concerned themselves with two related issues. First, there is the concept of a new dispensation, whereby the worship of the Old Testament period is replaced by the worship of the Christian dispensation. The allusion by Jesus to the imminent irrelevance of the sanctuaries in Samaria and Jerusalem provides the basis for a radical rejection of the concept of holy places. This shift towards the interior carries with it a rejection of the whole apparatus of the cult, whether the outward fabric of a holy building or the outward action of religious ritual. John Fawcett had previously stated quite bluntly:

It is well known, that under the former dispensation, a place appropriated to the worship of God was solemnly consecrated to him, and considered as holy in a ceremonial way . . . but this kind of holiness is not the object of our present attention. We consider it as peculiar to the Mosaic economy; as we find no trace of it, either enjoined or practised, by Christ or his apostles under the New Testament dispensation.[32]

Here is an expression of confessional identity which distances itself from those churches which it believes to be still worshipping under the Old Testament dispensation. This radical approach had led the Separatists to part company with the Puritans and seek a reformation of the Church 'without tarrying for any'.[33]

It would be a mistake to see this view as primarily a negative one. There is a Christo-centric focus which leads to the second issue which flows from the use of John 4.23–4. Gough asserted that, 'In every case, therefore, personal piety must be deemed an essential characteristic of a worshipper of Christ.'[34] Not only is there a new dispensation, but the work of Christ, and the pneumatological status of the believer as a recipient of the grace of God, provide a matrix for understanding Christian worship which is 'in spirit and in truth'. Outward aids to worship, whether buildings or actions, become secondary to the spiritual relationship between the worshipper and God. This is not a total rejection of buildings or liturgical actions as, for example, there is a clear distinction between the Baptist concern for the interior or spiritual dimension of worship and the radical interiority of the Quakers. There are indeed new means of grace to replace the sacrificial and ceremonial systems of the Old Testament, but they are always to be viewed from the pneumatological principle of John 4.24. So William Brock, in a circular letter to the Norfolk churches, also in 1845, invited his readers to see behind the components of worship the reality of a gracious God:

Unaided by the Spirit of truth, you cannot comprehend the things which are of God, because they are spiritually discerned. The prayer, the psalmody, the argument, the appeal, the Scriptures, the ordinances, are not grace – they are only the means of grace, the mere vehicles through which the God of all grace sends down the communications of his love. Rely then, implicitly and consciously, not in word only, but in deed and truth, upon God.[35]

The spiritual autobiographies of the Puritans and Calvinistic Separatists are locked into a concern about the destiny of the individual soul. They display a heart-searching *angst,* a need for assurance that the writer is a member of God's elect.[36]

Evangelicalism was often to express itself later in terms of the confession 'Jesus is my personal Saviour and Lord'. This individualistic spirituality can often manifest itself in a concern for sincerity in worship, as well as in a disregarding of external worship media, tendencies which were understandably increased during the period of persecution.[37] Justification is by faith, not the fulfilling of ritual actions in a special building, and individual believers must work out their own salvation 'with fear and trembling'.[38]

There are, however, further theological considerations. If worship is seen as an encounter with God, then, through praise and prayer, the reading of Scripture, the faithful preaching of the Word and consecrated listening, humanity approaches God. Yet this engagement is a result not of human but of divine initiative. According to the Particular Baptist *Second London Confession* of 1677, as well as the *Westminster Confession* and the General Baptist *Orthodox Confession*, the worship of God 'is to be made in the name of the Son, by the help of the Spirit, according to his will'.[39]

Here is a 'democratic' spirituality. The grace of God is the basis of the worshippers' confidence, not an ecclesiastically authenticated ministry or scrupulously followed ritual. It blossoms from the belief that there is no mediator other than Jesus Christ and that all believers have access to 'the throne of grace'. But this confidence is also built on the conviction that they and their forebears were worshipping God in God-ordained ways – as well as spirit, there must be truth.

Truth should not be understood only in intellectual terms. There is a relational dimension to truth, just as there is a spiritual reality distinct from the outward forms of worship. This is perhaps most clearly exemplified in the tradition of extempore prayer in which the worshipper, or the one leading others in worship, spontaneously expresses that which is heart-felt, as distinct from reading what has been composed by another. In the following passage from the prison writings of John Bunyan, he speaks of prayer as an ordinance which offers intimate communion with God:

> Prayer is an Ordinance of God, and that to be used both in Publick and Private; such an Ordinance, as brings those who have the Spirit of Supplication, into great familiarity with God; and is also so prevalent an action, that it getteth of God, both for the person that prayeth, and for them that are prayed for, great things. It is the opener of the heart of God, and a means by which the soul, though empty, is filled. By Prayer the Christian can open his heart to God as to a Friend, and obtain fresh testimony of God's Friendship to him.[40]

Here is a pneumatological understanding of prayer, an epiclesis which centres the event within a devotional relationship between the believer and God. Here is a marriage of duty and delight, for prayer is an ordinance of God and also a means of grace. Through this rendezvous, the believer learns new things at first hand about the faithfulness and friendship of God.

Significantly, Bunyan makes no distinction between public and private prayer, and sees it as a unified reality, whether in collective worship or private devotions. Commentators on the Reformation have suggested that the mediaeval laity became increasingly alienated from church worship because the words of the priest were indistinct and in a language which many could not understand. In the late mediaeval period, devotional practices, such as Books of Hours, developed which enabled members of the congregation to engage in their own private devotions during the service while other things were happening. Alistair McGrath suggests that much of the Reformation was a lay movement, stimulated in part by the increased education of the newly emerging professional classes.[41] The redefinition of ministry as non-priestly, worship in places other than historic church buildings, and an emphasis on the importance of everyday life, were all likely to contribute to a spirituality where the separation between the sacred and everyday life was eroded. This shift in how the world was viewed was particularly noticeable in the worship styles of the Separatists. Dignity in worship did not require formal ceremonial undertaken by an elite class, but could involve the participation of members of the congregation in leading parts of worship as well as in extempore prayer.[42]

In certain periods, Baptist and other Free Church worship, became more formal and fewer people participated in leading worship; at other times, the informal aspect of liturgical understanding seems to have reasserted itself. Perhaps it was inevitable that the gathering of large congregations was going to result in a worship culture which was formal because formality was deemed culturally appropriate for a large public event. Of course, an increased formality may also have arisen, at least in part, from the acceptance of a 'church' culture where certain modes of behaviour were deemed appropriate for church services. Conversely, in recent years, a culture of informality and the influence of television have affected many churches in the culture of worship. Intimacy and informality have become goals in a situation where microphones, and even big screens, can enable a relaxed delivery even in large auditoria. There may in fact be a connection between the culture of informality, even in large worship events, and the refusal to make a clear distinction between private devotion and public worship. So public prayer in modern evangelical worship services will often be unpolished and even hesitant, with rhetoric more suitable for a conversation among friends than the rhetoric of a courtier before a monarch. Such informality is frequently assumed to be a sign of sincerity and an indicator of the absence of pretence.[43] From a liturgical perspective, this has often been viewed as something of a disaster, and liturgical reformers have attempted to encourage a view of collective prayer which is structured by the dynamics of the worship service, crafted and prepared in advance. Worship in this Free Church tradition, however, is not seen as a rehearsed performance, so much as an activity in which people try to 'be real', and its prayer demands the same inextricable link between words and intentions as any interpersonal discourse. A part of this devotional concern is the conviction that worship and prayer must be sincere.[44]

The rise of the public address system and the culture of television are not the first examples of technological change to impinge on spirituality and worship. Christopher Hill reflects on the rise in individualism in the sixteenth and seventeenth centuries by commenting on the privatization of architecture:

> All roads in our period led to individualism. More rooms in better-off peasant houses, use of glass in windows . . . use of coal in grates, replacement of benches by chairs . . . Privacy contributed to the introspection and soul-searching of radical Puritanism, to the keeping of diaries and spiritual journals.[45]

However, we also need to listen to the writers in our study who do not refer to purity of purpose and sincerity of heart as examples of current philosophical thinking but as the claims of Scripture. We need to interpret *sincerity* in the context of personal religion, in the framework of a relationship with God in which integrity and sincerity are seen as dimensions of an interpersonal relationship.

John Fawcett dealt with the relationship of attitude to action in the course of a sermon discussing the holiness of the people of God and their worship. He saw this holistically, not like the ritual holiness of the Old Testament dispensation, but as the holiness of a people whose whole life is lived in relationship to God. The aims of the community, its doctrine and lifestyle, are all expressions of this holiness. The set-apartness of the Church is not a ritual separateness, dependent on various ritual actions, but a moral commitment to the ways of God, obedience to his ordinances and commitment to him in worship.

Fawcett does talk about outward actions and Christian conduct, but these actions are not the ritual actions of the sanctuary so much as the integral life of a community of disciples. He speaks about the various components of worship and offers the biblical evidence for these being ordained through precept or example. For example, the house of God must be a house of prayer and, within this framework, he claims that Jesus sanctioned congregational singing (after the Last Supper), preaching and hearing the Word (his sermon in Nazareth), and the ordinances of baptism and the Lord's Supper.

He then urges that these acts of worship should not be performed in a dull, negligent or formal manner. Worship is worship in spirit and in truth. It is accompanied by faith in God and is expressive of love – to others as well as to God. It must be sincere and upright, with every sin renounced and with a readiness to obey every divine command. It must not be lukewarm, but accompanied with fervency and ardour, performed in deep humility of mind – for the sacrifices which God will accept are those of a broken and contrite heart. 'In a word, reverence of God's majesty, hope in his mercy, and joy in his salvation, should accompany the several acts of devotion in the house of the Lord.'[46]

Matters of outward behaviour in worship still require instruction. Yet that instruction is about the *way* in which various actions are performed so that they may be sincere, or so that the worshipper may concentrate on them and thus be sincere. A sense of mutual responsibility within the worshipping community is suggested when William Brock argues that worshippers should behave in such a way that they do not distract their fellow worshippers. So the Baptists of Norfolk were told to complete their domestic arrangements before the day of rest so that they might arrive in good time for worship and not distract others by their late arrival.[47] Outward behaviour is to be regulated, not so that the correct ritual actions are performed, but so that the right inner attitude might be enabled:

> Cultivate, therefore, quietness of demeanour. Having taken your place in the sanctuary with gravity and sedateness, retain it in a manner that may be denominated devout, just indeed as men who are keeping their hearts with all diligence.[48]

His agenda is a straightforward one – that behaviour in the house of God may be worthy of the gospel of Christ – and he offers a solution through the consideration of 'punctuality of attendance, quietness of behaviour, deliberateness of action, attentiveness of disposition and prayerfulness of heart'.[49] This emphasis on deliberation is significant. He provides a commentary on each item within a normal Sunday morning service, thus providing the outline we have noted in Chapter 4, and in each case shows how the worshipper should appropriate what is done so that it becomes their own action. Prayer offered from the pulpit must become the worshipper's own prayer, and a song of praise should be offered 'in strains of cheerfulness, with joyful lips'. This deliberate owning of each part of worship requires concentration and attentiveness. The choir should not be preparing to sing before the preceding prayer has ended, and people should not be getting up to pray before the reading of Scripture has concluded:

> We call these things, evils, on account of the influence which they assuredly exert against our improving by the means of grace. When one thing is blended, even confounded with another, the impression left upon the mind is vague and indistinct. Nothing is treasured up, because nothing has been really received.[50]

We can see Brock's exhortation as an addressing of the perennial issue of congregational participation, in the hope of enhancing its quality, whether passive or active. The deliberation commended here demonstrates an earnestness which is evident in both the worship values discussed above. In devotion, a deliberateness of approach will be an expression of both the desire for sincerity and the desire to ensure that worship yields a sufficient spiritual benefit. With regard to Scripture, deliberation is an expression of that very attention which is the appropriate response to Scripture's authority.

In these two concerns – attention to Scripture and the concern for a devotional openness to the Spirit – we have values which each contribute to the spirituality of Baptist worship and which together stand in a polar relationship to one another. In one sense, attention to Scripture could be characterized as an outward obedience, though our examination of the notion of ordinance moves beyond that. Similarly, personal piety and devotion could be perceived as being primarily about inward spiritual concerns, but the important place given to sincerity attempts to ensure authenticity – the congruence of inward disposition and outward actions. Nonetheless, there is a creative tension between these two values – the dialectic between spirit and truth, in which our understanding of each is modified by the other.

These two values have been held together since the beginning of Baptist and Free Church life. In 1611, Thomas Helwys wrote in his *A Declaration of Faith of English People remaining at Amsterdam in*

Holland, 'That the church off CHRIST is a company off faithful people
1 Cor. 1.2, Eph. 1.1, separated from the world by the word & Spirit off
GOD . . . '[51] The separation from the church of the Elizabethan
Settlement occurred, according to Helwys, because of these two factors.
On the one hand, their reading of Scripture led them to a doctrine of the
Church which was incompatible with a state church and, on the other
hand, he believed that they had been led by the Holy Spirit. We have seen
how the Amsterdam worship valued spontaneity to the point of only
using Scripture in preparation for worship – a resolution of the tension
between these two values which was soon abandoned in favour of
worship in which Scripture had a more formal place. But the relationship
between these two themes has remained a feature in the development of
Free Church worship.

Fellowship and Kingdom: A Context and a Horizon

What is the relationship between the public and the private, between the
meeting house and the home? The polarity of Scripture and experience
interacts within the context of the Christian community, and this community looks beyond itself and its own concerns towards the will, or
Kingdom, of God. Here are two further themes, distinct and related: the
Church as a fellowship of believers, and a future hope which affects how
Christians see the world and what they pray for.

Holy People not Holy Places: The Church as Community

John Fawcett's sermon *The Holiness which becometh the House of the
Lord* was originally preached at the opening of a new church building in
Manchester in 1808. It is significant that on such an occasion he should
choose to preach on the people who would worship in that building,
rather than the building itself. In this he was standing in a tradition which
identified the Church with *people* – a tradition which originally called its
places of worship 'meeting houses'. After 1688, the number of meeting
houses inevitably increased, yet even in the times of great building
programmes and the development of architectural styles that reflected
the upward mobility of Nonconformist congregations, there was a func-
tional view of the building which refused to see it in sacramental terms.[52]
At its opening, a building would be *dedicated* but not *consecrated*, as
holiness was to be located in the congregation – in holy people, not holy
things.

In an ecclesiastical culture where worship and personal piety are inextricably linked, why did Baptists and other Free Churches come to regard the church building as a place in which to assemble to worship God, but not as a *holy* place? It is likely that this view of church buildings reflects the Reformation reaction to what were believed to be ecclesiastical abuses. Shrines, relics and indulgences were seen not only as examples of commercialism, but as proof of the satanic captivity of Rome. Worship was to be stripped to its bare essentials and God was not to be worshipped, as the *Westminster Confession* put it, 'according to the imaginations and devices of men'.[53] Worship in spirit and in truth meant a rejection of the material media which others saw as sacramental but which the Puritans and others saw as unscriptural and carnal.

Persecution in the early decades of Baptist church life almost certainly heightened the tendency to regard buildings and outward actions as being of secondary importance. During the period 1660–88, many congregations worshipped in secret, often in forests and other places far from the reach of snoopers or magistrates. Worship was vital and dangerous. To be a worshipper meant commitment and a readiness to suffer for the cause of Christ. This was worship in spirit and in truth, relying not on the sanctity of a building, but the faithfulness of a God of grace.

It is important to remember this ecclesial context when examining Baptist writings on worship because the Church is identified with the people who are worshipping, rather than an institution of which those worshippers form a part. In other words, the local congregation *is* the Church of Jesus Christ. While there is an understanding of the wider, or universal Church, the local congregation is the normative expression of the Body of Christ.

At the beginning of 2001 the Baptist Union of Great Britain encouraged its member churches and associations to express their life together through the celebration of a covenant service, an act of mutual commitment which was also undertaken at that year's annual assembly. It was claimed that this process of covenant-making was based upon a seventeenth-century Baptist practice.[54] It was also argued that worship was the appropriate place for the covenant nature of the Church to be celebrated, as 'We belong together because we are called by God. Our act of commitment in fellowship-sharing should therefore be as we worship God together.'[55] Baptist church life has a strong sense of community and some of this is expressed in the self-understanding which speaks of 'a gathered church'. The placing of the covenant renewal within worship, however, served to underline the nature of the church as *ekklesia*, for it is gathered by God and ought not to be simply a matter of human choosing.[56] This covenant is between churches – as (county) Association or as (national) Union – and mirrors the covenant relationship within a local church that is most clearly seen in the church meeting when members gather for the governance of the congregation. Yet this church meeting should not be seen as primarily a business meeting, even though mechanisms for decision-making will usually include the normal procedures of a business meeting. The decision-making is not primarily an exercise in collective will, but an attempt at communal discipleship in which the church gathered in meeting seeks to discern the mind of Christ.[57]

The communal nature of Baptist church life has been increasingly explored by recent Baptist writers, and the implications of this for our understanding of worship should not be lost.[58] Worship is a social activity, performed by a group of people assembled for that corporate purpose, though we must recognize that different patterns of worship are likely to express the communal dimension more or less explicitly than others. For example, Sunday worship in a large congregation will be communal in a different way from a weeknight prayer meeting in which most of those present participate actively by leading in extempore prayer.

Fawcett argued that the primary meaning of 'the house of God' in the New Testament is not that of a building set aside for worship, but the worshipping community itself:

> The holiness which becomes the house of the Lord in New Testament times relates not to the place of worship, but to the people concerned in the erection of such a place, and to those who assemble there for religious exercises. And as such, it may include holiness of intention, holiness of doctrine, holiness of worship, holiness of discipline, and holiness of practice.[59]

The behaviour of the members of the congregation in worship will indicate something about their view of worship but also about their view of the Church. When Brock urged Norfolk Baptists to be more intentional in their worship practices, his concern for attentiveness was partly the result of his conviction that dissenting congregations were too casual in their approach to worship, lacking the solemnity appropriate to the worship of God. Indeed, he pointed out that dissenting congregations compared unfavourably with Anglican ones in the matter of reverent behaviour, and insisted, 'it becomes us to do every thing in our power to render our services decorous and attractive'.[60] However, the informality of much Baptist worship, especially at the time of gathering immediately before the service begins, was to be seen later by Wheeler Robinson as a sign of the communal values which are an important part of Baptist church life. Like Brock, he contrasted the atmosphere with that of an Anglican service, but drew different conclusions:

> An Anglican, entering a Baptist Church for divine worship, might often be alienated by the seeming want of reverence . . . Deacons walk about unnecessarily, and even come to chat with people in the pews. The secretary gives out notices at an alarming length, and may intersperse a few remarks.[61]

While he does suggest that 'it would be better for Baptists to cultivate more reverence in the forms of worship', he then points out,

> Yet it must be remembered that the Church is a family as well as a building or a body, and that the vital warmth of human fellowship can be sanctified to high spiritual ends. Even if some of these people talk when it would be better for them to be silent, or err unconsciously in matters of taste, yet the weightier matters of gospel fellowship may be theirs.[62]

Some very practical advice was offered by F. F. Whitby, a prominent layman in the Western Association, in his president's address to the association meeting at Dorchester in 1903. He was concerned that prayers should not be too long and argued that praise singing should be undertaken actively and audibly, because 'the whole man – heart, soul and voice – should join'.[63] Like Brock, he was concerned that members of the congregation should consider the impact of their behaviour on the worship of others. Singers must not annoy their neighbours by singing loud and flat! Ostentation and slovenliness are both to be avoided and the organist should be in spiritual sympathy with the church – and will probably be a church member. The appropriation of each part of worship should continue with the members of the congregation listening actively to the sermon: 'There is worship both in preaching and in listening . . . As worshipping hearers, we need sympathy with the preacher. Prayer for the minister and his message is a great help here, even silent prayer while he is preaching.'[64] This is more than simple attentiveness, as though paying attention were a matter of learning as much as possible. Beneath this series of exhortations lies the assumption that the worship event is one in which the whole congregation plays its part, albeit in ways which are not necessarily outwardly obvious. Worshippers are not simply recipients, or a chorus to be brought into the drama of worship at certain points. Even listening to the sermon is an active process where the worshipper offers to God their openness to the divine Word.

In the Northamptonshire circular letter of 1777, John Ryland senior wrote of *The Beauty of Social Religion*, declaring,

> A Church of Christ is a peculiar society of gracious souls, who are called out of a state of sin and misery by the almighty Spirit of God, associated by their own free consent to maintain the doctrines of grace – to perform gospel worship and celebrate gospel ordinances, with the exercise of holy discipline to the glory of the divine perfections, and to promote their own usefulness and happiness in time and eternity.[65]

While he spoke of the Church as a voluntary society, 'for no man is naturally born into a Gospel Church', he also affirmed that a church 'consists in the diffusion of a divine nature through the souls of the members of this sacred society'.[66] This new life is made possible through Christ's redeeming death, and the invitation to worship comes as a call from the Spirit of God.[67] Here is an understanding of the local church in which worship is communal not only because of the covenantal relationship between its members but because of the work of the Spirit. The Free Church *locus classicus* for this is the promise of Matthew 18.20: 'Where two or three are gathered in my name there am I among them.' The result is a transcendence based not on holy place or circumstance, but upon an assembly of believers, as the Western Association's presidential address of 1911 made clear:

> There is no question of the consecration of the building when He condescends to enter; no doubt about the validity of sacraments where the real Presence is enjoyed; no need of bishops when the one Archbishop presides, no want of the Holy Ghost where He breathes upon the faces of His disciples; and no longing for communion unrealised, where souls are joined in mystical fellowship with Him. When these conditions are satisfied a Church is found.[68]

These affirmations are about the real presence of the risen Christ. Yet their biblical basis is seen to be in the act of assembling, in which his followers gather *in his name*. Here is the communal context in which we need to understand worship. This belief is not unique to Baptists, though it will find expression in a Baptist way. For example, the devotional theme we have just explored will remind us that the community of the Church is a community of persons in relationship, that the gathered assembly for worship will be the same community which exercises mutual care for its members and seeks to offer a shared witness to the gospel of Jesus Christ.

Concern for the Kingdom

This covenant community is not static or complete but has a future orientation, its 'eschatological horizon'. Once again, we are treading on ground which is common to all the churches, and yet it finds a particular expression in the spirituality which permeates Baptist worship. In John Fawcett's hymn about the Church which has often been called 'the Baptist anthem' and is still sung at international gatherings, such as meetings of the Baptist World Alliance, there is a mingling of ecclesiology and eschatology:

> Blest be the tie that binds
>   our hearts in mutual love;
> the fellowship of kindred minds
>   is like to that above.[69]

Here is an anticipation of heaven in which the present Church manifests something of that which is to come. This ecclesiology is characterized by Christ-like qualities and anticipates a future state through the way in which *koinonia*, fellowship-sharing, is expressed in this present earthly existence with its inevitable suffering:

> We share our mutual woes,
>   our mutual burdens bear,
> and often for each other flows
>   the sympathizing tear.

The continuing of fellowship is not only a sign of the future hope but an encouragement to those who long for it. The members are bound together even when they are apart and hope to meet again.

> This glorious hope revives
>   our courage by the way,
> while each in expectation lives,
>   and longs to see the day.

When Fawcett wrote this hymn, associations of Particular Baptist churches were still listing their common beliefs at the beginning of their circular letters and among them including the doctrine of 'the perseverance of the saints'. Fawcett's contemporary, John Rippon,[70] regarded congregational singing as an anticipation of heaven, as well as a joining with the eternal praise of the heavenly host, again linking the communal nature of worship with an eschatological hope.

This hope is not only communal but impinges on personal devotion through a concern for the individual believer's personal destiny. The agonizing of the Puritan spiritual autobiographies, and the rigorous desire for assurance which we find in works such as Bunyan's *Grace Abounding*, demonstrate how spirituality is not only about the present but about the future, indeed, the eternal. This hope remains an important dimension of Baptist spirituality, even when its Calvinistic basis is no longer present. The Evangelical emphasis on Jesus Christ as personal saviour again reinforces this theme of eternal hope as it affects the life of the individual believer. But the horizon of God's future also finds expression in a number of ways beyond simply faith in the life to come.

We have seen that the early Baptists shared with other groups a concern for the purity of the Church and its worship. This concern gave the Puritans their name and is primarily concerned with an eternal accountability. The Church should be pure not only so that she may be what her Lord wills her to be – but also so that she may appear pure and spotless as the bride of Christ (Ephesians 5.27). Church discipline needs to be understood in this ecclesial context as the integrity of worshippers, and the quality of their life together in fellowship, and of their daily lives, affects the quality of their worship.

There are two further ways in which a future orientation provides a horizon for worship. First, petitionary prayer should be seen as prayer for the Kingdom. A great deal of prayer in Free Church worship has been of this kind, sometimes reinforced by days of humiliation and fasting. The God to whom such prayer is offered is a God of particular providence, concerned about the details of his children's lives. Petitionary prayer assumes that things are not as they should be and that God wills them to be different. It recognizes the brokenness of the world which can only find resolution through the coming of the Kingdom. Here is a future orientation which hopes that God will act here and now, but which is always looking beyond the here and now. This holy dissatisfaction will often be accompanied by a sense of the provisional nature of the Church, what Bonhoeffer calls 'the penultimate',[71] and much of Baptist church life can carry this provisional nature. The voluntary aspect of covenant carries something of this, as does the desire to see the Church grow. *Stasis* is not a state which can easily be linked to Baptist ways of being church,[72] and this reveals the final and most obvious expression of eschatology – a concern for mission.

Concern for evangelism is a particular feature of Baptist life and worship, present from its early stages, though later to be influenced by the Evangelical Revival and other movements. The *London Confession* of

1644, for example, though a Calvinist document, presents the necessity of preaching the gospel to all people.[73] Each generation has envisaged worship where unbelievers are present.[74] There is evidence that Benjamin Keach, in the latter part of the seventeenth century, had 'regularly and effectively pleaded with his congregation to put their trust in Christ'.[75] In one of his sermons he appealed, 'Is not this Good News? Do you believe it? And is it in your Heart to take hold of the Promises of the Gospel? What Answer shall I return to him that sent me?'[76] The 1656 *Somerset Confession* had declared:

> That as it is an ordinance of Christ, so it is the duty of his church in his author-
> ity, to send forth such brethren as are fitly gifted and qualified through the
> Spirit of Christ to preaching the gospel to the world.[77]

Andrew Gifford senior (1642–1721), minister of the Pithay church in Bristol, was called by Joseph Ivimey 'the Apostle of the West, as he was the founder of most of the churches in Somerset and Gloucestershire'.[78] His ministry clearly demonstrated a missionary zeal, especially during a time of persecution. William Bagley, in the oration at Gifford's funeral, testified to the evangelistic nature of his preaching, which

> abounded with sublime thought and substantial divinity. He did not aim to
> indulge and please the fancy, but to warm and affect the heart, and inform the
> judgement in the great and necessary things of salvation. The sum and sub-
> stance of all his sermons were (as were the Apostles) Repentance and Faith. He
> desired to know nothing among his hearers, but Jesus Christ and him
> crucified; and at the close of his sermon, which was generally the most excel-
> lent part, he would offer Christ to sinners, and invite them to embrace him as
> offered in the most affectionate and pathetic manner.[79]

Gifford's grandson, Andrew, an influential London Baptist, was a friend of George Whitfield, Augustus Toplady and Howell Harris. His persua-sive preaching also presented Jesus Christ to congregations and invited sinners to repent and embrace his salvation for, 'When'er he preach'd, love streame'd thro ev'ry text.'[80] However, the influences of Hyper-Calvinism certainly affected this missionary concern in some parts of the country and had an impact in worship. The focus of a Calvinistic community celebrating their eternal election is going to be different from one which recognizes the Great Commission at the end of Matthew's Gospel as a divine ordinance which is still binding on the Church. This Scripture passage was particularly significant in the explanation Andrew Fuller and William Carey gave for the missionary vocation of the Church.[81] The result was the establishment, amidst much prayer and exhortation, of what would become the Baptist Missionary Society, and, as the years passed, the pulpit would often be used as a place of challenge, where men and women were called to missionary service.

The *Declaration of Principle* of the Baptist Union of Great Britain has expressed an important aspect of denominational identity and Baptist spirituality through its final clause that every Christian should play their part in the evangelization of the world.[82] Payne observes how the developing urban churches in the early nineteenth century initiated evening services which in turn became occasions for 'fishing for sinners', as distinct from the morning service which tended to concentrate on the edification of the saints.[83] He also notes the impact of revivalism from the first evangelistic campaign of Dwight Moody in 1873 with its continuing influence through the revivalist hymnody of Ira Sankey and others. The influence of Billy Graham and Willow Creek are examples from the late twentieth century of movements which have continued to encourage some Baptists to be concerned that worship should be a vehicle of evangelism.

This missionary concern inevitably looks beyond the life of the local congregation. Eschatology provides an element of instability whereby the worship of the Church can never be complete or self-sufficient. A closed circle will be an inadequate way of representing the worship of the Church as it leans towards God's future. This openness also makes possible the relationship between the cultic focus of the gathering for worship and the offering of daily life and the concerns of the world. This is the near horizon towards which worship peers, even as it looks beyond to the distant horizon of the coming kingdom.

Worship, Spirituality and Liturgical Theology

'Does Free Church worship have a theology?' In response to this question, it should be conceded that Baptist worship is not consciously constructed on the basis of a systematic theology of worship. However, in this exploration of the *spirituality* of Baptist worship a number of theological convictions have been gathered – core worship values which influence worship or are expressed in it. James McClendon has described the task of theology as:

> The discovery, understanding, and transformation of the convictions of a convictional community, including the discovery and critical revision of their relation to one another *and to whatever else there is*.[84]

In our examination of the things which matter to Baptists with regard to worship, we have explored some of the core convictions of a convictional community. In writings which have covered a period of nearly four hundred years, we have seen concerns expressed about *what* components should be included, or not included, in worship. More importantly, we have identified a group of values which not only affects the order of worship but the *way* in which that worship is undertaken. In gaining a theological understanding of worship, we have seen that the structure of worship, and the relationship of the various parts of a service, are less significant than the interaction of these core values – attention to Scripture, devotion, community and Kingdom.

The 'spirituality of worship' does not, of course, only refer to the theme of devotion. We have noted Philip Sheldrake's inclusive definition of spirituality as, 'the conjunction of theology, prayer and practical Christianity',[85] and our discussion has worked within the generous framework of this understanding. So the spirituality of worship is about the way in which what communities believe influences and is influenced by what they do and say in worship. It is about how they pray and how the events of the worship gathering influence and reflect the events of daily living. Sheldrake discusses the way in which the study of spirituality will deal with experience as much as with theology and enquires into which area should claim priority. In this he mirrors the debate within liturgical theology about the relationship of theology and worship, which was discussed in Chapter 2:

> The suggestion that experience has priority over theory needs to be nuanced. It is impossible to break open the hermeneutical circle in this way so as to establish a straightforward pattern of cause and effect. Experience itself is born of assumptions, theories and reflection. Yet it is possible to say that the Christian way began with events rather than with a shift of theory born of intellectual speculation.[86]

So what is the relationship of belief to Baptist worship? It is not merely that theology prescribes what is expressed in worship, nor that worship shows us what to believe. Rather, we should see worship as an embodiment of the spirituality of the community and as such a conjunction of prayer, thought and practice. Sheldrake speaks of a 'dialectical relationship' between worship and theology, similar to the theological method of Kevin Irwin and the interaction between the exposition of worship and its critique which I have proposed as a fourth stage of liturgical theology. Following this, we can say that worship both *expresses* and *nurtures* certain values.

In Part 3, we shall look at the component parts of free worship through the lens of this spirituality. Prayer and preaching, singing and sacrament will each express and nurture the values of the community. These comprise the *ordo* which, in turn, manifests the convictions and theology of this community. From these values we shall then begin to construct a liturgical theology – in a Free Church context.

Part 3

Embodied Theology

6

From the Heart

The Spirituality of Free Prayer

O how great a task is it, for a poor soul that becomes sensible of sin, and the wrath of God, to say in Faith, but this one word, *Father*! I tell you, how ever hypocrites think, yet the Christian, that is so indeed, finds all the difficulty in this very thing, it cannot say, God is its *Father*.

. . . here is the life of Prayer, when in, or with the Spirit, a man being made sensible of sin, and how to come to the Lord for mercy; he comes, I say, in the strength of the Spirit, and cryeth, *Father*. That one word spoken in Faith, is better than a thousand prayers, as men call them, written and read, in a formal, cold, lukewarm way.

Prayer, without the heart be in it, is like a sound without life; and a heart, without it be lifted up of the Spirit, will never pray to God.

John Bunyan 1662[1]

The picture of worship which we have so far uncovered is a panorama of evolving practices and developing interpretations. Now we are going to move closer to the action, by examining each of the main components of worship in turn. Over the next five chapters, we shall examine the practices and reflect on the spirituality of prayer, preaching, singing and sacraments.

The four core values of worship will provide a framework within which to explore these practices and their meaning. Each practice will express something of each value, yet in each case a practice will seem to express one of the values most clearly. So we will note, in due course, the eschatological nature of the sacraments, the attention to Scripture which is integral to preaching, and the ecclesial nature of congregational singing. First, we shall see how the tradition of free prayer expresses eloquently, even when the praying is hesitant, the devotional concerns of openness and dependence upon God.

The Practice of Prayer in Baptist Worship

The study of Baptist worship is far from straightforward. It is not normally expressed in written texts, so we cannot turn to a prayer book or ancient liturgy in order to examine its form or content.[2] This problem is particularly acute with regard to prayer, for most prayers in Baptist worship are examples of what may be called 'free prayer', in which spontaneously articulated prayers are offered by one person, or several persons, on behalf of the congregation. In this extempore prayer tradition, there is little evidence of what was said in particular prayers or even the manner in which those prayers were offered. There are few examples of transcribed prayers,[3] though with an increased use of written prayers and manuals for worship in the twentieth century, there is some additional, though not necessarily typical, data. As a result, we shall need to rely on the scanty descriptions of what happened in worship, together with a study of what has been said *about* prayer. Our starting point is an examination of the place of prayer in some of the worship services we reviewed in our historical survey.

The Place of Prayer in Baptist Worship

In the Amsterdam congregation of 1609, there were two Sunday services, each of 3–4 hours duration. The Bromheads' letter home which describes their services, simply records, 'we begin with prayer'.[4] This was followed by the reading of Scripture, its interpretation, and a discussion. After this preparation, even Scripture was put aside because the worship proper needed to be undertaken without any books at all.[5] Prayer then introduced a long period of inspired proclamation, eventually brought to a close by the first speaker who 'concludeth with prayer as he began with prayer'. After exhorting the congregation to give to the poor, and after a collection had been taken, the same speaker concluded with prayer. The only clue to the nature or content of the prayers is the position of each prayer in the sequence of events. Prayer is on each occasion offered by the same person appointed to lead this collaborative act of worship on that particular day.

   It would seem that the first two prayers were likely to have included an approach to God, invoking God's help with the preparatory Bible study and especially the 'prophesying'. The charismatic nature of the worship makes such an invocation very likely. The prayer before the prophesying was described as 'solemne', perhaps in recognition of its epicletic importance at the beginning of spontaneous worship. With this spirituality of dependence it is likely the prayer also included praise, confession and a claiming of the mercy of God. The third prayer, at the conclusion of the propheseying, probably focused on and applied the principles and truths which had been proclaimed. At some point, the petitions of the congregation were offered, both for themselves and for others. That this is the most likely place is reinforced by the indication that prayer was followed by an exhortation to give for the needs of the poor. Alternatively, the concluding prayer after the collection may have included such intercessions and petitions.

With this scant information, our speculation about the content of the various prayers must be tentative. Here is an event which the participants believed to be inspired and which began and ended with prayer. Prayer was, of course, free and unscripted, as were the whole proceedings.

The worship of the newly formed Paul's Alley church in 1695 was probably shorter in length and part of the service was led by someone other than the minister.[6] The meeting began with a member of the congregation being appointed to read a psalm, '& then to spend some time in Prayer'. After the sermon, the minister would pray and a psalm would be sung.

Prayer was linked to the opening of worship and we may speculate that it may well have evoked some of the themes of the preceding psalm. Similarly, the prayer following the sermon could have responded to themes presented in the preaching, but either prayer might have developed into petitionary and intercessory prayer.

The morning service at Isaac Watts' Bury Street Church in the second decade of the eighteenth century began with a metricated psalm sung by the congregation.[7] After this, a short prayer of invocation was offered, asking 'for the Divine presence in all the following parts of worship', and this was followed by an exposition of Scripture. After a hymn, the minister entered the pulpit and prayed:

> more at large, for all the variety of blessings, spiritual and temporal, for the whole congregation, with confession of sins, and thanksgiving for mercies; petitions also are offered up for the whole world, for the churches of Christ, for the nation in which we dwell, for all our rulers and governors, together with any particular cases which are represented.[8]

This is a full description of what came to be known as the 'Long Prayer' and which was the main form of free prayer in Nonconformist worship into the early part of the twentieth century. A century and a half after Watts, Charles Haddon Spurgeon was to advise his students that for this prayer 'ten minutes is a better limit than fifteen',[9] advice which implies it was often longer! Of particular note is the allusion to 'particular cases which are represented'. Here is an example of the pastoral localization of free prayer, though the size of the congregation often required special arrangements for informing the minister of specific needs in the congregation. After the sermon there was a short prayer and a benediction. As there had already been ample opportunity for petitionary prayer, it is more likely that this latter prayer followed on from the themes of the sermon, perhaps as a response in the form of personal consecration and the request for divine assistance in faithful living.

William Brock's account of Particular Baptist worship in the 1840s describes the beginning of the service:

> First, there is prayer, intended to seek more especially for the communication of the Holy Spirit upon the engagements of the whole day. That prayer, brethren, is offered in your name. Rightly understood, it must be regarded in fact as your own prayer. You do therein acknowledge your insufficiency to think anything as of yourselves, and you gratefully remember that your sufficiency is of God.[10]

Then, after a hymn and a Bible reading, 'there is another prayer in which supplications and intercessions, with giving of thanks, are made for all men, especially for the household of faith'. The service concluded after the sermon with a prayer and benediction. Again, the long prayer included requests both for the worshippers and others, though we should note the recurring pattern of invocation which places the whole service within the context of prayer. Brock called the Norfolk Baptists to a 'prayerfulness of spirit' and he suggests that if the experience of worship has not 'profited the heart' it is because of a 'negligence of devotion'.[11] He portrays the whole service as an encounter with God in which the worshippers are dependent upon divine grace and in which all the components, including the various prayers, are 'the mere vehicles through which the God of all grace sends down the communications of his love'.[12]

By the early twentieth century, little had changed except an increase in the number of hymns interspersed in the service. There was normally one long prayer, the opening of worship would sometimes include Scripture sentences and a prayer of invocation, and there would sometimes have been a brief prayer at the conclusion of the sermon. Some of the praying was now done in the hymnody, though the chief prayer was still a long collection of miscellaneous concerns and, as the century progressed, there were calls for the breaking up of this prayer into shorter prayers.[13]

In the two worship surveys of 1996 and 1997, there is evidence of considerable diversification in recent Baptist worship. Some remains 'traditional', while other worship shows the influence of Charismatic renewal or liturgical reform, and even some evidence of interaction and blending between these two movements. Indeed, it is possible that some liturgical reform has come into Baptist life as a result of Charismatic Baptists experiencing a positive encounter with Charismatic worship within liturgical traditions.[14] While only a tenth of churches offer prayer in the 'traditional' pattern of one main prayer, over 60 per cent of churches claim to have a prayer of praise and confession early in the service, followed by intercessions later.[15] A further 21 per cent intersperse prayers through the service in relation to other components. Here are patterns which *appear* to diverge from the supposedly traditional pattern of a long prayer though, as we have seen in our survey, prayer was rarely confined just to the 'long' prayer. The present separation of praise and confession from intercessions may well reflect the influence of the Liturgical Movement, with its encouragement for rational development through the service and for clear functions for the several parts. Alternatively, it could reflect an increased concern that praise should be a major component in worship.[16]

Though there was a small amount of correspondence concerning read prayers in *The Freeman* newspaper in the middle of the nineteenth century,[17] virtually all prayer in Baptist churches before the twentieth century was free prayer, but not all prayer was spontaneous. For example, Isaac Watts, in his *Guide to Prayer*, recommended that two extremes in prayer should be avoided.[18] On the one hand, we should avoid 'confining ourselves entirely to pre-composed forms of prayer' and, on the other, be wary of 'entire dependence on sudden motions and suggestions of thought'.[19] He defines 'extempore prayer' as what happens 'when we, without any reflection or meditation beforehand, address ourselves to God, and speak the thoughts of our hearts, as fast as we conceive them'. From this he distinguishes 'conceived', or 'free' prayer:

> when we have not the words of our prayer formed beforehand, to direct our thoughts, but we conceive the matter or substance of our address to God, first in our minds, and then put those conceptions in such words and expressions as we think most proper.

This conceived prayer may not involve a detailed working out of what will be uttered in public, but should include what he describes as 'premeditation' involving the preparation of the heart as well as a reflection on the subjects for prayer. According to the 1996 survey, those churches which normally used free prayer explained that about two-thirds of these were extempore. Therefore, about a third of free prayer currently offered in Baptist churches is sketched out or prepared in detail beforehand, 'conceived prayer' according to Isaac Watts, while over two-thirds is still offered spontaneously.[20]

Yet, whether free prayer is conceived or spontaneous, it is still quite different from either the use of service books or the reading of pre-composed prayers by the leader of worship. In addition, there are different forms of pre-composed prayer. First, there are those prayers and responsive sequences which are put in the hands of the congregation so that all might pray aloud using the same words. Second, there are those written prayers, published in worship manuals, or collections of prayers which the leader of worship may read as though their own. Finally, this material written by others needs to be distinguished from written prayers which have been prepared and written for the occasion by the person leading worship.

In the survey of worship practices, only 1 per cent of respondents said that prayers were *usually* read from a book, while just over half replied that prayers were *sometimes* read. Interestingly, only 42 per cent said that prayers were *never* read. This varied pattern suggests a significant modification of the extempore tradition, though it may only refer to the occasional use of written material.[21]

Liturgical developments in the nineteenth century, especially among the Congregationalists and the Presbyterians and which Horton Davies argues were a consequence of the Romantic and Tractarian Movements, seemed to have little impact on Baptist ministers and congregations. There were, however, a few notable exceptions, to which the architecture of some church buildings still bears witness.[22] However, worship manuals and books of resource material have been increasingly available since early in the twentieth century. As well as the wider publishing of local experiments, such as that of Henry Bonner and F. C. Spurr of Hampstead Road Church, Birmingham,[23] there were national attempts to offer assistance to those leading worship. Books were produced at first which simply, and very tentatively, offered an order of service for communion and for baptismal, marriage and funeral services. Prefaces tried to make clear that what was offered was not mandatory or an infringement of the freedom of local worship, but a resource to aid the worship leader.[24] Later examples developed beyond this simple provision to include other sequences for use in worship, such as the commissioning of deacons, as well as material to be used through the Christian year and prayers for various occasions.

This development can be seen clearly in the line of publications available to leaders of Baptist worship.[25] F. B. Meyer compiled a *Free Church Service Manual* which was published by the National Free Church Council. Around 1927 M. E. Aubrey, the general secretary of the Baptist Union, edited a similar, but rather fuller, volume entitled *A Minister's Manual* which was specifically intended for Baptists. In 1960 Ernest Payne and Stephen Winward produced *Orders and Prayers for Church Worship* which was to be reprinted several times and which included liturgical resources from the wider Church as well as a substantial number of sequences and prayers entitled 'Ordinances of the Church'. The book also included an influential introduction which was regarded as a classic statement on worship by those Baptists who were increasingly identifying with the issues of the Liturgical Movement.

In 1980 *Praise God* was published by the Baptist Union, but it did not seem to gain wide support, with many continuing to use copies of 'Payne and Winward'. *Patterns and Prayers for Christian Worship* was published in 1991 and benefited from an awareness of the cool reception which its predecessor had received.[26] As well as the increased need for a new book, following the changes in worship language and culture since 1960, Charismatic Baptists were now expressing a need for some written material to help with certain parts of worship, and these views were canvassed and incorporated in the developing of the book.[27]

But to examine the genres of written or free prayer, whether as 'conceived' or 'extempore', is only to discuss their forms. What of the *content* of prayer in Free Church worship? What have Baptists prayed for? In one sense, they have prayed for the same things as other Christians, but a classification of their prayers will help us identify some of the characteristics of prayer in Baptist and Free Church worship.

Types of Prayer

While there has been some necessary speculation in our historical survey of prayer in worship, there are a number of reasons to have confidence in the interpretations which have been given. Several references to prayer at the beginning of a service, such as the comments by William Brock,[28] suggest that it included invocation. In addition, his constant references to the congregation having a prayerful attitude throughout the service suggest a holistic concern that each constituent part should be regarded prayerfully. It is a short step from this devotional frame of mind to the offering of prayers linked to those several parts.

There is also a concern among writers on prayer that the different types of prayer be distinguished. This might suggest that such distinctions were not normally apparent in the prayers of their time, but it also indicates a concern that prayer should be ordered, purposeful and sincere. In his *Guide to Prayer*, Watts expounds the nature of prayer by delineating its various parts.[29] These he lists as:

- invocation
- adoration
- confession
- petition
- pleading
- profession or self-dedication
- thanksgiving
- blessing.

His detailed exposition of each not only reflects the rational and didactic framework within which he was working, but offers a theological exposition of prayer as the expression of our relationship with God. For example, invocation is interpreted as a declaration of the desire to worship God, as well as a request for God's assistance in that worship. Prayers of petition are to be offered for spiritual blessings as well as material provision and throughout there is a sense of dependence on God, Creator and Redeemer.

In the course of this exposition, Watts gives occasional and brief samples. They furnish us with fleeting glimpses of prayer offered by this influential figure. Here are two examples:

> *Invocation*: Lord, quicken us to call upon thy name. Assist us by thy Spirit in our access to thy mercy seat. Raise our hearts towards thyself. Teach us to approach thee as becomes creatures, and do thou draw near to us as a God of grace. Hearken to the voice of my cry, my King and my God, for unto thee will I pray.
>
> *Confession*: Thou, O Lord, art in heaven, but we are on earth; our being is but of yesterday, and our foundation is in the dust. What is man that thou art mindful of him, and the Son of man that thou couldest visit him? Man, that is a worm, and the Son of man that is but a worm! It is in thee that we live, move, and have our being: Thou withholdest thy breath and we die.[30]

From these we can see that his prayers were saturated with scriptural references, paraphrases and allusions. Watts had a strong sense of the holiness and majesty of God which, in his prayers as well as his hymns, interplays with an Evangelical[31] thanksgiving for salvation and a warmth of religious affections.

Later in the eighteenth century, two Baptists published addresses concerning prayer and both followed Watts in listing the component parts of prayer. For John Gill,[32] 'the several parts of prayer' are:

- Adoration (of the divine perfections).
- Confession and prayer for pardon.
- Petition.
- Thanksgiving.
- Deprecation of evils to which we are liable.
- Doxology.

A few years later, Benjamin Wallin declared, 'Prayer, in its simple and native idea, is no other than an address to the Almighty, on matters that concern us in the present or future state of existence.'[33] The manner or types of prayer differ according to the context, like branches. He itemizes these branches as,

- supplications, i.e. deprecations of evil to which we are liable
- prayers or petitions for every blessing we need
- intercessions or pleadings on behalf of others
- thanksgiving, without which we would be strangely forgetful of the innumerable benefits on us.

He points out that our intercessions should be for persons of all rank, including rulers, and even for our enemies.

In the transcribed prayers of Spurgeon and Maclaren, various aspects of prayer are expressed within a single monologue.[34] The use of several short prayers, each with a different subject or function, is a more recent development and reflects the ecumenical impact of litanies and collects.[35] Inevitably, written worship resources are likely to lead to shorter prayers with a greater degree of differentiation and focus of their content. Brevity and clarity of focus are characteristics even of the early service books mentioned above, which tentatively offered basic orders of service for pastoral offices and the ordinances. Of course, this may result as much from the dynamic of literary conciseness and a concern to leave the leader of worship opportunity to offer free prayer, as from a liturgical concern. From 1960 onwards the manuals encourage a thematic presentation of prayers, with the assumption that specific prayers will occupy an appropriate place within the liturgical rationale of a particular service.

We must remember that manuals of prayer are likely to be prepared by people with a greater liturgical consciousness and desire for order than perhaps the average minister. The 1996 survey suggested that over 60 per cent of churches claim to have an early prayer of praise and confession, followed later by prayers of intercession. While this reflects some differentiation on the basis of content and its place in the service, it is not far from the earlier practices where prayer occurred at the beginning and, more substantially, at a later point.

Public and Private Prayer

It is significant that, in his writing on prayer, John Bunyan made no distinction between prayer in collective worship and prayer in private devotions. Instead, he saw prayer as a unified reality:

> Prayer is an Ordinance of God, and that to be used both in Publick and Private; such an Ordinance, as brings those who have the Spirit of Supplication, into great familiarity with God . . . By Prayer the Christian can open his heart to God as to a Friend, and obtain fresh testimony of God's Friendship to him.[36]

We have already noted in the previous chapter that strand of Reformation spirituality in which the separation between the sacred and everyday life was eroded. The effect on worship of this shift in perception may be seen both in increased participation on the part of some members of the congregation and in the note of intimacy which may be found in prayers in which God is described as 'a friend'. While many liturgists will denounce what they see as slovenly worship practices, this tension predated Isaac Watts's *Guide to Prayer*,[37] and should be recognized as an aspect of the spiritual tradition which refuses to separate prayer in worship from the immediate and personal devotions of the 'closet'. Consequently, worship is not seen as a rehearsed performance, so much as an activity in which people try to 'be real', and its prayer demands the same inextricable link between words and intentions as any personal discourse.

Yet despite the importance placed on prayer in much writing and preaching, there seem to have been periods and places where its practice has degenerated. Benjamin Wallin preached in 1770 before a group of his fellow London ministers on 1 Timothy 2.8. He was concerned about the apparent decline in the prayerfulness of congregations and even hinted at the possibility of people coming into worship during the main prayer, ignoring the preceding worship as an unimportant preliminary to the sermon. He argued that lifting hands in prayer is not only biblical, but it would ensure that prayer was extempore, for the minister would not be able to turn the page of a prayer book![38] In addition, his meditation on *holy* hands led him to plead for an integrity of relationships and lifestyle. This integrity, he argued, is an important part of offering worthy prayer, for the conduct of worship cannot be separated from the holiness of the people of God. Such concerns over the quality of prayer in worship prompt us to turn to the spirituality of this tradition of prayer and to an examination of some of the theological concerns which are implicit in it.

The Spirituality of Prayer in Baptist Worship

> Prayer is a sincere, sensible, affectionate pouring out of the heart or soul to God through Christ, in the strength and assistance of the holy Spirit, for such things as God hath promised, or, according to the Word, for the good of the Church, with submission, in Faith, to the Will of God.[39]

Bunyan's definition of prayer is a full one and contains a number of themes which will help in the exploration of the free prayer tradition. First, prayer and worship must be offered with sincerity of purpose: prayer is 'a sincere, sensible, affectionate pouring out of the heart or soul to God through Christ'. Sincerity is required, as there is no place for pretence before the God who knows and sees all. True prayer is also 'sensible', for it needs to engage the mind and be rational in intent and expression. Prayer is an '*affectionate* pouring out of the heart or soul to God' and as such moves within the sphere of the religious affections. Bunyan will later suggest that prayer cannot be stimulated externally by a prayer book,[40] but here he states this concern positively. Prayer is an outpouring of the heart – not only is it emotionally charged,[41] but it flows from the depths of the person. John Fawcett later argued that the acts which take place in worship 'are not to be performed in a dull, lifeless, negligent and formal manner', because worship involves our relationship with God, a relationship of love:

> Holy worship is accompanied with faith in God, without which it is impossible to please him. It is expressive of love to his name; for if we are destitute of that, we want that holy and animating principle which is essential to true religion.[42]

Prayer and worship are places where our relationship with God is expressed and developed. This aspect of encounter is central to Bunyan's understanding of prayer and an important theme in our examination of worship. Here is intimate devotion: 'By prayer the Christian can open his heart to God as to a friend, and obtain fresh testimony of God's friendship to him.' The assurance of salvation, of being one of the elect, was an experience which some Puritans did not easily attain. Bunyan himself had agonized long about his standing before God, but here he declares that the experience of prayer is a means whereby the believer may have evidence of being accepted by God. In this he seems to anticipate later developments in Evangelicalism. Whereas the Puritans agonized about their eternal destiny, Wesley was to see the experience of conversion as evidence of God's acceptance. Here Bunyan seems to see the experience of prayer in a similar way – evidence of being accepted as a friend of God.[43] Later in 'I will Pray with the Spirit', he speaks of the relationship of the believer to God as that of a child to a parent and, with an allusion to Romans 8.14–17, he speaks of the work of the Holy Spirit in enabling the cry 'Abba'. Thus the discovery of a special relationship with God is made through the pneumatological dimension of prayer:

> No, here is the life of Prayer, when in, or with the Spirit, a man being made sensible of sin, and how to come to the Lord for mercy; he comes, I say, in the strength of the Spirit, and cryeth, *Father* . . . That one word spoken in Faith, is better than a thousand prayers, as men call them, written and read, in a formal, cold, luke-warm way.[44]

If religion only consisted in being a law-abiding citizen of the Kingdom of God, then outward behaviour would be the most important aspect of Christian living. Law can only regulate outward behaviour. However, seeing Christian living as entering into a family relationship with God is likely to lead to devotional expectations about that living which involve *attitudes* and *feelings*.

Finally, we must ignore neither the Christological focus nor the pneumatological context in which prayer is offered. Prayer is 'through Christ, in the strength and assistance of the Holy Spirit' and therefore epicletic. In this perspective, the distinction between divine and human aspects of worship breaks down. All human worship is, in one sense, a work of God, inspired and empowered by the Spirit. Nearly two centuries later, William Brock announced:

> The treasure is in earthen vessels, that the excellency of the power may be of God and not of us . . . The prayer, the psalmody, the argument, the appeal, the

Scriptures, the ordinance, are not grace – they are only the means of grace, the mere vehicles through which the God of all grace sends down communications of his love. Rely then, implicitly, and consciously, not in word only, but in deed and truth, upon God.[45]

Brock was to emphasize grace, while Bunyan referred to the assistance of the Spirit – each reflecting something of the mystical tradition within Christianity, a tradition closely linked to the devotional concerns of the Free Churches. Alexander Maclaren preached at the autumn assembly of the Baptist Union in 1901 on the subject of 'Evangelical Mysticism':

> as long as the truth of an indwelling Spirit stands in the fore-front of New Testament teaching, and as long as the insight of a pure heart leads into a region far above that to which ethics and reasoning carry, so long will the mystical element enter into all living Christian experience, and be a fundamental part of the Christian belief.[46]

How do these reflections on prayer relate to the worship values we have identified? In answering this question we shall begin with the theme of devotion and openness to the Spirit, where the connections are most obvious.

Devotional Prayer

Free prayer has historically represented a freedom from the perceived tyranny of liturgical forms and prayer book services – but it does not thereby imply an autonomous liberty which is self-indulgent or without discipline. Indeed, *free* prayer might even be a misnomer, except with regard to its form. This prayer is not free in the sense that the one praying is free to pray what he or she likes. Indeed, there is a sense of submission to, and dependence upon, God which finds expression in a concern for two particular characteristics – inspiration and sincerity.

Inspired Prayer

Bunyan states that prayer is 'in the strength and assistance of the holy Spirit' and points out that only prayer which is offered through the teaching and assistance of the Spirit will be according to the will of God.[47] He later argues that, 'There is no man, nor Church in the world, that can come to God in Prayer but by the assistance of the holy Spirit.'[48] In their account of the worship of the proto-General Baptist congregation in

Amsterdam, Hughe and Anne Bromhead express the concern that worship be a spontaneous, pneumatological experience, because 'only God's word and the lively voice of his own graces must be heard in the public assemblies'.[49] Even Scripture was put aside after the preparatory exposition because the worship proper needed to be without any books at all. The immediacy of encounter with God is so valued that the human words which are uttered, whether in prayers or prophesying, are seen as the promptings of the Spirit – 'the lively voice of his own graces'. The Bromheads claim that to use written prayers is to offer God a human invention, rather than the Spirit-inspired pleadings of spontaneous worship:

> to worshippe the true god after another maner then he hath taught, is Idolatrie. but god commandeeth vs to come vnto him heavy loaden wth contrite hartes to cry vnto him for oure wants &c Therfore we may not stand reading A dead letter in steade of powring foorth oure petitions . . . we must stryve in prayer wth continuance &c but we cannot stryve in prayer and be importunate wth continuance reading vpon a booke, Therfore we must not reade when we should praye . . . we must pray as necessitie requireth but stinted prayers cannot be as necessitie requireth, Therfore stinted prayer is vnlawful.

Here the inspiration of the Spirit will give the words and will also prompt an honest recognition of human need and a necessary dependence upon divine grace.[50] In such an understanding of prayer, books will only get in the way, 'because true prayer must be of faith vtterred wth hearte and lyvely voyce'. If God is wanting to inspire our worship here and now, then 'It is presumptuous Ignorance to bring A booke to speake for vs vnto god.' Romans 8.26 is often referred to in writings on free prayer, indicating the need human beings have for the activity of the Spirit to prompt their prayers. For example, Horton Davies points out that John Owen's *Discourse of the Work of the Holy Spirit in Prayer* is an extended sermon upon that text.[51]

From the perspective of spirituality, as we have already noted, free prayer is not actually 'free'. It should be open to, and therefore dependent upon, the inspiration of the Holy Spirit. Though free in form, free prayer ceases to be true prayer when such submission to the Spirit is missing:

> It is the easiest thing of an hundred, to fall from the Power to the Form; but it is the hardest thing of many, to keep in the life, Spirit and Power of any one duty, especially Prayer: That is such a work, that a man without the help of the Spirit cannot so much as pray once, much less, continue.[52]

John Gill was to make a similar point when he claimed that 'true, spiritual, fervent and effectual prayer' cannot be performed without 'the grace, influence, and assistance of the Spirit of God'.[53] However, while this was the majority view for most of the span of Baptist history, the tradition has been adapted in the last century, as we have seen, to provide some scope for pre-composed prayers. Whether this is viewed as a substantive change or a legitimate development of the tradition is an open question. Contemporary Baptists would see the one leading prayer as open to the Spirit in the work of preparation, and also 'free' to follow the Spirit's leading by setting aside prepared or written prayers during the service.

The preparation for worship has a devotional dimension and requires an openness to the Spirit. Spurgeon links the personal devotion of the minister with what is offered in preaching and public prayer: 'There is no rhetoric like that of the heart, and no school for learning it but the foot of the cross . . . But how dare we pray in the battle if we have never cried to the Lord while buckling on the harness!'[54]

Sincere Prayer

Although prayer is an *expression* of the relationship between the one praying and God, there is a sense in which it is also that person presenting themselves before God and therefore an episode in that relationship. Such prayer must be truthful both in what it expresses and in what it represents. Sincerity of prayer and purity of heart are important characteristics of true prayer for Bunyan, who explains:

> And why must *sincerity* be one of the essentials of Prayer which is accepted of God, but because *sincerity* carries the soul in all simplicity to open its heart to God, and to tell him the case plainly without equivocation; to condemn itself plainly without dissembling; to cry to God heartily without complementing.[55]

He is concerned that sincerity be evident in prayer as in other areas of Christian living. 'Sincerity is such a grace as runs through all the Graces of God in us, and through all the actings of a Christian . . . '[56] This is so obviously necessary in view of the one to whom prayer is addressed, for it is the heart that God looks at, and, 'While Prayer is making, God is searching the heart, to see from what root and spirit it doth arise.'[57]

Sincerity should, however, not simply be defined as truthfulness. It should refer both to speaking the truth and also to the level of engagement that the speaker will have in that truthfulness. The role of the religious affections is an important factor in gauging a prayer's sincerity, though outward signs of emotion cannot be interpreted as inevitable indications of heart-felt prayer. Bunyan argues that outward incoherence may well demonstrate true prayer and be an indication that the burden of meaning and emotion are too great for human language:

> A man that truly prayes one Prayer, shall after that never be able to expresse with his mouth or pen, the unutterable desires, sence, affection and longing, that went to God in that Prayer . . . The best Prayers have often more groans than words; and those words that it hath, are but a lean and shallow representation of the heart, life, and spirit of that Prayer.[58]

Outward incoherence will not necessarily mean inward incoherence, but may indicate an intuitive grasp of spiritual truth, or a deep engagement of the person's emotions. When Bunyan speaks of prayer being 'sensible', he refers more to an intuitive grasp of spiritual realities rather than to rationality or eloquence.[59] This inevitably raises the question of how such prayer, when offered in public, may be understood by others in the congregation and edify or build up the Church. Certainly, later writings on prayer tend to be more rationalistic in approach and it is made clear that a requirement of true prayer is that it be understood by others.[60] Yet, this concern for heart worship continues to present itself as a significant feature of writings on free prayer. When Spurgeon urges his students to prepare for worship rather than offer 'random' prayers, he regards the primary preparation as 'not the preparation of the head, but of the heart'.[61]

The spiritual congruence of a person's actions is also an aspect of sincerity. 'Authenticity' may be a more apt designation for the sincerity which includes the person's life as a whole and not simply their heart in the moment of prayer. When Wallin proclaims that 'holy hands' are required in the offering of acceptable prayer, he recognizes that this cannot simply refer to innocence, but rather to a concerted desire to turn away from sin.[62] This integrity of life is a part of the relationship between God and the believer, and links prayer and living in a holistic way.

The sincerity of prayer finds further expression when that prayer is pastoral and expressive of the needs and desires of a particular congregation at a particular time. Bunyan ridiculed the notion of prayers prescribed for particular feast days because they could not be expressive of the needs of any particular congregation on a particular day:

> But here now, the wise men of our dayes are so well skill'd, as that they have both the *Manner* and the *Matter* of their Prayers at their finger ends; setting such a Prayer for such a day, and that twenty years before it comes.[63]

Consequently, the mouthing of generalities, rather than the articulating of specific and relevant petitions, is seen as an example of gross insincerity, as well as a stifling of the Spirit's inspiration. Free prayer is free to be contextual and timely, as we shall see when we examine its communal nature.[64]

Belief in the *inspired* nature of free prayer is dependent upon a prior belief that prayer will spring from the relationship between the person praying and God. To be open to the Spirit requires not only discernment, but also a desire to discern and a willingness to follow. The valuing of *sincerity* is a concern not simply for public truth, but for truthfulness and integrity between persons. Free prayer, by its dependency, submission and desire for authenticity, suggests a spirituality grounded in the personal relationship between the believer and God.

This relationship is a dynamic, for there is an interaction between the person and God which expresses itself not only in the offering of specific petitions, but also in the demands which God is perceived to make on the life of the one praying. This relationship, because it is *personal*, cannot stand still, and a particular prayer should be seen not so much as a manifestation of eternal truth, as an episode in the groaning of creation, a stage on the person's journey of faith and an event in which God acts. In this view, prayer is part of the drama of salvation, for transforming both the world and the worshippers, and to this eschatological theme we now turn.

Kingdom Prayer

As well as expressing devotional concerns, prayer has a future orientation, a concern for the Kingdom of God. This is especially evident in the petitionary emphasis which is likely to be prominent in any view of prayer which stresses dependence upon God. The pouring out of the heart, which is central to Bunyan's definition of prayer, is 'for such things as God hath promised, or, according to the Word, for the good of the Church'. If prayer is devotional in seeking the presence of God, petitionary prayer is eschatological in seeking the 'not yet'.

The prominence of petitionary prayer within the Protestant tradition has been highlighted in the work of the German phenomenologist Friedrich Heiler. He distinguishes between what he calls *mystical prayer* and *prophetic* or *evangelical prayer*.[65] He argues that, for the mystic, the devotional life comes to a climax in extraordinary experiences, while the life of piety in the prophetic tradition is lived in communion with God through faith and moral duty. On the one hand there is the present experience of communion with God and on the other there is the wrestling with his will, the bringing of requests to a God who has invited us to ask, to seek and to knock.

It is possible to adapt Heiler's distinction between two traditions of prayer by identifying the general characteristics of these and applying them as two *aspects* of prayer. When he speaks of 'the mystical tradition' we may speak of prayer as *communion* and when he speaks of 'the prophetic tradition' we may speak of *petition*. The tension between them is one which can be found in worship as a whole.[66] Although communion is integral to the nature of prayer as relationship, much free prayer is concerned with petitions of one sort or another. This is consistent with Heiler's claim that the Protestant tradition of spirituality tends towards making requests of God. As such it demonstrates a future orientation, for petitionary prayer is asking that a situation be changed by the activity of God. Such prayer embodies a dissatisfaction with the present and expresses a desire for a future changed by God and is therefore eschatological in nature.

There is, however, a third category which is reflected in some of Heiler's analysis, but which is not developed by him – what we might call *dialogue*. In his discussion of petitionary prayer in the prophetic tradition, Heiler points out that there will sometimes come a point of submission, where the one requesting certain things will reach a place where they acknowledge the will of God and submit to it.[67] Bunyan, despite his readiness to pour out requests to God, observes that these petitions must be 'with submission, in Faith, to the Will of God'. In other words, not only is there a possibility of the world being changed as a result of petition, but of the petitioner being transformed. This dynamic process is, perhaps, more likely to take place in a form of prayer which allows a free engagement and articulation of the worshippers' concerns and their response to their encounter with God and his revealed will. While it is easier to envisage such a transformation occurring in the prayers of an individual, the psalms of lament are increasingly recognized as offering a biblical model which can be used to good pastoral effect in corporate worship. In using such a psalm, the congregation is able to follow what may previously have been an individual journey from complaint through transformation to trust and praise.[68] Just as we may see communion as an expression of the devotional values we have identified, so the transformation of the worshipper may be seen as an expression of the eschatological values we have also claimed are significant for Baptist worship.

The devotional theme of communion reminds us of the centrality of

God in all worship, yet God invites us to bring our requests and to pray for his Kingdom. So this meeting with God leads to prayer requests for the worshippers and for God's world which lead us beyond worship itself to the life of creation. Yet this praying for the world cannot remain a series of unchanged demands because the encounter with God leads to ourselves being changed and to a change in the things for which we ask and the way in which we ask. This transformation not only changes our understanding of the world and of ourselves, but also leads us back to God and to communion.

Worship is *central* to the totality of Christian experience but is not to be mistaken for the whole. There are mystical aspects to worship – moments of adoration, thanksgiving and dedication. Yet the prophetic and biblical model of petition and dialogue encourages worshippers not to separate worship from the rest of life. Worship must be God-centred, but it also needs to be Kingdom-focused. The worshipper should not only be lost in love for God, but discover a passion for God's Kingdom to come and God's will to be done. The love of God should lead to the love of neighbour as expressed in Jesus's summing up of the law (Mark 12.28–31). Here is both rest and movement, relationship and action – communion, dialogue and petition.

Communion is God-centred and yet, when it is truly God-centred, the worshipper will be led to the concerns which are God's concerns, namely God's love for the world. Similarly, petition results in a struggling encounter with God in which more of the divine will is revealed and in which the worshipper is changed. In order to pray that God's Kingdom might come, the worshipper must be prepared for the Kingdom to come in part through his or her own transformation. That transformation will lead not only to communion, but to a life of service and the living-out of kingdom values.

Scriptural Prayer

We have already recognized a tension between the demands of Scripture and the experiential concerns of personal religion. Nonetheless, there are important linkages in this dynamic relationship. Proponents of free prayer have argued that this was the only kind of prayer which they could see in Scripture, particularly returning in their expositions of prayer to various parts of the eighth chapter of Romans. Committed to the notion of ordinances, they claimed that there was no biblical precedent for liturgical forms, and Vavasor Powell, the Welsh itinerant evangelist, argued that if the imposition of such liturgies could not be justified from Scripture, then 'it is no less than Will-Worship'.[69]

Attention to Scripture carries a devotional dimension in the worshipper's prizing of the Word of God. A willingness to submit assumes a commitment to the God who is believed to be revealed in Scripture and an acceptance of divine authority which is itself a relational characteristic which may be expressed in prayers of dedication and offering.

In the few sample prayers we have examined there is a profusion of scriptural phrases and ideas. While free prayer may, according to Bunyan, legitimately be expressed in sighs and groans, its more usual expression is in a catalogue of biblical images and quotations. While this may be regarded as a cultural phenomenon, it would be a mistake to miss the spirituality to which it points. We have seen how there is little distinction to be made by Baptist writers between extempore prayer in worship and private devotions. This erosion of a division between personal piety and public worship is also evident in the way in which the use of Scripture in those personal devotions is reflected in the scriptural language of public extempore prayer. There has, in fact, been recent interest in the relationship between personal piety and public worship, though it is often the liturgical nurturing of personal spirituality, rather than the influence of personal spirituality on worship.[70]

Communal Prayer

Apart from recent borrowings from other traditions, prayer in Baptist worship will rarely be the unison utterance of a whole congregation. It is more likely to be the solo voices of ministers and others who lead that congregation in prayer in a representative way. Sometimes in public worship, but more often in other gatherings such as prayer meetings, a range of individuals will be encouraged to pray on behalf of the assembly. Proponents of liturgical prayer might regard this as individualist and lacking in any sense of worship being 'the work of the people'. However, we must understand that those leading in prayer are doing so as representatives in the belief that the whole congregation is praying, even though only one voice might be heard. A vocal 'Amen' at the close of prayers will be one way in which some congregations supply evidence that what has been uttered by one voice is actually a communal action. Other congregations might murmur words of assent, such as 'Yes Lord', as the prayer proceeds. Using White's helpful distinction between 'active participation' and 'passive (or receptive) participation' on the part of the congregation, we can say that, generally, Baptist congregations will participate passively in free prayer, despite the examples of active involvement just given. Nonetheless, what White means by passive participation is not wholly passive but rather an absence of outward actions or words on the part of the congregation.[71] Indeed, as well as contributing the prayer itself, the representative leader is also modelling a way of praying which will influence the spiritual formation of members of the congregation.[72]

Discussing the prayer debates of the seventeenth century, Horton Davies argues that liturgical prayer and free prayer reflect two quite distinct ecclesiologies. While 'the former stresses the corporate nature of the Church in "Common Prayer", the latter emphasizes the need of individuals in a family Church'.[73] He suggests that liturgical prayer will express commonalities such as credal statements, and collects which pray for graces required of all Christians, while free prayer will give voice to the particular needs of individuals. Relying on Troeltsch's distinction between 'church' and 'sect' he argues that 'free prayer suggests not Israel but the remnant, i.e. the compact unit of the congregation as a worshipping family'. This insight does not question the communal nature of Baptist worship but helps clarify the understanding of that community as covenantal. The congregation is not seen as a crowd, but as a group of individuals in relationship with one another.[74] Thus 'public worship' can be a misnomer for Baptist congregations for while that worship is open to the public it is also an expression of interpersonal relationships. This domestic aspect of Baptist worship also bears a close relationship to the lack of division between public and personal prayer already noted.

This sense of family finds particular expression in Baptist worship in prayer for 'the needs of the saints', the 'long prayer' that often included particular requests for members of the congregation. In 1996, almost 90 per cent of churches said most services would include prayers for individuals in the fellowship.[75] John Skoglund, a contemporary American Baptist, speaks of 'localized' prayer being made easier by free prayer.[76] Isaac Watts claimed that such openness to the needs of a particular congregation is not possible with prescribed prayers for they will be either general or inaccurate:

> It is much sweeter to our own souls, and to our fellow worshippers, to have our fears, and our doubts, and complaints, and temptations, and sorrows represented in most exact and particular expressions, in such language as the soul itself feels when the words are spoken.[77]

The *ad hoc* nature of this prayer enables it to be the prayer of *this* local church, the needs and aspirations of *this* group of people on *this* particular day.[78] As well as giving expression to the devotional and epicletic nature of free prayer, this pastoral praying manifests a concern for the local congregation as a community whose members are called to care for one another and which expresses that care through its petitions.

7

Living Word

The Spirituality of Preaching

Not a sound was heard but that of the preacher's voice – scarcely an eye but was fixed upon him – not a countenance that he did not watch, and read, and interpret, as he surveyed them again and again and again with his rapid, ever-excursive glance. As he advanced and increased in animation, five or six of the auditors would be seen to rise and lean forward over the front of their pews, still keeping their eyes upon him. Some new or striking sentiment or expression would, in a few minutes, cause others to rise in like manner; shortly afterwards still more, and so on, until, long before the close of the sermon, it often happened that a considerable portion of the congregation were seen standing – every eye directed at the preacher, yet now and then for a moment glancing from one to the other, thus transmitting and reciprocating thought and feeling: – Mr. Hall himself, though manifestly absorbed in his subject, conscious of the whole, receiving new animation from what he thus witnessed, reflecting it back upon those who were already alive to the inspiration, until all that were susceptible of thought and emotion seemed wound up to the utmost limit of elevation on earth – when he would close, and reluctantly and slowly resume their seats.

Memoir of Robert Hall (1764– 1831) by Olinthus Gregory,
prefixed to vol. 4 of Hall's *Works*

Christian preaching is a practical expression of the authority of Scripture. While interpretations of this doctrine have varied among Baptists, as among other Christians, the recognition that Scripture carries an authority for the Church is fundamental to an understanding of preaching and its place within worship. As Horton Davies explains,

the 'opening' of the scriptures occupies the central position in Puritan worship. The importance of preaching consisted in the fact that it was the declaration by the preacher of the revelation of God, confirmed in the hearts of the believers by the interior testimony of the Holy Spirit.[1]

The awesome aim of preaching is, therefore, to explain Scripture and apply divine revelation. Understood as a revelation of the divine will, Scripture has been used to set norms for faith and practice within the Christian community, but this should not be understood in an overly legal way. Scripture has also been seen as essentially life-giving – the revelation of God's will and a testimony to his saving acts and promises, especially in Jesus Christ. Preaching is a means by which this life-giving revelation of God is communicated and shared.

Here are two approaches to Scripture. One the one hand, it can be seen as a repository of objective, heteronomic commands which will structure Christian living and belief. On the other hand, it can be seen as a devotional treasury in which we can find words of life to nourish and transform those who read and hear. Both approaches are important, and preaching is an event which can both communicate authoritative information and provide a place of encounter with God.[2]

To see Scripture as a source of authoritative teaching is close to the notion of ordinance which we have already seen to be as a significant factor in the ordering of Separatist and Baptist worship.[3] A community which combs the Scriptures in search of such ordinances and then organizes its life and witness on the basis of what is found, is a community which is trying to take seriously the authority of Scripture. Here is an example of spirituality, of 'the conjunction of theology, prayer and practical Christianity', as the reading of Scripture leads to the structuring of Christian living both inside and outside the Church. In worship, preaching is where the connections are made between this source of authoritative truth and daily life, and it has been accorded particular prominence in Baptist and Free Church worship.

The Independent, Thomas Goodwin, was clear that the communication of preaching was far more than imparting information, and included 'experimental, saving, applying knowledge'.[4] We shall need to explore these devotion concerns in order to understand something of what preaching means in Free Church worship, but first, we shall turn to the *practice* of preaching among Baptists – its development, its varieties and especially its dominance.

The Practice of Preaching in Baptist Worship

Free prayer is difficult to study because it is not often recorded and, by definition, has not used a written script. But it is not only prayer which proves elusive. The problem for the student of preaching is different.

There exist many sermon scripts, often widely published. However, we need to distinguish between the written text of the sermon and the *event* of preaching.[5] It is possible to read the script of a sermon and yet have no clear idea as to what the preaching event was like. The words may be the same, but the personality of the preacher and the level of enthusiasm with which the words were delivered or received will affect the nature of the preaching event. For example, this contemporary account of Joseph Stennett's enthusiastic and extempore preaching offers a considerable contrast to the polished rhetoric of his published sermons:

> And when at the close of a discourse he came to reason with sinners about their unhappy condition, and to set before them the generous proposals of the gospel, together with the fatal consequences of their impenitency; he would so mix his tears with his expostulations, as the affections of but few in the assembly could remain unmoved.[6]

Similarly, John Gill's published sermons do not reflect the fervour evident in John Rippon's account of Gill's early funeral orations:

> In preaching funeral sermons, and on other extraordinary [i.e. special] occasions, when he was a young man, and surrounded with large congregations, his exertions have been such that the people have conveyed to him, as well as they were able, three or four handkerchiefs to wipe his face, in one discourse.[7]

This contrast between written record and contemporary account means that we should be cautious in only using sermon texts for examining the development of preaching in worship. Instead, we shall again examine the services we have already reviewed and supplement them with various statements about the nature of preaching and practical advice to aspiring and active preachers.

The Development of Preaching in Baptist Worship

There are hints in the description of the English exiles' worship in Amsterdam of emphases which later came to characterize the General Baptists. After the preparatory Bible study prayer, the Bible and other books were put aside, and

> after a solemne prayer made by the .1. speaker, he propoundeth some text ow^t of the Scripture, and prophecieth ow^t of the same, by the space of one hower, or thre Quarters of an hower. After him standeth vp A .2. speaker and prophe-

cieth ow^t of the said text the like tyme and space. some tyme more some tyme lesse. After him the .3. the .4. and the .5. &c as the tyme will geve leave.[8]

Horton Davies suggests that the Baptists were responsible for introducing the practice of a running expositional commentary during the reading of Scripture.[9] This seems to have begun with the Smyth and Helwys congregation, though it became a feature of wider Puritan and Particular Baptist worship and survived into the nineteenth century, with the 'expositions' of C. H. Spurgeon preceding his 'sermons'. The Bromheads' account seems to indicate that, after preparatory Bible study, a text was announced from the passage studied and expounded. This was then followed by an extempore sermon, first from the one leading and then from others who preached extempore from the same text. Most of the four-hour service, after the initial reading and discussion, seems to have been taken up with preaching. The word 'prophecieth' probably means 'preaches' as this seems to have been the usual meaning of the word in the seventeenth century.[10] In understanding the word as synonymous with 'preaching' there is a hint of both inspiration and authority, as the one prophesying may be seen to speak on behalf of God and by divine prompting. The spontaneity of the preaching, and the Bromheads' use of the phrase 'the lively voice of his own graces', may suggest something comparable to the modern Charismatic understanding of prophesy as inspired utterances. However, the prophesying in Amsterdam appears to have been more expositional than oracular.

The Separatist congregation described in 1641 in *The Brownist Synagogue* reportedly had two preachers expounding the same text, and Lambe's congregation had a number of speakers.[11] However, by the end of the seventeenth century General Baptist worship seems to have resembled the worship of the other Nonconformists, except that there was no unison hymn singing. The reference to preaching is brief and straightforward in the constitution of the Barbican church formed in 1695:

> In the morning about half an hour after nine, some Brother be appointed to begin the Exercise in reading a Psalm, & then to spend some time in Prayer; & after yt to read some other Portion of H. Scripture, till the Minister comes into the Pulpit; and after Preaching and Prayer to conclude with singing a Psalm.[12]

Leadership was shared between a member of the congregation who was designated to lead the worship, and a minister, who was to preach. The allusion to preaching is brief and suggests a formalization in line with other groups, with the preaching undertaken by a minister who delivers the sermon from a pulpit. It is difficult to map the trajectory of development from Amsterdam to this point, though we know that it was subject to a climate of diverse experiment during the Commonwealth, followed by the constraints of persecution after 1660.[13]

A slightly more extended service at Bury Street carried the same characteristics as the Barbican service:

> In the morning we begin with singing a psalm, then a short prayer follows to desire the Divine Presence in all the following parts of worship; after that, about half an hour is spent in the exposition of some portion of scripture, which is succeeded by singing a psalm or an hymn. After this the minister prays . . . Then a sermon is preached, and the morning worship concluded with a short prayer and the benediction.[14]

It has already been noted that there would usually be a hymn after the sermon but, because of Watts's nervous disorders, the hymn was placed earlier, after the exposition. Here is a pragmatic approach to the order of service, and the response to the sermon now rests upon the short prayer rather than the congregational hymn. There is an explicit reference to an exposition of Scripture, distinct from the sermon, though whether they are both on the same passage is not clear.

This exposition lasted for about half an hour and, from contemporary sources, we know that the sermon was usually of an hour's duration, often with an hour glass attached to the pulpit. So, in each service, at least an hour and a half consisted of homiletic material in one form or another.

Horton Davies suggests that the prevailing culture of the so-called 'Age of Reason' might have influenced dissenting preaching, because 'the most consciously intellectual and apologetic element in the service of worship, the sermon, took on an exaggerated importance'.[15] Worship became the attendance at 'the Lord's Day Lecture'[16] and the other activities of worship were often seen as preliminaries to the rational sermon, in which elegant form and rational argument were prized. While Particular Baptists and Independents may not have been as affected by the prevailing rationalism as General Baptists and Presbyterians, many of whom became Unitarian, Benjamin Wallin's critique of worship attitudes among Baptist congregations suggests that intellectual stimulation may well have been more greatly prized than devotion by some of the Baptists of his time.

Yet the picture is more complex, and the climate of Baptist theology and devotion in the eighteenth century a far from uncontested field. The middle of the century saw a rising concern for revival, with the ministries of Whitefield and Wesley providing an encouragement to those already inspired by the New England writings of Jonathan Edwards. London seems to have been a centre of Hyper-Calvinism. Raymond Brown has observed that

> John Gill and John Brine were men of immense influence [who] diverted the thinking of many Particular Baptist ministers into patterns of occasionally abstruse high Calvinism and caused the good news to be a matter for arid debate rather than confident proclamation . . . In 1748 Whitefield told Dodderidge that 'sweet invitations to close with Christ' were 'the very life of preaching,' though he observed that anyone who introduced the note of entreaty into a sermon would soon be 'dubbed a Methodist on account of it.'[17]

Baptist life in the West of England, Midlands and North seems to have enjoyed a continuing Evangelical identity with a warm spirituality. Such devotion is evident in the circular letters of the Northamptonshire Association during the period in which Andrew Fuller and William Carey were so influential.[18] In the 1814 letter, written by Robert Hall junior, worshippers were exhorted to a devotional approach to the hearing of the Word.[19]

Similarly, in 1845, William Brock exhorted Norfolk Baptists to a devotional, but critical, attentiveness to preaching: 'You are to take heed *how* you hear; not thoughtlessly, not indolently, not superstitiously receiving whatever may be advanced, but receiving it with observation and care.' His description of the sermon clearly presents it as an exposition of Scripture which is not merely rational but potentially life-giving in its power: 'Then comes the exposition, or the discourse intended to build you up in your most holy faith, and to open the Scriptures to the understanding of the people, that they may become wise unto salvation by faith in Jesus Christ.'[20]

The nineteenth century has often been described as 'the age of preaching' and Charles Haddon Spurgeon, for example, preached to ten thousand people each Sunday. It has been suggested that the advent of more popular evening services led to a less formal preaching style,[21] and Spurgeon once said, 'I wish to lay the formalities of the pulpit aside and talk to you as if you were in your own houses.'[22] In stark contrast to the forthright sermons of Spurgeon, with their numbered heads and strident images, was the topical preaching of John Clifford and the expository and mystical preaching of Alexander Maclaren who, after careful exegesis involving philological examination and a survey of critical literature, would turn to the message. Now the hours of spiritual wrestling and intellectual concentration in the study and the time spent with treasured volumes of Carlyle and Browning bore fruit . . . as exposition turned to application and finally to appeal and the Word was transformed from external authority to a dynamic penetrating the preacher's and his hearer's innermost being.[23]

In the twentieth century, wider cultural changes again affected the culture of worship, and the place of the sermon was influenced by a widening of education, a developing secularization and an increasing informality encouraged by radio and television. Where once sermons had been expected to last one hour, they were now expected by many to last less than half that. Yet still, in the middle of the twentieth century, the sermon was likely to represent nearly half of the time available for the service.

By the late 1990s further cultural changes were evident and less than 40 per cent of sermons were preached from a pulpit. Over a third of preachers used an overhead projector, at least sometimes, to illustrate the message, and nearly three-quarters of congregations would listen with a Bible provided for their use. A similar number spoke of preaching as 'teaching', and nearly 95 per cent claimed that the preaching was usually closely based on the Scripture reading.[24]

Teaching and Proclamation

While proclamation and teaching are seen by some biblical commentators[25] as distinct activities in the primitive Church, with *didache* being delivered within the church community for its edification and *kerygma* being proclaimed outside it in mission, both these forms of preaching have tended to be present in Christian worship. *Teaching* is an inevitable part of the interpretative process when the explication of Scripture is seen as the explaining and applying of divine revelation. However, the announcing of God's Word is a present event, and therefore *proclamation*, as well as the interpretation of past oracles.[26]

The kerygmatic presentation of the gospel, accompanied by invitations to faith, has been evident in a continuous Baptist tradition since the seventeenth century,[27] when Benjamin Keach, for example, 'regularly and effectively pleaded with his congregation to put their trust in Christ'.[28] Emmanuel Gifford, ministering at the Pithay Church in Bristol in the first quarter of the eighteenth century, would, at the close of his sermons, 'offer Christ to sinners and invite them to embrace him as offered in the most affectionate and pathetical manner'.[29] The preaching of Spurgeon was a clear example of evangelism within the worshipping community, and his sermons, though often very doctrinal, usually included an appeal to the worshippers to respond to divine grace. In the 1996 survey, over 46 per cent of churches described their preaching as 'evangelistic', 53 per cent described it as 'challenging' and 37 per cent as 'inspirational'.[30]

On the other hand, that same survey showed the largest number of churches, over 70 per cent, using the word 'teaching' to describe their preaching. Certainly, the *form* of many published sermons over the years has suggested a high level of didactic purpose, though, of course, sermons containing didactic material are more likely to commend themselves for publication than other types of sermon. Influenced by the structure already established by the Puritans, Baptist sermons have often been divided and subdivided into teaching points. In his advice to the students of his 'Pastors' College', Spurgeon asserted:

> Sermons *should have real teaching in them,* and their doctrine should be solid, substantial, and abundant . . . If we speak as ambassadors for God, we need never complain of want of matter, for our message is full to overflowing. The entire gospel message must be presented from the pulpit; the whole faith once delivered to the saints must be proclaimed by us . . . Nothing can compensate for the absence of teaching; all the rhetoric in the world is but chaff to the wheat in contrast to the gospel of our salvation.[31]

It is significant that a preacher noted for his missionary concern and evangelistic passion should extol the virtues of comprehensive doctrinal teaching. Yet Spurgeon saw the presentation of doctrine as the proclamation of God's saving grace, which led to an invitation to respond to the divine goodness. Such preaching was not only a presentation of the gospel for the unconverted, but also a means of building up the saints in their faith and in their faithful living.

The challenges of preaching to a congregation with varied needs are clear in the advice given to preachers by Hercules Collins in 1701.[32] In commenting on 2 Timothy 2.15, that a pastor should study in order to be 'a workman that needeth not to be ashamed, rightly dividing the Word of Truth', he exegetes 'dividing' as a metaphor suggestive of the dividing of a sacrifice by the priest, or the sharing out of a meal by parents among their several children. The implication is that some of the text has truth suitable for some people and other parts contain truths relevant to the needs of others. The role of the preacher is to apply the rich resources of the scriptural text to the various needs of the congregation:

The word imports thus much, that Ministers should so divide the Word of Truth, as to give every one their due Portion . . . You must seek the Sinner's Conversion, the ignorant Man's Instruction . . . In a word, some must be fed with Milk, some with strong Meat: Food for Strong Men, and Milk for Babes.[33]

Here is a double diversity. The gospel must be preached for the conversion of sinners and the varied needs of the saints must be met by relevant and judicious expository preaching – proclamation and teaching. Yet even the teaching is more than simply instruction, and will include the proclamation of divine grace as well as the clarification of divine commands. The purpose of 'teaching' is 'edification', for one of the functions of preaching is the building up of the Church through the instruction, exhortation and challenge of Christian believers. This pastoral task of edification is an important link between the role of pastor and the task of preaching. Nonetheless, the diversity of any congregation provides a context within which the preacher attempts to meet a variety of pastoral needs and usually both teaching and proclamation will be in evidence.[34]

The Dominance of Preaching

Preaching has often dominated much Baptist and Free Church worship, tending to take a relatively large proportion of the time allotted for each service. In mid-eighteenth-century London, Benjamin Wallin admonished worshippers for sometimes arriving late, as though the preceding worship were unimportant,[35] and, over a century later, Spurgeon encouraged his students to give adequate attention to worship and not allow the sermon to unduly dominate.[36] There are a number of factors which help to explain this situation.

Scripture is regarded as the primary vehicle through which God addresses humanity, and preaching the means whereby it will be given a contemporary and living voice. Thus the 'hearing of the Word' is a regular theme in Baptist writings as it assumes the readiness of a congregation to be open to the voice of God through the voice of the preacher.[37]

The phrase 'hearing the Word of God' assumes that authority is not only to be found in Scripture as it is read, but that in some sense the Word of God is to be encountered through the words of the preacher. The Puritans had defended preaching over the simple reading of Scripture, as Thomas Goodwin, for example, argued:

It is not the letter of the Word that ordinarily doth convert, but the spiritual meaning of it, as revealed and expounded . . . There is the letter, the husk; and there is the spirit, the kernel; and when we by expounding the Word do open the husk, out drops the kernel. And so it is the spiritual meaning of the Word let into the heart which converts it and turns it unto God.[38]

Evangelical religion carries a high expectation of personal change. While this is seen as a work of grace in the Spirit's ministry of regeneration and sanctification, the role of preaching is central in the testimonies of many Christians. Consequently, there is a high expectation that God will work, as well as speak, through the preaching and hearing of the Word.

In a tradition in which other components of worship have often been perceived as 'preliminaries' to the preaching of the Word, many ordinary Christians have found the *ad hominem* nature of preaching more palatable, and even entertaining, than some of those other components. The tradition which began by suspecting visual images developed a culture where people were more concerned for articulated, conceptual forms of communication, than sacramental, non-verbal expressions of spiritual reality.

The dominance of preaching in Baptist worship is demonstrated not only by the proportion of time given to it, but through its identification with the calling to ministry.[39] The testing of a person's call to ministry has, for Baptists, always included the testing of a person's gift of preaching. While preaching may not be perceived as the primary gift of a particular individual, the idea of a pastoral ministry without the call to preach is a notion foreign to a tradition in which Scripture is so important. In the early Baptist period, this testing also applied to those who were licensed as preachers without a call to pastoral office. In the seventeenth and eighteenth centuries, any believing themselves to be called to preach were usually listened to in private by the Church, which then voted as to whether or not the person's sense of vocation was verified by the community.[40] When the Northern messengers were asked in March 1706 whether a person could take upon themselves (without a call mediated through the Church) 'the Office of the Ministry in Preaching the Gospel & Administering the Ordinances of Baptism & the Lord's Supper', they gave nine reasons why this could not be, including:

Because truely Called Ministers are Ambassadours for Christ in the great work & message he send them about But those that take that great work upon themselves not truely Called thereto cannot be reputed so But does their own work and goes in Ambassie for themselves.[41]

When asked whether preachers were authorized to administer the ordinances of baptism and the Lord's Supper simply by virtue of their authorization to preach, the messengers of the Northern churches in 1704 ruled that 'those whom the Church Approves to preach the Gospel may also Administer the Ordinances of Baptism and the Lord's Supper Preaching being the main and principall Work of the Gospel'.[42] This assertion that preaching is 'the principal work of the gospel'[43] demonstrates an important aspect of the Reformation tradition which, in the Free Churches, has often been symbolized by a central pulpit. The preaching of the Word was seen as a primary manifestation of the gospel, while the Lord's Supper was seen as an embodied form of that same gospel. Calvin argued that the Lord's Supper should always be accompanied with preaching, for otherwise it becomes a 'dumb show'.[44] William Bradshaw had claimed to represent the general Puritan position when he stated:

> They hould that the highest and supreame office and authoritie of the Pastor, is to preach the gospell solemnly and publickly to the Congregation, by interpreting the written word of God, and applying the same by exhortation and reproof unto them. They hould that this was the greatest worke that Christ & his Apostles did.[45]

Yet this dominance should not lead to an unnecessary division between preaching and the rest of worship. Prayer, for example, should not be regarded as worship in a way that preaching is not.[46] If preaching is *not* regarded as worship then it can be open to misinterpretation as entertainment, or as merely a commentary on the supposedly primary events of worship. However, the whole of the service should be interpreted liturgically, including the sermon, and this may be illustrated by the dynamic movements which occur within preaching as an act of worship.

The most obvious movement is from preacher to congregation. The *form* of preaching is that of an individual addressing a crowd, or at least a representative figure addressing a group. Yet even here the nature of the event might vary, as the way in which the sermon is delivered can affect the relationship between the preacher and the listeners. For example, eye contact with the congregation may suggest a contextuality which enables the sermon to address *this* congregation, in this place, at this time. If, however, the sermon is read with no great attempt to engage in an interpersonal way with the congregation, it could be judged an essay of a general nature arising out of the preacher's reflection on Scripture, a generalized confessional statement which is simply overheard by the congregation.

There are other movements in addition to the flow between preacher and listeners. There is the claim that in preaching, God addresses those who listen.[47] The authority accorded the sermon is greater than that given to an address in other contexts, for it is in some sense perceived to be 'the Word of God' and not merely the opinions of a human being.[48] Similarly, there is a flow from Scripture to the present moment, as the Scripture reading is expounded and applied.

The movement of God upon the worshippers is not only through the divine voice of Scripture at the point of inspiration and writing. Both in the reading of Scripture and in preaching, the *testimonium Spiritus Sancti internum* provides a theological explanation for the hearing and believing of the Word,[49] in which the internal work of the Spirit in the hearts of the listeners enables them to hear not only the external voice of the preacher, but an inner voice applying the Word to them and inviting an appropriate response.

The dynamic movements within the preaching event should not only be thought of as being in a 'downward' direction, whether from God or the pulpit! The preacher not only delivers the sermon to the congregation but offers the preaching in an 'upward' direction to God. The invocatory prayer is one expression of this and, by their readiness to listen and respond, the members of the congregation also make an offering which belies the passive role which is often assumed.[50] The members of the congregation offer to God their readiness to respect and listen to the preacher, and this attentiveness, and the preparation for obedience, is most properly understood as an offering to God. Preaching is a complex event in which even those who *appear* to be passive may play an important and active role.

To describe worship as a meeting of the divine and human, and preaching as a significant place of encounter, helps us to understand some of the links made by Baptists and other Free Churches between the call of people to ministry and the preaching of the Word. The messengers of the Northern churches in 1706 identified the commissioned nature of the preaching ministry and argued that it should be under the authority of a God, who equips and commissions, and of a Church which tests and ordains.[51] This guarding of the pulpit is significant. Preaching is perceived as a mode of pastoral ministry in which leadership is exercised, the Church built up and the community nourished. It is also a handling of the divine oracles and an event through which God is expected to speak.

The Spirituality of Preaching in Baptist Worship

How do these preaching practices and their interpretation express something of what Baptists and others believe? How do the core worship values interact in the event of preaching? The polarity between an attention to Scripture and a concern for devotion and the experiential dimensions of faith are particularly significant. However, because in preaching we are already dealing with the first value, attention to Scripture, the polarity is not so much between external authority and internal testimony as between rational understanding, or explanation, and affective response.

Preaching, Rationality and Scripture

Attention to Scripture is clearly going to have a particular relevance for preaching and the role of Scripture within worship. We have already seen that this attention has been partly expressed through the notion of scriptural ordinances governing the practice of worship. Preaching is no exception to this principle of ordering because it is seen as an activity commanded and exemplified in Scripture.[52] Preaching is perceived as an activity in which scriptural truth is announced, and therefore carries not only the authority of the preacher, resulting from their status in the Christian community, but the authority of the Scriptures upon which the preaching is based.

The liturgical function of preaching could be broadly described as the exposition of Scripture.[53] In that exposition, rationality plays a large part, offering a particular approach to the reading of Scripture for the purposes of preaching. This rationality may be in the way Scripture is interpreted, but also in the development of biblical and doctrinal teaching from that interpretation. Thus reason is one of the ways in which Scripture is comprehended and received by the community, though rationality has a particular role in the development of didactic preaching.

Despite the diverse elements in preaching, the notion of teaching for edification is a central and continuing feature. Spurgeon urged his students, 'Take care that your deliverances are always weighty, and full of really important teaching.'[54] Whether Christians need to be educated in the basics of the faith or invited to move from milk to meat (Hebrews 5.12–14), whether those who are despairing need to be lifted up, or those who are without hope need inviting towards faith, the notion of teaching provides a basis for each of these pastoral actions. Doctrinal preaching, understood as teaching, should therefore be seen as either the norm or the rhetorical base upon which other homiletic devices are founded. This assumes that rationality is a major feature of our humanity and that God addresses us and invites us to respond within a rational framework. We misunderstand preaching if we do not recognize that its provenance is human rationality, whatever intuitive or affective shoots might spring from this ground. Rationality can nurture devotion, and both are needed in any adequate understanding of faith.[55]

This doctrinal emphasis is not the conveying of credal information, as though the main purpose of the preacher was to load the minds of the congregation with a 'body of divinity',[56] but a presentation of the gospel and an invitation to respond to the God whose gospel it is. John Fawcett claimed that such doctrine must be Christocentric and theocentric:

> No doctrine, we trust, will ever be preached in this house, but that which sets forth Christ and him crucified, as the Alpha and Omega, the first and the last, in the salvation of men . . . That is holy doctrine which gives due honour to the rich and sovereign grace of God in the salvation of men. No doctrine will become this house, which teaches a man to trust in his own heart, to go about to establish his own righteousness as the ground of acceptance with God, or to mingle works and grace together as causes of salvation.[57]

Spurgeon told his students not to give undue weight to esoteric aspects of doctrine, but to concentrate on what was pastorally relevant to their congregations. He claimed that finer points of doctrinal dispute are

> practically of very little concern to that godly widow woman, with seven children to support by her needle, who wants far more to hear of the loving-kindness of the God of providence than of these mysteries profound; if you preach to her on the faithfulness of God to his people, she will be cheered and helped in the battle of life; but difficult questions will perplex her and put her to sleep . . . Brethren, first and above all things, keep to plain evangelical doctrines; whatever else you do or do not preach, be sure incessantly to bring forth the soul-saving truth of Christ and him crucified.[58]

The *pastoral* function of preaching is the building up of the Church, and the faith and living of its members.[59] Long before Spurgeon directed his students to concentrate on central doctrines which had a pastoral value, Hercules Collins proclaimed edification to be a central function of preaching:

> Meddle with controversies and doubtful matters as little as may be in public

auditories, lest you puzzle your hearers and hinder their edification; insist on those points that tend to sound belief, sincere love to God, and a holy conversation.[60]

Here is what we may call a 'qualified rationality'. While preaching needs an intellectual framework, the intention of that preaching should be directed to the building up of the congregation, the improving of their understanding of spiritual truths and the nurturing of their faith.

The rational character of preaching can often be found as much in the *structure* of the sermon, as in its *content*. As heirs to the Puritan tradition, Baptist preachers have continued to expound a text, subdivide its meaning into a number of heads and apply its truth to the lives of the hearers. The Westminster Assembly's *Directory for the Public Worship of God*[61] was concerned that doctrinal structures would have a priority above exegetical schemes, for 'In analysing and dividing the text', the preacher 'is to regard more the order of matter than of words'. It also offered a clear formula[62] of 'Doctrine, Reason and Use' as a pattern for sermons which was followed closely by Hercules Collins and which is worth quoting at length. Having expounded 2 Timothy 2.15, Collins explains how his sermon illustrates these homiletical principles.

> Consider my whole Method in speaking, 1. To the Penman of the Epistle. 2. To the Time when written. 3. The Occasion. 4. The Scope . . . 2ndly Consider how your text coheres and depends on what goes before it, but stand no longer upon it than what may make your way plain to the Text: Some have spent so much time upon a Context, that by that time they came to their Text the hour was almost gone . . . 3rdly Make an exact Division of your Text . . . 4thly Explain any difficult terms, but spend not time needlessly in Explanation, if things are easily understood without it. 5thly Raise as many doctrines as your Text will allow, and make what good use you can of every one of them, but insist most on the chief Scope of the place. 6thly Your *Doctrine* being laid down, prove it from the Word of God by 2 or 3 Scriptures; because *in the mouth of two of three Witnesses every truth is established*. After you have prov'd it, then lay down the *Reasons* and the Arguments of the Point why and wherefore it is so . . . And then, what *Use* you make, let it be always natural from the Doctrine, and draw as many Inferences from it as it will bear; for they are generally very divine things. Mark one thing, that all Doctrines will not afford the same Uses. There is, (1.) The Use of information. (2.) Caution. (3.) Trial and Examination. (4.) Refutation. (5.) Instruction. (6.) Reprehension. (7.) Exhortation, with its motives and directions. (8.) Admiration. (9.) Consolation. Now you must consider which of all these, or any other Uses, will be most naturally handled from your Doctrine.[63]

While there is a concern to make clear the text, the primary function of this method is to develop a doctrinal presentation in which other texts will be marshalled to support what is argued and pastoral application made. This is a methodology which roots the sermon in the text and urges the preacher to move beyond the text to its spiritual meaning, or doctrine, and its relevance for the hearers. Here is rationality in the form of schematization, logic and application in the reading and explaining of Scripture. While this detailed schema has not been widely used beyond the eighteenth century, the division of a discourse into heads has survived and remains a feature of preaching in Baptist and other, especially Evangelical, circles, where the expectation is that sermons will teach Christian belief and offer instruction about Christian living.[64]

Rationality is not to be restricted to the preacher. The proto-General Baptist congregation in Amsterdam included in its worship an opportunity for the hearers to discuss the sermon, particularly in relation to its handling of Scripture. While this activity was to disappear from Sunday worship,[65] probably through growing numbers and a process of formalization, there is a link between the *intention* of this activity and the critical listening which William Brock encouraged his Norfolk congregation to bring to every sermon:

> You are to take heed *how* you hear; not thoughtlessly, not indolently, not superstitiously receiving whatever may be advanced, but receiving it with observation and care. And you are to take heed *what* you hear, distinguishing between things that differ, and applying then as your emergencies may require . . . With much urgency we ask you to do this.[66]

Here is an active role for the congregation, which is exhorted to sift what it hears, testing and questioning the words offered as 'the Word of the Lord'. The preacher encourages his hearers to use their minds and, in so doing, he removes any automatic authority that the preacher might have. The sermon must be sensible, scriptural and persuasive. This sifting of what is heard is not new with Brock. Indeed, the emphasis on the Church as a fellowship of believers encourages responsible listening and assessment, and this attitude can be seen in the testing of new preachers and potential ministers.[67]

The commitment to rational preaching is also demonstrated in the concern for the education and training of ministers and preachers. Collins cautioned his hearers against calling 'an ignorant, unlearned, inexperienced person', as 'that unction and divine anointing which may make a person a true believer, may not be sufficient to make him a minister'.[68]

In the seventeenth and eighteenth centuries there was debate as to whether a preacher should prepare a particular sermon, or whether preaching should be wholly extemporaneous. The messengers of the Western churches, meeting in Taunton in July 1654, did not wish to rule out the possibility of 'the immediate ministry of the Spirit of Christ', but affirmed that proper preparation should be the norm:

> We judge that he may lawfully, and it is his duty, to wait on the Lord in the reading and meditating on the scriptures, as opportunity and occasion gives him liberty, and whatsoever the Lord is pleased to give in both for matter and manner, he may communicate to others as the Spirit gives him utterance, II Tim. 2.15, 3.17, Eccles. 12.9f. yet notwithstanding by this we deny not the immediate ministry of the Spirit of Christ in the churches.[69]

Collins interpreted 2 Timothy 2. 15 as a direct command that the preacher should study so that the expounding of the Word would be worthy. He spoke of study as an ordinance and proposed a number of 'doctrines':

> That study is an ordinance of God.
>   That the Scriptures of Truth are the foundation of a Minister's study.
>   Men's great design and end in study should not be to get men's hums and applause by quaint and eloquent speech, but above all to please God and win souls.
>   Those that study so as to approve themselves to God their Master, and rightly divide the Word of God, will be delivered from all shame, and rather gain themselves honour and boldness.
>   All persons who will undertake to preach without study are not likely to approve themselves to God their Master, nor rightly divide the Word of Truth, but rather expose themselves and the cause of God in their hands to shame and contempt.[70]

This is not the place to narrate the story of dissenting academics, though the very concern for an *educated* ministry implies a recognition of the part played by rationality in the exercise of ministry in general and preaching in particular.[71]

We have seen how there has been a recurring concern that doctrinal preaching should build up the hearers and lead them to the saving gospel and the grace of God. Preaching should be of use to the congregation – not a demonstration of the preacher's erudition or an examination of esoteric matters. Both a concern for pastoral usefulness and a concern that doctrinal preaching should lead people to God suggest a conviction that theological truth is more than simply intellectual, and that all the study, schematization and rationality are intended to serve the soterio-logical and pastoral priorities of the gospel. Spurgeon argued:

> True preaching is an acceptable adoration of God by the manifestation of his gracious attributes: the testimony to his gospel, which pre-eminently glorifies him, and the obedient hearing of revealed truth, are an acceptable form of worship to the Most High, and perhaps one of the most spiritual in which the human mind can be engaged.[72]

Understanding should invite and nurture faith, and doctrinal preaching should present the person and work of God in such a way as to elicit awe and thanksgiving, repentance and faith. The rational aspects of preaching should lead to a comprehension of grace and a stirring of the heart in response to God, a spirituality which includes both head and heart. Reason is not an end in itself. Nor is truth, except in so far as it is to be found in God, and must be approached by persons who have been reconciled and redeemed and who have learned the reasoning and language of the heart. So Caleb and Hugh Evans, in their manifesto appealing for donations for the newly formed Bristol Education Society in 1770, qualified their argument for an educated ministry by speaking of 'the usefulness and importance of learning in *subordination* to what is more essentially requisite to the ministerial character'.[73] And in the sermon occasioned by his father's death, Caleb Evans spoke of his father's aims as a tutor, 'as not merely to form substantial scholars but as far as in him lay he was desirous of being made an instrument in God's hand of forming them, able, evangelical, lively, zealous ministers of the Gospel'.[74] Such a holistic vision encourages us to explore the impact of the second value, namely, preaching in Baptist worship as expressive of, and influenced by, a concern for devotion and the affective dimensions of Christian experience.

Devotion and Preaching

The nature of an address is fundamentally affected by the liturgical con-text in which it is delivered, and because a sermon is the kind of address which expects a response, vehicles of congregational response are usually provided.[75] The part of the service which follows the sermon may well illuminate the intentions of the preacher, particularly if the preacher has been the person responsible for planning the rest of the service. The selection of a particular hymn as a vehicle of congregational response, or the themes of a prayer, are likely to tell us something about where the preacher hoped the sermon would lead the congregation: to repentance, for example, or faith, confession or commitment.

Again, what comes immediately *before* the sermon can also tell us something about what kind of event preaching is believed to be. If the reading comes immediately before the sermon, and is even read by the preacher, then the implication is that the sermon is expected to have a relationship to that reading, whether or not this is borne out in what follows. Similarly, the offering of prayer immediately prior to the sermon suggests that the preaching is viewed from a devotional perspective. It is indicative of a belief that the preacher needs divine assistance and the hope that the words uttered will somehow be God's Word to the members of the congregation, and that their reception of what is said will be inspired by the operation of the same Spirit who has inspired the preacher. In 1659, the messengers of the Western churches, gathered in Wells, claimed that prayer before the sermon is a duty, and even went so far as to call it an 'ordinance'.[76]

It will be helpful to examine the devotional dimensions of preaching from the two distinct perspectives of preacher and congregation.

The Devotion of the Preacher

When prayer is offered before the sermon, it is only the public expression of all the prayer which may have preceded the worship event and accompanied the preparation of the service. Spurgeon devoted a lecture to the personal prayer life of the preacher[77] and in his lecture on the choice of a text, he asserts that this activity is one which should be inspired by the Spirit.[78] He was emphatic that prayer is an essential ingredient in the preparation for preaching:

> Praying is the best studying . . . Pray over the Scripture; it is as the treading of grapes in the wine-vat, the threshing of corn on the barn floor, the melting of gold from the ore. Prayer is twice blest; it blesseth the pleading preacher, and the people to whom he ministers. When your text comes in answer to prayer, it will be all the dearer to you; it will come with a divine savour and unction altogether unknown to the formal orator to whom one theme is as another.[79]

Here is pragmatic, pastoral experience as well as spiritual guidance. Spurgeon recognized that the commitment of the preacher was a vital factor in the efficacy, or at least the persuasiveness, of the preaching.

Preparatory prayer articulates a preacher's sense of dependence upon God. It may also express the belief that the welfare of the congregation is primarily met through the gracious activity of God rather than through the efforts of the preacher.

The character of the preacher and dependence upon God are not restricted to the immediate task of preparing a particular sermon, but have a wider relevance to the spirituality of being a pastor or a preacher.[80] The exercising of spiritual gifts is an important part of this, but, to use Pauline imagery, there is a need for the fruit of the Spirit as well as the gifts (Galatians 5.22–3 and 1 Corinthians 12.1–11 *inter alia*). Hercules Collins had urged his London audience 'that all the churches may take a great care to choose pastors after God's own heart' and explained the devotional dimensions of true preaching:

> Let us preach and prophesy according to the proportion of faith and know-ledge, speak experimentally and feelingly; that which comes from the heart is generally carried to the heart, then it is we preach to edification . . . Get your hearts sincerely affected with those things you persuade others to, that your hearers may see that you are in good earnest, and that you deliver nothing to the people but what you are willing to practise yourselves, and venture your salvation upon.[81]

Worship should be of the heart, sincere and affective. Collins applies this to preaching in such a way that the spiritual reality of the event cannot be separated from the spiritual realities of the preacher's heart. Here again is a spirituality which claims that the integrity of external behaviour is dependent on inner motivation, in which the actors are participating internally as well as externally. The motivation, intentions and devo-tional status of the speaker cannot be separated from the words spoken.

Yet the preacher should also be a person of the gospel, redeemed by the gospel, with a personal story of grace to recount, with evidence of the sanctifying work of the Spirit in their lives. They are to speak 'experi-mentally', with personal experience of God and the living truth of the Scriptures which are being expounded. The preaching is to be from heart to heart, because this is the arena of God's grace and the point of great-est communion with, and offering to, God. When asked what the qualifications were for one who was to preach to either believers or unbe-lievers, the Northern messengers, as well as stipulating sound doctrine and competence in leading worship, replied, 'He must be endued with a competent measure of converting grace effectually wrought in his own soul.'[82]

This concern that the preacher should have a living, personal faith is a central feature of the tradition. Baptist ecclesiology defines the Church as 'the fellowship of believers', and the reserving of baptism for believers has, among other things, functioned as a sign of this conviction. The concern for the sincerity, integrity and vital faith of the preacher is of a piece with this ecclesiology and the spirituality which undergirds it. In a believer church, the preacher will, of necessity, be a believer. There is no activity in worship which has a spiritual reality independent of the devotional integrity of those who are participating. Baptists, and other Evangelicals, have resisted any doctrine of *ex opere operato*, arguing that the faith of the minister *is* a relevant condition for the due order of worship.

Preaching is an activity ordained by God in which sinners may come to faith and in which believers can be built up. There is an efficacy in preaching which can be seen as parallel in some way to the sacramental theology of other traditions. Thus John Fawcett proclaimed, 'The gospel is to be preached for the obedience of faith; it is the gospel of repentance, and the power of God unto salvation; faith cometh by the hearing of it, and they are helped much by it who have believed through grace.'[83] But what of the other actors in the event of preaching? The members of the congregation also play their own part and devotional concerns figure for those who hear the word, as well as for those who announce it.

Devotion and the Congregation

It is significant that some Baptist writers have spoken of the ordinance of preaching as a means of grace whereby God graciously encounters men and women. Robert Hall, in his 1814 circular letter, reminded his readers that 'the ministry of the gospel is the appointed instrument of forming the spirits of men to faith and obedience'.[84] The previous year, the Northamptonshire circular letter had been *On Reading the Word of God*,[85] but Hall suggests that it is the preaching, more than the reading, which is likely to be efficacious:

the living voice of a preacher is admirably adapted to awaken attention, and to excite an interest, as well as apply the general truths of revelation to the various cases of Christian experience and the regulation of human conduct. When an important subject is presented to an audience, with an ample illustration of its several parts, its practical improvement enforced, and its relation to the conscience and the hearts insisted upon with seriousness, copiousness, and fervour, it is adapted in the nature of things, to produce a more deep and lasting impression than can usually be expected from reading.[86]

The members of the congregation also have a responsibility to play their part so that communication might be effectively undertaken. William Brock exhorts congregations to an 'attentiveness of disposition'. 'We want you, beloved, to give all diligence to what is said in the sanctuary, whether in preaching, praise or prayer.'[87] He invites his readers not only to listen critically, but also to meditate upon what they hear so that they might apply the Word to their own situation.[88] This edification of the believer is more likely if that believer has prepared for worship, as, according to Hall, 'no true Christian will neglect to preface his attendance on social worship with secret prayer'.

> Pastors and people would both derive eminent advantages from such a practice; they in their capacity of exhibiting, you in your preparation for receiving the mysteries of the gospel.[89]

He implores his readers not only to listen to their preferred forms of preaching, but to be impartial in their hearing of the Word, so that they might be open to the full counsels of God.[90]

This readiness to be open to whatever is preached is a form of integrity in which the hearer can display sincerity by being receptive without the constraint of ulterior concerns. This sincerity of purpose will also express itself in not assuming that distasteful challenges might only apply to their neighbours:

> Hear not for others, but for yourselves. What should we think of a person who, after accepting an invitation to a feast, and taking his place at the table, instead of partaking of the repast, amused himself with speculating on the nature of the provisions, or the manner in which they are prepared, and their adaptation to the temperament of the several guests, without tasting a single article?[91]

The hearers of the Word are also worshippers, and their reception of the Word is in a spirit of devotion, humility and expectation. There should be an attention and openness to the Word, for even critical listening is a devotional activity, as hearers listen for God's Word to them personally – promises of grace to give them hope, divine commands to challenge their behaviour, and divine instructions to direct their feet. As the whole person is called to respond to the preaching of the Word, then we must again speak of 'the worship of the heart'. Words need to be more than understood – they need to be assimilated in meditation and prayer. This devotion is not simply an engaging of the emotions, but a total orientation towards God. Devotion includes the readiness to be challenged: 'Hear the word of God less in the spirit of judges than of those who shall be judged by it.'[92] Both the preaching and hearing of the Word are places of encounter between God and his people.

The exposition of Scripture through the exercise of reason and the development of didactic preaching, together with the devotional engagement of both preacher and congregation in the event of preaching, are the main ways in which the worship values influence preaching in Baptist worship. However, the ecclesial and eschatological dimensions are also in evidence.

Preaching in the Church

The distinction between the 'sermon' and 'preaching' distinguishes between text and performance and emphasizes the nature of preaching as event. Preaching cannot take place without a congregation. This is illustrated in the architecture of Baptist chapels and meeting houses, which have usually been designed as auditory spaces in which the pulpit is central, both for practical, acoustic reasons and as a symbol of the centrality of the Word and its proclamation. Towards the end of the nineteenth century a few Baptist chapels began to resemble Anglican churches, with apses, central communion tables and side pulpits. However, these were a minority, probably reflecting the aspirations of upwardly mobile benefactors.[93] Galleries have often been built in such a way that the only location in the building visible from every seat is the pulpit – a physical sign not only of performance on the part of the preacher but of hoped-for attentiveness on the part of the congregation.

Despite the apparently passive nature of the congregation during preaching,[94] James White's distinction between 'passive' and 'active' participation may not be so helpful here. While the participation is silent, the members of the congregation are invited by Brock to spend their entire time in the church sanctuary 'baptized in the purest spirit of dependence upon the grace of God'.[95] As we have seen, he was also concerned that the congregation engage with the sermon by sifting what was said by the preacher, so as to appropriate the Word of God to their Christian living.

Although Baptist ecclesiology views the Church through the lens of the local congregation as a covenant community, it could be argued that this ecclesial value is less evident in the act of preaching where the congregation appears as a crowd rather than as a covenant community. Nonetheless, the pastoral relationships between preacher and congregation may well be in evidence in the selection of Scripture readings which are relevant to the needs of the particular congregation, as well as in the content of the sermon, its illustrations and its exhortations.[96]

While evangelistic preaching will present the gospel to the unconverted members of a congregation, the preaching which is directed at church members will probably be formational in character, edifying people through teaching and exhortation. Although most of this preaching will be directed at the needs of individual Christians, helping them in discipleship and growth in grace, some preaching will be directed to the church as a whole and as such will serve as an instrument of pastoral leadership. The congregation is the *ekklesia*, disciples called out and gathered by Jesus Christ, and as it assembles in worship, it is addressed by the incarnate Word through the human utterances of the preacher.

Kingdom Preaching

Preaching is eschatological. It has a future orientation founded on the belief that it will be effective – that it will make a difference and that the lives of the hearers will bear testimony to change. Preaching is an instrumental action designed to effect a change of heart and mind, to direct actions and to further the will and rule of God through the free response of the hearers. While all preaching should be seen from this eschatological perspective, there are two particular homiletical aspects which most clearly illustrate this concern for the kingdom.

First, there is the *ethical* dimension of preaching which seeks to encourage an improvement in the lifestyles and actions of the disciples of Jesus. We have seen how petitionary prayer looks beyond worship to a resolution within the purposes of God: the same can be said for worship viewed through preaching. Exhortation to Christian living, prophetic challenges to injustice, encouraging people to expect more of God – all these point beyond worship itself, and usually imply a required response of practical action. Just as the Orthodox speak of 'the liturgy after the liturgy',[97] so preaching challenges worshippers to see worship as a focus of that living before God which is the offering up of the whole of life. In 1814, Northamptonshire Baptists were encouraged to

> Go to the house of God with a serious expectation and desire of meeting with something suited to your particular state, something that shall lay the axe to the root of your corruptions, mortify your besetting sins, and confirm the graces in which you are most deficient.[98]

The eschatological note of judgement, as an encouragement to repentance and growth, is even more explicit a little later when Hall's readers were reminded, 'every one of us must give account of himself to God, and every man must bear his own burden. *Is not my word as a fire, saith the Lord, and as a hammer that breaketh the rock in pieces?*' Here, through preaching, the congregation is led to the point where they can offer in prayer eschatological petitions and cry to God for help in the amending of their lives and the seeking of his Kingdom.

Second, the *evangelistic* function of preaching seeks to proclaim the gospel of Jesus Christ and invite those who have not yet done so to repent and believe the gospel. We have noted that this kerygmatic tradition runs from the seventeenth century and, even though High Calvinists saw it as inappropriate, it has been exemplified in such preachers as Benjamin Keach, the Giffords, Spurgeon and many others. In the nineteenth century, the development of the evening service provided an opportunity for more varied congregations to hear a gospel challenge and, later, the revival hymns of Ira Sankey, for example, were often used for such occasions.[99] While the invitation to respond to the gospel has always been a part of this evangelistic preaching, the influence of Finney, which has been mediated through such American preachers as Dwight Moody and Billy Graham, has influenced much Baptist worship by encouraging the opportunity for a personal response on the part of the hearers during the service. The invitation for someone to enquire further or to make a commitment of faith by walking to the front of the church during the service may be widely seen in Evangelical churches. The influence of Charismatic renewal may have altered the way in which such responses might be expressed, but the liturgical concern to provide such opportunities remains, underlining the missionary expectation of preaching on such occasions.[100]

Preaching is an event which requires both a preacher and a congregation but in which the outward activity is primarily undertaken by the preacher. We now turn to the third component of Free Church worship, namely congregational singing, in which the congregation becomes the primary agent in worship.

8

With Heart and Voice

The Spirituality of Congregational Song

Blest be the tie that binds
    Our hearts in Christian love;
The fellowship of kindred minds
    Is like to that above.

Before the Father's throne
    We pour our ardent prayers;
Our fears, our hopes, our aims are one,
    Our comforts and our cares.

We share our mutual woes,
    Our mutual burdens bear,
And often for each other flows
    The sympathizing tear.

When for awhile we part,
    This thought will soothe our pain,
That we shall still be joined in heart,
    And hope to meet again.

This glorious hope revives
    Our courage by the way,
While each in expectation lives,
    And long to see the day.

From sorrow, toil and pain,
    And sin we shall be free;
And perfect love and friendship reign
    Through all eternity.

John Fawcett, 1740–1817[1]

Just as we have approached worship through a study of prayer an preaching, so now we shall explore worship through the practice and spiritual-

ity of the congregational hymn. Both popular and academic studies of hymnody abound.[2] The biographical circumstances of composition,[3] the literary character of the verse,[4] the devotional nature of the texts,[5] the marriage of words and tunes,[6] the history of editorial alterations[7] and the editorial rationale of hymnbooks[8] have all been the subject of scrutiny and publication. By contrast, this chapter examines the *liturgical practice* of congregational singing in Baptist worship, and its spirituality.[9]

We have seen that there is a difference between the written text of a sermon and the event of preaching. A similar distinction can be made between hymn texts and the event of congregational singing. When hymn texts are studied in isolation they will primarily provide information about the authorial intentions of the various hymn writers, or the response of the reader, rather than the *use* of those texts by congregations and their leaders. Congregational singing is a communal event and its shared nature is of particular significance in any discussion of the liturgical function of hymnody.[10] It is this practice and its implied spirituality which will be explored here.

In the historical review, we saw that the proportion of each service spent in congregational singing has increased steadily since the seventeenth century. This singing provides an opportunity for a group of people to utter the same words at the same time. While those words will have a variety of possible meanings, or at least a variety of nuances, and while verbal imagery and musical expression will have their own potency, the fundamental event is that of people joining together with the same words at the same time. In the act of singing together, a group of people becomes united in thought and utterance. Other traditions use congregational responses, the reciting of creeds and the joint reading of prayers, but these mechanisms of congregational activity have not been widely used within the Free Churches or among Baptists. Although the oft-quoted words of Bernard L. Manning speak of the way in which hymns connect congregations to the faith of the past or to the wider Church, his words also highlight the way in which hymns function in a Free Church service in a way which is somewhat equivalent to the role of liturgical responses in other traditions:

> Hymns are for us Dissenters what the liturgy is for the Anglican. They are the framework, the setting, the conventional, the traditional part of divine service as we use it. They are, to adopt the language of the liturgiologists, the Dissenting Use.[11]

Much has changed since those words were written, but the main point remains: hymns have provided a liturgical form in Free Church worship which enables congregations to articulate corporate acts of praise, corporate prayer and corporate confessions of faith. Indeed, Cecil Northcott argues that the development of liturgical rites in the early Church provided limited scope for the use of hymns in public worship, with the congregation's participation taking other forms.[12] Eventually, in the post-Reformation rediscovery of hymn singing, Baptists and Independents were to be at the forefront of the British strand of this hymn renaissance.

  Despite the existence of Baptist hymn writers, there has never been a corpus of 'Baptist hymns' which has expressed or nourished an identity for the denomination in the way that the Wesleys' hymns have done for Methodists.[13] Even John Rippon's *Selection*, which was so widely used in Britain and North America at the end of the eighteenth century and the early decades of the nineteenth, mainly comprised hymns from non-Baptist sources. Baptist hymn writers were included in considerable number, but they still represent a minority when placed alongside the hymns harvested from existing hymnbooks from across the churches. As a supplement to the *Psalms and Hymns* of Isaac Watts, not a Baptist himself though influential among them, the basis of Rippon's selection of hymns was clearly stated in his preface:

> It has given me no small pleasure, to unite, as far as I could, different Denominations of Ministers, and Christians on Earth, in the same noble Work, which shall for ever employ them above. It has not been my Enquiry, *whose* Hymns shall I choose, but *what*, Hymns; and hence it will be seen, that Churchmen and Dissenters, Watts and Tate, Wesley and Toplady, England and America sing Side by Side, and very often join in the same Triumph, using the same Words.[14]

Later hymnbooks have contained an even wider ecumenical representation, although arguably the actual mix of hymns in a particular hymnbook will represent some reflection of denominational identity, if only through the intentions of the editors. Using a common hymnbook has inevitably provided a cohesive influence for Baptists and, for example, the publication of *The Baptist Church Hymnal* in 1900 was designed to aid and express the integration of Particular and General Baptists.[15] By way of contrast, the 1996 worship survey indicated that barely a quarter of the Baptist Union's churches were using *Baptist Praise and Worship* and that sales of the new denominational hymnbook in Baptist churches were eclipsed by the sales of *Mission Praise* and *Songs of Fellowship*.[16] This might suggest a loosening of denominational cohesion, though cause and effect are far from clear in the interaction of denominational

unity and hymnbook loyalty. These questions of identity and the changing nature of denominational life, however, must remain secondary for
us here as we explore the nature of Christian worship.

The Practice of Hymnody in Baptist Worship

The two main strands of Baptist witness held different views about congregational singing, and their stories need to be told separately.

The General Baptists

General Baptists were radical in their opposition to what they perceived
to be 'forms of worship' and this included the practice of corporate
singing. Information is scarce, but it seems that the only singing which
was permitted in worship was of a solo nature. This was probably
sung spontaneously, not metricated but based on remembered biblical
phrases, as Edward Drapes seemed to suggest in 1649: 'To singe Psalmes
in the Gospel is a special gift given to some particular member in the
church, whereby he doth blesse, praise, or magnifie the Lord through
the mighty operation of the spirit.' Ephesians 5.18–19 was given as the
biblical basis for such singing which is, 'To be performed I say, by one
alone, at one time to the edification one of another and therefore it is an
ordinance flowing from a cheerfulle heart . . . '[17] Thomas Grantham set
forth in 1678 a number of reasons against 'musical singing with a multitude of voices in rhyme and metre',[18] and the 1689 General Assembly
denounced congregational singing as 'carnal formalities'.[19] A denomination in which many would move away from doctrinal orthodoxy within
a few years, it was fiercely conservative in its rejection of innovations in
worship. However, by 1733 the practice of congregational singing was
beginning to gain ground and the Assembly of that year did not consider
it sufficiently fundamental to be the cause of breaking fellowship.[20]

The negative attitude towards congregational singing had a number of
sources. In the Amsterdam congregation of Smyth and Helwys, even the
Bible was put aside once the worship service began. When Scripture was
later expounded, it could only be quoted by memory, so we can assume
that any solo singing was likely to be a spontaneous rendering of remembered passages from the Psalms set to tunes made up at the time because
Smyth had declared, 'Wee hould, that seeing singing a psalme is a part of
spirituall worship therefore it is vnlawful to have the booke before the

eye in time of singinge a psalme.'[21] Later, Grantham was to argue that what churches should sing 'must be the Word of God, or that which is according to it . . . seated in the *soul* of the Christians, and not as it may be read unto them out of a Book only, and then repeated by them'.[22] He also cautioned that singing other men's words, in which he included metricated psalms, 'opens a gap for forms of prayer'.[23] Such negative attitudes were still in evidence in the middle of the eighteenth century and were a contributory factor in the new Evangelical General Baptists, who were greatly influenced by the fervour and hymn singing of the Methodist movement, breaking away from the old General Baptists to form their New Connexion of General Baptists in 1770. A collection of hymns was soon gathered by them, supplemented by Samuel Deacon's *Barton Hymns* in 1785[24] and later replaced by a series of hymnbooks including collections by John Deacon of Leicester and Dan Taylor, the leader of the New Connexion.[25] Between 1785 and 1787, an exchange of pamphlets over hymn singing occurred between Gilbert Boyce of the old General Baptists and Dan Taylor, whom he had previously baptized. However, W. R. Stevenson, editor of the late nineteenth-century *Baptist Hymnal*, claimed that, 'By the close of the Eighteenth Century . . . singing, as part of public worship, had become universal among the General Baptists.'[26]

The Particular Baptists

The worship of the Particular Baptists probably resembled the worship of that wider group of Calvinistic Dissenters from which they had separated over baptism, but to which they continued to belong and with which they continued to share fellowship. While congregational singing was not universal among this group of Baptists, what singing did originally take place consisted of metricated psalms, as did psalm singing at this time within the Church of England. The Baptist association meeting at Bridgwater in February 1655 declared, 'that singing of psalms is an ordinance of Christ, to be performed in the Church of Christ by the saints' and, 'singing is, when the soul being possest with the apprehension of the goodness and mercy of God, doth make a joyful noise to his praise'.[27]

There is more information available for the period after 1660 when, despite the dangers of persecution, congregational psalm singing clearly took place, though not in every congregation. The records of the Broadmead church in Bristol contain a number of references to congregational psalm singing, and the record for 6 June 1675 comments, 'They sing without any one to read ye Psalme to them', as most of the congregation brought their psalm books and did not require lining out.[28] When a joint meeting was proposed with the Pithay church in 1675, some of the members of that church 'were ready to sing Psalms with others beside the church'. However, a minority 'of them could not sing in Metre as [the Psalms] were Translated' and asked permission to keep their hats on or to retire while singing was in progress. The churches resolved that those who wished to act in this way should not participate in joint services as their uncooperative behaviour might be divisive.[29]

It was, however, in a congregation which had not corporately sung psalms that the practice of *hymn* singing began, though its progress was slow.[30] Benjamin Keach, a former General Baptist, became pastor of a Particular Baptist Congregation in Southwark, which grew and eventually built a meeting house at Horsleydown. He believed that congregational singing was an ordinance of Christ and, sometime between 1673 and 1675, persuaded the church to permit the singing of a hymn at the close of the Lord's Supper. Six years later the church agreed to hymn singing on 'public Thanksgiving days', and by about 1690 they agreed to sing the praises of God every Lord's day. These were not psalms, but hymns in manuscript form, mostly composed by Keach himself.

It is true that other congregations had regularly sung psalms,[31] and that some of the Fifth Monarchists had occasionally introduced their own hymns into worship during the Commonwealth.[32] In addition, others had obviously written hymns before Keach,[33] but the Horsleydown congregation was the first to use hymns as a regular feature of weekly worship.[34] A small minority of the congregation objected and one of their number, Isaac Marlow, printed *A brief Discourse concerning Singing*.[35] Keach replied with the publication of *The Breach repaired in God's Worship*[36] and a publication war ensued.[37] The First General Assembly of Particular Baptists debated the matter in 1689, but the debate was inconclusive. The pamphlet controversy had become so heated that the 1692 Assembly appointed a committee to examine the pamphlets. It ruled that the most acrimonious ones should be withdrawn, and appealed for peace. While the substantive issue was not formally decided, a measure of peace was restored and the eventual upshot was an increase in the number of singing congregations.[38] Keach noted in 1700 that many churches had adopted singing, and in the next half-century the practice gained ground, becoming 'a principal mechanism whereby dissenting worship was to secure that congregational participation in worship which was to characterize its quality'.[39]

At the beginning of the eighteenth century Isaac Watts wrote and published a body of hymns and Scripture paraphrases which commended themselves to many churches, including those of the Particular Baptists.[40] Dissatisfaction with the old paraphrases led Watts to publish *Hymns and Spiritual Songs* in 1707, and in 1719 he published *The Psalms of David imitated in the language of the New Testament and applied to the Christian state and worship*. The title of this later work demonstrates that Watts was concerned with far more than improving the quality of the poetry sung in worship. He was a pastor and a theologian, anxious that the congregation should not be invited to sing inappropriate words. He believed that Christian devotion is not helped by singing all the words of all the psalms, as many contain words which are 'extreamly Jewish and cloudy, that darkens our Sight of God the Saviour: Thus by keeping too close to *David* in the House of God, the vail of *Moses* is thrown over our Hearts'.[41] While he saw the psalms as a devotional treasure which reflect and express many of the moods of the believer, he found the invectives and curses, which some of them contain, intrusive and unacceptable for worship. These he either omitted or spiritualized as warfare against sin. The result was a corpus of material which blended paraphrased psalms and Scripture passages with devotional hymns acceptable to many of a Calvinistic or Evangelical persuasion.[42] After his death in 1748, both works were commonly bound in one volume and called *Dr Watts's Psalms and Hymns*. This remained the main hymnbook for most Particular Baptists and Independents well into the nineteenth century.[43]

In 1769 John Ash and Caleb Evans produced their innovative *Collection of Hymns adapted for Public Worship* known as the 'Bristol Hymnbook', which included a significant number of Watts's hymns, together with the original hymns of others such as Anne Steele and Benjamin Beddome.[44] This achieved some success, though their inclusion of hymns by Watts meant that some congregation declined to buy hymns they already had in *Dr Watts's Hymns and Psalms*! It was John Rippon who saw the pastoral and marketing opportunity for publishing a supplement to Watts in 1787 and *Rippon's Selection* joined Watts as the staple diet for most Particular Baptist churches until the middle of the next century.[45] It contained a wide range of hymns from authors of various Protestant denominations, organized under various theological headings, thus aiding the worship of the churches by providing a means of hymn selection. Among the Baptist authors represented were Anne Steele, Samuel Stennett, Daniel Turner, Benjamin Beddome and John Fawcett. In the following four years, leading up to the publication of an accompanying tune book, over 20,000 copies of the *Selection* were to be sold. By 1800 it had reached its tenth edition which was enlarged by a further sixty hymns, particularly with additions adapted 'to Village Worship, to Monthly Prayer Meetings for the spread of the Gospel, to Missionary Meetings, and to the chapter of hymns before and after the Sermon'.[46]

Another book which laid claim to denominational loyalty was John Haddon senior's *A New Selection of Hymns* (1828), which offered its profits for helping widows and orphans of Baptist ministers and missionaries. It also included some of the new hymnody, notably early hymns by James Montgomery and Bishop Heber. This in turn was succeeded by other semi-official books, until, as Payne claims, the 1883 edition of *Psalms and Hymns* 'rapidly replaced both Rippon's *Selection* and *The New Selection,* as well as a number of other lesser known books'.[47]

The Institution of the Hymnbook

Ian Bradley places the modern hymnbook, with its pairing of hymns and tunes, alongside the penny post and the railway system as a great achievement of the Victorian 'quest for order, efficiency and ease of communication':

> From modest origins as a tool of reforming clergy wishing to improve congregational worship, the hymnbook became one of the central institutions of Victorian religion, defining the identity of different denominations and church parties and providing a handbook for doctrine and devotion which, if sales provide any indication, had more influence and impact than any other category of publication.[48]

The publication in 1900 of the *Baptist Church Hymnary* attempted to provide one denominational hymnbook for the Baptist Union of Great Britain and Ireland, a body which had in 1891 reached the culmination of a unity process between Particular Baptists and the General Baptists of the New Connexion. This unifying intent was pursued in subsequent books, through to *Baptist Praise and Worship* in 1991.[49] It is not clear how thorough the monopoly of the denominational books was, though anecdotal evidence suggests it was considerable. However, in the early part of the twentieth century, Sankey's *Sacred Songs and Solos* enjoyed considerable popularity in some Evangelical circles, though sometimes as a supplement. We have already noted that by 1996 a relatively small number of churches were using the latest denominational hymnbook, *Baptist Praise and Worship,* while over three-quarters were using the Evangelical and Charismatic collections *Mission Praise* and *Songs of Fellowship.*[50] A considerable number of churches were using several hymnbooks or projecting hymn texts so that very recently published material might be used.

This present situation, which has moved away from the use of a single denominational hymnbook, prompts us to survey the two centuries in which hymnbooks were so significant and to enquire as to the effect these books had on worship. First, hymnbook collections have provided a catholicity to the worship of a local congregation. In a tradition where there is little or no use of liturgical material representing the wider Church, hymnbooks have provided devotional material both from the past and from authors in other communions. This catholicity is not only achieved through the resources of the wider Church being made available to a local congregation, but also through the local congregation joining in a communion of praise with different Christians in different places and at different times, praising God with the same words.

Second, because catholicity is a dimension of the relationship between the local congregation and the universal Church, even the relations with other churches of the same denomination are a partial embodiment of that catholicity. So the 1900 publication was explicitly an attempt to unite a uniting denomination, not unlike the later work of the Methodists in the 1930s.[51] While Baptist churches continue to express and nurture their interrelatedness in a variety of ways, it must be acknowledged that singing from a common denominational hymnbook is no longer one of them.[52] The editors of *Baptist Praise and Worship* admitted in their preface that they were entering an uncertain and competitive market.[53] Six years after publication, barely a quarter of the Baptist Union's churches were using the new denominational hymnbook and after ten years it had gone out of print. In so far as there is a sense of identity now expressed and engendered through congregational singing by Baptists, it is not to be seen primarily in a denominational identity made possible by a denominational hymnbook. Instead, there is a sense of belonging to a wider, Evangelical community which is expressed and engendered by the songs many Baptists now share with a wider Evangelical constituency.[54]

Third, worship has been enriched by hymnbooks which provide tools for the selection of hymns for a particular service. Alphabetical tables of first lines and thematic contents pages have combined with subject titles above hymns and marginal scripture citations to provide a liturgical apparatus which can aid the leader of worship. Underlying this assistance is an implicit belief that a hymn should be selected on the basis of its content and that its usefulness is in expressing the sentiments anticipated at a particular point in the service.

Finally, hymnbooks have provided a link between public and private devotion. They enable people to sing together and as such are an expression of corporate worship. But some hymns have also been assimilated into personal devotions and have provided a resource for private prayer and meditation, just as John Wesley offered his *Collection of Hymns for the use of the people called Methodists* as a 'body of experimental and practical divinity'.[55] As the hymns prayed in private are the same hymns sung in public worship in the sanctuary, the hymnbook has brought the wider, or catholic, Church to bear on those devotions as well as the nuances of corporate worship. The extent to which the hymnbook has been used for this should not be exaggerated, but it has offered the possibility of taking home the worship of the church.[56]

The Practice of Singing

This private use of the hymnbook also alerts us to a potentially private dimension in the public singing of hymns. The nature of verse, the potency of its imagery and open-ended meanings could be perceived as leading to a collection of individual experiences of singing, with people holding their own books and extracting their own privatized meanings. Here we trespass upon a borderland of semantic distinctions between 'individual' and 'personal'. There will be aspects of the event which are shared, such as the words uttered, the musical sound performed and the liturgical context before and after the hymn. But there will also be aspects which are not shared, such as the personal response of the individual worshipper to that context, their life experience and their encounter with God, as well as their reading of the hymn text. In this borderland, the way in which hymns are sung can affect the balance between these different aspects. For example, it can be argued that the use of projected texts may increase the sense of togetherness in the congregation as all look physically at the same set of words, instead of each inhabiting the semi-private world of the individual book in their hands.

Each method of singing has pastoral losses and gains. Before there were hymnbooks in the hands of the congregation, the words were 'lined out' by a leader. The congregation sang the psalm or hymn with the words of each line given out just in time for it to be sung by the congregation. This did make for a shared event, but musically it was probably dismal, and meaning was often suspended as phrases and ideas which continued from one line to the next were interrupted.

It appears that lining out, commended as an interim accommodation to limited literacy by *The Westminster Directory of Public Worship*,[57] continued to be the majority practice at least until late in the eighteenth century. However, in 1707, Watts had explained that, 'I have seldom permitted a Stop in the middle of a Line, and seldom left the end of a Line without one, to comport a little with the unhappy Mixture of Reading and Singing, which cannot presently be reformed.'[58] He was older, more famous and more assertive in *The Psalms of David* where, in an 'Advertisement to the Readers', his views were made very clear to those who used his hymns: 'It were to be wished that all Congregations and private Families would sing as they do in foreign Protestant Countries, without reading Line by Line.'[59] The advertisement continued to be published with the psalms through the century, even through the preface itself was excluded from the combined edition. It appears that lining out was a British custom and it was to take a long time to change the worship habits of the people. The advent of mass-produced hymnbooks, however, together with rising literacy rates, will undoubtedly have helped the transition to uninterrupted congregational singing, though pleas for the ending of lining out continued. In 1769, the Preface to Ash and Evans's Bristol hymnbook commended an end to lining out and the editors saw the possibility of books in the hands of the congregation as one of the opportunities which the distribution of the book would afford.[60]

Change was obviously slow. In 1787, Rippon quoted Watts in the preface to his *Selection* and also cited a group of London ministers who, at the beginning of the century, had advocated the abandonment of lining out. But Rippon remarked that by the time he was writing, 'I have the Pleasure to remark that this Practice is gaining Ground in some Congregations of the first Note in London, at Bristol, and elsewhere – and it is hoped that it will soon become pretty general where it can be conveniently introduced.'

Another change in the way hymns were sung was in the posture of the congregations. It appears that until the time of Rippon's books most congregations sat for singing and stood for prayer, after the continental custom. However, some directions on musical performance by a Mr T. Walker in Rippon's 1791 tune book inform his readers that, 'the best *position* for singing is undoubtedly that of standing, as it gives the greatest ease and liberty to the voice'.[61] The same writer suggests that tunes should be pitched for the comfort of both trebles and basses, an intimation which may suggest that in some congregations part singing was already happening. The introduction of 'fugal' tunes from the Methodists, together with the example of their hearty singing, must have influenced the Baptists in time.[62] Similarly, the inclusion of hymns with a greater variety of metres ensured a corresponding variety in the tunes used and a greater need for instrumental support.[63]

With increasing congregations, the introduction of organs, though controversial, was understandable, though the vast congregations of the Metropolitan Tabernacle still managed with a precentor when J. S. Curwen described its worship in 1880.[64] Regarding organs, he commented that within living memory people could remember when there were hardly any outside the Church of England, but that since the Methodists, Independents and Baptists had introduced them, 'the adoption of them has been steady and unchecked . . . we can hardly doubt that, in a few years, unaccompanied singing will seldom be heard'. In time, the use of organs imposed a musical conformity on worship which has only been seriously challenged in recent decades with the advent of new song material. The syncopated rhythms of modern worship songs demand new instrumental provision and the amplification of voices, as the contemporary music culture permeates and changes the culture of worship. Yet this is not without precedent, as the music hall style of Sankey's *Sacred Songs and Solos* indicates.[65] What *is* changing is the amount of music in worship and the corresponding effect that this has on the experience and interpretation of worship. Baptists are not alone in this, but are part of what might be called a 'pan-Evangelical' shift in worship culture.

The Place of Hymns in Worship

Ernest Payne's description of Baptist worship, as 'scripture, prayer and sermon, interspersed with hymns',[66] masks a process of change in the number, nature and placing of hymns which has subtly affected the experience of worship.[67] It is probable that the spontaneous singing of the seventeenth-century General Baptists happened during times of prayer and was not programmed into a prearranged order. At the beginning of the eighteenth century, Particular Baptists and Independents began worship with a congregational metricated psalm and the sermon was followed by a psalm or hymn, prior to the closing prayer.[68]

Keach first introduced a hymn at the end of the Lord's Supper, following the biblical precedent that Jesus and the disciples sang a hymn before they left for the Mount of Olives (Matthew 26.30). When, finally, he introduced a weekly hymn into Sunday worship it was again at the end of the service, this time after the sermon. Although this had the additional pastoral advantage of promoting unity by enabling any who might have conscientious objection to congregational singing to leave, its position after the sermon was a logical place to offer the congregation an opportunity to respond to the preaching of the Word. That this was the customary place for congregational singing is reinforced by the hymns which some ministers wrote for the congregation to sing in response to the sermon. The large output of both Benjamin Beddome at Bourton-on-the-water and John Fawcett at Wainsgate had their origins in this practice.[69] Fawcett explained in his Preface to the 1782 collection of his hymns:

> When I have digested my thoughts on some portion of God's word, I have frequently attempted to sum up the leading ideas, in a few plain verses, to be sung after the sermon; so that they might be more impressed on my own heart, and on the hearts of my hearers.[70]

It is interesting to compare these sentiments with the lines of George Herbert, some of whose devotional poetry has later been used as hymns. In relation to the use of verse *vis-à-vis* the sermon he wrote:

> A verse may finde him, who a sermon flies,
> And turn delight into a sacrifice

These lines were quoted by Keach, Bunyan and Baxter as well as others.[71] At the beginning of the twentieth century, there were likely to be at least four hymns for Baptist congregations, usually occurring at the beginning of worship, after the reading and before and after the sermon.[72] By 1996, however, less than half of Baptist congregations were relying solely on this 'interspersed hymn' pattern in worship. Instead, many had begun to incorporate blocks of worship songs alongside the traditional hymns, and for a few, the blocks of song were the staple diet.[73]

When they are interspersed, hymns can interact with the other parts of the service, offering a pattern of word and response in which the congregation expresses the human response to the encounter with God.[74] The shape of a 'Charismatic style' service is, however, quite different, with an extended period of singing followed by preaching and then either open worship, a 'ministry time' or led prayer. The songs of an extended sequence are sometimes a collection of favourites, but often they will have a planned internal dynamic, with prayers, devotional prompts or

Scripture verses flowing from one song to the next. These sequences, often led by musicians, will frequently be introduced with a phrase such as, 'And now for a time of worship', as though prayer and preaching were not worship. If challenged, those making the announcement would probably demur from such an interpretation. Yet the practice does suggest an understanding of worship as *praise,* a restrictive understanding which does not account for many of the actions which take place within the worship event. This is not peculiar to Baptist worship but reflects the wider Charismatic and Evangelical scene.[75]

Critics of contemporary worship songs will often complain that they are 'too subjective', concentrating on the needs, hopes and desires of the worshipper, rather than the 'public truth' of the gospel or the nature of God. Calvinists responded in a similar way to the work of Charles Wesley, and his hymns were slow to appear in significant numbers in Particular Baptist hymnbooks.[76] Similarly, the inclusion of Sankey hymns was slow and in fact many churches seemed to use his book as a supplement to the denominational hymnbooks for events other than Sunday services, when evangelism was a key concern, or for Sunday evenings.[77]

It is often argued that hymns tend towards objectivity and songs towards subjectivity. This is a considerable simplification, as many traditional hymns are intensely subjective. Yet there is some truth in the distinction, partly resulting from the contrast in form. The hymn form may be said to express a linear progression of ideas, from the beginning of the hymn through to the end, and rationality will be a feature of such thematic progression. With such thought progression, it does not usually make sense to repeat the hymn. On the other hand, many songs consist of one or two stanzas which are repeated, often a number of times. Such circularity of utterance is possible because of a single idea or network of images. There is little progression of thought and so the idea can be repeated in such a way as to produce an intensifying of that idea in the mind of the worshipper. This has similarities with the way in which evangelistic choruses in the songs of Sankey and others often expressed words of dedication and response so that the devotional intensity of the singing event might be increased . This comparison is no accident, as the modern worship song developed from what were called, in the earlier decades of the twentieth century, 'choruses', and the word is still applied by many people to worship songs. Those choruses were in fact one-verse songs which had been removed from devotional hymns where they operated as a chorus or refrain.[78]

Yet both objective and subjective hymns can impress moods and ideas onto the worshippers. To proclaim doctrinal truth is to expose oneself to it, and to sing subjective songs is to invite oneself to enter into their devotional intent. Hymnody offers us an intersection between the shared faith of the community and the personal experience of the individual worshippers. That intersection is an important place where issues of faith, encounter, belonging and sincerity meet and leads us to a consideration of the spirituality of congregational singing in Baptist worship.

The Spirituality of Congregational Singing in Baptist Worship

Each of the worship values is evident in congregational singing and we shall again use them as a way of organizing our study. As a concerted activity, in which the members of the congregation actively participate together, the best way to begin this exploration is by examining the ecclesial dimension of hymn singing.

With One Voice

By its very nature, congregational singing is a communal activity in which the congregation participates actively and concertedly in worship. Both these features are significant. The congregation gives open utterance and, through the words and music, *actively* participates in worship in a more obvious way than anywhere else in Baptist worship, where liturgical responses are not often used.[79] We have seen that there has been a gradual increase in the proportionate amount of singing in Baptist services, a trend which has accelerated in recent years.

This participation is also *concerted*, with the members of the congregation singing the same words at the same time. This expresses something of the nature of the congregation as *ekklesia*, the liturgical assembly which is called out and gathered for worship by God. There is a dimension of personal experience during the event of communal singing, a fact we shall explore in the context of devotion, but there is also a *shared* experience which heightens the individual worshipper's awareness of others and encourages a sense of belonging and community. Consequently, congregational singing both *expresses* the nature of the Church as a covenant community, acting in agreed and concerted ways, and *nourishes* that ecclesial identity. This is not to say that communal singing creates community – crowds can sing without being made into community – but the shared event of congregational singing can contribute, along with other factors, to the formation and enhancement of local worshipping communities. For example, John Bell argues that the musical pulse makes it easier for people to sing together than to speak together in a concerted way and that, coupled with songs which are associated with particular communities, this concerted singing helps to create communal identity.[80]

We may therefore speak of the spirituality of congregational singing as 'communal spirituality'. It is a joint activity and a shared experience. Joint singing expresses an interdependence which should characterize relationships within the Body of Christ. Indeed, we might speak of the 'sacramentality' of congregational singing, for it is an embodiment of what the Church is called to be, through being a sign of mutuality and of the sharing of gifts.[81] The shared nature of communal singing, however, goes beyond the realm of shared musical experience, as the congregation gives joint utterance to words which express the faith of the Christian community.

Shared Proclamation

Just as the Nicene Creed begins with '*We* believe in God . . . ', uniting all who utter those words in a fellowship of theocentric accord, so the singing of hymns which articulate the faith of the Christian community, or express the redeemed experience of individual believers, unites those who sing in a shared community of faith.

This proclamation takes a number of forms. For example, it can have a credal structure which confesses some aspect of Christian belief. Yet this singing is more than simply a credal announcement. The shared vulnerability of performance can be formative in creating a community in which gifts are exercised in a context of mutual acceptance and trust.[82] To sing the faith is not to describe it, but to announce it and identify with it.

Hymn singing can be simultaneously both a celebration of the gospel and its proclamation. Indeed, the very celebration is a part of what is proclaimed and shared, for it is an expression of good news. This gospel is the good news of Jesus Christ and its incarnational character usually results in a narrative form. The birth, ministry, death, resurrection and ascension of Jesus Christ will have significant sections in those hymnbooks which are thematically ordered. But, as with credal hymns, singing the story of Jesus is more than imparting narrative information. To sing together this story is to identify with it, both as individual disciples and as a community which seeks to be patterned after Christ. This is corporate devotion, and an identifying with the gospel story can be significant when those who have not made a commitment of faith share in this singing of faith. Having provided various arguments as to why singing should be allowed in congregations which comprise both believers and unbelievers, John Gill declared:

> To add no more, this ordinance has been an ordinance for conversion; I have known it to be so, and so have others besides me; and a good reason this is why it should be continued publickly in our churches, and unbelievers be admitted to an attendance on it.[83]

Proclamation which can lead to such personal transformation may well include the narrative of personal faith as well as the biblical narrative. Testimony can play its part, both in the proclamation of God's gracious activity and in the leading of others to open themselves to such gracious encounter:

> Amazing grace! How sweet the sound
>   That saved a wretch like me!
> I once was lost, but now am found,
>   Was blind, but now I see.[84]

The singing of these words will, for some members of a congregation, engage them in an act of remembering God's gracious dealing with them personally in the past and may well lead to thanksgiving as well as proclamation. For others, the words will function as an invitation to enter into the mystery of grace.

Shared Spirituality

The spirituality of congregational singing is an ecumenical spirituality. Only a small proportion of hymns sung by Baptists have been written by Baptists, so most congregational singing uses material from other parts of the Christian Church. This has been the case from the first use of hymnbooks in the Baptist community, beginning with the widespread reliance on Isaac Watts, the Independent, and Rippon's claim to have consulted over ninety published hymnbooks in the search for supplementary hymn material.[85] Even the controversial C. H. Spurgeon boasted that his *Our Own Hymnbook* did not exclude work on the basis of its origins, but included material chosen for its intrinsic value:

The area of our researches has been as wide as the bounds of existing religious literature. American and British, Protestant and Romish – ancient and modern. Whatever may be thought of our taste we have used it without prejudice; and a good hymn has not been rejected because of the character of its author, or the heresies of the church in whose hymnal it first occurred; so long as the language and the spirit commended the hymn to our heart we included it, and believe that we have enriched our collection thereby.[86]

Often, worshippers will be unaware of the source of the material they are invited to sing and, indeed, the early hymnbooks did not include the authors' names beside the hymn texts. Yet named or unnamed, the material which represents the beliefs and devotion of the wider Church draws the local congregation into the fellowship of that wider Christian community.

Singing in the Kingdom

Through congregational song the Church not only proclaims the Kingdom of God but participates in its reality. This is the bold claim that hymn singing is eschatological! Isaac Watts, in his preface to *Hymns and Spiritual Songs*, claimed, 'While we sing the Praises of our God in his Church, we are employ'd in that part of Worship which of all others is the nearest a-kin to Heaven; and 'tis pity that this of all others should be perform'd the worst upon Earth.'[87] He expands the theme of dissatisfaction at some length, and it was the poor quality of psalm singing in practice which provided the matrix for his great achievement as a hymn writer. Yet his unhappiness with current psalm singing was heightened by his belief that such singing should bring the congregation in tune with heaven. This is not simply a poetic fancy which draws a parallel between the worship of the Church militant with the worship of the Church triumphant. It is also a statement about the communion of saints and the identity of worshippers as creatures who attain fulfilment in their praise of the creator. John Rippon was later to make a similar point, by claiming that the singing of praise was a higher activity than prayer or hearing the word of God:

It is generally allowed, that of all the services in which good men on earth can be engaged, none is more sublime and elevating than singing the praises of God. In *hearing the word* of God, we place ourselves at his feet as the children of ignorance, hoping to be made wise unto salvation: Performing the *work of prayer* we are only Beggars of a superior class; but when the *highest praises* of

God, in our mouths, are inspired with gratitude to him who sitteth upon the throne and to the Lamb, then we rise above the lower forms of Christianity, wear a character more illustrious than the wrestling Jacob, the petitionary Samuel, or even the almost omnipotent Moses, being assimilated to Saints and Angels, all happy and triumphant before the throne of God; made blessed of him and wishing him blessed.[88]

To sing the praise of God is to unite with the heavenly host which is forever praising God. Although Baptist congregations may not often use the words of the *Sursum Corda*,[89] there is a sense in which, when they unite in songs of praise, they are joining 'with angels and archangels and all the company of heaven', singing, 'Holy, holy, holy, Lord God of Hosts'.

Praise also anticipates the eschatological completion in which all creation will acknowledge and praise God, a foretaste of heaven as represented in the Revelation of St John, where God is on the throne and all bow in worship and cry out in praise. Rippon uses the image of festal pilgrims approaching the holy city with singing and in so doing suggests that our singing praises to God is an anticipation of our own home-coming, an anticipation of the completion of earthly pilgrimage.[90] These eschatological expectations offer us another way in which to understand the singing of praise in an age when the Kingdom is both *now* and *not yet*. As one writer on the Psalms has expressed it, 'Praise and thanks are in a sense the *final* word, the direction one is headed in the relationship with God.' And again,

> That is so *theologically*, because in praise more than any other human act God is seen and declared to be God in all fullness and glory. That is so *eschatologically*, because the last word of all is the confession and praise of God by the whole creation. And that is so for *the life of faith*, because praise more than any other act fully expresses utter devotion to God and the loss of self in extravagant exaltation of the transcendent Lord who is the ground of all.[91]

Praise is both a direct address *to* God and a statement *about* God. To praise God as creator and redeemer is to announce God as creator and redeemer, a constitutive action which makes real that which is indeed real, though hidden from the eyes of the world. Following Mowinckel's cultic interpretation of the Psalms, Walter Brueggemann claims that to praise God *as* sovereign is to make a world in which God *is* sovereign.[92] This has political, as well as devotional, consequences which are close to the radical import of the early Christian confession 'Jesus is Lord' in a world in which Caesar was proclaimed as Lord, and to the radical Separatist concern for 'the crown rights of the Redeemer'.

This constitutive role for singing in worship is not limited to praise. We have already seen how a concern for mission should be regarded as a Kingdom concern and we would do well to note the role singing has played in evangelistic endeavours. This Kingdom activity is not limited to special evangelistic events, but includes those dimensions which have formed a feature of much congregational worship among Baptists in the last century and a quarter. This can be illustrated by the way in which each of the denominational hymnbooks since 1900 have included sections which include hymns which can articulate an invitation to personal faith, as well as hymns which can offer vehicles for responding to that invitation.[93] Thus singing offers a role for the Church not only in announcing the Kingdom but in being an instrument for the coming of that Kingdom.

Singing with Heart and Voice

A devotional response to the gospel may take various forms. The worshipper may feel gratitude and offer thanksgiving; they may experience hope in their distress and offer prayers of petition; they may respond in faith and offer their life's commitment; or they may be brought back to the overwhelming love of God and re-dedicate themselves to following Jesus Christ. We have seen how the first congregational singing for Baptists was introduced at the close of the service. While there were pragmatic and pastoral reasons for this, it also provided a vehicle of response to the sermon, a response which could take any or all of these various forms.

Hymns, Spontaneity and the Nature of Inspiration

The early opponents of hymn singing, among both the Particular and the General Baptists, used similar arguments. Some Particular Baptists, like Isaac Marlow and Robert Steed,[94] even objected to singing psalms and, like the General Baptists, saw the paraphrasing and metrication as an unacceptable human device. Others were prepared to sing metricated psalms but were uneasy about hymns which they saw as an unacceptable human construction. John Briggs urges us to recognize the good intentions of the opponents of singing: 'Those concerns were essentially to protect the freedom of the Spirit in giving life to worship, to protect the nature of the believing community, and to ask people to sing only that with which they could honestly identify.'[95] Both sets of opponents saw psalms and hymns as the introduction of forms of worship and it must be admitted that in this they were correct. Bernard Manning's equating hymns with liturgy has a point, and in the nineteenth century, correspondents in *The Freeman* argued that it was permissible to use read prayers in worship because many hymns were pre-composed prayers.[96] The introduction of hymn singing initiated a transitionary process in which free worship was to be redefined.

Steed and Marlow claimed that arguments in favour of pre-composed songs could also apply to prayers and that Keach was in effect introducing 'set and stinted forms' of prayer into what should be free worship.[97] The singing they favoured seems to have been a form of spontaneous song which was seen as a high form of extempore prayer, perhaps like the Welsh *hwl*, which is a sung extension of passionate preaching. If such singing is seen as the high point of prayer, then to replace this with formal singing undertaken by everyone, whatever their spiritual state, may well be seen as replacing inspiration with organization. It is no wonder that Keach and others argued their case from the belief that congregational singing was an ordinance and therefore something which required obedience, rather than an elevated spiritual state. Keach quoted I Corinthians 14.15, where both prayer and singing are 'with the Spirit', and went on to define inspiration in a way which embraces more than the spontaneous: 'There is no Duty nor Ordinance of the Gospel, that can be performed acceptably to God without the Spirit, or the gracious Influences thereof.' He continued by conceding,

> There may be, 'tis plain, an extraordinary Spirit of Prayer at some times, and an extraordinary Influence in Preaching, and an extraordinary Occasion to perform those Duties likewise, and so in Singing: But must not we therefore be found in performance of each of these Duties at any other time? . . . we ought to strive to be filled with the Spirit, that we may both Pray, Preach, and Hear also. But sometimes we have not those fillings of the Spirit in such measure as at other times, yet we must Pray, Preach, Hear, and Sing also; for the Argument or Motive of Singing, (as of our other Duties,) doth not lie in our being so exactly qualified to do it, or in our extraordinary fitness for the Duty, but in the requirement of God, 'tis his Ordinance . . .[98]

The argument here is similar to that of Isaac Watts in his *Guide to Prayer*, where he offers a method for those who feel themselves ill-equipped for extempore prayer and argues that we cannot always have a special grace of inspiration.[99] Perhaps both Keach and Watts are examples of a generation which saw the need for a spirituality which was capable of being taught, handed on and implemented without the need of special inspiration.[100] If the fundamental value for the Separatists was 'spiritual worship', rather than the narrower equating of inspiration with spontaneity, then that spiritual character was now maintained by a concern that worship still be from the heart, though the sustaining grace of God and the operation of the Spirit were still necessary for true worship to take place even when engaging with an ordinance as a duty.[101]

Singing from the Heart

The importance of sincerity has been a significant theme running through Baptist debates about worship from the beginning. The opposition to set prayers included two arguments flowing from a commitment to sincerity. There was a concern that words written by someone in a particular situation would not be relevant to those praying with, or singing, those words in another circumstance. This was regarded as a kind of second-hand devotion, wearing the borrowed clothes of another, a practice which was seen as lacking in integrity and verging on hypocrisy. However, half a century later, John Gill was to argue that the different details of a particular psalm or hymn could suit the different circumstances of the individual members of the congregation. Now the claim to sincerity was maintained by arguing that each part of the psalm expressed the concerns of different members of the congregation.[102]

In addition, there was a scrupulosity which built its critique of singing on an assumption that spontaneity was a necessary indicator of inspiration. This was coupled with a particular understanding of the biblical teaching that goodness flowed from *the heart,* and could not be achieved through outward actions: 'for it is out of the abundance of the heart that the mouth speaks' (Luke 6.45). The concern of the Amsterdam congregation that spiritual worship was hindered by the use of words before the eyes, even those of Scripture, was echoed in the pamphlet of the Particular Baptist Robert Steed, who argued that the words to be sung should come from within a person, not from a printed page:

> Because the Lord hath expressly declared that this religious Singing ought to proceed from the word *dwelling richly in them,* Col. 3.16. And from being *fill'd with the Spirit,* Eph. 5.18. Now if they may or ought to sing by a set, stinted, composed Form that is before them; it is then but reading or hearing of a Psalm or Song read to them.[103]

This desire for integrity in worship is the hinge on which turns the relationship of the singers to that which is sung. The transition from not using the words of others in worship, to embracing them as a vehicle of congregational praise and personal devotion, was complex. Some Particular Baptists, as we have seen, probably sang psalms from the beginning of their independent Baptist existence, as it was the worship they had known as Independents. Others, together with the General Baptists, were suspicious for the reasons we have reviewed. Yet after the heated debates of the 1690s, Particular Baptist churches soon embraced both psalm and hymn singing.[104]

In looking at the way hymns function in worship, as with a discussion of prayers, it may be helpful to distinguish between the categories of *expressive* and *impressive* utterances. Steed and others believed that singing needed to *express* that which was in the heart, just as Bunyan had argued over the nature of prayer. Yet the use of hymns and songs *impresses* on the singer a series of phrases, ideas and images which are then offered to God as the worship of the one who has just read, but not written, them.[105]

As the proportion of sung material in contemporary worship increases, it is important to examine how such increased singing functions, both within the service and in the spirituality of the congregation. The linked songs of a worship sequence provide a liturgy in which the worshippers together express various sentiments and offer prayers to God. The notion of *communion* is particularly significant here, not only with regard to the words of particular songs, but in the repetition of much song material. This repetition has some of the features of meditation, just as silence in other traditions offers worshippers the opportunity to assimilate and develop those words which have been uttered corporately. So the Roman Catholic Louis Bouyer saw the silence after the responsorial psalm as an opportunity for such personal assimilation.[106] Similarly, Paul Bradshaw comments on Cassian's account of monastic daily worship in fifth-century Upper Egypt where the monks shared periods of silent prostration after each psalm. Bradshaw uses this as an example of private worship within a corporate setting and contrasts this monastic tradition with the liturgical communality of daily prayer in Jerusalem.[107] In song sequences, the repetition, moments of silence, vocal solos and instrumental links provide the means through which worshippers can engage more deeply with the words they have sung.

> Here might I stand and sing,
>   no story so divine;
> never was love, dear King!
>   Never was grief like thine.

This is my friend
  in whose glad praise
  I all my days
could gladly spend.[108]

Many hymns are of an affective, devotional nature, and worship songs are even more likely to be so. Much of the criticism levelled at them is about a perceived lack of theology and a playing on the emotions.[109] Yet, arguably, the use of song material is little different from the use of architecture, liturgical gesture or other symbols. Each provides a field of aesthetic nuance, communal memory and directed devotion which is intended to lead the worshippers into an experience of God and the gospel. What is significant for our study is the use of such material within a community of faith which has prized inner religion and has been suspicious of orchestrated worship.

Evangelical Warmth

Although the hymns of Wesley took some time to be used in significant numbers among Particular Baptists, Baptist hymn singing has increasingly been identified with Evangelical concerns about personal faith and the relationship of the believer to Christ. We have seen that evangelistic preaching was present, to some extent, in the seventeenth century and, similarly, many of Watts's hymns from the beginning of the eighteenth century express great warmth and were, as we have seen, widely used by Baptists. Later in that century, many of the hymns of Anne Steele to be included in Rippon's *Selection* are marked by a significant devotional intensity, especially in respect of the believer's relationship to Jesus Christ and his atoning work.[110]

Although there is not a significant corpus of Baptist hymns, there is nonetheless a 'centre of gravity' in the hymns which have been selected for Baptist books. The *Baptist Hymn Book* and *Baptist Praise and Worship*, though their content reflected recent liturgical developments, also included a few Sankey hymns – and the latter a number of worship songs. As for the respective contents, it is interesting to compare the way in which hymn texts were edited in *Baptist Praise and Worship* with editorial concerns in the United Reformed Church's *Rejoice and Sing*. Both books were published in 1991 by the same publisher, the Oxford University Press. While the URC book attempted to avoid military imagery and exclusive language, the Baptist book made a very limited attempt at inclusive language and instead attempted to change linguistic archaisms such as 'thee' and 'thou'. This was presumably because of a concern for 'relevance' and 'accessibility' – values which signify an enduring Baptist commitment to personal evangelism and which reflect something of the informal culture of contemporary Evangelical worship.

Scriptural Song

Early Baptists who sang in worship were keen to demonstrate that their singing practices carried scriptural warrant, and this concern was heightened by the controversy which surrounded the introduction of hymn singing.

The Particular Baptist *Second London Confession* of 1677 and 1689 referred to 'singing with grace in our Hearts to the Lord' as one of the parts of worship 'to be performed in obedience to him, with understanding, faith, reverence and godly fear'.[111] In the dispute over hymn singing, Keach argued that such singing was a divine ordinance[112] and this was also argued by John Gill sixty years later. He made the additional point that sung praise was an ordinance distinct from other forms of giving praise:

> Let us now consider this action of the tongue, or voice, as perform'd religiously, and we shall find, that singing of God's praise is speaking out his praise musically; or it is an expression of it, with the modulation of the voice; and so is an ordinance distinct from prayer, praise, giving of thanks, and inward spiritual joy.[113]

In the dispute between Keach and his detractors, a variety of arguments ranged across the interpretation of Scripture and the worship experience of the different parties. The practice of the early Church was reconstructed from different perspectives and the claim that congregational singing was a divine ordinance was debated with considerable vigour. This was far more than a disagreement over theological terminology. While the debate had hermeneutical and theological features, its intentions and concerns were a matter of spirituality. Was congregational hymn singing an example of obedience to God and his ways, or an indulgence in fanciful inventions which replaced divinely ordained worship? Attention to Scripture was a key value for both sides in the debate.

The scriptural nature of congregational singing, however, goes far beyond the question of warrant. The earliest metricated songs were, as we have seen, psalm paraphrases, and the concepts, imagery and language of many hymns are markedly scriptural. Indeed, *Baptist Praise and Worship*, as other modern hymnbooks have done, included an index of scriptural allusions, though it was far from comprehensive. Beyond these obvious borrowings, many hymns are anamnetic in their recounting of biblical narrative and in the proclamation of the kerygmatic testimony of Scripture.[114] This is not surprising when we reflect on the structure of hymn and song texts and the way in which they provide a vehicle of theological expression for the congregation. Development is a key aspect of hymns and songs, though each genre addresses it differently. In a worship song, the development of the worshipper's experience occurs through repetition and reinforcement. In a hymn, the worshipper is taken on a journey through the thought progression of the text. Sometimes this will be of a narrative nature, sometimes it will follow the experience of the hymn writer or a number of related doctrinal themes. However, because the words are intended to be put into the mouth of the worshipper, they need to be words which can readily be accepted and appropriated, as well as words which can easily be seen as orthodox, and words which will bear singing more than once. In each of these dimensions, the use of Scripture is important. Because Scripture is the normative vehicle of divine revelation available to the Church, it is the primary source of themes for the praise of the Church, as well providing the most widely acceptable vocabulary for that praise.

Congregational singing, prayer and the reading and preaching of Scripture form the main building blocks of Baptist worship, and we have examined the practice and spirituality of each of these activities in turn. However, before we explore how the worship values interrelate in the worship we have studied, providing the raw materials for the next stage in our liturgical theology, we need to examine another aspect of worship. We have already seen that the Eucharist is less centre-stage in Free Church worship than in other traditions. That is not to say that its place is unimportant, and any study of worship which ignores either the Lord's Table or the baptistery will be distorting the worship life of the community. So we now turn to the sacramental life and, in particular, to the way in which the practices of the table and the pool bear witness to the faith of those who gather.

9

In Memory of Me

The Spirituality of the Supper

As soon as the afternoon public service was concluded, such as chose to go home went. Such as chose to be spectators went up the galleries. The outer gate was fastened for the avoiding interruption; always hurtful in public worship, particularly so in the Lord's-supper-time. Mary Norris, the servant of the church, covered the table with a clean linen cloth, and sat thereon bread in a basket, the crust being taken off: two borrowed silver cups: and three pints of red port wine. The pastor took his seat at the upper end of the table. The deacons next him, two on each hand. The elder men-members at the table. The younger men in the pews on the pastor's right hand. The women in pews at his left. The pastor began with a short discourse on the occasion, nature, benefits, etc. of this ordinance.

Then he read 1 Cor. xi. 23 till he came at the words '*took bread*', then, taking the bread in his hand, he read '*and when he had given thanks*' and said, 'Let us do likewise,' on which, the congregation rising, he gave thanks. This ended, and the church sat down again, he added, '*When he had given thanks, he brake it:*' and broke the bread. During which he spoke of the sufferings of Christ, etc. Then, delivering the plates of bread to the deacons, he said, '*Take eat; this is my body, which is broke for you: do this in remembrance of me.*' The deacons then carried the bread round to the members: during which the pastor and all the church sat silent. The deacons at their return took bread and ate: the pastor last of all because the servant of all. After he had eaten the bread he rose again and added, taking the cup into his hands, '*After the same manner also he took the cup.*' The congregation rising again he gave thanks again. Then he poured the wine from the bottles into the cups, discoursing as while he broke the bread. The deacons rising at the close, he gave them the cups saying '*This cup*' and so on the end of the 26th verse. After the deacons returned, and were seated, they drank, and last the pastor: all sitting silent from the delivery of the cup to the deacons. The pastor rising subjoined, Our Saviour and his disciples '*sang a hymn and went out,*' let us do likewise. An hymn or psalm was then sung: after which a collection for the poor was made: the blessing added: and the assembly dismissed. The whole time was about three quarters of an hour.

The Stone Yard Meeting House, Cambridge
28 June 1761[1]

Each denomination carries in its communal life and worship something of that culture in which it originated and came to mature identity. Baptists are no different in this, and the plainness of their buildings bears silent testimony to cultural perspectives which influence the way in which they and other Free Churches view the world of worship. Where other churches might have an altar, they have a table, where others process, their leaders slip into their respective places at the beginning of worship, and where others face east, Baptists face the preacher – and, increasingly, the musicians.

One way of explaining this contrast might be to speak of Catholic worship as having something of the temple about it, while Free Church worship is more reminiscent of the synagogue. This is, of course, a huge generalization as Catholic worship developed from a number of strands, including the upper room and the synagogue. Yet it achieved maturity at a time when its official status in the Roman empire allowed it to expand in scale to fill a basilica and to express itself through the ceremonial of the large public space. Something similar can be claimed for Anglican worship as it developed in the public space of the parish church. The Free Churches, however, began more recently in secret and developed in the age of the Enlightenment, a culture in which word was vital and symbol was suspect. Here was scant pageantry or ceremonial, little talk of 'sacrifice', but much of 'remembrance'. There is also a Free Church culture of reaction, in which a protest movement not only prizes its own values but is careful to avoid the values it has rejected in parting company with others. This culture of reaction is apparent in the seventeenth century with regard to baptism and the rejection of a state church, and, for example, in the nineteenth century with a rejection of the sacramental and ceremonial expressions of the Eucharist in the Oxford Movement.

Many Baptists are suspicious of the word *sacrament*, and even today there will be those who say, 'Baptists don't have sacraments, we have ordinances.' The truth of the matter is that throughout their history there has been considerable diversity among Baptists concerning sacramental theology. The rough labels of 'Calvinist' and 'Zwinglian' have been used to identify the mystical and the memorialist ends of this spectrum.[2] While there is a modern recognition that Zwingli's eucharistic theology was richer than simply bare representation, the label is helpful in naming a perspective in which the elements are seen as 'mere' representations of the gospel. We cannot map this diversity or follow the evolving interpretations in detail, but we do need to understand the concerns which undergird the differences of view if we are to understand both the meanings Baptists give to the Supper and to baptism and the context in which Baptist practices continue to affect ecumenical relations.

Sacrament and Ordinance

The word *sacrament* is a casualty of denominational polemic, and those Baptists who have rejected its use have often done so by rejecting the interpretation they believed other Christians have given it. Sometimes they were correct in turning away from what they believed to be magic or superstition, but the rejection of sacramental language has also been a form of reductionism. Too often interpretations of the Eucharist or baptism have been reduced to an *illustration* of the gospel, an expression of subjective faith or an opportunity to encourage commitment.

The General Baptists of the seventeenth century followed John Smyth in his use of the word 'sacrament'. We should not make too much of this, however, as he explained,

> 73: . . . the outward baptism and supper do not confer and convey grace and regeneration to the participants of communicants: but as the word is preached, they serve only to support and stir up the repentance and faith of the communicants till Christ come . . .

Yet this is more than a subjective appropriation of a sign, for he continues,

> 75: That the preaching of the word, and ministry of the sacraments, representeth the ministry of Christ in the Spirit; who teacheth, baptiseth, and feedeth the regenerate, by the Holy Spirit inwardly and invisibly.[3]

Nonetheless, the Generals continued to use the word sacrament, though their interpretation of it tended towards the symbolic. In contrast, the *Second London Confession* of the Particular Baptists followed closely the text of the *Westminster Confession*. The words 'sacrament', 'seal', 'pledge' and 'sacrifice' were excluded, and 'sacramentally' was replaced by 'figuratively'. However, this was not to be the whole story. Benjamin Keach said that in the Supper 'there is a mystical Conveyance of Communication of all Christ's blessed Merits to our Souls through Faith', and neglect of the supper leads to a 'Loss of Communion with Christ'.[4] In his *Baptist Catechism*, which was approved by the General Assembly of Particular Baptists, the Lord's Supper is called an 'effectual means of Salvation', by virtue of 'the blessing of Christ, and the working of the Spirit in those that by faith receive'.[5]

Hercules Collins also adopted a 'Calvinistic' approach to the Supper. He speaks of 'the remission of sins' being 'sealed' and 'We are as verily Partakers of his Body and Blood, through the working of the Holy Ghost, as we do perceive by the Mouth of our Body, these holy Signes in Remembrance of him.' We become 'Flesh of his Flesh, and Bone of his Bones'.[6]

Like Collins, Benjamin Beddome was able to use the word sacrament in his eighteenth-century catechism: 'The outward and ordinary Means whereby Christ communicateth to us the benefits of Redemption are his Ordinances, especially the Word, Sacraments and Prayer, all which are made effectual to the Elect for Salvation.'[7] In 1802 Andrew Fuller was able to write on behalf of Northamptonshire Baptists: 'Sin is washed away in baptism in the same sense as Christ's flesh is eaten, and his blood drunk, in the Lord's Supper: the sign, when rightly used, leads to the thing signified.'[8]

Even more striking is the language of Robert Hall, the great preacher who argued that, to consider the Lord's Supper as a mere commemoration is to entertain a very inadequate view of it:

> it is a feast upon a sacrifice, by which we become partakers at the altar, not less really, though in a manner more elevated and spiritual, than those who under the ancient economy presented their offerings in the temple. In this ordinance, the cup is a spiritual participation of the blood, the bread of the body of the crucified saviour . . . It is first a feast upon a sacrifice, in which we are actual partakers by faith of the body and blood of the redeemer offered upon the Cross.[9]

However, there was such a reaction against the sacramental theology of the Oxford Movement that within decades of the statements of Fuller and Hall, Baptists were concerned to present the Supper as primarily a remembrance of what God *had* done and baptism as primarily a witness to the faith of the one being baptized. We have already seen how the word *ordinance* has a prominent place in the formation of Free Church worship. Now the word was taken and given a new meaning by contrasting it with *sacrament*. Previously the Lord's Supper could be seen both as an ordinance, which was performed because it was commanded, as well as a sacrament, which signified the operation of grace in the present as well as the past.[10] By the mid-nineteenth century most Baptists would emphasize the human actions of remembrance, witness and commitment, rather than the activity of God through bread, wine and water.[11] Ironically, this reductionism needed to rely even more on the notion of ordinance because, beyond the various subjective benefits, there was little to commend these liturgical actions other than their requirement by divine command. In so far as communion with God was seen to be an aspect of these rites, it was a spiritual union of mind and heart, assisted by the subjective support of the elements and actions. This was a mystical union in which the rites were a helpful, though not essential, support.

The individualism of the age, coupled with an evangelical emphasis on conversion, accentuated this notion of 'ordinance' as a common-sense interpretation of baptism and the Lord's Supper. Yet despite the dominant mood of Free Church anti-Catholic reaction, there was still diversity of sacramental theology. For Baptists it was represented by the towering figures of Charles Haddon Spurgeon and John Clifford.[12] For Clifford, the influence of the Supper was subjective, while Spurgeon, though able to engage in polemic against the Catholic revival, presented a rich sacramental theology:

> The priest who celebrates mass tells us that he believes in the real presence, but we reply, 'Nay, you believe in knowing Christ after the flesh, and in that sense the only real presence is in heaven; but we firmly believe in the real presence of Christ which is spiritual, and yet certain.' By spiritual we do not mean unreal; in fact, the spiritual takes the lead in real-ness to spiritual men. I believe in the true and real presence of Jesus with his people, such presence has been real to my spirit. Lord Jesus, Thou Thyself has visited me. As surely as the Lord Jesus came really as to His flesh to Bethlehem and Calvary, so surely does he come really by His Spirit to His people in the hours of their communion with Him.[13]

Such sentiments became more widespread as the early twentieth century progressed, with a growing number of voices calling for a richer and more biblical approach to these matters than the prevailing memorialism. Henry Wheeler Robinson encouraged his readers to reread the New Testament and to take account of the close links between references to baptism and to the Holy Spirit.[14] In 1937 a committee reporting to the Council of the Baptist Union concerning a union proposal with Congregationalists and Presbyterians was able to speak of baptism as 'a means of grace' and urged Baptists to reconsider sympathetically 'a more sacramental, i.e. Calvinistic, view of both baptism and the Lord's Supper'.[15] Such an exhortation is an indication both of changing views among some theologians and church leaders and of a prevailing rejection of sacramental categories among the churches. Through the remainder of the twentieth century there was a gathering momentum in the use of sacramental language, though the spectrum of opinions is still wide. Some of the influences which have led to the embracing of more sacramental categories are the continuing work of biblical studies,[16] increased ecumenical contact and the various phases of the Charismatic Movement. The emphasis of this movement on the contemporary activity of the Holy Spirit has directly challenged the reductionist mindset of the modernist era with its limiting of the sacraments to subjective experience.

Sacramental Theology

Recent decades have seen considerable attention being given to reflection on the meaning of the sacraments. Yet this reflection has come not so much through an embracing of so-called 'sacramental theology' as from a sustained exploration of the meaning of baptism and the meaning of the Lord's Supper. Liturgical theology has its part to play in this process which, to some extent, sidesteps the old debates.

Neville Clark argued in the 1950s that we should enquire into the meaning of baptism and the meaning of the Eucharist *per se*, rather than interpret them in the light of a separately arrived at definition of 'sacrament'.[17] This is true to a point, but categories of thought need to be critiqued and expanded if people are to be enabled to embrace different interpretations of the baptism and the Supper. The Charismatic challenge is an example of this, as is the ecumenical learning which can come with increased contact and shared worship. However, systematic theological reflection also has a role to play. While sacramental theology may be informed and transformed through a detailed study of the biblical foundations and developing practices of each sacrament, sacramental theology can also assist the interpretation of baptism and the Supper through the provision of a framework of understanding. Clark was concerned that a pre-existent sacramental theology might operate as a sieve through which to squeeze the biblical and liturgical facts. While such distortion must be avoided, sacramental theology can operate as a palette of colours to enliven our representation of baptism and the Supper. All interpreters will inevitably work with a pre-existent sacramental theology, whether high or low. The question is whether or not that theology is adequate to the task, whether the palette is rich enough or realistic enough for a worthy portrayal.

A theologian who can help us in this is the Roman Catholic Edward Schillebeeckx, who, in his *Christ the Sacrament of the Encounter with*

God, uses the notion of sacramentality as a way of linking God's activity in Christ to his activity in and through the Church. He argues that the incarnation is the primordial sacrament of God's saving encounter with humanity:

> The man Jesus, as the personal visible realization of the divine grace of redemption, is *the* sacrament, the primordial sacrament, because this man, the Son of God himself, is intended by the Father to be in his humanity the only way to the actuality of redemption . . . Human encounter with Jesus is therefore the sacrament of the encounter with God.[18]

Schillebeeckx argues that the word *sacrament* should operate in three distinct, though related ways. The first is to denote Jesus Christ as the bodily, sacramental presence of God, coming in saving power and inviting a human response. The second is to speak of the Church, the Body of Christ, as a sacrament of encounter in which Christ is manifest in the people of God, graciously accessible in saving power. The third use is the traditional one, which refers to '*the* sacraments' celebrated by the Church, which he claims are in reality the action of Christ. If the incarnation of the eternal Word in the historic Jesus of Nazareth is the primordial sacrament of the encounter with God, these sacraments of the Church become, for Schillebeeckx, the earthly vehicle of this encounter in the present.[19] James Empereur argues that these sacraments enable the Church to be this sacramental reality: 'As communal symbols sacraments call for participation. Through this participation the church as sacrament is created and the liturgy is the expression of it.'[20] Because they are centred in Jesus Christ who is the primordial sacrament of the encounter with God, the Lord's Supper and baptism enable the contemporary Church to encounter Christ in the present and to *become* the Church, the Body of Christ. Geoffrey Wainwright speaks of 'patterning', in which

> The sacraments may therefore be seen as the ritual expression of a pattern which is set by Christ and whose intended scope is nothing less than the universal divine kingdom.[21]

The churches of the Reformation reduced the number of sacraments from the mediaeval seven to the two 'dominical' sacraments of baptism and the Eucharist.[22] These were the two ritual actions in which Scripture testified to explicit instructions being given by Jesus to his disciples[23] and it was for this reason that they were called 'ordinances'.[24] But they are also dominical in their fundamental focus in the life, death and resurrection of Jesus Christ. They are dominical in the way in which they both express and enable the relationship of Jesus Christ to the Church to be one of Lordship: a relationship in which the character of the Church as a community can manifest some of the character of Jesus Christ.

In this and the following chapter we shall examine both the practices of the Lord's Supper and the baptism of believers, and the spirituality implicit in them. There is a continuing need for practice and theology to interact so that practices can be understood and the theology they embody scrutinized. Here liturgical theology may have a reforming consequence but, for the moment, our primary concern must be description and interpretation.

The Practice of the Lord's Supper

Unlike many parts of the Church, most corporate worship in Baptist and Free Churches is not eucharistic. Much of our study has acknowledged this characteristic, noting with James White that it should influence our liturgical theology in a way which is quite distinct from the liturgical theology of the Anglican, Orthodox or Catholic traditions. It is not helpful, however, to call this worship 'non-eucharistic', as that would be to name it with a negative rather than taking seriously its actual content and rhythms.

A monthly communion service is the pattern experienced by most Baptist worshippers,[25] and this represents a recurring, central feature of the worship of a local church, even though it is not as prominent as in some other Christian traditions. It is helpful to distinguish the Lord's Supper as being *central* rather than *normative*. It is central in the sense that it recurs regularly and attendance is normally regarded as an important responsibility of church membership. Further, the disciplinary fencing of the table in the early centuries indicates a close relationship between the Supper and the church. It has a unique place within the worship of a Baptist church, but it is not more fully worship than other services.[26] We need to remember that, in the seventeenth century, a monthly celebration may have been a more frequent occurrence than what was available in the parish church.[27] Its character was certainly different, with its emphasis on a symbolic meal.[28] This communal character is important in understanding the function of the Supper as an expression of Baptist ecclesiology and as a focusing of that ecclesiology in the death and resurrection of Jesus Christ.[29]

The Development of the Lord's Supper

There are few early witnesses to the Lord's Supper in Baptist churches and we need to make the most of what hints are available. The distinctions between General and Particular Baptist worship is important in any reconstruction, because we need to give adequate account of the closeness of the Particular Baptists to other Calvinistic dissenters as well as recognize the radical nature of General Baptist worship with its restorationist concerns. So the Generals practised footwashing as an ordinance until the middle of the eighteenth century, as well as agape meals attached to the Lord's Supper. These love feasts may often have been celebrated in homes with the Eucharist following immediately after a meal. An informant described a service in a large private house in Bishopsgate Street in 1645 which began with prayer and the laying on of hands, after which a meal was served and, while the cloth was still on the table, the Lord's Supper was administered.

Three decades later, Thomas Grantham gave a detailed outline of the Lord's Supper which is remarkably similar to that found in the *Westminster Directory*:

Preaching and prayer, as on other occasions
Preparation of the elements on the table
Exhortation 'to due Humility and reverence'
Statement of the authority for and institution of the supper
Statement of its 'mystical signification' regarding the cross of Christ
Statement of the spiritual qualifications necessary for all partakers

Taking and blessing of the bread
Fraction and words of institution
Distribution and reception of the bread
Taking and blessing of the cup
Libation and words of institution
Distribution and reception of the cup
Exhortation to gratitude
Prayer of thanksgiving
Fellowship offering
Hymn of praise[30]

We should remember that while there is continual referencing to Scripture, no books would have been used in the service. So words of institution would have been either memorized or paraphrased. The structure is recognizable to modern readers and can serve as a generic pattern along-side which we can note variations from time to time. In particular, some occasions would have been simpler and included fewer elements.

The hymn referred to by Grantham would have been the extempore singing of an individual, probably the elder conducting the service. However, we have seen that regular congregational hymn singing began in a Particular Baptist church in 1668 when Benjamin Keach introduced a hymn at the conclusion of the Lord's Supper. His argument was based on ordinance: the gospel accounts tell us that Jesus and the disciples sang a hymn before they left for the Mount of Olives. The practice spread steadily and, in 1697, Joseph Stennett published his *Hymns in Com-memoration of the Sufferings of our blessed Saviour, Jesus Christ, com-posed for the celebration of His Holy Supper.*

Churches would usually hold two services each Sunday in the morning and the afternoon. Evening worship was not common until the advent of gas lighting in the cities in the early nineteenth century. The common practice was for the afternoon service to include, or be followed by, the Lord's Supper once each month. The two congregations which united in the Barbican in 1695 agreed to meet at 9.30 am and 1.30 pm. The unit-ing agreement stated that 'on the Breaking-Bread-Days the Psalm to be omitted in the Afternoon till the Conclusion of the Lord's Supper'.[31]

Some churches would prepare for this monthly event by holding a preparatory service during the previous week. So the Broadmead church would meet for prayer on the Wednesday before the Lord's Supper,[32] and Isaac Watts's Bury Street congregation would meet on the Friday after-noon before the first Sunday of the month to hear a sermon and conduct the pastoral and business affairs of the church, such as the admission or disciplining of members.[33] The service was conducted by one of the pastors:

Words of institution read from either Matthew 26 or 1 Corinthians 11
Minister takes the plate of bread and offers a prayer of blessing
Breaking of the bread 'into small pieces, as big as walnuts', saying:
   'This is the body of Christ, or the emblem or figure of the body of
   Christ, which was broken for you: take it and eat ye all of it, in
   remembrance of our Saviour who dies for us'
Distribution to the congregation by deacons and others appointed
Pouring out of the wine into at least one of several cups
Prayer of blessing on the cup
Distribution of the wine to the congregation
Psalm or hymn sung by the congregation

Collection for the poor
Prayer responding to pastoral requests made by members of the con-
gregation
Prayer of thanksgiving
Benediction[34]

Several details are worthy of note. First, the words of institution are
read as a narrative framework for the rite and the church records explain
that this is in order that they 'may ever be kept in mind to regulate every
part of the practice'. This is quite different from Christian traditions in
which the words of institution are contained *within* the eucharistic
prayer. This Free Church practice is significant for at least two reasons.
On the one hand, it illustrates the ordinance nature of the event with the
scriptural warrant preceding the sacrament. On the other hand, it
increases the sense of re-enactment in which the events of the upper room
are repeated in the church. The drama is not primarily one of celebration
but of a Bible story enacted in obedience to Jesus Christ. In some
churches, as at Bury Street, the whole passage was read and then the
relevant words repeated with the bread and the wine. In others, such as
at the Cambridge church described at the beginning of the chapter, the
words of institution were interrupted by the relevant actions, such as the
prayer of thanksgiving coming after the first mention of Jesus giving
thanks. In both cases the scriptural words provide a framework for
anamnesis, though the focus is on the death of Christ *through* the story
of the upper room.

  Second, the congregation receives the bread and wine seated as though
for a meal, rather than kneeling, which was considered to imply an undue
veneration of the elements. Third, a distinction is made between prayers
of blessing for the bread and the cup, and a prayer of thanksgiving at the
end. We can only speculate, but this may suggest a sacramental emphasis
in the prayer of blessing in which God was asked to bless the material
bread and wine. The church at Cambridge simply had two prayers of
thanksgiving, for bread and wine respectively. The offering of separate
prayers for bread and wine probably reflects the ordinance concern to
re-enact exactly what has been recorded in Scripture as the events of the
upper room. So a literal reading of I Corinthians 11.25 ('Likewise he
took the cup after supper, saying . . . ') resulted in two prayers because
the 'likewise' was understood as referring not only to the taking of the
cup but also to the manner of the taking, that is, with a prayer of thanksgiving. These prayers have often been led by deacons. Finally, having
been examined in private and agreed at the previous Friday's meeting,

new members were received into membership immediately before the Lord's Supper.

It is instructive to place alongside this account of the Lord's Supper in the congregation where Isaac Watts was pastor, one of his hymns written for the conclusion of such a service:

> Jesus invites his saints
>   to meet around his board;
> here pardoned rebels sit and hold
>   communion with their Lord.
>
> Here we survey that love
>   which spoke in every breath,
> which crowned each action of his life,
>   and triumphed in his death.
>
> The holy bread and wine
>   maintain our fainting breath,
> by union with our living Lord,
>   and interest in his death.
>
> Our heavenly Father calls
>   Christ and his members one;
> we the young children of his love,
>   and he the first-born Son.
>
> We are but several parts
>   of the same broken bread;
> our body has its several limbs,
>   but Jesus is the head.
>
> Let all our powers be joined
>   his glorious name to raise;
> pleasure and love fill every mind
>   and every voice be praise.[35]

Although occasional hymn texts, such as this one, reflected the symbolism of the Supper, most early communion hymns dwelt on the death of Christ and its significance for the believer rather than the sacrament through which that atoning death was being remembered.

There seem to be fewer changes in the overall practice of the Lord's Supper than in other services of worship, probably because its form was governed by the words of institution and the concern to be faithful to the biblical narrative. But changing circumstances inevitably led to shifts and variation. The Supper has continued to be the place where new members are received, though the fencing of the table in church discipline has largely disappeared, as attitudes to discipline and inclusivity have changed. The Lord's Supper continues to be the place where the fellowship of the Church is eloquently expressed through the reception of new members, thanksgiving for those who have died, prayers for the sick and those in need and, latterly in some places, the sharing of the peace. Well into the twentieth century, many churches continued the practice of collecting members' identity tickets so as to keep a record of faithful attendance or absence from the Lord's table.

The replacement of the afternoon service by one in the evening led in time to some people only attending one service each week, and to the practice of monthly morning and monthly evening communion services. Ernest Payne argues that lay presidency was not common until the nineteenth century, though Baptists would now tend to be out of step with other traditions on this matter.[36]

The second half of the nineteenth century saw the introduction of non-alcoholic communion wine as Baptists and the other Free Churches were strongly committed to the temperance movement.[37] In the first decade of the twentieth century individual communion glasses began to replace the common cup in response to concerns over public health and hygiene. The intervening century has seen some regret at the loss of symbolism in this development and various practices have been introduced to compensate for the individualization of the event. In particular, drinking simultaneously after all have been served, has been a widespread way of dealing with this matter, though some congregations, especially smaller ones, have begun to return to a common cup.

The twentieth century has also been a period where printed manuals for the use of ministers and other leaders have provided the historian with a means of mapping the development of what has, at each time of publication, been officially regarded as good practice, though the extent to which the orders of service have been followed by congregations cannot easily be determined. M. E. Aubrey's *A Minister's Manual*, first published in 1927, follows a simplified version of the outline which has continued since the seventeenth century:

Reception of new members (and thanksgiving for any who have died)
Scripture sentences
Words of institution
Prayer of thanksgiving
Distribution of the bread (though no fraction is mentioned)

Distribution of the wine
Prayer
Hymn collection for the poor
Benediction

While there is considerable simplicity and little ornamentation in this order, the structure remains remarkably stable. The book offers only a limited number of prayers and other words, so we may speculate that its provision of an outline service was provoked by the lack of structure in the practice of some churches. The order includes only one prayer of thanksgiving, though we have noted that the practice of separate prayers of thanksgiving for the bread and the wine was widespread.

The lack of any reference to breaking the bread is significant as it plays down the sense of ritual action. The influence of the liturgical movement was to be far more evident in the next manual edited by Ernest Payne and Stephen Winward in 1960. This influence was found not only in the provision of prayer material from the wider Church,[38] but in the structuring of the service where the contribution of Gregory Dix is in evidence.[39] Not only is the breaking of the bread indicated, but also the raising of the cup so that the full symbolism of the rite may be marked and experienced by the congregation and the 'shape of the liturgy' made clear. The 1980 publication *Praise God* offered imaginative and ecumenical material, and this was evident in its order of service for the Lord's Supper through the inclusion of the sharing of the peace.

By this time, however, a more profound change had occurred in most churches through the drawing of the Supper into the main worship service. Liturgical renewal was taking place across the denominations. Whereas the centrality of the Eucharist was celebrated by Catholics through its translation into the vernacular, and by Anglicans through the development of parish communion as the main service of the week, for Baptists and other Free Churches that centrality was expressed in the moving of the Supper from an after-meeting of the faithful, to the climax of the main Sunday service. This was the preferred option in the material provided by Payne and Winward and in the same year Neville Clark presented the detailed order for Sunday eucharistic worship which we noted in Chapter 4.

Of course, the monthly interval remained for most, and sometimes it appeared as a culmination rather than a climax! But this shift of context was to have various consequences for Baptists and for the other Free Churches. Many churches had operated an open table since before the open and closed communion controversy of the early nineteenth century.[40] That policy was now widespread and would be expressed by inviting 'all those who love the Lord Jesus irrespective of denomination' to share in the communion. With this now occurring in public worship, the passing of time would see those who had made a faith commitment, but who had yet to be baptized, receive bread and wine. In addition, the ecumenical debate concerning the admission of children to the table has a particular dimension for Baptists and their ecumenical relationships because their children will not have been baptized.

Increasing denominational diversity was reflected in the breadth and flexibility of *Patterns and Prayers for Christian Worship*, which was published in 1991. This offered three patterns for the Lord's Supper, each of which was a service of word and sacrament. Of particular note was the second pattern's attempt to link the novelty of the sharing of the peace with those other elements which have traditionally expressed the fellowship nature of the sacrament: the reception of new members, prayers for the needs of the fellowship and the collection for the needs of the fellowship.[41] The third pattern was intended for 'those who set the Lord's Supper within a more informal and participatory approach to worship' and was particularly suitable for Charismatic congregations. This pattern offered a structure accompanied by some prompts which would relate to the worship culture of some congregations. For example, after the words of institution it is suggested that members of the congregation might 'offer one-sentence prayers of thanksgiving for God's mighty acts in Jesus'.[42] This pattern also links the peace with other expressions of Christian fellowship, but here they are grouped after the communion in order to express the fellowship with each other which is made possible through participating in the redeeming work of Christ.

Questioning Practices

Amidst the diversity of Baptist eucharistic practice, it is difficult for a commentator to view each practice as being of equal merit. There will inevitably be areas where a critique of worship will lead to a concern for reformation and renewal. What is important is that the diverse practices are given a voice and that each voice be given serious liturgical and theological attention and the implied spirituality understood. Such detailed attention is not possible here, but a number of pastoral and theological observations may be made before moving to an exploration of the spirituality inherent in the mainstream Baptist practices at the Lord's Table.

Baptists have tended to hold an antipathy towards the notion of ritual action. Their reaction to the doctrine of transubstantiation, their rejection of authorized prayer book worship, and their concern for sincerity have led them into simple, and often abstract, forms of worship. When this is remembered, it is remarkable that we have found such consistency in the form of the Lord's Supper over nearly four hundred years. We have seen how the narrative framework of the words of institution have been largely responsible for this, but behind the words we need to recognize the authority of an ordinance in which the command is most explicit: 'Do this in memory of me.' In recent years, a growing attention to drama has encouraged some churches to increase congregational participation by making the symbolic actions more prominent.

But the ritual questions remain and are closely related to our reflections on the nature of sacramental action. None dispute that there is symbolism in the Supper, and most agree that God can use that symbolism in the effective operation of the Holy Spirit in the life of the believer. But how do we account for this activity of God in the Lord's Supper and to what extent is this divine activity associated with particular human actions? Are the eucharistic actions performative or expressive? Do they achieve some objective result in the spiritual realm or are they primarily an expression of the faith of the Church? Baptists, as other Christians, will differ in their response to these questions, but face them they must. Indeed, it has already been suggested that the Charismatic movement provides a conceptual framework of divine activity which makes it possible to see some performative meaning in these actions. It is already present in the ministry of healing and in the laying on of hands with prayer for leaders and others; it has yet to be fully appropriated for the interpretation of this central activity of Christian worship, the Lord's Supper.

Associated with the interpretation of the actions at the Supper is a more general question concerning the nature of the event as a whole. In most Baptist churches, the Lord's Supper is observed rather than celebrated; the mood is one of quiet reflection rather than enthusiastic celebration. In recent years, there has been an increasing ecumenical emphasis on the resurrection of Jesus Christ, yet the mood at a Baptist communion service remains primarily one of introspective remembrance of his death. The theme of a meal, with the congregation remaining seated, may increase the sense of community, but it does not easily enable the celebration of the victory of Christ or the exploration of the cosmic consequences of that victory. Baptists have tended to be resistant to more frequent celebrations of the Supper,[43] and this may partly be because the quietism of the service is at odds with the upbeat mood of much Sunday worship. Like many evangelicals, they are determinedly activist and the reflective and unvaried nature of the Supper may only be sustainable on a monthly basis. Pastorally, this raises two questions. First, how might Baptists be encouraged to explore other cultural patterns of celebrating the Lord's Supper so that the practice is truly one of celebration? And second, if the Supper is only observed monthly, how is the paschal mystery experienced in regular Sunday worship?

This latter question is vitally important and this study of Baptist worship is an attempt to understand how that worship, Sunday by Sunday, testifies to the faith of the Church and the gospel of Jesus Christ. However, we shall now turn to the spirituality of the Supper and ask how its practices bear witness to what the Church believes about God and about itself.

The Spirituality of the Lord's Supper

What theological meaning are we able to ascribe to the Baptist way of gathering around the Lord's table? As in other aspects of worship, that meaning is to be found in the values we have already identified. We have seen a consistency of shape and content as we have followed the development of the Lord's Supper in English Baptist churches over several centuries, and have recognized that those recurring patterns bear witness to the scriptural authority which has inspired and framed the eucharistic actions, providing continuity and consistency. It is to this authority that we turn first.

Remembering Jesus Christ: Attention to Scripture

Scripture frames the eucharistic actions and provides more of a liturgical structure than at any other point in Baptist worship. The words of institution, from either 1 Corinthians 11 or one of the Gospel parallels, are read as the biblical basis of the ordinance. It is not possible to stress too much the importance of these words of institution. They direct and limit the practice of the Supper, enabling the congregation to participate in the drama of the upper room as well as participate in the drama of salvation in Christ. Not only the eucharistic prayer, but the whole of the Supper is anamnetic, as memory and participation merge. Here is an attention to Scripture which is not only attention as concentration but attention as involvement.

The sense of re-enactment is strong, as the seated congregation become the assembled disciples.[44] The president at the table, surrounded by seated deacons, utters the words of Jesus and then offers a prayer of thanksgiving and those deacons distribute the bread and wine. Here is a good illustration in worship of James McClendon's claim that believer-church ecclesiology involves a 'shared awareness of *the present Christian community as the primitive community and the eschatological community*'.[45] We may compare this with the comment of C. H. Dodd:

> At each Eucharist we are *there* – we are in the night in which He was betrayed, at Golgotha, before the empty tomb on Easter day, and in the upper room before he appeared; *and* we are at the moment of His coming. with angels and archangels and all the company of heaven, in the twinkling of an eye at the last trump.[46]

Here is not only remembrance and participation, but eschatological anticipation as well. Yet within this cosmic and eternal canvas, the picture which is painted is one which is determined by Scripture. So attention to Scripture not only confirms the status of the Supper as a divine ordinance, it also structures its performance and reception. The consistent pattern of the Lord's Supper bears eloquent witness to the seriousness with which Baptist congregations take Scripture and especially those words of Jesus: 'Do this in memory of me.'

Communion with Christ: Devotion

In each Christian tradition, devotional expression and intent are likely to be significant aspects of each Christian's approach to the Eucharist. This devotional experience, however, is even more evident in Baptist and Free Church celebrations of the Supper, largely because the themes of proclamation and celebration are so subdued.[47] Quiet remembrance and personal prayer express and enable a *subjective* engagement with the Eucharist which will be significant in any theological explanation of the Supper's sacramental meaning. As William Kiffin explained in 1681, 'the performance of all duties will be of no value to any man further than Christ is enjoyed in them'.[48] It has already been noted that many Baptists tend to a 'Zwinglian' interpretation of the Supper, though that designation begs various questions and is not representative of all Baptists.[49] The nineteenth century saw Baptists react against the Oxford Movement in such a way as to heighten the memorialism of the Lord's Supper. Thus Alexander Maclaren wrote:

I, for my part, am contented to be told that I believe in a poor, bald Zwinglianism, when I say with my Master, that the purpose of the Lord's Supper is simply the commemoration, and therein the proclamation, of His death. There is no magic, no mystery, no 'sacrament' about it. It blesses us when it makes us remember Him. It does the same thing for us which any other means of bringing Him to mind does. It does that through a different vehicle. A sermon does it by words, the Communion does it by symbols.[50]

This 'low' view may be contrasted with C. H. Spurgeon's commitment to 'the real presence' of Christ, and the other, more sacramental interpretations of such as Hall and Fuller.

But whatever the theological understanding of the operation of grace and the sacramental nature of the Supper, we may see in it the Church gathered around the paschal mystery of Christ crucified, raised and ascended. The Church is addressed by the gospel and its life thus shaped by Jesus Christ. And here individual Christians meet their risen Lord through the fellowship of the meal and the gospel meaning of the elements. Both high and low interpretations of the Supper have tended to intensify devotion – high views through a belief in the real presence of Christ and low views through an emphasis on subjective faith and the importance of the scriptural symbols in enriching that faith.

Most Baptists have resisted identifying the presence of Christ with the bread and wine and have preferred to locate the divine presence among those gathered around the table, both collectively and individually. While Wheeler Robinson explained that 'the Communion Service is fundamentally a memorial rite', he added,

> it is much more than this . . . It renews obedient loyalty, and it establishes and mediates fellowship, both with God in Christ and with fellow-members of His Body. It implies the real presence of the risen Lord by His Spirit, and Baptists might join . . . Richard Hooker in saying, 'The real presence of Christ's most blessed body and blood is not, therefore, to be sought for in the Sacrament, but in the worthy receiver of the Sacrament.'[51]

This feeding of the believer's relationship with Christ, together with an ethical self-examination, is a significant aspect of personal communion with Christ in the Lord's Supper. Together with private devotions, based on Scripture reading and prayer, and regular communal worship and preaching, the Lord's Supper is a place of nourishment. For the Church, this is a rite which represents to its members the costliness of their salvation and invites them to respond in heart-felt gratitude and love. Thus Anne Steele wrote:

Yet while around his board we meet,
And worship at his glorious feet;
O let our warm affections move
In glad returns of grateful love.

Yes, Lord, we love and we adore,
But long to know and love thee more;
And while we taste the bread and wine,
Desire to feed on joys divine.[52]

Here she speaks of the religious affections being aroused by an encounter with Christ's costly love. The tasting of bread and wine play their part in the communication of this divine appeal, but the event is primarily presented as an intense focus of the ongoing relationship of the believer with Christ. The religious affections are again used to explain the spiritual dynamic of this communion in John Sutcliffe's circular letter of 1803:

> But we know that you are not satisfied with what is externally decent. Spiritual worship is the object of your concern. God is a spirit, and he requires that those who worship him, should do it in spirit and in truth. Spiritual worship includes in it the exercise – the right exercise of the heart. At the table of the Lord, there is work for spiritual reflection. Everything relative to the character, especially his death, claims your serious attention. Spiritual reflection should be accompanied with holy affections. Of all the objects, none like the cross, to excite, to call into exercise our inmost feelings . . . To him who gave his life a ransom, it becomes you to devote your lives.[53]

At the communal meal with its emphasis on the redemptive work of Christ, which is itself eschatological, we find the call to holy living as well as the devotional offering of the heart – and both are in response to the cross. In Baptist practice, heart worship will be unlikely to have much outward expression at the Lord's table. However, through reflection and prayer the excited affections may encourage believers to offer themselves anew for obedient discipleship in God's service.

So the devotional concern for sincerity and integrity of life is not only evident in the practice of self-examination and penitence. It is also evident in the encounter with God's costly love in the cross of Christ and the consequent strengthening of a faith which inspires not only devotion, but the sacrificial living which should follow.

Fellowship in Christ: The Church as Community

When it gathers around the Lord's table, the Church as 'the fellowship of believers' expresses something of its true self as community. The framework of a communal, albeit token, meal is in itself a powerful symbol of fellowship, but this communality is also expressed in other ways. During the Lord's Supper new members of the congregation will be welcomed. Here also prayer will often be offered for the needs of individual members who may be sick or in need, and a money offering will be collected to meet the needs of the poor.[54] The Lord's Supper is a place where the Church acknowledges its identity as a community before God with obligations of mutual care.

Historically, this care was sometimes exercised in the form of discipline. All members of a local congregation were expected to attend worship on a regular basis, and absence without due cause was a matter for censure and even removal from the role of members. Such absence was seen not only as disobedience to a divine ordinance and a lack of loyalty to Jesus Christ but also as a sin against the fellowship.[55] Absentees were often visited so that they might be brought back into the fellowship. This discipline could be seen as an *external* monitoring of attendance and the lifestyle of church members. It was a juridical and pastoral means of maintaining the character of the Church as a community which reflects Jesus Christ and which looks forward to the Kingdom. But we might say that this character of the Church is also patterned *internally* by the devotional dynamic of the Supper.

The horizontal emphasis of a meal, with all seated and the table encircled by president, deacons and congregation,[56] enriches the devotional notion of communion with the additional meaning of community. Being 'in communion' means being in communion with one another as well as with the Lord of the Church. While a little under a fifth of contemporary Baptist churches in 1997 shared the peace on a regular basis,[57] that element eloquently expresses the communal dimension of the Supper which has been present for Baptists since their origins as covenanted communities.[58]

The Church is able to be an instrument of the will of God because its members respond to God's love and so put themselves at his disposal. It is no accident that in the early, rural expressions of Baptist church life, the Lord's Supper and the church meeting were often held on the same Sunday afternoon. Heart worship, if it is genuine, will result in a dedicated life. For the Church, this can mean moving from the table of the Lord to a meeting in which his Lordship is expressed through pastoral planning, fellowship caring and stewardship. Here the values combine, as obedience to scriptural commands, personal piety and faith in God's future are worked out in community.

Until He Comes: Concern for the Kingdom

The Pauline words of institution end with the eschatological affirmation, 'For as often as you eat this bread and drink the cup, you proclaim the Lord's death until he comes' (1 Corinthians 11.26). Here is a Kingdom meal and, according to Mark, Jesus sees the Passover cup as anticipating the Messianic banquet (Mark 14.25). The Eucharist is, despite its anamnetic structure, fundamentally eschatological in orientation. Despite its structure as a re-enactment of the *Last* Supper, it is, in fact, the *Lord's* Supper as, this side of the resurrection of Jesus, the Church communes with its risen Lord and proclaims the mystery of salvation. This eschatological transformation invites the gathered community to live Kingdom values and have Kingdom hopes.[59]

In the early centuries of Baptist life, the community which gathered at the table had a discipline with a future orientation. A member might be excluded from the table because of some public sin from which they needed to repent and which dishonoured the Church. This exclusion was seen as a pastoral measure with the intention of bringing repentance and a change of lifestyle, and was usually justified by reference to Matthew 18.15–18. The ecclesial character of the Supper was apparent when exclusion from the table became exclusion from membership of the Church if repentance and reconciliation did not occur.

Again the values combine. Here is a linking of community and Kingdom, as concern for the purity of the Church and the eternal destiny of its members coincide. But here also is a concern for the integrity of life and heart as the outward obedience to the commands of Christ in daily living becomes part of the eucharistic offering. Changing social and pastoral attitudes have today resulted in such measures being very rarely implemented in British Baptist churches, though it is important not to lose the intention of this discipline. It is a way of seeing the Lord's table as a place where believers are invited to examine their hearts and actions, after the injunction of Paul in 1 Corinthians 11.27–32, before presenting themselves for communion with their Lord.

The eschatological dimension has yet to be fully realized in Baptist celebrations of the Supper. The cosmic proportion of the work of Christ, especially as it may be expressed in the sacramental use of bread and wine, is not usually given adequate attention. Bread and wine are not only for the nourishment of the saints, or symbols of the sacrifice of Christ, but symbols of the material stuff of the universe. Here is an anticipation of the end of the work of Christ, both in the sense of its intent and its completion, when creation and redemption join hands. From such a liturgical expression might flow not only an instilling of hope in a threatening world, but a transformation of how that world is viewed. That God uses the material elements of bread and wine is significant for a Christian tradition which has tended to emphasize subjective faith and abstract worship. Cosmic communion may also lead to a political spirituality in which mission and devotion belong together. Anticipating God's Kingdom need not only mean waiting for it, but seeking it in prayer and serving it through action in the created world.

The Supper of the Lord

The meanings of the Supper are to be found and united in its central meaning as the *Lord's* Supper. Here is an overarching reality which gives meaning to the whole of Christian experience and the life of the Church. Just as in all the Church's Sunday worship disciples gather 'in the name of Jesus', so at the table all that happens and is said centres on Jesus Christ and especially his death and resurrection. All the values we have discussed relate to the central, Christological meaning of the rite. All the imagery is earthed in the story of Jesus and the New Testament interpretations of its meaning. The narrative structure is the Gospel narrative and the spiritual centre is of communion with the one who broke bread with his disciples, was crucified and raised and now meets again his disciples in the breaking of bread (Luke 24.35).

Despite the sense of re-enactment, Baptists have not seen the president as representing Jesus. Yet they have emphasized the Supper as a meal in which Jesus Christ is the host who welcomes his guests. Although the eighteenth and nineteenth centuries saw considerable debate over the question of open and closed communion,[60] the overwhelming practice today is to invite 'all those who love the Lord Jesus Christ and seek to follow him' to share in the Supper, irrespective of whether they are members of a Baptist church or have been baptized as believers. This ecumenical openness is often justified on the grounds that it is the *Lord's* table and not the table of the Church.[61] While this seems to raise questions about the relationship of the Church as the Body of Christ to its

Lord, it nonetheless expresses an evangelical directness which refuses to place the Church *between* believers and their Lord.

This ambiguity of Church and Lord suggests an area for future exploration in Baptist theological reflection. For example, reflection on the implications of Jesus Christ being not only the Lord of believers but head of the Body, the Church, might challenge some of the practices of Baptists and other Free Churches. Headship could suggest a different and more intimate relationship than Lordship, and this may have a consequence for the way Baptists view worship and the practices which link worship and the day-to-day life of the Christian community. For example, the connection between being a Christian, sharing in the Supper and belonging to the Church needs to be explored. However, Lordship must always be qualified by a towel and a cross, and the nature of this Lordship is made clear in the Supper, for it is broken bread which is distributed. The new covenant is made possible by the sacrificial death of the one who is named and owned as 'Lord'.

Buried with Christ

The Spirituality of the Pool

This day the two churches of Walden and Cambridge met by mutual consent at Whittlesford to administer the ordinance of baptism. This church sometimes administers baptism in public (as now) in the presence of many hundreds of spectators; so John the Baptist administered it: sometimes in private; so S. Paul administered it to the jailor, though never in the night, because we are not only not persecuted, but we are protected by law. Circumstances must determine when a private, or when a public baptism is proper. Previous to this, twenty-five persons had professed their faith and repentance to the church at Walden; and twenty-one had done the same at Cambridge; and all had desired baptism by immersion. Dr Gifford, at ten o'clock, mounted a moveable pulpit near the river in Mr Hollick's yard, and, after singing and prayer, preached a suitable sermon on the occasion from Psalm cxix.57. After sermon, the men retired to one room, the women, to two others, and the baptizer, Mr Gwennap, to another, to prepare for the administration. After about half an hour, Mr Gwennap, dressed as usual (except a coat, which was supplied by a black gown made like a bachelor's) came down to the waterside. He was followed by the men, two and two, dressed as usual, only, instead of a coat, each had on a long white baize gown, tied round the waist with a piece of worstead-binding, and leaded at bottom that they might sink: they had on their heads white linen caps. The women followed, two by two, dressed as usual, only all had white gowns, Holland or dimity. Their upper-coats were tacked to their stockings, and their gowns leaded, lest their clothes should float. Mr Gwennap sang an hymn at the waterside, spoke about ten minutes on the subject, and then taking the oldest man of the company by the hand, led him to a convenient depth in the river. Then pronouncing the words, I baptize thee in the name of the Father, and of the Son, and of the Holy Ghost, he immersed the person once in the river. Robinson stood in a boat, and, with other assistants, led the rest in, and, having wiped their faces after their baptism, led them out. Mr Gwennap added a few words more after the administration at the water-side, and concluded with the usual blessing.

Church Book, Stone Yard Meeting, Cambridge
10 April 1767[1]

It started as a nickname, but it stuck. Baptists baptize believers only – yet naming them after this distinctive position masks a number of ambiguities and ironies.

Baptists have indeed stood over and against much of the world Church for the best part of four hundred years. Yet it is ironical that they have usually been more concerned with the *who* and the *how* of the baptismal rite than with its meaning. They have been convinced that baptism should only be administered to those who have repented of their sins and professed a faith in Jesus Christ, and they have insisted that the proper method of administering the rite is by immersion in water. Both these concerns have dominated Baptist writings on baptism until recent years. This was understandable, as a minority movement will need to use bold language to justify its separation from the rest of the Church over such matters. Much of the polemic has been founded on what Baptists have believed to be the requirements of Scripture. Yet often debate has not developed into dialogue because the various parties have handled Scripture differently. Despite recent ecumenical dialogue, differences of theology and practice remain, and in this chapter we shall explore some of the theology embodied in the baptism of believers.

Further ironies complicate the distinctive Baptist witness. For example, Baptists are not the only group within world Christianity to practise the baptism of believers only. Many evangelical and Pentecostal groups share this practice and this is arguably evidence that their witness over the centuries has been heard and increasingly shared by others. If others share their practice of baptism, what makes Baptists distinctive? On the one hand, the answer to this question has to be sought away from baptism, particularly in the area of ecclesiology. Baptists are distinct from other evangelical groups by the way in which they are church. (After all, there are many denominations which share the practice of infant baptism but which are distinguishable from one another for other reasons.) On the other hand, Baptist distinctiveness can indeed be located in the practice of baptism because its interaction with various aspects of the life and mission of a church leads to subtle changes of emphasis. For example, a commitment to baptism as the baptism of believers has ensured a continuing emphasis on evangelism and discipleship. But before we explore these meanings, we must clarify the practice of baptism among Baptists and sketch its development and explanation.

The Practice of the Baptism of Believers

All parts of the Christian Church will, from time to time, baptize those who have come to conscious faith. Often this will be in a missionary context where the person has not been raised in a Christian setting and has therefore not previously been baptized. What makes Baptists, and other baptistic groups, distinct is their radical rejection of infant baptism as an acceptable or appropriate practice of the Church.

This rejection of infant baptism is crucial to understanding the Baptist place in the wider Church. It provided the basis for separation from others in the seventeenth century and it remains a crucial factor in the relationship of Baptists to other Christians in the contemporary ecumenical scene. Baptists remain out of step and even those with strong ecumenical commitment recognize the baptismal divide must be addressed if progress is to be made in other areas.[2] For example, Baptists continue to be troubled by talk of 'common baptism' as the basis for future unity or increased ecumenical convergence.

From the perspective of liturgical theology, the problem of 'common baptism' language is particularly acute. Because liturgical practices embody particular theologies we should expound a theology of baptism from a study of the way in which baptism is practised. Such an inductive approach is likely to lead to a range of theologies of baptism. For many, this will simply be a difference of emphasis. Not so for Baptists, for the rejection of infant baptism is a fault line which results in such different baptismal practices that the theologies which are embodied on either side of that fault line will be quite different.

A study of key ecumenical texts suggests that this is not widely acknowledged. For example, the historic Lima document, *Baptism, Eucharist and Ministry*,[3] begins the section on baptism with a scriptural exposition of the meaning of baptism and follows this with a discussion of the various denominational practices of baptism. Nowhere is there an exposition of the theology embodied in these various practices. This has encouraged talk of 'one baptism' and can lead to a lack of ecumenical listening. It can also lead to the questionable view that baptism can be used as a *means* towards greater ecumenical recognition, rather than an ecumenical challenge which itself needs to be faced.[4] In contrast, this chapter will take the inductive route from practice to theology, for it is primarily an exercise in liturgical theology rather than a faith and order discussion. So what do Baptists do when they baptize – and what does it mean?

The Development of the Baptism of Believers

The early Baptists wanted to reorder the Church on scriptural principles, and this biblicism underlay their attempt to explain and practise baptism in a way which was consistent with their reading of the New Testament. We can identify at least three historical and theological stages in the journey from membership of the established church to a full Baptist position:

1 Separation from the established church in order to form a society of believers.
2 Separation from other such societies in the belief that true baptism is the baptism of believers only.
3 Belief that the mode of baptism should be by immersion.

This process was true for both the General and the Particular Baptists as they separated from other separatist groups. Smyth and Helwys's congregation was distinct by 1608 when, on their emigration, they failed to join with other congregations in Holland. Similarly, the first Particular Baptists, who left Henry Jacob's Separatist congregation in the 1630s, did so over the question of who was eligible for baptism as well as their unease with a baptism received in the 'apostate' Church of England.[5] Each step was overtly a consequence of searching the Scriptures to find evidence for the nature of the Church, the subject and then the mode of baptism. Yet we can also see here a process whereby the nature of the Church was being clarified as a fellowship of believers.

The Fellowship of Believers

Henry Wheeler Robinson, in the early part of the twentieth century, argued that all forms of the rite of baptism administered to infants assume a passive role for the recipient. While reviewing the different interpretations of the baptism of infants in different churches, he asserted:

> The Baptist position is not simply a new phase of this succession of interpretations; it stands outside of them all as *the only baptism which is strictly and primarily an ethical act on the part of the baptized*. As such, it is the only type of baptism which is properly consistent with the logic of 'Separatism' and the whole idea of a separated Church of Believers.[6]

This interpretation may well go beyond the self-understanding of those first Baptist congregations. They came to a Baptist position as a direct result of reading the New Testament and believing that the only valid interpretation of its practice and commands was the baptism of those who professed faith in Christ. Yet this very reading was based upon the assumption that believers must be obedient to the divine ordinances and that this would therefore apply to baptism as well as to other matters concerning Christian living. Baptists have argued that in this they are simply being faithful to Scripture. In true Renaissance and Reformation method, they have returned to the original sources and critiqued and emended contemporary practices accordingly. They have jumped over the centuries of church tradition and doctrinal development and have appealed to a plain reading of the biblical material. This question of method is of vital importance in any ecumenical discussion and Baptists need to listen and reflect on questions of tradition and authority, even as they ask others to reflect on the Baptist concerns about the nature of the Church and the authority of Scripture.

Historically and theologically, the belief that the Church was com- posed of believers converged with the conviction that believers should be baptized according to New Testament teaching. The mode of entry to the Church became an expression of the nature of the Church – a community obedient to Scripture, comprising those who, after repentance and the response of faith, choose to follow Jesus Christ. Wheeler Robinson con- tinued:

> The Baptist stands or falls by his [*sic*] conception of what the Church is; his plea for believers' baptism becomes a mere archaeological idiosyncrasy, if it be not the expression of the fundamental constitution of the Church. We become members of the living Body of Christ by being consciously and voluntarily baptized in the Spirit of Christ – a baptism to which witness is borne by the evidence of moral purpose and character as the fruit of the Spirit.[7]

We have already noted that much Baptist polemic has been concerned with *who* should be baptized and *how* they should be baptized, rather than with theological meaning. Yet sometimes these arguments over the form of baptism have led to reflections on the purpose and meaning of the rite.

Baptism and Scripture

As early as 1611 Thomas Helwys wrote, 'That Baptisme or washing with Water, is the outward manifestacion off dieing unto sinn, and walkeing in newnes off life. Roman. 6.2, 3, 4. And therefore in no wise apperteyneth to infants.'[8] It was important for the writers of the 1644

Particular Baptist confession to designate baptism as an ordinance. They had recently taken the serious step of 're-baptizing' their members, but still wanted to affirm as much common ground as possible with those Independents who suspected them of ecclesiastical and sacramental anarchy.[9] Therefore they claimed to be faithful to the New Testament: 'That Baptisme is an Ordinance of the new Testament, given by Christ, to be dispensed onely[10] upon persons professing faith, or that are Disciples, or taught, who upon a profession of faith, ought to be baptized.'[11] This claim was consistently made through the confessions of the seventeenth century. The 1656 confession claimed, 'It is the duty of every man and woman, that have repented from dead works, and have faith towards God, to be baptized, that is dipped or buried under the water . . .'[12] The word 'duty' alerts us to the theme of obedience. Indeed, this obedience is not only to Scripture but to the Christ who said 'Go and baptize'.[13] Obedience to the command had an internal meaning which reflected and nourished a distinctive spirituality.

This can be illustrated by comparing the Particular Baptist *Second London Confession* of 1677/89[14] with the corresponding sections in the *Westminster Confession*.[15] In many places the Baptist document follows the text of the *Westminster Confession* verbatim, but there are nonetheless significant differences.

There is no mention in the Baptist confession that baptism can only be administered once. This was not an encouragement to repeated administration, but a reflection of the historical reality that many who espoused the Baptist cause did so having been brought up within a different church. Their baptism as believers was, and remains today, viewed by other churches as a re-baptism. However, those early Baptists did not regard the previous rites they would have received as infants as true baptism, because they understood baptism to be ordained in the New Testament as the baptism of believers. Their own baptism, therefore, would not have been seen by them as re-baptism but as a first baptism.

Naturally, the Baptist document contradicts the Westminster text over who may be baptized – which in turn probably reflects a reaction to the growing Baptist voice of the 1640s. While the Baptist confession does not repeat the explanation of baptism as a means of admission into the Church, other references to the Church speak of it comprising members who are 'visibly manifesting and evidencing (in their profession and walking) their obedience unto the call of Christ' and are 'in professed subjection to the ordinances of the Gospel'.[16] While baptism may not have been seen as a rite of admission, it was seen as a necessary prerequisite for membership and obedient discipleship. Dipping is advocated not only as the mode demonstrated in Scripture,[17] but as an eloquent sign of the gospel.

There is, in addition, a greater subjectivity in the Baptist text than in its Westminster precursor. In the earlier text, baptism is 'a sign and seal of the covenant of grace', whereas the Baptist statement portrays it as, for the one baptized, 'a sign of his fellowship with him [Jesus Christ], in his death, and resurrection'. In fellowship with Christ, the believer repents as well as trusts – for the baptism of believers is perceived to express more adequately the dual response of repentance and faith than a rite administered to infants who, though born in sin, are not able to either repent or exercise faith. It is intriguing that the Baptists changed the Westminster phrase 'to walk in newness of life' to the longer 'to live and walk in newness of life'.[18] Perhaps the words 'to live' were intended to convey a more dynamic way of life than one of mere obedience suggested by the moral term 'walk'. Here again is obedience in dialogue with devotion, as the nuance of this expanded phrase implies a life transformed into something new in which ethical obedience is the fruit of devotion.

Immersion

There are tantalizingly few descriptions of how people were baptized in the early period of Baptist history.[19] The first congregations continued the practice of sprinkling over the head, though the candidates were now adults. However, by the early 1640s the practice had developed to the total immersion of the candidate in water. The language of 'dipping' was soon common and rivers and ponds were the main places where water in abundance – and depth – was available. This inevitably made the practice very public and no doubt contributed to a climate in which heated public debates flourished. Through the eighteenth century, most baptisms continued to be held in the open air and the description from Cambridge at the beginning of this chapter provides a good account. Some London churches shared indoor baptismal facilities from the end of the seventeenth century, though baptisteries constructed in individual church buildings were not common until the last few decades of the eighteenth century.[20] Eventually, as more purpose-built Baptist meeting houses were built, so provision was made for baptisms which required plenty of water. Some rural chapels which were surrounded by a burial ground had baptisteries dug in the chapel grounds, with water diverted from a convenient stream by means of pipes and sluice gates. This offered an eloquent resonance from Romans 6.3, with candidates being buried with Christ amidst the graves of the community.

Urban chapels would be more likely to provide a baptistery, often with elaborate arrangements to safeguard the modesty of the candidates. Usually the baptistery was a tank placed under the dais in front of the central pulpit and was usually covered by flooring when not in use. This has remained the practice in Britain, though some modern buildings, revealing the influence of liturgical renewal, contain an open baptistery which is often in a prominent position.[21]

There is no clear picture of *how* the candidates were submerged. Contemporary practice is for the candidate to stand in waist-deep water side-ways on to the baptizer who supports them with an arm around the back of their waist while holding their clasped hands in front. Then, after the words, '*Name*, I baptize you in the name of the Father and of the Son and of the Holy Spirit', the candidate is pulled backwards into the water and as soon as they are completely submerged they are pulled back upright. Often they will descend to the pool from one set of steps and leave the pool via steps on the opposite side, so symbolizing a new beginning: 'Therefore we have been buried with him by baptism into death, so that, just as Christ was raised from the dead by the glory of the Father, so we too might walk in newness of life' (Romans 6.4). We cannot know whether these actions represent an early practice or a later development. Perhaps in a river or pond the candidate might have been led out to fairly deep water and their head simply lowered at the appropriate time. What has been important is that the person is submerged, though pastoral exceptions on medical grounds are not unusual.

Baptism as Worship

Baptists differ in their view of how baptism relates to church membership. Is baptism an *initiation* into the Church or a *prerequisite* before a person may be admitted to the membership of a local congregation?

Those who view baptism as a prerequisite for membership see no need to associate the rite with the reception of the baptized person into church membership. The emphasis is on baptism as a testimony to the gospel of Christ, the faith of the candidate and their obedience in following the command and example of Jesus Christ. The notion of ordinance, as distinct from sacrament, is particularly strong in this view. What matters is that the person is obedient.[22] At some point in the future they may formally join a church, but will not necessarily do so.

The practice which reflects and embodies these views is one in which persons are baptized without then being received into the membership of a local church. Such a service will usually be called a 'baptismal service' and will include the preaching and the baptism. A simple order for such a service may look like this:

Opening worship
Prayer
Scripture reading
Sermon
Hymn
Baptism
  Introduction
  Testimonies of the candidates
  Baptism
  Appeal to others in the congregation to respond in faith to the
  gospel
 Closing hymn
 Benediction

Some churches will baptize immediately those who come forward and offer themselves for baptism. Others will counsel them and baptize them on a future occasion after due preparation. In this service there is a strong emphasis on evangelism through the proclamation of the gospel and the challenge of the faith of new believers. This challenge is often embodied not only in the moving witness of the baptism itself, but in the candidates' account of their own faith journey. Just as normally these churches will probably see the preaching as the climax of a regular service, so now baptism is regarded as such a climax. In both cases the hope is that the challenge at the close of a service will lead to members of the congregation making a commitment to accept Jesus Christ as their own personal Saviour and Lord.

    Yet it would be unfair to see in this liturgical event a wholly subjective approach to Christian believing. The testimonies are an incarnation of the gospel in which truth about God is communicated through an account of God's working on the lives of those testifying. This is a sharing of the experience of God's grace. The focus is on a God who in love seeks those who are lost and offers them a way to return to fellowship, and baptism is presented as the outward, communal expression of that inward journey of repentance and trust which is the road that every believer must travel.

    In contrast to all this, there is a sacramental approach which regards baptism as initiation into the Body of Christ. This implies an ecclesiology in which it is incomprehensible to see someone as a Christian and not recognize their belonging to the Christian Church. Consequently, a person will be welcomed into membership either during the Lord's Supper in the same service or at the next monthly communion service. This is the practice commended by the Doctrine and Worship Committee of the Baptist Union of Great Britain. It is the majority practice of the churches of the union[23] and the practice which will be commended in what follows.

Such a view of baptism, in which baptism into Christ is also initiation into the Body of Christ, may take one of two forms. Either a baptismal service will be held after the pattern of that which has just been outlined above, though the baptism may come before rather than after the preaching,[24] or there will be a service in which the Lord's Supper is also included and in which the newly baptized are received as members of the local congregation. Such a baptismal service with the Supper might proceed as follows:

Opening worship
Reading
Sermon
Hymn
Baptism
   Introduction
   Questions to the candidates (and sometimes testimonies)
   Prayer
   Baptism
Leader and newly baptized leave to change their clothing
Hymn
Prayers of response and intercession
Offering
   Leader and newly baptized re-enter. The newly baptized may bring bread and wine to the table which can be received as the offering is brought forward
Invitation to the Lord's Supper
Hymn
Prayer of approach, and/or sharing of the peace
Reception into membership
   Questions to the newly baptized and church members
   Right hand of fellowship
   Laying on of hands *(These two items may be reversed.)*
Communion
Hymn
Dismissal and blessing[25]

Here baptism is clearly part of a process of initiation. The candidates, accompanied by the congregation as witnesses and companions, undertake a journey which begins with praise, and continues through the reading and preaching of God's saving acts. Then they confess their faith and are baptized. As the congregation continues in prayer, the candidates change and dress, preparing themselves for a new life within the community of God's people. They return to the sanctuary bearing the bread and wine for the feast of communion and are welcomed into membership. They receive the laying on of hands for blessing and commissioning as the work of the Spirit is made clear in bringing them to faith, encountering them in baptism and enabling them for witness and service. They take their place for communion with Christ and with his people as bread and wine are shared. Along with the rest of the congregation they are then sent out into the world as witnesses and servants of the gospel.

The laying on of hands is a practice which had fallen into disuse but which is now being re-introduced quite widely. In Britain, it was commended in the official worship manual *Order and Prayers for Christian Worship*,[26] though its widespread adoption has been more recently encouraged by the Charismatic movement, with its common use of the laying on of hands to accompany prayer for individuals. In *Patterns and Prayers for Christian Worship* (1991) both of the proposed baptismal patterns included the practice, and in 1997 nearly 40 per cent of churches claimed to include this practice in a baptismal service.[27] Many early General Baptists practised the laying on of hands, both in association with baptism, where its emphasis may well have been one of commissioning, and as a regular preliminary to open worship, where the emphasis would have been one of invocation of the Spirit to prompt and inspire the worshippers. By the time the practice was discontinued early in the eighteenth century, there had been disputes between churches as to whether it was a necessary component of baptism and thus an essential precondition of membership.[28]

Before we explore the meaning of baptism in worship, we should note an extreme view which does not regard baptism as worship at all, at least, not in its corporate, ecclesial meaning. John Gill, one of the leading proponents of High Calvinism in London in the mid-eighteenth century, strongly defended baptism as an ordinance which was binding on all believers.[29] Yet he argued that it 'is not a church ordinance':

> I mean it is not an ordinance administered in the church, but out of it, and in order to admission into it, and communion with it; it is preparatory to it, and a qualification for it; it does not make a person a member of a church, or admit

him into a visible church; persons must first be baptized, and then added to the church . . . a church has nothing to do with the baptism of any, but to be satisfied they are baptized before they are admitted into Communion with it.[30]

Ernest Payne claimed that each generation had included some who were ready to treat baptism as 'the divinely ordained means of entry into the visible church', as well as others who stressed its individual significance, citing Gill as an example of the latter.[31] Gill clearly saw no place for baptism within the worship of the Church. While the view of baptism as a prerequisite for membership has continued in some quarters, Gill's individualistic emphasis has been tempered by the now universal practice of including baptism in the regular worship of local congregations, even when that worship is sometimes outside the church building for the purpose of public witness. So even when it is not followed by reception into membership, baptism is an action of the Christian community and it is to a discussion of what meaning it holds for that community that we now turn.

Sacrament or Ordinance?

Chapter 9 contained a brief discussion of Baptist attitudes to the language of sacrament as a way of interpreting baptism and the Lord's Supper. Much of the writing on baptism in recent decades has been from a sacramental perspective.[32] Some, especially those who have had close ecumenical relations, find sacramental language provides a rich vocabulary for expressing the layers of meaning which they perceive in the practice of baptism. Others are cautious, however, concerned about what they see as the danger of ritual to claim for human action what should be wholly subject to the sovereignty of God.[33] Often this concern has been focused in a rejection of the phrase *ex opere operato*. While this rejection has assumed a more mechanical interpretation than has usually been offered by Catholic exponents, the concern has been clear. Salvation is the work of God and cannot be manipulated by human actions, and should not be controlled by ecclesiastical authorities. This caution embodies a concern for the freedom of God and a democratic spirituality which prizes the direct access of the believer to God through Christ.

These concerns, however, need not preclude a sacramental interpretation of baptism in which the Church, the candidate and God may all be seen as partners. Baptists have historically presented baptism as an action of the candidate in response to the gospel. At times, they have been criticized for presenting baptism as a human work rather than as a place of divine grace. This criticism is misplaced, because they have not located salvation in the act of baptism but in God's saving action in the cross and resurrection of Jesus Christ and in the operation of the Holy Spirit in the life of the Christian. However, Baptists need to pay increased attention to the other partners in this 'rendezvous of grace'.[34] What is it that the Church does as it gathers for worship and baptizes men and women in the name of the triune God? And what is God doing in all this? Whether or not the word 'sacrament' is used in answer to these questions, the very questions lead to theological reflections which other parts of the Church would normally describe as 'sacramental theology'.

Testimony or Initiation?

We have already noted the diversity of views among Baptists concerning the relationship of baptism to membership of the Church. That membership is expressed in the membership of a local congregation. The gathered nature of Baptist ecclesiology means that to be a church member requires enrolment in a local society of believers. Membership is incarnate. Most Baptists are agreed that baptism is a prerequisite for such membership, though there are historical and ecumenical variations which will be discussed below.

Doctrinal differences continue: is baptism *initiation* into the Church, or is it a simply a duty of the individual Christian and a *prerequisite* for membership? The rise of evangelicalism accentuated the view that baptism testifies not only to the gospel of Christ but also to the personal faith of the candidate. But does baptism make someone a member of the Church? This is where questions of diversity impinge upon theological questions about what is theologically coherent and what is good and best practice. Official British Baptist publications through the latter parts of the twentieth century have urged a necessary link between baptism and membership.[35]

One modern prayer, suggested for use immediately before baptism, concludes:

> Send your Holy Spirit that this baptism may be for your servants a union with Christ in his death and resurrection that, as Christ was raised from death through the glory of the Father, *they* also might live new *lives*. Send your Holy Spirit anew upon *them* that *they* may be brought into the fellowship of the Body of Christ and may grow in Christ's likeness.

Baptists have a distinctive ecclesiology to present to the wider Church, a contribution which would be strengthened, not weakened, by the inclusion of liturgical and sacramental perspectives. For example, the local nature of the Church is enhanced when we see it constituted in the gathering for worship and as it crowds around the pool to celebrate the gospel of Jesus Christ which has been made incarnate in the life of the community. Before God, the Church celebrates what God has already done. That is why baptism is the baptism of believers, the baptism of those who have already received the saving grace of God. But before God, the Christian community also invokes the powerful presence of its creator and redeemer: here, in the midst of the Christian community God is invited to act. This action is not dependent on ecclesiastical authority, but the faithful preaching of the gospel and the open reception of the work of the Spirit. This is Church. Indeed, this is Church as local community – not self-electing and consumer driven – but gathered by God. If baptism is viewed as a sacrament of community, then all that is expressed and symbolized in baptism is shown to be a statement about the nature of the Church as the community of the baptized.

Other questions remain. What are Baptists doing when they practise an open membership which welcomes other Christians? On what basis do those Christians become part of this community and what significance is afforded their own baptism as infants? What of the ecumenical offence which is caused by the so-called re-baptism of those who seek to be obedient to their understanding of the requirements of Scripture? What grounds for convergence is there between Baptist convictions concerning baptism and the testimony of the rest of the Christian Church? These questions are beyond the scope of this study, which is concerned with baptism as worship. We now turn, therefore, to the values which are evident in this worship and which are embodied in the baptism of believers.

The Spirituality of Baptism

Baptist worship is worship in community, a life together formed and enlivened by the interaction of reading Scripture and an openness to God. These values have a momentum which moves beyond worship towards the horizon of God's Kingdom and a concern for mission. Each is evident in baptism as practised by Baptists and it is to the spirituality of this practice that we now turn.[36]

Go and Baptize: Attention to Scripture

We have already seen how an attention to Scripture played a crucial role in the developing of a Baptist position in the seventeenth century and in the continuing persistence of this minority group. Baptists believed they were being obedient to God, and that the majority of Christians were being, in this matter at least, disobedient to the clear testimony of Scripture.[37] This stance depended, of course, on a particular approach to the authority of Scripture where the plain meaning took priority over the nuances of later interpretation in the tradition and doctrinal development of the Church.

Baptists and other Free Churches followed the Calvinist route of only permitting in worship that which could be regarded as a command or an example of Scripture and a number of practices came to be regarded as ordinances. However, the Lord's Supper and baptism have been regarded as having unique authority as practices explicitly commanded by Jesus Christ, commands which continue to be binding on his followers.[38]

For baptism, the dominical command is located in the closing verses of Matthew's Gospel where Jesus commissioned the eleven disciples to go and make disciples of all the nations. Baptists increasingly related baptism to evangelism, conversion and the response of faith. At the beginning, however, it was seen as a matter of obedience. How could a church be holy if it failed to obey the command of Jesus Christ?

After the great commission, Baptists have tended to turn to the accounts of the early Church and especially Acts 2.38, where again the link with evangelism is explicit. After the preaching of Peter on the day of Pentecost the crowd asks him what they should do in response to his presentation of Jesus as the Messiah who has been vindicated by God through the resurrection. His reply is, 'Repent, and be baptized every one of you in the name of Jesus Christ so that your sins may be forgiven.' Thus Baptists have argued that baptism requires a similar response in all those who are to pass through the waters. While this argument requires various interpretative assumptions,[39] it is reinforced by the theology of such passages as Romans 6.3, where the rite is seen to symbolize the dying of the old, sinful self.

Beyond these scriptural gleanings, the story of Jesus's own baptism ought to be more central in Baptist expositions than has sometimes been the case. The theme of burial has tended to be more dominant than the theme of following, and may reflect a greater emphasis, in some circles, on the Pauline themes of atonement and forgiveness rather than on the discipleship theme of the Gospels.[40]

Yet Scripture has provided the narrative framework for the practice of baptism among Baptists, as well as the metaphorical and theological context within which it has been interpreted. This is less explicit for baptism than for the Lord's Supper, where the words of institution form a part of the rite. At the table, Paul's account in 1 Corinthians 11.23–6 or one of the Gospel narratives is used either as the introduction to the eucharistic meal or as a narrative framework which encompasses it. While the liturgical celebration of baptism may not be as structured as this, it will probably include Scripture readings, or at least an introduction which will base the practice in a number of Scripture passages such as the baptism of Jesus, the great commission, Peter's dialogue with the crowd on the day of Pentecost, or the death, burial and resurrection motif of Romans 6.[41] So the account of a baptismal service in Cambridgeshire in 1767, which opens this chapter, recounts how the person administering the baptisms 'spoke about ten minutes on the subject' at the waterside before the baptisms, and recent manuals have both included introductions which explain the meaning of the rite, and referred to stories and explanations in the New Testament.[42]

Devotion: The Baptism of Disciples

Baptists have normally seen faith as more than a matter of doctrinal assent. They have looked for evidence of experiential faith, a change of lifestyle and a transformation of values indicative of a work of God in the life of the believer. For this reason, it may be helpful to talk not of the baptism of *believers* so much as the baptism of *disciples*.[43] The word 'disciple' makes more explicit an emphasis on obedient faith and the desire to follow Jesus Christ, and baptism can then be seen as an embodiment of such discipleship. Indeed, the early emphasis on baptism as an ordinance, and the requirement that faithful followers should be obedient in presenting themselves for baptism, make this clear. So the *baptism of disciples* may be seen as a challenge to believers to obey the baptismal command of Christ (Matthew 28.19) and to obey the example of Christ (Mark 1.9 and parallels). To see baptism in terms of discipleship also encourages a view of baptism as the beginning of a life which is lived communally in relationship with Jesus Christ. After union with his death and resurrection (Romans 6.3f.), the new disciple follows Christ in fellowship with other disciples, who together form the Body of Christ.

Neither the *Westminster Confession* nor the Baptist confessions saw baptism as conferring salvation, as this was a gift of God to all those subject to the divine election. While there was believed to be an efficacy of grace in baptism, neither the administrator nor the subject of baptism could force the divine hand through the ritual action. The grace conferred is a gift of the Holy Spirit and, in the case of Baptists, assumes the presence already of saving faith – as was clearly stated in the 1656 *Somerset Confession*:

> THAT in admitting of members into the church of Christ, it is the duty of the church, and ministers whom it concerns, in faithfulness to God, that they be careful they receive none but such as do make forth evident demonstration of the new birth, and the work of faith with power.[44]

The faith which should be evident prior to baptism is not simply an assent to creeds or even a holy and moral lifestyle. 'Evident demonstration of the new birth, and the work of faith with power' suggests a change in the person which can best be described in terms of conversion, or evidence of the Spirit of God changing the quality of the person's life. Two years earlier, the same association of churches which had produced the 1656 confession met in Taunton. The records of the meeting include queries submitted by the churches and the response of the assembled company, including:

> Query 4. Whether any are to be received into the church of Christ only upon a bare confession of Christ being come in the flesh and assenting to the doctrine and order laid down by him?
> Answer: they may not be admitted in such terms without a declaration of an experimental work of the Spirit upon the heart, through the word of the Gospel and suitable to it, being attended with evident tokens of conversion, to the satisfaction of the administrator and brethren or church concerned in it, Acts 8.37, Rom. 10.9f., Acts 19.18, Luke 6.44f., Matt. 3.7f.[45]

We have seen how Baptist worship should be understood within a framework of personal faith and the expectation of a living encounter with God. Such an experiential spirituality can also be seen in this early association meeting where membership of the Church requires evidence 'of an experimental work of the Spirit upon the heart', together with 'evident tokens of conversion'. Here is a dynamic view of the Church where its members are, even at the point of entry, testimonies to the creative work of the Spirit. The 1644 confession had been at pains to point out that such faith is not a human work, but a gift of God to the sinner who is 'dead in sinnes and trespasses'. Yet saving faith becomes possible because the transformation of the sinner's life is brought about 'by no lesse power, than that which raised Christ from dead'.[46]

The expectation that such faith should *precede* baptism and membership has certain consequences for the understanding of baptism and the nature of the Church. Both Particular and General Baptists saw salvation as the gracious work of God operating in the believer's life.[47] Those who repented and believed would still need to be faithful to the divine ordinances – they would need to obey the command of Christ and be baptized and enter into a covenant relationship with others to form a society of saints, a visible manifestation of Christ's Kingdom.

Baptism was therefore seen as a sign of that which was already accomplished in the person's life, an act of obedience and the conferring of blessing through a closer fellowship with Christ, made possible by that very obedience and by an identification with Christ in his death, burial and resurrection. Again we can see the interaction of personal faith and a willingness to be obedient.

For the Church, this would mean that the ecclesial body was a fellowship of those who had already been brought to life by the work of God, through repentance and faith. Members of the Church were viewed, not as passive recipients of ecclesiastical grace, but as active recipients of divine grace who had banded together to be faithful followers of Christ, obedient to his laws and available to God as instruments of his purposes.[48]

The Church as Community: The Fellowship of Baptized Believers

Baptists view the Church as a fellowship of believers. It is 'the community of the baptized', a community marked by an obedience to Scripture and a valuing of personal faith.

The pastoral process which surrounds the practice of baptism in most local churches today illustrates how baptism can be a sign of the communal nature of the Church.[49] After a person has come to faith they will ask for baptism and church membership. Usually the church meeting will appoint two representatives to visit and interview the person, in order to discern the living reality of their faith and to establish that they understand what they are doing, and that they accept the duties and privilege of church membership. Those visited will normally have attended preparation classes to help them understand much of this, though the visitors would require some evidence of personal faith, not simply an understanding of the issues. The visitors will then report to the church meeting, which would decide on the appropriateness of baptism and membership.[50] Provided the outcome of the meeting is positive, the

person is baptized in a Sunday service and usually received into membership during the next celebration of the Lord's Supper, whether at the
close of that service or on the next appointed day.[51] Though not uni-
versally followed, this pattern of preparation for baptism and reception
into membership was accepted practice for the majority of Baptist
churches in the 1996 survey.[52]

There is considerable diversity among Baptists concerning the relationship between baptism and church membership. On the one hand,
there are churches which baptize without necessarily receiving people
into membership and, on the other, there are churches which admit
people into membership who have not been baptized as believers. The
latter practice reflects a long tradition within English Baptist church life,
in which an openness of spirit has enabled some local churches to admit
to membership both those baptized as believers and also those who have
been members in good standing of other churches. This is not an acceptance of infant baptism, but an acceptance of fellow Christians who give
evidence of faith and demonstrate a life of discipleship.[53] Open membership churches now represent a majority within the Union and, in some,
this openness has resulted in some people being admitted to membership
without any form of baptism. However, official publications have criticized this practice and have called for one which reflects what they see as
the 'true' meaning of baptism – incorporation into the Body of Christ. So
a recent report of the Baptist Union's Doctrine and Worship Committee
asserted:

> this baptismal beginning will include initiation as a member of the whole
> Church of Christ, since the Church is inseparable from the 'Body of Christ'
> into which the person has been baptized (1 Cor. 12.12–13). *There should thus
> be no baptism without membership in a church which is a local manifestation
> of the universal Body of Christ.*[54]

The twentieth century has seen an increasing emphasis on baptism as the
means of entry into the Church, though this process is completed by
reception with 'the right hand of fellowship' and sometimes the laying on
of hands.[55] A number of studies by Baptists have interpreted baptism as
initiation,[56] and the logic of linking a believer church and the baptism of
believers has been stressed[57] alongside the use of historical precedent and
scriptural argument. So, after an exposition of various scriptural themes,
Morris West argued:

> Our Baptist forefathers, who drew up the 1677 Confession . . . speak of the
> baptized believer being engrafted into Christ. It is fairly clear that for them this

signified linking with the fellowship of the Church, as well as appropriating the benefits of Christ's life, death and resurrection.

In the light of all this we need to ask ourselves seriously whether baptism unrelated to church membership is either scriptural, or according to Baptist History and Principles.[58]

Just as the baptism of believers is an expression of the Church as a fellowship of believers, so the baptism of believers also functions as an embodiment of an Evangelical understanding of the Christian life and of the Church. Wheeler Robinson suggested:

The baptism of believers by immersion has not only emphasised conscious faith as essential to the Church, but it has also, by its symbolism, constantly recalled men to the foundation of the Gospel in history, the death and the resurrection of Jesus Christ, which, as Paul argued, are represented in the act of the believer's immersion and his rising from the waters of baptism. That act, constantly repeated before the eyes of Baptists, has taken the place of any formal creed, and helped to keep them an evangelical Church, without any authoritarian confession of faith. Like the Lord's Supper, it has preached the Lord's death until He come, whilst leaving believers free, in successive generations, to interpret afresh the meaning of that redemptive death.[59]

As well as an act of obedience on the part of the individual believer, baptism is seen here as having an ecclesial function. It is not only directed towards the believer as incorporation into the Body of Christ, but is also directed reflexively back to the Church itself. In baptism the Church is addressed, as the mystery of salvation in Christ is represented and as the nature of the Christian life as immersion into Christ is re-enacted. Pastorally, this often results in the rededication of some in the congregation who relive their own baptism through the baptism of another. It may also result in the decisive act of someone coming to faith through hearing the testimony of God's grace in another's life and through witnessing it in their baptism.

The Church is patterned after Christ and its identity as a gospel community is made clear and made possible in baptism. The baptism of Jesus is not only his immersion in the waters of the Jordan, but his immersion in the mission of God and his immersion in death (Mark 10.38 and Luke 12.50). Increasingly, baptism is being seen in the wider Church as a symbol of the whole of the Christian life.[60] Christians are therefore called to 'live out their baptism', and such a phrase has both devotional and ethical dimensions. Baptism embodies both the believer's relationship with Jesus Christ and a readiness to bear costly witness to Christ. Here immersion eloquently points to the waters of chaos which can threaten not only the Kingdom of God but those who are its messengers and citizens.[61] But baptism includes the lifting from this chaotic flood, as Christ was raised from the tomb, and points to the final victory which the Church proclaims and in the hope of which it lives.

Concern for the Kingdom: To the End of the Age

Scripture shapes baptism through its narratives and metaphors which give a form to fellowship with Jesus Christ. The Christian Scriptures are the Word of God because they testify to *the* Word of God made flesh in Jesus of Nazareth. Baptism is an immersion into the life, death and resurrection of that eternal Word of God uttered for the salvation of the world. Here is an *anamnesis* in which the baptism and burial of Jesus are re-enacted and shared by the new disciple. While Scripture operates in the act of remembering, this *anamnesis* is also an act of participation, as the disciple follows the example of Christ by being baptized and shares the cosmic drama of burial and resurrection. This is both the beginning of a new life and the basis for it.

Within four years of the adoption of immersion as the method of baptizing believers, its symbolism was being seen as a sign of the gospel. The 1644 confession stated:

> The way and manner of the dispensing of this Ordinance the Scripture holds out to be dipping or plunging the whole body under water: it being a signe, must answer the thing signified, which are these: first, the washing the whole soule in the bloud of Christ: secondly, that interest the Saints have in the death, buriall and resurrection; thirdly, together with a confirmation of our faith, that as certainly as the body is buried under water, and riseth againe, so certainly shall the bodies of the Saints be raised by the power of Christ, in the day of the resurrection, to reigne with Christ.[62]

Baptism presents the eschatological dimension of the Christian gospel. It symbolizes salvation and an eternal hope which is focused in the mission, cross and resurrection of Jesus Christ. But this future orientation is not only on a cosmic canvas: the metaphor of discipleship itself carries a future orientation. A disciple will be concerned to learn from the mentor, moving from ignorance to knowledge. The disciple will follow the master in a meaningful direction, away from the present to somewhere else, a citizen of the colony of heaven (Philippians 3.20).

Baptism offers a sacramental focus for mission. As the ordinance of repentance and faith, it is a means of responding to the gospel invitation to believe and follow Jesus Christ. Yet the very enactment of baptism is an evangelistic event through which further disciples come to faith. This kerygmatic function highlights the liturgical meaning of baptism not only for the one being baptized, but for the community of the Church and its guests.

Baptism also functions as a sacrament which defines the Church as a community, as well as a sacrament of initiation for the person being baptized. This community is called to be redeemed by Christ's death and resurrection, incorporated into his life by the work of the Holy Spirit. Communally and individually, all its members are called to follow Christ's example and observe Christ's commands. The baptism of believers enables and expresses the Church as a community of believers who are disciples of Jesus. Such an emphasis on personal response has sometimes been criticized by members of other traditions as an expression of 'faith as works', but that is to ignore the role that the doctrine of election and the role of the Holy Spirit play both in those early confessions of faith and in subsequent Baptist writings about faith. What we may say is that the baptism of believers has functioned as a part of the Church's proclamation of the gospel of Christ and has been a liturgical focus of the invitation to personal discipleship and a life of fellowship 'in Christ'.

Finally, baptism is immersion into the name of the Triune God, it is a sacrament of grace in which God is encountered and it is a sacrament of community in which the Trinitarian identity of the Church is expressed. Baptists claim to be scriptural in their *practice* of baptism, but the baptism of believers is also scriptural in its testimony to Christ and in its focus on the call to discipleship. It is a sacrament of response. While there have been periods when Baptists have over-emphasized this particular dimension, we should not ignore it in order to provide a corrective. As a divinely ordained means of human response to the saving work and call of Christ, baptism by immersion shows the character of that response to be one of whole-hearted consecration.[63] Obedience and devotion belong together.

Part 4

Liturgical Theology

11

The Community of Disciples

A Free Church Liturgical Theology

The church is the Lord's house; the materials of it are all his own. Every lively
stone in it is purchased with the price of the redeemer's blood, 'Ye are bought
with a price.' The Lord is the architect of this spiritual edifice. He prepares the
materials for it with his own gracious hands. Believers are the workmanship
of God, created in Christ Jesus unto good works. He has laid the foundation
of it, which therefore must be suitable, safe, and sure. The wonderful structure
is not erected on the sliding sand, but on the solid rock. Isaiah xxviii. 'Thus
saith the Lord God, behold I lay in Zion for a foundation a stone, a sure
foundation, &c.' 'Other foundations can no man lay than is laid, which is
Jesus Christ.' . . .

   Of this house, Jesus Christ is the only Lord and Governor; so that on this
account also it may be justly called his own house. He is the King in his holy
hill of Zion. The laws, the orders, and the ordinances of this house are all of
his appointment.

John Fawcett 1808[1]

What Christians believe is embodied in the things they say and do when
they gather for worship. In our study of worship in the Baptist community in Britain, we have explored some of the convictions of that
community – not only their beliefs about worship, but also about God
and the Church and the world. Where does this lead us and what shape
and content will we find in a liturgical theology which follows from this?

Worship as Theology

Every attempt to present the Christian faith is contextual, affected by the
stance of the writer and the needs of the situation. Similarly, liturgical
theology is contextual in that it reflects the concerns and the history of
the community upon which it is based. This chapter will attempt to draw
together the various strands that have emerged in our study in order to

offer a presentation of Christian faith. As such it reflects the experience of a particular community, yet it is an example of *Christian* believing and so should be recognizable not only to members of other Free Churches but to Christians from all traditions.

Free Church worship expresses certain beliefs held by the Free Church community and, at the same time, encourages that community in areas of shared meaning. Worship has a formational function, though the factors which create meaning and influence faith are themselves complex. The 'primary speech' of worship, nuanced and laden with metaphor, both expresses the community's faith and forms the worshippers in the Christian life. Yet when we have established the liturgical facts and begun to reflect on their meaning, the tasks of systematizing and testing still remain to be attempted. Are the affirmations consistent with one another and are they congruent with other expressions of Christian doctrine?

In Search of an Ordo

In Free Church worship there is considerable fluidity, but much of the 'text' of a service, in the sense of all that happens, as well as all that is said,[2] is lost once a service is over. Many Baptists are not overly concerned with the *sequence* of worship components, even when they are concerned for order in the sense of orderliness. This is a characteristic of much Free Church worship and means that we are not able to use the running order of services as a primary means of discovering embodied theology. The theology in this worship is not so much found in the sequencing of the liturgical units, as in the values which influence the *content* of those units and the *way* in which they are performed. For example, free prayer by its very freedom tells us things about the spirituality of the Free Church tradition. As a result, we have needed to use descriptions of worship, together with a number of commentaries on worship, in order to discover what the concerns of Baptists have been.[3] These concerns, or values, are the undergirding principles which shape the worship. They represent an *ordo*, a pattern in worship which expresses something fundamental about the patterns of faith of the community.

Four values have been tracked through prayer and preaching, singing and sacraments. First, we recognized the importance of Scripture and a concern for its perceived commands. This was not simply an intellectual acknowledgement of the authority of Scripture, but *attention* to it, a recognition that Scripture as an embodiment of the Word of God requires obedience and faith. This written word provides a framework of external requirements which should have authoritative weight in the forming of Christian faith and practice.

In tension with this heteronomic authority, there is the devotional concern for personal faith and piety. The experiential dimension of faith influences much Free Church worship. Our use of the word 'devotion' has implied a cluster of related themes. There is the theological concern that worship be inspired by the Holy Spirit, as well as the relational concern that worship be understood as a personal encounter with God, the affective concern that worship should be 'from the heart', and the ethical concern that personal behaviour be congruent with this devotion.

The dialectic relationship between obedience to scriptural commands and devotional 'heart worship' provides a dynamic field which gives a certain character to Baptist worship, though this will be shared by other Christian groups. In particular, the Evangelical nature of the Baptist community is both exemplified and nourished through the dialogical relationship between the requirements of God and the opening of the heart.

This interaction of Spirit and Scripture is located within a Christian community in which fellowship and relationships are highly valued. Such worship should not be understood as complete in itself, for it always needs to look towards the horizon of God's Kingdom. This future orientation is expressed in a variety of ways, from the concern for a saving relationship with Jesus Christ, to petitionary prayer for God's will to be done, to the missionary commitment which drives the Church to action and is expressed in worship through a concern for relevance, challenge and response. The activity of worship itself may embody Kingdom values and participate in, as well as testify to, the *missio Dei*, inviting a response to the gospel and participation in new life in Christ.

These values represent the underlying *ordo* of Baptist worship. However, as we have already claimed, because that worship is Christian worship they also bear some relationship to characteristics identified in other forms of Christian worship. For example, they bear a considerable likeness to the characteristics of the liturgy identified by Kevin Irwin. Within his own Roman Catholic context, Irwin argues that the 'theology of liturgy' contains three strands – the *epicletic,* the *anamnetic* and the *ecclesiological*[4] – three theological principles which underpin his understanding of liturgy. Worship is *anamnetic*, a remembering and making present of God's gracious and saving actions which bridges the past, present and future. The liturgy is *epicletic*, derived from and dependent upon the action and power of the Holy Spirit, and it is *ecclesiological*, as 'it is always an act of the Church's self-understanding and self-expression'.

The parallels between Irwin's typology and the four Baptist values of this study are striking. The worship of which Irwin speaks is eucharistic, though these principles do represent fundamental aspects of Christian worship in general.[5] We may compare his *anamnesis* with the Baptist attention to Scripture, *epiclesis* with the concern for devotion and the Spirit, and *ecclesiology* with the Baptist understanding of the Church as primarily manifested in the local congregation.

Where the present study has travelled further than Irwin, is in offering a fourth principle, namely, that worship is *eschatological*. Concern for the Kingdom rescues the community from settling in the present and locates hope, not in its own achievements, but in God's future. This eschatological dimension can, of course, be identified and substantiated within Irwin's own tradition, just as Schmemann and others have done for their own.[6] Indeed, Irwin speaks of how *anamnesis* bridges past, present and future in such a way as to encompass both our concern for attention to Scripture and an eschatological concern for the Kingdom. These similarities illustrate how the values evident in worship among Baptists, far from being unique to that worship, demonstrate its catholic nature.

These values also interact with one another, modifying and transforming their respective influences in an interaction which illuminates the study of this worship. *Attention to Scripture* provides the basis for various worship practices as well as providing the substantive content of preaching. It furnishes not only the narrative framework for the Lord's Supper and baptism, but also the metaphors which texture the congregation's understanding of those sacraments. However, Scripture also provides nourishment for personal faith and, as such, feeds the epicletic dimension of worship. In addition, it addresses the community by offering the promises which encourage a Kingdom hope.

Similarly, *devotion and openness to the Spirit* seek the Spirit's activity in the application of scriptural truth so that it might be the word of life. This devotion leads not only to a delight in God but to a strengthening of the bonds of affection within the fellowship of the Church – as well as a prizing of the Spirit and the gifts and fruit which build up the Church. Praying for one another, whether in worship, prayer meetings or personal devotions, is an important intersection of the devotional, communal and eschatological values and often features in lists of the duties of a church member.[7] Eschatologically, personal faith trusts a faithful God who will bring in the Kingdom, and is ready to testify to the work of God in a person's life and give an account of the hope in which they live.[8] Such faith will pray urgently for the coming Kingdom, as well as for the working of God's will in the present time.

A concern for the community of the Church will encourage collaboration in seeking the will of God through Bible study and church meeting. The fellowship of the Church is concerned for the well-being of its members, and this pastoral dimension will affect its worship, centred as it is around the preaching of Scripture. Devotionally, personal faith assists in building up the Church, as Christian devotional living is modelled in community and those young in the faith are nurtured and enabled to grow.

Eschatologically, a commitment to fellowship in the Church will transform the nature of the evangelistic task, with the local church seen as a missionary congregation.[9] Its worship will look outwards to a human community which is broken and divided by sin and it will pray for that wider world and seek to be a sign of the Kingdom to the world through its own fellowship life and worship.

This brief account of the ways in which the values interact in worship indicates something of the vitality of that worship. However, can this interaction be represented by an overarching theme? What is the heart of Baptist worship and is it recognizable to other Christians?

Jesus is Lord

The earliest distinctively Christian confessions were 'Jesus is the Christ' (i.e. Messiah, Mark 8.29) and 'Jesus is Lord' (1 Corinthians 12.3). Indeed, all distinctively Christian theology flows from this fundamental affirmation. In his discussion of revelation, Karl Barth argues that the doctrine of the Trinity arose out of the naming of Jesus as 'Lord'. He quotes Adolf von Harnack approvingly, 'Confession of Father, Son and Spirit is . . . the unfolding of the belief that Jesus is the Christ',[10] and suggests that this is historically accurate in terms of the development of dogma. His main argument, however, is that because God's self-revelation is as 'the Lord' – God's own self reveals God's very self – the designation of Jesus as Lord implies an immanent and not only an economic doctrine of the Trinity.[11] To acknowledge Jesus as 'Lord' is to move inexorably towards a Trinitarian doctrine of God, and the characteristics of worship will include this doctrinal richness and even feed it.[12]

This central Christian affirmation promises to offer a way of holding together the various themes we have explored, an integrating of the values embodied in Baptist worship. It also enables us to develop a liturgical theology which connects with other Free Churches and the wider Christian community. Both these aspects are important. The confession that 'Jesus is Lord' can provide us with a theological framework in which to place our reflections on worship, but it is also a central theological theme in its own right.

Yet the confession is more than simply a theological statement. To affirm the Lordship of Jesus will have consequences for authority, behaviour, communal identity and ways of viewing the world – consequences which resonate with each of our worship values. Clearly, Baptists have no monopoly on this theme[13] and it is a conviction which expresses something of what the Church believes about itself. This is true in relation to the Lordship of Christ – both liturgically, in that all prayer is offered 'through Jesus Christ our Lord', and ecclesiologically, in that the Church comprises the community of disciples of Jesus and is also designated 'the Body of Christ'.

Christian worship is distinguished from all other examples of worship in this regard – it is in the name of Jesus Christ. While this can be demonstrated from the experience of worship, its foundation is both in the proclamation of the Church, i.e. the gospel is the gospel of Jesus Christ (Mark 1.1), and in the promise of Jesus: 'For where two or three are gathered in my name, I am there among them' (Matthew 18.20). Barth claims that, 'there is a Christian community with its special distinction and service to the extent that Jesus Christ assembles it and is present with it by his Spirit.'[14]

Yet, because liturgical theology is the establishing and explaining of the faith of the Church through a study of its worship, this faith will normally have a concrete, denominational form.[15] Such a study of worship involves the study of particular worship in a particular community and provides a resource for speaking about the faith of that community as it is expressed in its worship. Thus the study of *Baptist* worship, for example, provides data for a Baptist theology, or at least some insights into the faith of the Baptist community. This is not as partisan as it might seem, for there is a long tradition of recognizing the contextual nature of the dogmatic task. Early in the nineteenth century, Friedrich Schleiermacher argued that, 'Dogmatic Theology is the science which systematises the doctrine prevalent in a Christian Church at a given time',[16] what James McClendon calls 'the convictions of a convictional community'.[17] In this view, theology becomes an exercise in explicating the faith of a specific community, rather than the attempt to establish generic

Christian doctrinal statements. While these need not be competing
theological agendas, the place of authority in the theological enterprise
becomes problematic the more complex its community of reference. This
is why working inductively from a particular denomination's worship
has its attractions.

We may see the values which have been identified in Baptist worship as
key aspects of what is important to many Baptists, what James
McClendon refers to as 'convictions'. He has also written on this subject
with James Smith and argued that convictions are usually held in
groups.[18] We have seen how these values, or convictions, interact to
constitute the faith and spirituality of the Baptist community as it is
expressed in worship. This interaction is what McClendon and Smith
speak of as 'a conviction set', and it is significant that they locate the
coherence of the set in the life of the community:

> the glue that binds convictions into a single set is their mutual relation to the
> life of the person or (normally) the life of the community in which he or she
> shares. The unity of conviction sets is the rough but vital unity of shared life,
> the narrative in which they cohere.[19]

But they also argue that these sets of convictions cohere in what they call
'a presiding conviction'. This notion provides a way of understanding
how the confession 'Jesus is Lord' can be seen as an overarching reality
which integrates the values embodied in worship.[20] Indeed, McClendon
elsewhere argues that,

> Christian doctrine – and Christian theology in its doctrinal mode – begins and
> ends with the confession, *Iesous Kyrios,* Jesus is Lord. But that confession
> by itself is a nonesuch, a word in an unknown tongue; uninterpreted it says
> nothing to us. To see its force we must see this ancient conviction tightly
> woven into a broad tapestry of other Christian convictions.[21]

We now understand how the Lordship of Jesus Christ, as 'a presiding
conviction', relates to worship. Even when most of the worship material
is drawn from the Old Testament, such as psalmody, Christian worship
is celebrated from this side of the resurrection of Jesus of Nazareth.
Christian prayers usually end with the formula, 'through Jesus Christ our
Lord', or variations on it. This is not a magical incantation guaranteed to
provide petitionary success, but a kerygmatic affirmation that Christian
worship is through the mediatory service of Jesus Christ and that the
liturgical assembly is an assembly which bears his character. Of course,
to speak of worship as being in the name of Jesus Christ is not to move

away from a Trinitarian interpretation of that same worship. Thomas's confession before the risen Christ, 'My Lord and my God', is significant in opening a new world for worship and for dogma (John 20.28). The followers of Jesus gather to worship the Christ-like God and their service is inspired by the Spirit of Jesus.

Churches of Christ

How does the theme of the Lordship of Jesus Christ find expression in the life and practice of Christian communities? And, as we have approached this study through the worship of Baptists in particular, how has that community given expression to this presiding conviction?

The introduction of the *First London Confession* of the Particular Baptists in 1644 began: 'To all that desire the lifting up of the name of the Lord Jesus in sinceritie, the poor despised churches of God in London send greeting, with prayers for their farther increase in the knowledge of Jesus Christ.' The revised edition of 1646 was even more Christocentric in its designation of the congregations: 'A Confession of faith of seven congregations or churches of Christ in London, which are commonly (but unjustly) called Anabaptists. Published for the vindication of the truth, and information of the ignorant . . .'[22] This focus on Jesus Christ is one which has remained a feature of Baptist spirituality. He is the mediator of God's salvation, the unique 'sonne of God the father, the brightnesse of his glory, the ingraven forme of his being . . . by whom he made the world, by whom he upholds and governs all the workes hee hath made'.[23] It is little wonder that the confession should end with the claim that the signatories 'desire to give unto God that which is Gods, and unto Cesar that which is Cesars'.[24] Later, the phrase 'the Crown rights of the Redeemer' was to become a way of explaining why Baptists and other dissenters found themselves in conflict with the civil authorities in a time of persecution, for Christ, as Lord of all, as well as Lord of the Church, requires the ultimate loyalty of his subjects and followers. Brian Haymes suggests, 'To say "Jesus is Lord" is to utter what can amount to subversive doctrine', and illustrates the point with examples from the history of Baptist dissent.[25]

The power of the theme has been continually reinforced by its devotional dimension. An elegy published on the death of Andrew Gifford junior describes this Christological devotion:

When'er he preache'd love stream'd thro' ev'ry text,
   And all his soul was on the Saviour fix'd . . .
O how he spake of Jesu's matchless charms,
   And welcom'd sinners to his tender arms.[26]

The acknowledgement of Christ's Lordship is related to the experience of Jesus as Saviour so that submission to his rule becomes a matter of love responding to costly love. This responsiveness is central to the idea of a covenant community in which there is an intersection of God's covenant with humanity and the covenant between the members of a gathered church. When Leonard Champion preached his presidential address before the Baptist Assembly in 1964, he was concerned about the current state of Baptist worship and exhorted the gathering to consider how worship might 'proclaim the power and presence of the living Christ' so that 'in our churches it is again an experience of the living Christ'.[27]

The *Declaration of Principle* of the Baptist Union, dating from 1938 in its final form, actually begins with the Lordship of Christ:

> That our Lord and Saviour, Jesus Christ, God manifest in the flesh, is the sole and absolute authority in all matters relating to faith and practice, as revealed in the Holy Scriptures, and that each Church has liberty, under the guidance of the Holy Spirit, to interpret and administer His laws.[28]

The Declaration is not a creed, designed for use in worship,[29] but an instrument of unity for the strengthening of ties between the churches. It is, in effect, an expression of spirituality because it combines belief with practice, placed as it is within the constitution of the Union, and as such offers us a further clue to what Baptists regard as important.

In a recent commentary on the Declaration, the then principals of the Baptist colleges in England offered this interpretation of the first clause: 'our final authority is a *person*, Jesus Christ. It is not a book, nor a creed, nor even a basis of faith – but a *person* in whom God expresses himself fully.'[30] The authors then linked this theme with the Barmen declaration in its defiance of the idolatry of 'German Christianity': 'Jesus Christ, as he is witnessed to in Holy Scripture, is the one Word of God whom we have to obey in life and death.' We have already noted that the theme of the Lordship of Christ needs to be understood from a wider perspective than simply a doctrinal one, for it is a theme which also carries existential and ontological meaning. To name Jesus Christ as Lord is to affirm not only that he is Lord of the Church and Lord of the universe, but that he requires obedience and trust from those who acknowledge his Lordship.

So how does this theme interact with the values we have identified? The *Declaration of Principle* is significant in the way in which it links Christ and Scripture. While Scripture testifies to Jesus Christ, he is affirmed as 'the sole and absolute authority in all matters relating to faith and practice'. Here is a Christological hermeneutic reminiscent of Barth's presentation of the three forms of 'the Word of God',[31] which subordinates the written word to the incarnate Word. There is also a Trinitarian dimension because, while churches have liberty of interpretation, that liberty is under the guidance of the Spirit.

The Lordship of Christ is particularly clear in the realm of personal devotion, and the Evangelical spirituality which runs through Baptist life is redolent with appeals to accept Christ. Christian worship, by its very Christian identity, will bear witness to the Lordship of Christ. If we were to study specific hymn texts, we would see that many place Jesus Christ at the devotional centre, and the baptism of believers is an intensely Christocentric event in which pneumatological dimensions have only more recently been affirmed.[32]

As the fellowship of believers, the Church gains its identity as a gathered Church, as *ekklesia*. Yet it does not gather itself but is called by Christ, who forms it into his Body. Here he exercises authority because those gathered are his disciples, a community of followers who not only trust him for salvation, but also offer themselves in his service.

But Jesus Christ is Lord of all, not only Lord of the Church. His Lordship is over all authorities and powers and he calls his people to live under that authority. The *Declaration of Principle* implicitly bears witness to the closing verses of the Gospel of Matthew in which the risen Christ claims all authority in heaven and on earth and then commissions the disciples:

> Go therefore and make disciples of all nations, baptizing them in the name of the Father and of the Son and of the Holy Spirit, teaching them to obey everything that I have commanded you. And remember, I am with you always, to the end of the age. (Matthew 28.18–20)[33]

This commission, which has been so important in Evangelical identity and in much Baptist church life, places the task of mission – work for the Kingdom – under the authority of Christ.[34] To name Jesus as Lord in worship has implications for the way in which the world is viewed,[35] as well as for the priorities which are acknowledged within the corporate witness of the Church.

Worship and the Vocation of the Church

The meaning of the statement 'Jesus Christ is Lord' will vary according to the arena in which it is confessed. We may speak *cosmically* of Christ being 'Lord of all things', or *politically* of Christ as being Lord over all earthly rulers, or *devotionally* of Jesus Christ as being the 'personal Lord and Saviour' of an individual believer, or *ecclesiologically* of Christ being Lord or Head of the Church.[36] We have seen how the Declaration of Principle affirms this Lordship over the Church by stating that, 'our Lord and Saviour Jesus Christ, God manifest in the flesh, is the sole and absolute authority in all matters pertaining to faith and practice'.

In the language of McClendon and Smith, this Lordship is the presiding conviction of the Baptist community, and should be the presiding conviction of any Christian community. It has both liturgical and ecclesiological dimensions. We noted in Chapter 1 that liturgical theologians have argued that worship embodies the nature of the Church. The Lutheran theologian Gordon Lathrop asserts that, 'To interpret the meaning of the assembly is to interpret the meaning of "church" and the church's faith.'[37] This stresses that worship is communal and is an action of the Church acting corporately.[38] Such activity of the Church in worship is both an expression of what the Church believes and an expression of what the Church is – and is becoming. Margaret M. Kelleher claims that 'liturgical action discloses the beliefs, values, commitments, relationships, memories and hopes which are constitutive of the church as a community', arguing that liturgy is an 'instrumental act of meaning', and that:

> Liturgy is not to be understood as an instrument for putting theories into practice. It is rather to be understood as an action in which the Christian collective subject performs its shared meaning, appropriates its common memory and hope and continually creates itself as a community of meaning. Liturgical praxis is an example of incarnate meaning.[39]

This collective action is an expression of what the Church is in its historical actuality, its humanness.

On the other hand, the liturgical action demonstrates the eschatological hope of what the Church seeks to be, while also providing a means by which the Church attempts to move towards such a future reality.[40] Again, according to von Allmen, 'by its worship the Church becomes itself, becomes conscious of itself, and confesses itself as a distinct entity. Worship thus allows the Church to emerge in its true nature.'[41]

In studying the Church and its worship, it is important to distinguish between the actuality of the Church's life and its vocation or aspirations. It is the eschatological perspective which enables us to see worship not only as an embodiment or expression of the Church as it is, but also as an instrument for its sanctification, a means by which it might, through grace, become more truly itself.[42] Geoffrey Wainwright remarks,

> For the Christian community, meaning is in the making: life is oriented towards God's ultimate purpose, and history-making is the way to the attainment of that purpose for both individuals and humanity as a whole; the most characteristic Christian rituals are therefore predominantly transformative in character, actions that signify divine grace coming to begin and continue the shaping of active recipients into the people God is calling them to become. Christian ritual is thus marked by eschatological tension.[43]

So if worship expresses what the Church is called to be, what do the themes we have identified say about the calling of the Church. What kind of community confesses that Jesus Christ is Lord and how do the values shape that community?

The Witness of the Community of Disciples

It should be clear that what is intended is not a partisan essay in denominational doctrine, but an approach to Christian theology through the testimony of a particular Christian community. The faith of this community is a witness to the faith of the Church of Jesus Christ, and one of the primary purposes of the seventeenth-century confessions was to explain the faith of the Baptist community to the wider Church, and to do this in such a way that the wider community would recognize in that faith the faith of the Church of God.[44] The Baptist Union of Great Britain was a founder member of the British Council of Churches and of the World Council of Churches,[45] and in 1948 its council declared that Baptists

> have always claimed to be part of the one holy catholic Church of our Lord Jesus Christ . . . In the worship, fellowship and witness of the one Church we know ourselves to be united in the communion of saints, not only with all believers upon earth, but also with those who have entered into life everlasting.[46]

Nonetheless, we need to ask if there is a distinctive Free Church voice, a mode of believing or a way of being the Church which is expressed in worship and in the values we have identified.

What kind of church do these values suggest and to what kind of faith does it bear witness? While other Christian communities might place the centre of their ecclesial understanding in a notion such as 'communion' or 'incorporation', a church which confesses the *Lordship* of Christ through the set of convictions we have identified may well be characterized by the notion of 'discipleship'. This is not to suggest an 'either/or' distinction between churches. Indeed, in the second edition of his *Models of Church*, the Roman Catholic Avery Dulles favoured the designation 'community of disciples'.[47]

Lordship implies obedience, following and discipleship. Baptist and Free Church disciples gather as *ekklesia* for worship, and they gather as *ekklesia* for mutual discernment and governance in church meeting. Here is communal discipleship in prayer and decision-making. In both these spheres the Church looks forward to the Kingdom of God. In prayer it prays for God to act, and in church meeting it seeks to align itself to the divine will. This is an eschatological community, a group of people bound together in Jesus Christ, attempting to be disciples. This is the Church and it cannot be understood apart from these perspectives. Its common life is the contemporary life of the disciple band following Jesus, and the contemporary life of the apostles sent out in mission with the promise of Jesus Christ to be with them always.

To speak of the Church as a community of disciples has a number of advantages. It presents the Church as a convictional community but, especially, it defines that community in terms of its relationship to Jesus Christ. That community therefore reads the gospels as members of the disciple band, learning from Jesus but also seeking to be faithful followers.[48] Ernest Best suggests that the primary objective of Mark in writing the first connected narrative of the earthly life of Jesus was pastoral, 'to build up his readers as Christians and show them what true discipleship is'. He argues that for Mark,

> a true understanding of discipleship depends on a true understanding of Jesus. True discipleship is also to be explained in terms of a relation to Jesus ('Follow me'), and this may be another reason he has chosen to do his pastoral counselling on the basis of the traditions about Jesus rather than through a letter or homily.[49]

Yet, from this side of the resurrection, the disciples' relationship to Jesus Christ is inevitably different from that of those he called to follow him during his earthly mission. Wolfhart Pannenberg argues that that the authority of the earthly Jesus alone cannot be the basis for a Christology because his claims to authority, both explicit and implicit, required a future verification. Therefore Pannenberg argues that, although Jesus claims 'that survival or destruction in the coming judgement by the Son of Man would be decided on the basis of one's relation to him', 'everything depends upon the connection between Jesus' claim and its confirmation by God'.[50] As well as being an inauguration of the future Kingdom, the resurrection of Jesus therefore becomes this verification in which God 'confirms the pre-Easter activity of Jesus'[51] in such a way that he may legitimately be called 'Lord and Messiah'.[52] Following the resurrection, *Kyrios* (and *Maran*) expanded in meaning so that, as we have seen, *Iesous Kyrios* may well have been the earliest baptismal creed.[53] Consequently, we may see post-resurrection discipleship and Lordship as two sides of a single relationship,[54] though Lordship carries a wider meaning than simply the person who is followed by disciples.[55] But how do the convictions, the worship values, relate to this Lordship?

This is the community which seeks to live under the Lordship of Jesus Christ and here it lives within the creative tension of Scripture and experience. It participates within the biblical narrative as it tries to be obedient to the Lordship of Christ mediated through the testimony of Scripture. But it also seeks a personal engagement with the living God and requires the living voice of the Spirit as well as the commands of the written word. Here is an interplay in which objective and subjective factors interact and exchange identities, for the reading of Scripture requires the Spirit's testimony and the experience of God can only be recognized through the testimony of Scripture.

These convictions, in the first instance, point us towards ecclesiology, a distinctive way of being church.[56] Further study might explore what distinctive theological perspectives might relate to such an ecclesiology. For example, the implications for the doctrine of God which follow from an emphasis either on devotion or on the attention to Scripture might be fruitfully developed. Similarly, the place of special providence implied by an emphasis on petitionary prayer might also influence the presentation of dogmatic theology shared with other Christian traditions. An existing example of such convictional influence on dogmatic presentation can be seen in the way that McClendon *begins* his Dogmatics with eschatology.[57] An additional example might be the claim that Evangelicalism needs to be understood in the light of a concern for evangelism – another way of claiming that the Church and its faith can only be understood in the light of its vocation.

Yet even here we are dealing in shadows, or at least structures, for the content of Scripture and experience have not been named, nor the character of the community, nor the characteristics of the Kingdom. All these are to be found in Jesus Christ, which is why the Church is called to be a community of his disciples. To repeat what has already been said, this is not a *Baptist* Jesus, but the Lord of all and the Lord of the whole Church.

The Sunday Gathering of Disciples

The Lordship of Jesus Christ as the presiding conviction in Christian worship means that worship in his name will be worship which bears his character. The whole of worship, not only the sacraments, is instrumental in forming the Church in its vocation – to be the Body of Christ and to be a foretaste and sign of the coming Kingdom. This study has tried to illustrate how Free Church worship has an identity which includes, but which is larger than, sacramental categories. The weekly experience of most Protestant worshippers is of a service of the Word and not a eucharistic celebration, as we have seen James White observe. Any liturgical theology based on such worship will take account of sacramental expressions, as has been attempted in Chapters 9 and 10 above. But the heart of the Free Church Sunday gathering is, most Sundays, to be found elsewhere.

It is best not to call this gathering 'non-sacramental worship', as that would define it with a negative, and would assume a norm which is not representative of this Free Church tradition. Sometimes it is called 'the service of the Word' or 'public worship', but each of these limits the understanding of the event. The former suggests a dominance of Scripture and the latter merely implies that it is open to people beyond the congregation. Instead, we might use the word 'gathering' to describe an event which is simply that – a gathering of people for a common purpose. Or we might add the word 'Sunday', not only to indicate the timing of the event, but to suggest something of its meaning – worship on the 'eighth day', a gathering made possible by the resurrection of Jesus Christ, a gathering of new humanity to celebrate a new creation.[58]

What, then, is the spirituality of this Sunday gathering? What theology is implicit in its practices and what faith is expressed? How are the values embodied in the gathering of disciples to hear the Word of God, in their offering of praise and their prayers of petition? How will a Free Church liturgical theology, reflecting on worship in the Baptist community, give an account of the faith of the Church?

Attention to Scripture: Gathering around the Word

In Christian theology, Scripture has an authority as 'the Word of God' because it is the primary means whereby we have access to Jesus Christ who is the eternal Word of God.[59] So McClendon writes, 'The Bible is the book of Jesus Christ, a book that is about him, a book that finds its interpretative key in him, a book that points as witness to him.'[60] One characteristic of worship, according to Irwin, is that it is anamnetic, a remembering which is more than merely bringing to mind, for it carries a sense of participation and involvement. Scripture will not only be read and preached, but will permeate worship through, for example, quotations in prayers, sung paraphrases and the narrative framework of the ordinances. However, the most obvious and foundational place for Scripture in worship is in its reading and its proclamation. Here God addresses the gathered disciples and, by the work of the Spirit, applies his message to contemporary hearts and lives. Here will be promise and invitation, rebuke and judgement. Here incarnation of the Word of God in Jesus Christ is brought to his followers again, that it might be incarnate in their own living.

The Lordship of Jesus Christ is central to worship because the Triune God has been revealed through him. This does not narrow the content of the Word but focuses it as through a lens. So Scripture will testify to creation and the redemption of the Hebrew slaves; to exile and return, to cross, resurrection and anticipated glory. Yet these Scriptures, written over centuries, are viewed through the lens of Jesus Christ. All proclamation must centre on him, all exposition of the written word must bear witness to the living Word, just as all psalmody must be with reference to what God has revealed and done in Christ.[61]

Yet we have seen that the conviction which is brought to worship is not simply the authority of Scripture but attention to it. This is best understood within its role of testifying to Jesus Christ. Attention to Scripture, once interpreted through a Christological hermeneutic, becomes attention to Jesus as Lord. Gathering around the Word is not only a gathering in order to listen to Scripture, but it is a gathering around the living Word, Jesus Christ. It is here that we find a resolution between the dialectic tension of Scripture and devotional experience, for even the approach to Scripture is relational. Disciples bring a readiness to obey – yet this obedience is to Jesus Christ, the Word of God made flesh, whose story is the heart of Scripture. Faith is not simply *belief that* the promises of Scripture are true, but *trust in* the one who comes to us through Scripture. Attention to Scripture leads to devotion: a loving desire to delight in the one to whom Scripture bears witness.

Devotion: Open to God

Worship is a place of encounter in which the worshippers are invited to worship 'in Spirit and in truth'. We have seen how the Free Church tradition has placed a high premium on the concern that this should be sincere worship and worship that is open to the Holy Spirit. Extempore prayer is a sign of this epicletic dimension, in which worship can be explained as a participation in the life of the Triune God.

The Spirit testifies to the Lordship of Jesus Christ, for 'no one can say "Jesus is Lord" except by the Holy Spirit' (1 Corinthians 12.3). This acclamation is more than a liturgical formula, though it is at least that, for affirming Jesus as Lord will carry implications for the life of a disciple. Following Jesus means displaying the same qualities of love as him, displaying a glorious servanthood and being prepared to walk the way of the cross. These are not codified requirements, though they are to be found in Scripture. Rather, they are to be understood as part of the loving dynamic which is part of the devotional life and which finds expression in worship through adoration and consecration. Therefore worship which testifies to the Lordship of Jesus Christ will require these devotional elements, with opportunities for a congregation both to express love of God and to offer rededicated lives.

Devotion also requires truthfulness through the confession of sin, which becomes not so much a juridical transaction as the healing of a broken or disfigured relationship. This reconciliation is made possible through the cross and resurrection of Jesus Christ. 'He is our peace' (Ephesians 2.4). Yet devotion asks more of the worshipper than confession of sin alone. There is a concern that worship should be sincere, not only through a lifestyle which is congruent with the affirmations of worship, but through a transparency and honesty of heart in worship itself. Confession then becomes the fruit of honest self-examination in which the worshipper acknowledges the omniscient scrutiny of God and in which love requires not dissembling but truthfulness. Baptists have not tended to follow the Genevan tradition of beginning worship with a prayer of confession[62] or of using the Collect for Purity from the *Book of Common Prayer*. Indeed, distinct prayers of confession are probably a fairly recent practice,[63] though the hints we have of prayer material from writers such as Bunyan, Watts and Maclaren suggest a considerable penitential component.[64] Such penitence in worship assumes the atoning work of Christ and so, by implication, whenever sins are confessed and forgiveness sought in his name, Jesus Christ is proclaimed as saviour.

As well as the need for sincerity, we have seen that our concern for devotion has contained within it a sense of dependence on God, not only for daily living, but in the actions of worship itself. So extempore prayer assumes a reliance upon the Spirit. Similarly, the prayers of preparation before corporate worship begins also imply a recognition that worship must be 'in the Spirit', an event in which the worshippers are open to and reliant upon the activity of God. When we speak of 'encounter' in worship we must understand this in a more subtle and complex way than simply the meeting of two parties, as it includes the enabling of human worship through the inspiration of the Holy Spirit. Thus the movement towards communion with God is not a programme of human striving but an epicletic process in which the worshippers open themselves to the possibility of participation in God. Such participation is dependent on the sovereignty of God as there cannot be any *ex opere operato* assumptions about prayer and communion.[65] In all this, Jesus is the human face of God, and encounter is not primarily with the Spirit but with Jesus Christ through the Spirit. Devotion is a free and trusting response to the generous and costly love of God manifest in him. Worshippers bring a readiness to be open to God – this their first offering.

The Church as Community: Fellowship-Sharing

The covenant nature of church life is an expression of the *koinonia* of the Holy Spirit. While worship may take place in many different contexts and with different types of gathering, its normative expression is in the gathering of a local congregation.[66] Even when there is no formal local church covenant, the constituted organization of the church provides a covenantal framework within which fellowship and sharing can prosper.

These 'horizontal' relationships which comprise a congregation are only truly understood when seen within the 'vertical', new covenant inaugurated by Jesus Christ. This church is a community, but it is a community of disciples. The barriers of class, gender and race which are torn down in the new creation of the Church are torn down by the cross of Jesus Christ (Ephesians 2.13–22; and Galatians 3.28). In addition, it is the epicletic nature of worship which enables it to be truly communal, because it is the Spirit of God who works through the ministries of the Church, enabling different individuals to contribute to the building up of the community (1 Corinthians 12.4–11). Yet this Spirit is the Spirit of Jesus, for the gifts of ministry to the Church are the gifts of Jesus Christ (Ephesians 4.7). This is why, according to Paul, the Church is the 'Body of Christ' – an image which relates to the diversity of ministries and *charismata* within the unity of the Christian community (Romans 12.5–8; 1 Corinthians 12.12–27; and Ephesians 4.1–16).

Worship is a 'gathering' of disciples and by its very nature is communal. But we shall misunderstand that gathering unless we acknowledge that it is 'in the name of Jesus'. It is a gathering initiated by the hospitality of a God who calls and invites, and it is the fruit of the Spirit of unity who gathers people into life-changing community. But the centre of that community is Jesus Christ, through whom God reveals himself and to whom the Spirit bears testimony.

Concern for the Kingdom: The Messianic Community

When his disciples asked Jesus to teach them to pray, he taught them a prayer which was full of eschatological yearning.[67] While worship will have a devotional focus in its communion with God, it will also have a quality which resists staying in the present moment. For example, petitionary prayer is always about the future, even if it is only the next moment. Even the proclamation of God's saving acts or the celebration of divine goodness are in some sense eschatological, for they are the establishing of a sign of the Kingdom amidst the present realities of a fallen but redeemed world.[68] Petitionary prayer can, however, become self-seeking, and worship introverted, unless its petitions are clearly understood as eschatological, as prayer in the service of the Kingdom. Human requests become worship as the praying of the Church offers God its commitment to his Kingdom and its yearning that the Lordship of Jesus Christ become manifest in answered prayer and in new signs of the Kingdom breaking into the present.

This Kingdom-orientation of worship is closely connected to the notion of the Church as a community of disciples, as well as to the theme of the Lordship of Jesus Christ. Jürgen Moltmann, for example, speaks of the Church as the 'messianic community' and of worship as a 'messianic feast' because it anticipates the messianic banquet, a common biblical image for God's End. Disciples are called to celebrate counterculturally, as: 'The messianic feast is the Lord's song "in a foreign land".'[69] Again, the character of the Church is intimately linked to the person of Jesus Christ. In so far as it follows the Messiah, praying for and serving his coming Kingdom, the Church is the messianic community. Indeed, it can only be this by virtue of its relationship to the Messiah and not through any independent means of its own.

This concern for the Kingdom will also mean that the Church looks beyond its own communal life in prayer and mission. Although the evangelistic use of worship is seen by some as a distortion of its purpose, Baptists have long seen worship as an appropriate place for evangelism. Thus Keith Jones, reflecting on the challenge of the Anabaptist tradition for contemporary Christians, prefers the title 'a gathering church' to the usual 'gathered church',[70] because it suggests a community which is being changed and increased through the dynamic work of the Spirit. The notion of 'gathering', as distinct from 'gathered', also suggests a community which is defined more by its centre than by its circumference. This centre is Jesus Christ who continues to say, 'Follow me', drawing men and women into a community of disciples. As a Kingdom activity, mission becomes a form of discipleship and an out-flowing of prayer in which God is petitioned to hasten the Lordship of Jesus Christ.[71]

The contemporary relationship between worship and mission is problematic in many Free Churches. Sometimes worship is distorted by focusing the event on a presentation of the gospel which is pragmatic and owes more to the techniques of entertainment than to the riches of the Kingdom. Sometimes mission ignores worship and concentrates on the salvic benefits for the individual. These dangers can best be avoided by a recognition that both mission and worship are eschatological in nature. They embody and serve the coming Kingdom of Jesus Christ and it is in his invitation, and the gathering work of the Spirit, that the missiological relevance of worship will be understood and the rich spirituality of mission experienced.

These reflections about worship lead us to a place where we must recognize the Christ-shaped nature of Christian believing. We have been led *into* worship rather than *beyond* it. But the place we have reached is holy ground and we must take off our shoes and bow down long before we begin to understand. To see worship as doxological has become something of a truism in contemporary theology. Yet its truth can no longer be denied. Liturgical theology, whether undertaken in the Free Church community or the Orthodox Church or wherever, leads us to a knowledge of God which is scriptural and devotional, communal and eschatological. It leads us to a knowledge of God which is expressed in words and yet leads us beyond explanation to wonder and awe. Such reflection begins *in* worship; indeed, it begins as reflection *on* worship, but then *becomes* worship. This theology offers us an exciting and awesome prospect.

12

Free Worship – Living Faith

Continuing Hopes and Questions

It has sometimes been the boast of Episcopalians that Churchmen go to their churches to pray and worship God, but that Dissenters merely assemble to hear sermons. Our reply to this is, that albeit there may be some professors who are guilty of this evil, it is not true of the people of God among us, and these are the only persons who ever will in any church really enjoy devotion. Our congregations gather together to worship God, and we assert, and feel no hesitation in asserting, that there is much true and acceptable prayer offered in our ordinary Nonconformist services as in the best and most pompous performances of the Church of England.

Moreover, if the observation be meant to imply that the hearing of sermons is not worshipping God, it is founded on a gross mistake, for rightly to listen to the gospel is one of the noblest parts of the adoration of the Most High . . . . Nevertheless . . . there are meeting-houses in which the supplications are neither so devout nor so earnest as we desire; in other places the earnestness is so allied with ignorance, the devotion so marred with rant, that no intelligent believer can enter into the service with pleasure. Praying in the Holy Ghost is not universal among us, neither do all pray with the understanding as well as with the heart. There is room for improvement, and some quarters there is an imperative demand for it.

Charles Haddon Spurgeon 1879[1]

In worship, the Christian community expresses its communal faith and nurtures the faith of its members. Worship is an embodiment of theology, not in the sense that it translates into worship practices previously agreed theological statements, but in the sense that it expresses in its practices what the Christian community believes. This liturgically embodied expression of faith is complementary to the dogmatic statements of the Church. If the explanatory language of theologians is indeed theology, so the poetic language of worship and its attendant symbolism is also theology, though in a different mode of expression.[2]

It is my hope that the exploration in this book will encourage those who lead worship and those who participate in worship to reflect on the theological meaning of what they are doing. Its scope and its achievements have been limited, but if it inspires others to join in the task of exploring faith through the practices and experiences of worship, I will be well satisfied. There is much need for theological reflection on Free Church worship. In addition, much will be gained if those from more 'liturgical' traditions are able to see free worship in a new way.

Nothing has been completed here. Indeed, there is much that remains to be started. In these closing pages I shall offer a possible approach to a theology of worship from a Free Church perspective. Here also are some of the questions which will continue to exercise any who seek to map out the common ground between worship and theology.

Questioning the Tradition

We began by recognizing some of the difficulties which face a student of Free Church worship. On the one hand, the contemporary scene offers much variety. Diversity offers its challenges, not least when we have to make decisions about the scope of a particular study or the boundaries of a particular tradition. On the other hand, the oral nature of free worship means that we have very limited resources for reconstructing the worship events of previous ages.

Historically, there are many gaps in the story of Baptist and Free Church worship. But Schmemann's observation that liturgical theology must begin with history is well made and the present study has been grounded on the principle that liturgical theology needs to be established from the practice of worship rather than based upon independently developed theory. There is much scope for historians who wish to trace what clues we have about the worship of our Free Church forebears. Because spirituality is embodied and embedded in the stories of communities, there is the promise of much reward for those who attempt such detective work – and for those who will be able to reflect on the fruit of their labours. It has fascinated and frustrated me that so much published church history writing is about personalities and politics, structures and strategies rather than spirituality and worship.[3] Yet if worship is truly central to the life of the Christian community, then it ought to feature more in the work of those who research and present the story of that community.

There are intriguing philosophical questions which it has not been possible to pursue here. The concern for simplicity in worship could usefully be explored in relation to the cultural and philosophical context of the Reformation and the development of Separatist churches. Was the rejection of ceremony simply a reaction to mediaeval excesses, or was it the result of dualistic attitudes to spirit and matter, or indeed an example of early Enlightenment rationalism? Why have Free Church people and Evangelicals so often equated sincerity with informality; and what of the suspicion of outward devotional aids such as pre-composed prayers? At one level, the answers may appear simple, at another, they lead into a large agenda of philosophical and cultural enquiry.

The reforming of worship practices is far from straightforward, not least because the Free Churches do not normally acknowledge a central, ecclesiastical authority.[4] At a practical and pastoral level, we need to ask how the study of worship and the exploration of its theology might inform and influence our practice of worship. One possible way forward is to see liturgical theology as the basis for a critique of current practices. The question of authority is complex, but the recognition that worship embodies theology enables us to critique particular worship in the light of the strengths or weaknesses of the theology so embodied – or through the ability of those particular worship practices to obscure or to communicate the faith of the community.[5] For example, the core worship values we have identified offer one way of understanding worship within the Baptist community and the beginning of a reform process which could be sensitive to the Baptist tradition.[6]

Theological reflection should move beyond the descriptive Free Church liturgical theology which has been offered so far, and beyond the descriptive exposition espoused by Schmemann, towards the development of a Free Church theology of worship. And it is to this task we now turn briefly.

From Is *to* Ought?

Alexander Schmemann and a significant number of liturgical theologians distinguish between 'liturgical theology' and 'a theology of worship'.[7] The former is an important task in rediscovering vital links between worship and theology, and its primary role is as an exposition of the faith of the Church. By contrast, the theology of worship is viewed as a critical exercise in which worship is explained and reformed by means of norms which have been established elsewhere. This distinction partly arises from the view that liturgy is a manifestation of Tradition in which the *lex orandi* is seen as the bearer of the *lex credendi*. Schmemann harks back to the patristic period in which catechesis and mystagogy expounded the faith of the Christian community.

This perspective is closely related to the discussion about modes of theological activity and, in particular, the distinction between 'primary' and 'secondary' theology. The former is seen as an articulation of faith and the latter as an approach which requires a degree of critical distance from the 'object' of theological enquiry. Maxwell Johnson observes that 'Schmemann's theological model, therefore, is much closer to preaching than it is to lecturing, more at home in the pulpit than in the mediaeval or modern theological academy'.[8] Consequently, Schmemann did not seek to reform the Orthodox Liturgy but was rather concerned with 'the much needed "reconciliation" and mutual reintegration of liturgy, theology and piety'.[9]

Even in his own writings the distinction between descriptive and normative theological activity is not as clear as Schmemann claims. For example, his attempt to identify what he calls the *ordo* has a normative dimension as he seeks to establish the essence of worship and thus provide a means of interpreting its components, distinguishing that which is integral to the meaning of the liturgy from the accretions of custom and circumstance.[10] He declares, 'In our liturgical practice there are things which to many people seem to be the age-old tradition of the Church, but which in fact distort this tradition.'[11] A theological synthesis, by its very nature, attempts to provide meaning and explanation, and is likely to contain a movement which presses towards normative claims. To attempt coherence is to try and bring order to the practices upon which reflection is taking place. Conversely, if reform is to be an organic development within the tradition, then the explanation of that tradition is an important part of the reform process, as Schmemann exemplifies by his attempt to identify the underlying *ordo* which will make possible the interpretation of the parts of worship. Johnson comments that, 'in spite of his reluctance to offer a "theology of liturgy", it is precisely a theology of liturgy that Schmemann provides, an elucidation of the "correct" theological vision, norms, and principles which not only govern the liturgical celebration but function as the sources for theology itself'.[12]

While what *is* must not be confused with what *ought* to be, liturgical theology as a synthesis of the theological meanings of worship inevitably presents a vision of what worship really is and, as such, presents a vision which claims to order worship and not merely reflect it. Exposition is more than description.

Because the implications of Schmemann's work go beyond the limits he wishes to place upon it, it can be argued that even his own writings encourage the development of a theology of worship. However, the importance of such a theology is underlined when reflecting on Free Church worship and its theological inheritance. As children of the Reformation, the Free Churches have normally wanted to apply the test of Scripture to their worship and their theology.[13] Geoffrey Wainwright argues, as we have seen, that Protestants in general have been less persuaded by the notion of *lex orandi, lex credendi*, as 'Protestantism characteristically emphasizes the primacy of doctrine over the liturgy.'[14] When Baptists expound Baptist worship they are not attempting the same thing as when Orthodox theologians expound the Orthodox Liturgy. For the Orthodox liturgical theologian, the Liturgy offers an 'epiphany' of the faith of the Church in the sense that it manifests that Tradition which is understood as 'the life of the Holy Spirit in the Church'.[15]

Our exposition of Free Church worship is more modest for it only claims to explain the theological meaning of worship among Free Churches; indeed, it has been even more limited to the worship of a single denomination. The community values which have been identified may, however, be regarded as a Baptist, and largely a Free Church, tradition and therefore understood as a portrayal, albeit partial, of the faith of the Baptist and Free Church communities. Any development of a Free Church theology of worship should begin with these values. The liturgical theology we have begun to sketch can provide the foundation upon which such a theology of worship might be constructed. However, in developing a theology of worship which is integral to the Free Church tradition, this construction will need to include a dialogue with Scripture, as well as with the voices of other traditions.

In his attack on the notion of a theology of worship, Schmemann objects to what he sees as the reifying of worship as an object to be dissected. However, the doctrinal critique of worship is a natural part of the Protestant tradition, with its principles of *sola scriptura* and *ecclesia semper reformanda*, and therefore a normative theology of worship is an appropriate aspiration for Free Church reflection on worship. Provided liturgical theology, derived from an engagement with the worship practices of the Free Church community, plays its part in this, Schmemann's other concern, that a theology of worship ought not to be developed apart from the experience of worship, would also be addressed.[16]

Worship as Meeting and Seeking

How might we approach the task of developing a Free Church theology of worship? As well as an upward movement from practice and experience, there is need for a downward, critical movement, as the liturgical phenomena of worship are tested against a systematic theology which can claim to be founded on the witness of Scripture. The act of reflection will be invested with an authority which enables the resultant 'theology of worship' to be both normative and, in some sense, scriptural. In other words, liturgical theology will provide the agenda, or content, and Scripture and theological reflection the criteria for this theological enterprise.

A number of contemporary approaches to such a theology begin by attempting to define worship.[17] Provided we see the use of such definitions as a starting point, or the setting of the theological agenda, we can use liturgical theology as the means of establishing this – an agenda which will then need to be tested against Scripture and dogmatic theology. Establishing an agenda from the liturgical theology which has been presented here could result in the kind of starting point formulated in the following statement:

> Christian worship is a gathering of the Church in the name of Jesus Christ and in the power of the Holy Spirit in order to meet God through Scripture, prayer, proclamation and sacraments and to seek his Kingdom.

This summary identifies worship as an event in which God is encountered, though the complexity of that encounter is only hinted at. It is *Christian* worship because it takes place 'in the name of Jesus Christ', and the primary means by which the encounter is structured are identified. Most importantly, it clarifies the purpose of the gathering – it is 'to meet God . . . and seek his Kingdom'. Both devotion and eschatology are placed on the agenda. This seeking of the Kingdom provides a fundamental orientation because worship is centred in God and in the rule of God. Praise is the outward acknowledgement of this, but it is also expressed in prayer through the name of Jesus and prayers for God's will to be done. A seeking of the Kingdom is also to be found in the attention to Scripture and a devotional response to the love of God.

Here is a framework within which to build a more adequate account of worship, and it has the virtue of containing only those elements which we have used in our study of worship. It indicates the need to take seriously the worshipping experience of the Church – for the worship values are represented here and offer the opportunity for a dialogue with Scripture and the pastoral needs of the particular context within which such a theology of worship might be undertaken. Just as liturgical theology moves from the detail of historical events and liturgical components to a synthesis which gives meaning to the whole, so a theology of worship will move in the opposite direction, from theological overview and the study of Scripture to the explanation of liturgical detail and the scrutiny and possible reforming of current practice.

Space here only permits an arguing for the importance of such a theology of worship and for suggesting how such a theology might be undertaken.

Ecumenical Sharing and Ecumenical Equivalence

This book has approached worship from the perspective of a particular tradition. In an ecumenical age this may appear partisan, but its intention has been quite other. We have seen how Schmemann and others have insisted that liturgical theology must begin with history. But whose history?

The Liturgical Movement has tended to encourage the search for a common history in the early centuries of the life of the Church. Sometimes this has led to claims for a generic theology which places normative claims on present-day Christians. So the worship described by Justin Martyr in the second century provides the basis for Gordon Lathrop to construct a common *ordo* for all Christians.[18] Similarly, a reconstructing of the relationship between church and synagogue led Schmemann to develop his presentation of the *ordo* as the interaction of the Eucharist with liturgical time.[19] More recently, the attempt to identify an 'ecumenical *ordo*' has reinforced the centrality of the Eucharist and again raised questions of what constitutes Christian worship. For example, is the Eucharist a necessary focus for weekly worship? If so, then the worship of many Free Churches must be seen as sadly deficient. James White has offered a robust critique of this supposed ecumenical liturgical consensus. He argues that many Free Church traditions have been marginalized by the attempt to undertake generic liturgical theology, especially in judgements made concerning the frequency of eucharistic celebration or participation:

If we take seriously the premise that the way people pray expresses what they believe, then we have to be very deliberate in accepting the vast diversity of actual prayer practice, especially in North America. In trying to marginalize the worship life of so many millions, we have violated one of the basic motifs of *lex orandi*. But if we respect the varieties of prayer, it will change significantly the way liturgical theology is done.[20]

This book has offered a way of doing liturgical theology which is in dialogue with ecumenical partners but which is sensitive to the nature of Free Church worship. Three further observations may be offered. First, while most churches will see the Eucharist as a central feature of their worship, this may not mean a weekly cycle. While Schmemann and others have made much of the eschatological nature of Sunday as 'the eighth day', we have seen how most worship has an eschatological dimension. This is not restricted to the Eucharist. Further, the Eucharist can be central to a worshipping community without it needing to be weekly.

Second, we have identified an *ordo* as a cluster of values rather than a structure for worship. This is the most likely way of giving a systematic explanation of Free Church worship and enables us to see patterns in the diversity, as well as offering normative criteria for guiding practice and reform. Any ecumenical consensus on an 'ecumenical *ordo*' will need to take account of the fluidity of some worship and then will need to find patterns in ways which are not structural.

Third, ecumenical reflection on worship must take account of contextualization and culture. Diversity needs to be respected not eliminated. In particular, we need to distinguish between an *ordo* and the various local expressions of that *ordo*. In what ways do different practices in different places express the same affirmations of Christian believing? How can we take account of ecumenical equivalence?

Just as Gordon Lathrop says we are not faithful to the past by simply using the same words,[21] so the same practice will not say the same things in different denominational contexts. We need to take account of synchronic, as well as diachronic, variety. For example, a tradition which is not 'incarnationally literate' may struggle with a sacramental rite as a regular, indeed normative, expression of Christian worship. But how is the *ordo* to be expressed in such a culture? The question itself implies an *ordo* which is *behind* or *within* the practices and so is culturally conditioned. At what point is, for example, the Eucharist *as* Sunday worship an expression of the *ordo* in some, albeit most, traditions and to what extent is it part of the *ordo* itself?

Christians tend to have a 'home base' from which they understand various theological and confessional issues. These attitudes also include cultural and philosophical perspectives – ways of viewing the world. For example, some Christians find it difficult to cope with diversity, which they see as disorder. Others struggle with ecclesiastical authority, which they view as oppression. Such judgements can be as much philosophical and cultural as they are theological.

Conversely, different Christian traditions view the world from the perspective of Word and some from that of sacrament. This point is not one of either/or, but the base position from which a tradition views the world. Both perspectives may be biblical, orthodox and crucial – yet historical circumstances in which a confessional tradition might have originated, or undergone significant transformation, will affect the way the world is viewed culturally as well as theologically.

For example, while icons can testify to the incarnation, as their defendants in the iconoclastic controversy asserted,[22] we can also see that the development of icons took place in a society where pictures were vital communicators of the gospel to a largely illiterate populace. This is not to deny the 'sacramental' potential of icons, but simply to note the cultural context within which such potential emerged.

Conversely, preaching and storytelling can be seen as an expression of the prophetic way in which God has addressed humanity. Here is the divine Word which does not return void but creates the universe, invites the faithful, admonishes the wayward and is the word of life. Yet these theological insights were also culturally encouraged at the Reformation through the development of printing and increasing literacy.[23]

Alternatively, the world can be viewed from the perspective of the Spirit of God, who blows where the Spirit wills, testifies to Jesus Christ, raises him from the dead and today inspires words and actions and transformed lives. A Pentecostal liturgical theologian might legitimately claim that divine activity evident through the exercising of *charismata* in worship was a fundamental aspect of the Christian worship recorded in the New Testament[24] and should be a component of any ecumenical *ordo*.

So a reading of John 1.14 might favour a sacramental claim for liturgical norms – as the Word *became* flesh. So Maxwell Johnson has argued in discussing the need for an ecumenical *ordo* of word and table:

what is at stake here [is] . . . a particular theological understanding of God and how God acts incarnationally and *sacramentally* in history and the church. The ecumenical liturgical theologian can no more view that foundational understanding of how God is believed to act as 'one option among several'

... the liturgy we celebrate bears the Trinitarian–christological orthodoxy of the historic Christian tradition and proclaims and expresses that understanding of God who acts by means of Word *and* Sacrament in our Sunday and festal assemblies.[25]

But what is the meaning of that '*and*'? Johnson and Lathrop argue that the Sunday gathering should always include both word and meal and that the 'and' represents a part of the core *ordo* – that this weekly conjunction is a sign of the Word made flesh, of the incarnational way in which God has chosen to work in history and in the Church. Surely the meeting on the eighth day should testify to God's new creation made possible through the incarnation of the Word?

Edward Schillebeeckx has presented a fine foundation for such an argument, linking the Church's sacramental actions with Christ, the primordial sacrament.[26] However, the affirmation of God's sacramental action in Christ *need not* lead to the sacramentalist conclusions that every Sunday gathering is a conjunction of word and meal.

The importance of the Eucharist may be expressed by weekly celebration, or even daily, or it may be expressed through preparation for a festival, such as Lent before Easter, or self-examination and devotion before a Presbyterian quarterly celebration.[27] This is not to argue for such occasional celebration, or even to suggest that the two traditions see the Eucharist's importance in the same way, but it is to observe that the *ordo*, and in particular the 'and' between word and meal, may stretch over a wider time span than the gathering and dismissal each Sunday.

What is being argued is not that weekly celebration is in any way inappropriate, or that it doesn't express the *ordo*, but that it is not the *only* expression of an *ordo* where word and table are 'in apposition', where the Sunday gathering is 'a communal gathering meeting around two poles'.[28] Releasing Free Church worship from the heavy criticism of the supposed ecumenical *ordo* frees us to recognize in its Sunday gathering a rich testimony to the full counsels of God.

Theological reflection requires logical rigour. But such rigour must ensure that we do not confuse expressions of faith for faith itself. Contemporary debates about the contextualization of Christian worship are one example of this concern, but another may be found in the liturgical implications of the ecumenical question, 'What are the limits of legitimate diversity?'

Free Worship as an Ecumenical Gift

This study has been unashamedly denominational. It has explored Free Church worship, through a study of one denomination, and identified a set of convictions about worship. The theological task has been concerned with the convictions of a convictional community, but in what sense and to what extent are those convictions to be shared with other communities within the Christian Church? Ecumenical dialogue has to some extent already begun, for this book has been undertaken in an ecumenical context. The method employed for studying Free Church worship is a modification of one developed by an Orthodox liturgical theologian. At different stages, when theological reflection has been undertaken, Roman Catholic, Lutheran and other voices have been heard.[29]

How might these Free Church convictions be presented? They could be offered either as a loose cluster of concerns or as the more compact definitional statement presented earlier in this chapter. Alternatively, they could be presented as a model alongside other models, and we shall conclude with a discussion of this approach, for it offers a way in which a denominational cluster of insights can make a contribution in the ecumenical arena in an ecumenical spirit.

James Empereur identifies a number of models of liturgical theology, such as the *institutional*, *sacramental* and *proclamation* models, among others.[30] To these I would like to add a *discipleship* model of liturgical theology.[31] He insists that 'all models work best when they are seen as inadequate'[32] and that they should be seen as complementary and self-correcting. As different views of the same reality, they complement and enhance one another, while reminding us that they are views of the reality of worship and not the reality itself.

> Models are like windows in a house. Reality is what one sees through the windows. But one cannot look out of all the windows at the same time. To get an adequate view of reality, one must wander from window to window and get a composite view.[33]

This is particularly helpful as a way of understanding how a denominational perspective might contribute towards an ecumenical discussion, for it assumes an ecumenical process which operates through reconciled diversity rather than through general consensus.

An initial sketch of the discipleship model of liturgical theology might look something like this:

Christian worship occurs when, with attention to Scripture, in openness to the Spirit of God and in covenant community, disciples gather
in the name of Jesus to meet God and to seek his Kingdom.

This model sees the Church as a community of disciples who yearn
for the Kingdom of God, seek to express the Lordship of Jesus Christ
in their common life and worship with its creative tension between
Word and Spirit, between scriptural command and loving encounter.

These two statements are only a beginning, but they could well act as
an invitation for other Christians to experiment with this model as it
interacts with their own liturgical tradition. These statements could be
augmented by speaking of the way in which, within the Free Church
tradition, these values have been expressed, particularly, for example,
with regard to free worship and extempore prayer which express devotion, dependence and liberty in the Spirit – and a view of preaching in
which God addresses the congregation and its members.

Any church which uses this discipleship model to explore its own worshipping life will need to question itself concerning matters of personal
devotion, attention to Scripture and a communal approach to worship –
worship which will express itself not so much in scripted responses, as in
covenantal relationships, improvisatory prayer and testimony.

This is not an invitation for those in liturgically formal traditions to
replace their own worship with Free Church worship, but it is an invitation to participate in their own worship as members of an eschatological
community of disciples who struggle with Scripture and yearn to come
closer to God and to his will. Such a dialogue would enrich ecumenical
understandings of Christian worship because it would begin to release
the stuttering Free Church voice, which has either been silent, or else has
not been heard by those whose liturgical voices have for so long been
so eloquent. It is in exploring the riches of *each* tradition that we gain
a larger vision of the worship of *all* God's people. This exciting and
nourishing endeavour is only just beginning.

Notes

Chapter 1

1. 'The Manner of Attending to Divine Ordinances' in The Circular Letter from the Ministers and Messengers of the Several Baptist Churches of the Northamptonshire Association, assembled at Dunstable, 11, 12, 13 June 1805, pp. 2–4.

2. John Updike, *Couples*, London: Penguin Books, 1969, pp. 41f.

3. Jean-Jacques von Allmen, *Worship: Its Theology and Practice*, London: Lutterworth Press, 1965, p. 42.

4. Allmen, *Worship*, p. 42.

5. For example, the post-baptismal catechesis of Cyril of Jerusalem or Ambrose of Milan may be seen as a type of liturgical theology as they instructed the newly baptized in the riches of Christian believing by instructing them in the meaning of worship and the sacraments. See Maxwell E. Johnson, 'Mystagogical Catechesis' in Paul Bradshaw (ed.), *The New SCM Dictionary of Liturgy and Worship*, London: SCM Press, 2002, pp. 330–1; and David Regan, *Experience the Mystery: Pastoral Possibilities for Christian Mystagogy*, London: Geoffrey Chapman, 1994.

6. In 2003 the reported world-wide membership was nearly 46 million. See *2003 Yearbook of the Baptist World Alliance*, Falls Church VA: Baptist World Alliance, 2003, p. 109. These figures do not include those attending worship who are not members of a local church and therefore do not include those who are children and others who will not have been baptized. An estimate equivalent to the method of counting in other denominations raises the figure to a little over 100 million.

7. See the discussion of James White in Chapter 3 below.

Chapter 2

1. Altered and printed as hymn 494 in *The Baptist Hymn Book* (1962).

2. Philip Sheldrake, *Spirituality and History: Questions of Interpretation and Method*, London: SPCK, 1995, p. 60.

3. Sheldrake, *Spirituality and History*, p. 41.

4. See, for example, Laurie Green, *Let's Do Theology*, London: Mowbray, 1990, and Paul Ballard and John Pritchard, *Practical Theology in Action: Christian Thinking in the Service of Church and Society*, London: SPCK, 1996.

5. H. E. Chandlee, 'The Liturgical Movement' in J. G. Davies (ed.), *A Dictionary of Liturgy and Worship*, London: SCM Press, 1972.

6. See John Fenwick and Bryan Spinks, *Worship in Transition: The Twentieth Century Liturgical Movement*, Edinburgh: T & T Clark, 1995, pp. 5–11, for a list of themes in the movement.

7. The nineteenth-century precursors to the movement, with their interest in the mediaeval Church, may be seen as a part of a more general gothic revival, while the twentieth century has seen much study of the early Church and its liturgical life. See Chandlee, 'Liturgical Movement', pp. 216–17 and Fenwick and Spinks, *Worship in Transition*, pp. 13–21.

8. Alexander Schmemann, *Introduction to Liturgical Theology*, Crestwood NY: St. Vladimir's Seminary Press, 1966/1996, p.15.

9. Louis Bouyer, *Liturgical Piety*, Notre Dame IN: University of Notre Dame Press, 1955 (published in the UK in 1956 as *Life and Liturgy*), p. 277.

10. See Thomas Fisch, 'Schmemann's Theological Contribution to the Liturgical Renewal of the Churches' in Thomas Fisch (ed.), *Liturgy and Tradition: Theological Reflections of Alexander Schmemann*, Crestwood NY: St Vladimir's Seminary Press, 1990, pp. 1–10.

11. Alexander Schmemann, 'Liturgical Theology: Remarks on Method' in T. Fisch (ed.), *Liturgy and Tradition: Theological Reflections of Alexander Schmemann*, Crestwood NY: St Vladimir's Seminary Press, 1982/1990, pp. 137–44, at 137–8.

12. Aidan Kavanagh, 'Response: Primary Theology and Liturgical Act', *Worship*, 57, 1983, p. 324.

13. Geoffrey Wainwright, *Doxology: The Praise of God in Worship, Doctrine and Life*, London: Epworth, 1980, p. 218. His use of the customary abbreviated version *lex orandi, lex credendi* provides scope to reverse subject and predicate and so enables priority to be given to either – though despite speaking of a mutual interplay, he seems to want a doctrinal control of worship.

14. For a discussion of the use of the *lex orandi* argument by various liturgical theologians, see Maxwell E. Johnson, 'Liturgy and Theology' in P. Bradshaw and B. Spinks (eds), *Liturgy in Dialogue: Essays in Memory of Ronald Jasper*, London: SPCK, 1993, and for a discussion of those arguments in relation to Prosper's argument, see Paul V. Marshall, 'Reconsidering "Liturgical Theology": Is there a Lex Orandi for all Christians?', *Studia Liturgica*, 25, 1995, pp. 129–51.

15. Schmemann doesn't use the language of 'primary' and 'secondary' theology but makes a similar distinction by speaking of 'Scholasticism', which is his way of referring to what others have called 'secondary' theology. See Alexander Schmemann, 'Theology and Liturgical Tradition' in T. Fisch (ed.), *Liturgy and Tradition: Theological Reflections of Alexander Schmemann*, Crestwood NY: St Vladimir's Seminary Press, 1963/1990, pp. 11–20, p. 13. Cf. Aidan Kavanagh, *On Liturgical Theology*, Collegeville MN: Liturgical Press, 1984, pp. 74f., and David W. Fagerberg, *What is Liturgical Theology? A Study in Methodology*, Collegeville MN: Liturgical Press, 1992, pp. 16f.

16. Alexander Schmemann, 'Liturgy and Theology' in T. Fisch (ed.), *Liturgy and Tradition: Theological Reflections of Alexander Schmemann*, Crestwood NY: St Vladimir's Seminary Press, 1972/1990, pp. 49–68, p. 54.

17. Fagerberg, *What is Liturgical Theology?*, p.44.

18. Philip Sheldrake cites, as examples, Paul Tillich, David Tracy, Bernard Lonergan, Karl Rahner, Hans Urs von Balthasar, Jürgen Moltmann, Wolfhart Pannenberg, Rowan Williams and Andrew Louth. Philip Sheldrake, *Spirituality and Theology: Christian Living and the Doctrine of God*, ed. S. Sykes, London: Darton, Longman & Todd, 1998, pp. 65–95.

19. Sally McFague, *Metaphorical Theology: Models of God in Religious Lan-*

guage, Philadelphia PA: Fortress Press, 1982, pp. 118f.

20. For a discussion of prayer as primary speech in a psychological sense, see Ann Ulanov and Barry Ulanov, *Primary Speech: A Psychology of Prayer*, London: SCM Press, 1985.

21. David Power, 'Two Expressions of Faith: Worship and Theology', Concilium, 82, 1973, pp. 95–103, p. 101.

22. Power, 'Two Expressions of Faith: Worship and Theology', p. 99. See the synthesis in Edward J. Kilmartin, *Christian Liturgy: Theology and Practice*, vol. 1: *Systematic Theology of Liturgy*, Kansas City: Sheed & Ward, 1988, p. 97, and also Wainwright's discussion of Edmund Schlink's establishing five categories (prayer, doxology, witness, doctrine and confession) with the claim that theological statements can change their meaning when transferred from one category to another. Wainwright, *Doxology*, p. 280, and Edmund Schlink, *The Coming Christ and the Coming Church*, Philadelphia PA: Fortress Press, 1968, p. 16. For an overview of the various approaches to liturgical theology, see James L. Empereur, *Models of Liturgical Theology*, Bramcote, Nottingham: Grove Books, 1987, and *Worship: Exploring the Sacred*, Washington DC: Pastoral Press, 1987, and Kevin Irwin, *Liturgical Theology: A Primer*, Collegeville MN: Liturgical Press, 1990.

23. Alexander Schmemann, 'Liturgical Theology, Theology of Liturgy, and Liturgical Reform' in T. Fisch (ed.), *Liturgy and Tradition: Theological Reflections of Alexander Schmemann*, Crestwood NY: St Vladimir's Seminary Press, 1969/1990, pp. 38–47, p. 40. He resists the formulation of a theology of worship to which the liturgy must 'comply'. He argues that when theology is applied to liturgy it is primarily in order to discover truth about God rather than about worship. Also, because in the Orthodox tradition the task of theology is 'to find words adequate to the mind and experience of the church', this experience of the Church has its 'living focus and expression . . . as Truth revealed and given, and as Truth accepted and "lived", has its *epiphany*, and that is precisely the function of *leitourgia*'.

24. Johnson, 'Liturgy and Theology', p. 206.

25. Irwin, *Liturgical Theology*, p. 47.

26. Paul F. Bradshaw, 'The Reshaping of Liturgical Studies', *Anglican Theological Review*, 72, 1990, p. 482. Paul Marshall argues, 'The overarching problem with primary theology is that its view of liturgy is unilateral and not at all what we might call interactive or multivalent.' Marshall, 'Reconsidering "Liturgical Theology"', p. 135. He further suggests, 'In Fagerberg's view, the job of primary theology is to ask, "what happened?" not "what ought to have happened?"', p. 137.

27. See David W. Bebbington, *Evangelicalism in Modern Britain: A History from the 1730s to the 1980s*, London: Unwin Hyman, 1989, pp. 184–91, and George E. Ladd, *The New Testament and Criticism*, London: Hodder & Stoughton, 1967, p. 55.

28. Kevin Irwin, *Context and Text: Method in Liturgical Theology*, Collegeville MN: Liturgical Press, 1994, p. 44.

29. He defines 'the liturgical fact' as a matter of 'liturgical history' by which he seems to mean the establishing of a normative tradition though historical enquiry. See Schmemann, 'Liturgical Theology: Remarks on Method', p. 144. However, he has more material to work with, with the texts of the Divine Liturgy and the various *typica*, than a Free Church counterpart has available.

30. Schmemann, *Introduction to Liturgical Theology*, pp. 20ff. He quotes the

nineteenth-century Russian liturgical pioneer Archbishop Filaret of Cherigov, who claimed, 'It is evident that liturgical theology must begin with the historical study of worship . . . A theory of worship in the Church which does not rest on historical data is in itself false, and is also harmful in its consequences.'

31. Schmemann, 'Liturgical Theology: Remarks on Method', p. 144.

Chapter 3

1. Thomas Grantham, *Christianismus Primitivus: or, The Ancient Christian Religion, in its nature, certainty, excellency, and beauty, (internal and external) particularly considered, asserted, and vindicated &c*, London: Francis Smith, 1678, Part 2, p. 2.

2. While broadly referring to those who dissented from worship in the Church of England, it originally referred to those clergy who refused to conform to the *Book of Common Prayer* and were ejected from their livings in 1662. By the nineteenth century it had become synonymous with 'Free Church' as in the phrase 'Nonconformist conscience'.

3. Of course the situation varies in different parts of the world.

4. Ernest A. Payne, *Free Churchmen, Unrepentant and Repentant and Other Papers*, London: Carey Kingsgate Press, 1965, p. 3.

5. Clearly there will be legal limits to acceptable behaviour – even for churches – but these legal limits will relate to practices which contravene the laws of the land other than any legal restrictions relating to religious belief. Modern examples of such restrictions would be child protection legislation and financial accounting procedures. What Free Churches would not accept are civil restrictions on the church's worship, the propagation of its beliefs or the joining of that church though conversion and conscience.

6. However, see Nathaniel Micklem (ed.), *Christian Worship: Studies in its Meaning by Members of Mansfield College*, London: Oxford University Press, 1936; and Raymond Abba, *Principles of Christian Worship with Special Reference to the Free Churches*, Oxford: Oxford University Press, 1957. For Baptist contributors, see below.

7. James F. White, *Protestant Worship: Traditions in Transition*, Louisville KY: Westminster John Knox Press, 1989, p. 14.

8. Fenwick and Spinks, *Worship in Transition*, p. 8.

9. There have, of course, been studies of daily prayer though this is beyond the limits of the present study which is primarily about Sunday worship. See Paul F. Bradshaw, *Daily Prayer in the Early Church*, London: Alcuin Club and SPCK, 1981; Robert Taft, *The Liturgy of the Hours in East and West: The Origins of the Divine Office and its Meaning for Today*, Collegeville MN: Liturgical Press, 1986; and George Guiver, *Company of Voices: Daily Prayer and the People of God*, London: SPCK, 1988.

10. White, *Protestant Worship*, p. 15.

11. This is not to ignore the fact that there will be repetition in the use of hymns and the expressions of the prayers, but that repetition has a basis in human behaviour rather than in theological motive.

12. He defines the term as 'that significance which, apart from its own immediate content, each [element] acquires as a result of its place in the general sequence or

order of worship', Schmemann, *Introduction to Liturgical Theology*, p. 19.

13. Irwin, *Context and Text*, p. 53. For various contributions to a discussion of improvisation and inculturation in the liturgy see Mary Collins and David Power, *Liturgy: A Creative Tradition*, Concilium, Edinburgh: T & T Clark, 1983.

14. Irwin, *Context and Text*, p. 56.

15. See *The Baptist Union Directory 2002–2003*, Didcot: Baptist Union of Great Britain, 2002 and the 2003 *Yearbook of the Baptist World Alliance*, Falls Church VA: Baptist World Alliance, 2003. By definition, those baptized will be old enough to confess their own faith in Jesus Christ.

16. That is, a form of modified Calvinism in which human free will is affirmed.

17. See Barrington R. White, *The English Separatist Tradition: From the Marian Martyrs to the Pilgrim Fathers*, London: Oxford University Press, 1971; and *The English Baptists of the Seventeenth Century*, Didcot: Baptist Historical Society, 1983/1996; and Kenneth R. Manley, 'Origins of the Baptists: The Case for Development from Puritanism-Separatism' in William H. Brackney and Ruby J. Burke (eds), *Faith, Life and Witness: The Papers of the Study and Research Division of the Baptist World Alliance, 1986–1990*, Birmingham AL: Samford University Press, 1990, pp. 56–69, though Watts argues for the likelihood of a link between the Lollards and Anabaptists and the General Baptists. Michael Watts, *The Dissenters: From the Reformation to the French Revolution*, Oxford: Clarendon Press, 1978, pp.13–14, and 283–4.

18. See Horton Davies, *Worship and Theology in England: From Cranmer to Baxter and Fox, 1534–1690*, Grand Rapids MI and Cambridge: Eerdmans, 1970/1996, vol. 1, pp. 327–37.

19. See the evidence and arguments in Roger Hayden, 'Evangelical Calvinism among British Baptists with particular reference to Bernard Foskett, Hugh and Caleb Evans and the Bristol Academy, 1690–1791', unpublished PhD dissertation, University of Keele, 1991.

20. See, for example, John H. Y. Briggs, *The English Baptists of the Nineteenth Century*, Didcot: Baptist Historical Society, 1994, pp. 46–50 and 68–9, and Michael J. Walker, *Baptists at the Table*, Didcot: Baptist Historical Society, 1992, pp. 84–120.

21. Ernest A. Payne, *The Fellowship of Believers: Baptist Thought and Practice Yesterday and Today*, London: Carey Kingsgate Press, 1952.

22. Neville Clark, *Call to Worship*, London: SCM Press, 1960; and Stephen F. Winward, *The Reformation of our Worship*, London: Carey Kingsgate Press, 1964. In addition, see Ralph P. Martin, *The Worship of God: Some Theological, Pastoral and Practical Reflections*, Grand Rapids MI: Eerdmans, 1982; Michael H. Taylor, *Variations on a Theme: Some Guidelines for Everyday Christians who want to Reform the Liturgy*, London: Galliard; Stainer and Bell, 1973; and Jamie Wallace, *What Happens in Worship*, London: Baptist Union of Great Britain and Ireland, 1982.

23. Both were, for example, the founding Baptist representatives of the Joint Liturgical Group of Great Britain, with Clark serving from its inception in 1963 until his retirement in 1991.

24. Clark, *Call to Worship*, pp. 13 and 15.

25. However, see Paul F. Bradshaw, *The Search for the Origins of Christian Worship: Sources and Methods for the Study of Early Liturgy*, London: SPCK, 1992,

for a more recent and cautionary approach to historical liturgical enquiry.

26. See Taylor, *Variations on a Theme*, also Alec Gilmore, *The Pattern of the Church: A Baptist View*, London: Lutterworth Press, 1963, especially pp. 118–27 and Martin, *The Worship of God*, who uses biblical reflections alongside his patristic and pastoral considerations.

27. In the interests of clarity, a consistent use of terminology will be used in relation to the notion of *order*. *Order* shall refer to the principle of there being order, rather than disorder; *pattern* shall refer to the shape of a particular ordering of worship; *sequence* shall refer to the sequential order in which things follow one another, and *ordo* shall contain some of the ambiguity it currently reflects in ecumenical discussions, sometimes implying sequence, sometimes order, and sometimes an agreed list of ingredients. See, for example, Thomas F. Best and Dagmar Heller (eds), *Becoming a Christian: The Ecumenical Implications of our Common Baptism*, Geneva: World Council of Churches, 1999.

28. In the second half of the twentieth century, there has been considerable interest by British Baptists in exploring issues of shared identity. See Robert C. Walton, *The Gathered Community*, London: Carey Press, 1946; Gilmore, *Pattern of the Church* and especially the monograph by Brian Haymes, *A Question of Identity: Reflections on Baptist Principles and Practice*, Leeds: Yorkshire Baptist Association, 1986, which fuelled a continuing debate. See also the various reports of the Baptist Union of Great Britain Doctrine and Worship Committee on ecclesiology, ministry and baptism, as well as the work of the college principals, such as Richard Kidd, *Something to Declare: A Study of the Declaration of Principle*, Oxford: Whitley Publications, 1996. Alongside all this, and feeding it, has been the work of the Baptist Historical Society, its journal *The Baptist Quarterly*, and its long-term publishing projects.

29. While a number of Baptist 'ministers' manuals' have been published in the twentieth century, these offer patterns of worship for occasional services where some formality might be considered desirable. See Chapter 5. However, even these will be set aside by many Baptists.

Chapter 4

1. Reprinted in William T. Whitley, 'Paul's Alley, Barbican, 1695–1768', *Transactions of the Baptist Historical Society*, 4, 1914, pp. 46–54, especially pp. 46f.

2. For example, John H. Y. Briggs, 'English Baptists and their Hymnody: An Introduction' in W. H. Brackney (ed.), *Baptist Faith and Witness: The Papers of the Study and Research Division of the Baptist World Alliance, 1990–1995*, Birmingham AL and McClean VA: Samford University Press and The Baptist World Alliance, 1995, pp. 152–9.

3. For example, Raymond Brown, 'Baptist Preaching in Early Eighteenth Century England', *Baptist Quarterly*, 31, 1985, pp. 4–22.

4. A brief account which concentrates, however, on the seventeenth century can be found in Thomas R. McKibben Jr, 'Our Baptist Heritage in Worship', *Review and Expositor*, 80, 1983, pp. 53–69.

5. Horton Davies, *From Cranmer to Baxter and Fox; Worship and Theology in England: From Watts and Wesley to Martineau, 1690–1900*, Grand Rapids MI

and Cambridge: Eerdmans, 1961/1996; *Worship and Theology in England: The Ecumenical Century, 1900 to the Present*, Grand Rapids MI & Cambridge: Eerdmans, 1965/1996; and the earlier *The Worship of the English Puritans*, London: Dacre Press, 1948.

6. See, for example, Best and Heller, *Becoming a Christian*.

7. See James F. White, *A Brief History of Christian Worship*, Nashville TN: Abingdon, 1993, p. 87.

8. See the repeated use of this meaning in Frank C. Senn, *Christian Liturgy: Catholic and Evangelical*, Minneapolis MN: Fortress Press, 1997.

9. Schmemann, *Introduction to Liturgical Theology*, p. 40.

10. Schmemann, 'Liturgical Theology: Remarks on Method', p.144.

11. Thus he speaks of its being based on 'the combination of two fundamental elements: the Eucharist (with which all the other Sacraments are connected in some way), and that form of worship which in the language of western liturgics is called *officium divinum*, connected above all with the three cycles of time: daily, weekly and yearly', *Introduction to Liturgical Theology*, p. 41.

12. Thomas F. Best and Dagmar Heller (eds), *So We Believe, So We Pray: Towards Koinonia in Worship*, Geneva: World Council of Churches, 1995, pp. 6f.

13. Best and Heller, *So We Believe*, pp. 38–48.

14. Gordon W. Lathrop, *Holy Things: A Liturgical Theology*, Minneapolis MN: Fortress Press, 1993. See also his 'Koinonia and the Shape of the Liturgy', *Studia Liturgica*, 26, 1996, pp. 65–81, and a critique of these juxtapositions in Albert Gerhards, '*Koinonia* and the Development of the Liturgy: A Response to Gordon Lathrop', *Studia Liturgica*, 26, 1996, pp. 82–90, especially p. 84.

15. Schmemann, *Introduction to Liturgical Theology*, pp. 59–64.

16. See, for example, Lathrop's discussion of baptism and initiation in *Holy Things*, pp. 59f.

17. Best and Heller, *So We Believe*, p. 6.

18. Lathrop, *Holy Things*, p. 33. This principle is to be distinguished from the structural work of those who have used structural analysis in order to reconstruct the development of liturgical rites over time. See for example, Anton Baumstark, *Comparative Liturgy*, Oxford: Mowbray, 1958, and the work of the 'Mateos school' of liturgiology, especially Robert Taft, 'The Structural Analysis of Liturgical Units: An Essay in Methodology' in *Beyond East and West: Problems in Liturgical Understanding*, Washington DC: Pastoral Press, 1984, pp. 151–64.

19. Schmemann, *Introduction to Liturgical Theology*, pp. 41–5.

20. Lathrop, *Holy Things*, p. 49.

21. White, *Protestant Worship*, pp. 13–15.

22. Though see Chapter 9 below.

23. Payne, *Fellowship of Believers*, p. 96.

24. Some city churches would have used liturgical responses. See A. E. Peaston, *The Prayer Book Tradition in the Free Churches*, London: James Clarke, 1964, and, for example, Frederic C. Spurr and Henry Bonner, *Come Let Us Worship: A Book of Common Worship for use in Free Churches*, London: Kingsgate Press, 1930. However, this would have been a small minority strand within a larger, more unified tradition.

25. Christopher J. Ellis, *Baptist Worship Today*, Didcot: Baptist Union of Great Britain, 1999.

26. The survey was appended to the annual form requesting statistical information. 1,812 forms were returned, representing 85 per cent of the member churches. Thus the results represent far more than a sample from which projections might be made.

27. The results of this attitudinal study are also published in Ellis, *Baptist Worship Today*. See p. 25 for an account of how the sample churches were chosen.

28. Leland H. Carlson (ed.), *The Writings of John Greenwood 1587–1590, Together with the Joint Writings of Henry Barrow and John Greenwood 1587–1590*, London: George Allen & Unwin and the Sir Halley Stewart Trust, 1962, pp. 42–5 and 261. See also Davies, *From Cranmer to Baxter and Fox*, pp. 328–9 and 336.

29. Champlin Burrage, *The Early Dissenters in the Light of Recent Research (1550–1641)*, Cambridge: Cambridge University Press, 1912, vol. 1, p. lxii.

30. Letter from Hughe and Anne Bromheade to Sir William Hammerson of London, printed in Burrage, *Early Dissenters*, vol. 2, pp. 172–7. The term 'propheseying' had a number of meanings in the sixteenth and seventeenth centuries. It could be a synonym for 'preaching', as in William Perkins' *The Art of Propheseying* (1592, ET 1606). It could also refer to an open discussion, but its meaning here seems to suggest an extempore monologue. For further discussion, see Chapter 7.

31. 20 Sept 1608 cited in Burrage, *Early Dissenters*, vol. 2, p. 167.

32. But see p. 51.

33. See Davies, *From Cranmer to Baxter and Fox*, vol. 2, pp. 496f.

34. See Edward Drapes, *Gospel-Glory proclaimed before the sonnes of Men in the Worship of God*, London, 1649, p. 153.

35. Five churches wrote to the Waterlanders in 1626 and said that they couldn't hold a weekly Lord's Supper because there was not a full minister at each of the five churches. See William T. Whitley, *A History of British Baptists*, London: Kingsgate Press, 1923, p. 51.

36. See Davies, *Worship of the English Puritans*, p. 95. Whitley argues that the lack of reference to the reading of Scripture in worship in Grantham's review of General Baptist worship in 1678 (Grantham, *Christianismus Primitivus*) and the orthodox Creed of that year, is evidence that the plain reading of the Bible, without running commentary, was still not practised in the 1670s (*The Works of John Smyth, Fellow of Christ's College, 1594–8*, ed. W. T. Whitley, Cambridge: Cambridge University Press, 1915, vol. 1, pp. lxxxviif.).

37. In *The Brownists Synagogue*, 1641, and quoted in Watts, *Dissenters*, p. 75.

38. Edwards, cited in Murray Tolmie, *The Triumph of the Saints: The Separate Churches of London 1616–1649*, Cambridge: Cambridge University Press, 1977, p. 76.

39. *Fenstanton, Warboys and Hexham Records*, ed. E. B. Underhill, 1847, p. 272.

40. See Davies, *From Cranmer to Baxter and Fox*, vol. 2, p. 507.

41. See Abba, *Principles of Christian Worship*, p. 39, and Davies, *Worship of the English Puritans*, p. 141. For details of worship in Geneva, see William D. Maxwell: *An Outline of Christian Worship: Its Developments and Forms*, London: Oxford University Press, 1936, pp. 112–19, for Calvin's rites; and *The Liturgical Portions of the Genevan Service Book used by John Knox while a Minister of the English Congregation of Marian Exiles at Geneva, 1556–1559*, Edinburgh and London: Oliver & Boyd, 1931, for the worship of the English-speaking exiles.

42. See S. W. Carruthers, *Westminster Confession of Faith*, Glasgow: Free Presbyterian Publications, 1646/1994, pp. 372–86.

43. Davies, *From Cranmer to Baxter and Fox*, vol. 2, p. 434.

44. Roger Hayden, *The Records of a Church of Christ in Bristol, 1640–1687*, Bristol: Bristol Record Society, 1974, p. 48.

45. Hayden, *Records*, pp. 162f.

46. *Calendar of State Papers, Domestic*, 1674, 4 Nov., pp. 396–7, cited in Davies, *From Cranmer to Baxter and Fox*, vol. 2, p. 446.

47. An excerpt from the church book is reprinted in W. T. Whitley, 'Paul's Alley, Barbican, 1695–1768', *Transactions of the Baptist Historical Society*, 4, 1914–15, pp. 46–54. Horton Davies is probably not correct in describing the church as an amalgamation of two General Baptist congregations: Davies, *From Watts and Wesley to Martineau*, vol. 1, p.127.

48. Whitley, 'Paul's Alley', pp. 48f.

49. Ernest A. Payne, 'The Baptist Church near the Barbican', *Baptist Quarterly*, 39, 2001, pp. 132–45, p. 133.

50. Whitley, 'Paul's Alley', p. 47.

51. Whitley, *History of British Baptists*, p. 187; though see his comments on page 51 of Whitley, 'Paul's Alley'.

52. Whitley, 'Paul's Alley', p. 47.

53. On the similarity, see Davies, *From Cranmer to Baxter and Fox*, vol. 2, p. 507; and *From Watts and Wesley to Martineau*, vol. 1, p. 128; and Payne, *Fellowship of Believers*, p. 99. There are frequent references by historians to the way in which Particular Baptist and Independent worship were similar. The assumption is that both groups were Calvinists, and there is certainly evidence of the high regard in which Isaac Watts was held by many Particular Baptists.

54. From the Bury Street Church records, originally printed by John Rippon in *The Baptist Annual Register* of 1800–01 and reprinted in T. G. Crippen, 'From the Bury Street Church Records', *Transactions of the Congregational Historical Society*, 6, 1913, pp. 334–42.

55. Isaac Watts, *The Psalms of David, imitated in the Language of the New Testament, And apply'd to the Christian State and Worship*, London, 1719, p. v.

56. See the account of worship led by Richard Baxter in 1689: Davies, *From Cranmer to Baxter and Fox*, vol. 2, p. 457.

57. During shorter winter days it was sometimes held at noon. For a detailed description of the Lord's Supper in an eighteenth-century Baptist church see *Church Book: St. Andrew's Street Baptist Church, Cambridge 1720–1832*, ed. L. E. Addicott, L. G. Champion, and K. A. Parsons, English Baptist Records, Didcot: Baptist Historical Society, 1991, pp. 27–8.

58. Crippen, 'Bury Street Church Records', p. 334.

59. Crippen, 'Bury Street Church Records', p. 336.

60. There are, of course, some recent restorationist communities such as the Brethren and the Churches of Christ who celebrate the Supper weekly, as well as a few Baptist congregations.

61. Payne, *Fellowship of Believers*, p. 94.

62. William Brock, *The Behaviour Becoming the House of God*, Norwich: The Norfolk and Norwich Association of Baptist Churches, 1845, pp. 3f.

63. Brock, *Behaviour Becoming*, pp. 13–15.

64. Charles M. Birrell, *Life of William Brock D.D.*, London: James Nisbet, 1878, p. 131. Brock doesn't explain his calculation, though we might assume that he is including prayer meetings on church premises as well as long prayers in two services.

65. *Bloomsbury Chapel Year Book*, London, 1850.

66. *Bloomsbury Chapel Year Book*, London, 1862.

67. When the present writer began a ministry in a village on the edge of Cardiff, South Wales, in 1975 it was still the practice of the church for the organist to choose the hymns. Indeed, the practice continues, as music groups now often choose the worship songs for a service.

68. Charles Booth, *Life and Labour of the People of London*, vol. 7: *Religious Influences*, London: Macmillan, 1903, p. 125.

69. The term 'open table' refers to an open invitation to those present (often expressed in such words as: 'all who love the Lord Jesus Christ and seek to follow him') to participate in sharing bread and wine irrespective of denominational allegiance. This has become widespread, particularly in Britain, but, in the nineteenth century, there were robust debates between those who restricted participation in the Supper to those who had been baptized as believers (and sometimes even membership of a particular local Baptist church), and a more inclusive approach. For a discussion of nineteenth-century debates, see Walker, *Baptists at the Table*.

70. Ellis, *Baptist Worship Today*, p. 17.

71. For the use of Ministers' Manuals, see Chapter 6.

72. Clark, *Call to Worship*.

73. See, for example, the explanation of worship based on 'Approach to God', 'God's Word' and 'Our Response' in *Patterns and Prayers for Christian Worship*, Oxford University Press on behalf of the Baptist Union of Great Britain, 1991, pp. 12f.

74. Ellis, *Baptist Worship Today*, pp. 8 and 19.

75. Clark, *Call to Worship*, p. 54.

76. White, *Protestant Worship*, pp. 170–91.

77. White, *Protestant Worship*, p. 193.

78. Though these events soon became trans-denominational, they were begun by Presbyterians with their tradition of preparation for sacramental seasons.

79. White, *Protestant Worship*, p. 172.

80. Charles G. Finney, *Revivals of Religion*, ed. W. H. Harding, London: Morgan & Scott, 1835, p. 5.

81. Finney, *Revivals*, p. 313.

82. At the end of 1996, only 12 per cent of churches used *only* the Charismatic pattern of blocks of songs, but there were just over 44 per cent who used both traditional and Charismatic patterns at least twice a month respectively. However, if we examine another potential indicator of Charismatic concerns, we find that only 20 per cent of churches offered a regular 'ministry time', with 7.5 per cent offering a weekly opportunity and a further 12.7 per cent offering this at least once a month. However, this 20 per cent is less than half those churches that use blocks of songs at least twice a month. Ellis, *Baptist Worship Today*, pp. 17 and 24.

83. Gordon W. Lathrop, 'New Pentecost or Joseph's Britches? Reflections on the History and Meaning of the Worship Ordo in the Megachurches', *Worship*, 72, 1998, pp. 521–38.

84. However, it has been argued that the 'pure' form of the seeker-sensitive event

is self-consciously not wanting to place demands on the worshippers and that it is closer to entertainment than an event in which an encounter with God is anticipated. See Sally Morgenthaler, *Worship Evangelism: Inviting Unbelievers into the Presence of God*, Grand Rapids MI: Zondervan, 1995.

85. Lathrop, *Holy Things*, pp. 43–53.

86. Schmemann, *Introduction to Liturgical Theology*, p. 74.

87. The importance given to the Eucharist is illustrated by the way in which congregations prepared for its monthly celebration. The Broadmead church was not alone in holding a weekday prayer meeting before the monthly celebration of the Lord's Supper. See Hayden, *Records*, p. 54.

88. See Martin D. Stringer, *On the Perception of Worship: The Ethnography of Worship in Four Christian Congregations in Manchester*, Birmingham: University of Birmingham Press, 1999, pp. 150–2.

89. Vladimir Lossky, 'Tradition and Traditions' in Leonid Ouspensky and Vladimir Lossky (eds), *The Meaning of Icons*, Crestwood NY: St Vladimir's Seminary Press, 1952/1989, pp. 11–22.

90. Compare John Fawcett's use of 'ordinance', discussed in Chapter 5, with the more recent discussions, referred to in Chapter 3, which base the ordering of worship either on the theological, historical or ecumenical concerns of the Liturgical Movement, or on the evangelistic concerns of a missionary church.

91. White, *Protestant Worship*, p. 17.

92. I am grateful to the Revd Paul Roberts, formerly of Trinity College, Bristol, for the application of this phrase to the main sections of worship, in his unpublished lecture notes. Roberts distinguishes between this idea and 'superficial structures' by which he means the detailed items of worship. This distinction, borrowing language from anthropology and linguistics, is more than simply a way of talking about 'sections' because it suggests movement below the surface structures and Roberts is keen to use this dynamic concept to explore the negotiating of thresholds from one stage to another, relying as he does on Van Gennep's notion of the 'transliminal' (see Arnold van Gennep, *The Rites of Passage*, London: Routledge & Kegan Paul, 1960). Here we shall simply make the main distinction and recognize in it a dynamic movement.

93. See, for example, Friedrich Heiler, *Prayer: A Study in the History and Psychology of Religion*, London: Oxford University Press, 1932, pp. 345f.

94. Benjamin Wallin, *Gospel Requisites to Acceptable Prayer*, London, 1770, p. 22.

95. Charles H. Spurgeon, *Lectures to my Students: A Selection of Addresses delivered to the Students of the Pastors' College, Metropolitan Tabernacle*, London: Passmore & Alabaster, 1906, pp. 52–71.

Chapter 5

1. 'The Authority and Sanctification of the Lord's Day Explained and Enforced' in the Circular Letter from the Baptist Ministers and Messengers, assembled at Northampton, 6, 7, and 8 June 1786, p. 8.

2. See Christopher Hill, *A Turbulent, Seditious, and Factious People: John Bunyan and his Church*, Oxford: Oxford University Press, 1988, pp. 292–5.

3. Paul Fiddes, Professor of Systematic Theology in the University of Oxford, dis-

tinguishes between 'first-order' and 'second-order' theology, arguing that the former is found in 'the confession of the church in its worship, its creeds, its preaching, its works of love and its testimony through individual believers'. He illustrates this by pointing out how Karl Barth used the historic creeds (thus regarded as first-order theology) as a resource for his *Church Dogmatics* which are consequently second-order theology. See Paul S. Fiddes, 'Theology and a Baptist Way of Community' in Paul S. Fiddes (ed.), *Doing Theology in a Baptist Way*, Oxford: Whitley Publications, 2000, pp. 19–38, p. 24, and Karl Barth, *Church Dogmatics*, vol. I/1: *The Doctrine of the Word of God*, Edinburgh: T & T Clark, 1977, pp. 71–87.

4. Schmemann, *Introduction to Liturgical Theology*, p. 39.

5. James McClendon speaks of a 'conviction' as 'an embodied belief'. James W. McClendon Jr, *Systematic Theology*, vol. 1: *Ethics*, Nashville TN: Abingdon Press, 1986, p. 23. Here the spirituality which underpins and is expressed in Baptist worship is presented as a group of core values which interact in ways we shall explore later.

6. Ernest A. Payne and Stephen F. Winward, *Orders and Prayers for Church Worship: A Manual for Ministers*, London: Baptist Union of Great Britain and Ireland, 1960, p. xv.

7. Irwin, *Context and Text*, pp. 46–9. He says of this theology of liturgy that it 'describes what Christian liturgy is and what it does in terms of actualizing the reality of Christ's paschal mystery for the Church, gathered and enlivened by the power of the Holy Spirit'.

8. While implied by Irwin, it is explicit in his exposition of the epicletic dimension of worship: 'What really matters . . . in every act of liturgy is what God accomplishes among us through Christ in the power of the Spirit.' Irwin, *Context and Text*, p. 48.

9. See Donald F. Durnbaugh, *The Believers' Church: The History and Character of Radical Protestantism*, Scottdale PA: Herald Press, 1968/1985; and George H. Williams, *The Radical Reformation*, London: Weidenfeld and Nicolson, 1962.

10. See White, *Protestant Worship*, pp. 120–6, and Davies, *From Cranmer to Baxter and Fox*, vol. 1, p. 325.

11. 'Luther accepted the guidance of the Bible in doctrinal matters but refused to regard it as a directory of worship. Luther would admit in his worship any liturgical elements that were not inconsistent with the teaching of the Bible. Calvin would only accept what the Bible specifically warranted . . . Human additions were to be abhorred, for God had made known his will in the Scriptures.' Davies, *Worship of the English Puritans*, p. 19. He explains that, while the established church exemplified the Lutheran approach, the Puritans and Separatists followed Calvin. However, White suggests a more complex interpretation of Calvin, with the Separatists and Puritans going further and exercising 'a rigorous biblicism'. See John Calvin, *Institutes of the Christian Religion*, London: James Clarke, 1957, Book IV. X. 30, in vol. 2, p. 436; and White, *Protestant Worship*, p. 118.

12. See White, *English Baptists*, p. 119. The General Baptists in the Midlands produced a Confession of Faith, *The Orthodox Creed*, in 1678. It follows very closely the section which deals with the basis of worship, though it later paraphrases the remainder of the chapter in a way which reflects the more sombre worship of the General Baptists. For example it excludes the references to singing and refers to the 'solemn assemblies of the church'. William L. Lumpkin, *Baptist Confessions of Faith*,

Valley Forge PA: Judson Press, 1969, p. 328.

13. The opening of Chapter 22, 'Of Religious Worship, and the Sabbath Day', reprinted in Lumpkin, *Baptist Confessions*, p. 280. The confession offers a number of statements about the nature and meaning of worship (see especially Chapter 22, pp. 280–2). The chapter on worship and the Sabbath is a verbatim inclusion of Chapter 21 of the *Westminster Confession,* apart from some very minor textual differences, and three more significant phrases. (In the section on psalms, 'hymns and spiritual songs' are mentioned. This is not only a close quotation from Colossians 3.16 and Ephesians 5.19, but reflects the beginnings of congregational hymn singing among Particular Baptists. The other changes include the mentioning of Baptism and the Lord's Supper by name and the avoidance of the word 'sacrament', and a minor addition which says that the law of nature which sets apart a day of rest is 'by God's appointment'.)

14. Lumpkin, *Baptist Confessions*, p. 280.

15. By the nineteenth century, Baptists were using the word in a self-conscious attempt to distinguish it from 'sacrament'. Believing that they wished to distinguish something done in obedience to a divine command was quite different from an action interpreted by a sacramental theology of which they were suspicious. In the seventeenth century, the General Baptists appear to use the word 'sacrament' more freely than the Particular Baptists, as can be seen by comparing the respective creeds of 1677 and 1678. Lumpkin, *Baptist Confessions*, pp. 290 and 321.

16. Lumpkin, *Baptist Confessions*, p. 281.

17. See White, *Protestant Worship*, p. 118.

18. For examples, see Clark, *Call to Worship*, pp. 31f.

19. John Fawcett, *The Holiness which Becometh the House of the Lord*, Halifax, 1808, p. 25. Converted under the ministry of George Whitfield, Fawcett (1740–1817) was minister at Wainsgate, Hebdon Bridge, in Yorkshire, and became a leading figure among Particular Baptists in the north of England. He was instrumental in the training of ministers and was a significant hymn writer.

20. Compare the prayer from the Leonine Sacramentary of the Fifth and Sixth Centuries: 'Almighty and everlasting God, increase in us the gifts of faith, hope, and charity; and, that we may obtain what you promise, *make us love what you command;* through Jesus Christ . . . ' quoted in Philip H. Pfatteicher, *Liturgical Spirituality*, Valley Forge PA: Trinity Press International, 1997, p. 1.

21. Benjamin Keach, *The Breach Repaired in God's Worship: or singing psalms and hymns, and spiritual songs, proved to be an holy ordinance of Jesus Christ,* London, 1691/1700, p. 123.

22. This promise still requires, however, a devout and sincere attitude on the part of the worshippers. See the caution concerning 'unprofitable sabbaths' in Brock, *Behaviour Becoming the House of God*, p. 22.

23. While the issues around the notion of *ex opere operato* are more nuanced than this statement suggests, it fairly represents the view of many Baptists with regard to the relationship of outward action and inner disposition.

24. e.g. Matthew 6.5–8 and John 4.23–4.

25. But see Ellis, *Baptist Worship Today*, p. 7.

26. Such an exploration might include, for example, the use of Scripture in prayers – such as Paul Bradshaw's study of the use of the Psalms in daily prayer (Paul F. Bradshaw, *Two Ways of Praying: Introducing Liturgical Spirituality*, London:

SPCK, 1995, pp. 89–100) or the use of Scripture in the structuring of worship as in Winward, *Reformation of Our Worship*, especially pp. 12–31.

27. Allmen, *Worship*, p. 130, and Peter Brunner, *Worship in the Name of Jesus*, St Louis MO and London: Concordia, 1968.

28. *We Baptists*, Franklin TN: Baptist World Alliance, 1999, p. 23. Compare Brian Haymes who argues for three loci of authority: 'First, all true and ultimate authority is Christ's . . . Second, the Bible is authoritative, significantly more so than preacher, pastor or pope . . . Third, when it comes to the shape, direction and ordering of the life of the local company of believers then, as the Declaration of Principle has it, "each Church has liberty, under the guidance of the Holy Spirit, to interpret and administer his (Christ's) Laws".' Haymes, *Question of Identity*, p. 14.

29. H. W. Robinson, *The Christian Experience of the Holy Spirit*, London: Nisbet, 1928, pp. 181–3.

30. Thomas T. Gough, *Christian Worship*, the Circular Letter from the Ministers and Messengers of the several Baptist Churches in the Northamptonshire Association assembled at Olney, 1845, pp. 4f. Gough was pastor of the Clipston church from 1835 until 1869 and served as association secretary from 1863 until 1869.

31. Gough, *Christian Worship*, p. 5.

32. Fawcett, *Holiness*, p. 14.

33. Watts, *Dissenters*, pp. 26–34.

34. Gough, *Christian Worship*, p. 5.

35. Brock, *Behaviour Becoming the House of God*, p. 23.

36. See John Bunyan, *Grace Abounding to the Chief of Sinners*, ed. R. Sharrock, Oxford: Clarendon Press, 1666; Owen C. Watkins, *The Puritan Experience*, London: Routledge & Kegan Paul, 1972; and Charles L. Cohen, *God's Caress: The Psychology of Puritan Religious Experience*, New York: Oxford University Press, 1986.

37. See Davies, *From Cranmer to Baxter and Fox*, vol. 2, pp. 449–55.

38. For Evangelical spirituality, see David K. Gillett, *Trust and Obey: Explorations in Evangelical Spirituality*, London: Darton, Longman & Todd, 1993; James M. Gordon, *Evangelical Spirituality from the Wesleys to John Stott*, London: SPCK, 1991; and Bebbington, *Evangelicalism*.

39. Lumpkin, *Baptist Confessions*, p. xx.

40. John Bunyan, 'I will Pray with the Spirit', in *The Doctrine of the Law and Grace Unfolded: The miscellaneous works of John Bunyan series*, vol. 2, ed. Richard L. Greaves, Oxford: Oxford University Press, 1976, p. 235. Reproduced by kind permission of Oxford University Press.

41. Alister E. McGrath, *The Intellectual Origins of the European Reformation*, Oxford: Basil Blackwell, 1987, pp. 10–12; and *Roots that Refresh: A Celebration of Reformation Spirituality*, London: Hodder & Stoughton, 1991, pp. 44f.

42. The description of Thomas Lambe's General Baptist congregation in Edward's *Gangaena* describes a lively participation in discussing, and even interrupting, the sermon. Tolmie, *Triumph of the Saints*, pp. 76f.

43. Indeed, the 1996 and 1997 worship surveys indicated something of a culture of informality. See Ellis, *Baptist Worship Today*, p. 43.

44. It is interesting to compare secular discussions about the nature of sincerity. Hubert Read has difficulty in reaching a definition but concentrates on notions such as honesty, truthfulness and integrity. Lionel Trilling, on the other hand, argues that

'it refers primarily to a congruence between avowal and actual feeling'. He prefers the concept of 'authenticity' which 'suggests a more strenuous moral experience than "sincerity" does'. See Hubert Read, *The Cult of Sincerity*, London: Faber & Faber, 1968; and Lionel Trilling, *Sincerity and Authenticity*, London: Oxford University Press, 1972.

45. Christopher Hill, *The Century of Revolution: 1603–1741*, London: Nelson, 1961, p. 235.

46. Fawcett, *Holiness*, pp. 27f.

47. Brock, *Behaviour Becoming the House of God*, pp. 9f.

48. Brock, *Behaviour Becoming the House of God*, pp. 12f.

49. Brock, *Behaviour Becoming the House of God*, p. 6.

50. Brock, *Behaviour Becoming the House of God*, pp. 14–17.

51. Lumpkin, *Baptist Confessions*, p. 119.

52. See Clyde Binfield, 'The Coats Family and Paisley Baptists', *Baptist Quarterly*, 36, 1995, pp. 29–42, and Philip. Hayden, 'Nonconformist Meeting-Houses and Chapels', unpublished address to the Canterbury Archaeological Society, 1978.

53. Carruthers, *Westminster Confession*, p. 119.

54. *Covenant 21*, Didcot: Baptist Union of Great Britain, 2000, pp. 5f.

55. *Covenant 21*, p. 3.

56. Haymes, *Question of Identity*, p. 8.

57. *The Nature of the Assembly and the Council of the Baptist Union of Great Britain*, Didcot: Baptist Union of Great Britain, 1994, p. 6.

58. See especially, Fiddes, *Doing Theology in a Baptist Way*; Paul. S. Fiddes, Roger Hayden, Richard L. Kidd, Keith W. Clements, and Brian Haymes, *Bound to Love: The Covenant Basis of Baptist Life and Mission*, London: Baptist Union of Great Britain, 1985; and, from North America, Stanley J. Grenz, *Theology for the Community of God*, Grand Rapids MI and Vancouver BC: Eerdmans with Regent College Publishing, 1994.

59. Fawcett, *Holiness*, p. 15.

60. Brock, *Behaviour Becoming the House of God*, p. 5.

61. Henry W. Robinson, *The Life and Faith of the Baptists*, London: Kingsgate Press, 1946, p. 93.

62. Robinson, *Life and Faith*, p. 94.

63. F. F. Whitby, *Our Worship in the Light of our Principles*, Annual Report of the Western Baptist Association, 1903, p. 10.

64. Whitby, *Our Worship*, pp. 14f.

65. John Ryland, *The Beauty of Social Religion or the Nature and Glory of a Gospel Church*, the Circular Letter of the Northamptonshire Association, 1777, p. 3. John Ryland senior (1723–92) was a minister, author and schoolmaster in Warwick and Northampton and was a leading figure in the newly formed association in Northamptonshire and the surrounding counties.

66. Ryland, *The Beauty of Social Religion*, p. 4.

67. Ryland, *The Beauty of Social Religion*, p. 9.

68. A. R. Edwards, *The Church's Worship*, Annual Report of the Western Baptist Association, 1911, p. 8. Edwards was a prominent member of the Dorchester church and president of the association in 1911.

69. *Baptist Praise and Worship*, 472.

70. John Rippon (1751–1836) was a leading figure in the Baptist denomination.

As well as his contribution to Baptist worship through his *Selection* of hymns, he was influential through his publishing of *The Baptist Annual Register* between 1790 and 1802 which helped to gather and disseminate information about Baptist causes and thought and he was closely involved in the establishment of the Baptist union in 1812–13.

71. Dietrich Bonhoeffer, *Ethics*, London: SCM Press, 1955, pp. 103–10.

72. This is not to say that tradition, as custom, does not form much Baptist church life, but the basis for this is more to do with the human need for familiarity than with any sense of the perfection of the Church.

73. XXI, Lumpkin, *Baptist Confessions*, pp. 278f.

74. Note, for example, the seventeenth and eighteenth-century General Baptist concern for not singing in a mixed congregation and the nineteenth-century references to the presence of unbelievers in what by then was called 'public worship', such as in the letter of 'an unworthy worshipper' in *The Freeman* for 24 June 1857.

75. Raymond Brown, *The English Baptists of the Eighteenth Century*, London: Baptist Historical Society, 1986, p. 73.

76. Benjamin Keach, *The Display of Glorious Grace: or the Covenant of Peace*, London, 1698, quoted in Brown, 'Baptist Preaching', p. 16.

77. Lumpkin, *Baptist Confessions*, pp. 212f.

78. Joseph Ivimey, *A History of the English Baptists*, London, 1811, vol. 2, p. 546.

79. Quoted in Ivimey, *History*, vol. 2, p. 549. Bagley was co-pastor with Emmanuel Gifford of the Pithay church.

80. From an elegy by Richard Burnham, published at the time of Gifford's death and reprinted in Ernest A. Payne, 'An Elegy on Andrew Gifford', Baptist Quarterly, 9, 1938, pp. 54–7. See Chapter 7 for a further study of evangelistic preaching.

81. The opening section of Carey's *Enquiry* is concerned with the Great Commission and its continuing validity. William Carey, *An Enquiry into the Obligations of Christians to use Means for the Conversion of the Heathen*, Leicester, 1792, pp. 7–13.

82. *Baptist Union Directory 2002–03*, p. 7.

83. Payne, *Fellowship of Believers*, pp. 95–8.

84. McClendon, *Ethics*, p. 23.

85. Sheldrake, *Spirituality and History*, p. 60.

86. Sheldrake, Sykes, S., *Spirituality and Theology*, p. 86.

Chapter 6

1. Bunyan, 'I will Pray with the Spirit', pp. 252 and 256.

2. As was suggested in our discussion of method in Chapter 2, the 'worship text' which is available for our study comprises worship practices and commentaries on worship, rather than worship words.

3. Some prayers have been noted by a shorthand writer, though, in at least the case of Alexander Maclaren, the one praying was unaware of this at the time. See Charles H. Spurgeon, *Spurgeon's Prayers*, Fearn, Ross-shire: Christian Focus Publications, 1993; and Alexander Maclaren, *Pulpit Prayers*, London: Hodder & Stoughton, 1907; and *Pulpit Prayers (Second Series)*, London: Hodder & Stoughton, 1911.

4. The letter is printed in Burrage, *Early Dissenters*, pp. 172–7.

5. John Smyth had earlier established the principles underlying this practice when he claimed that, because 'wordes and syntaxe are signes of thinges, and of the relations and reasons of things . . . it followeth that bookes or writinges are in the nature of pictures or Images & therefore in the nature of ceremonies: & and so by consequent reading a booke is ceremoniall'. John Smyth, 'The Differences of the Churches of the Seperation: containing a description of the Leitovrgie and Ministries of the visible Church' in W. T. Whitley (ed.), *The Works of John Smyth fellow of Christ's College 1594–8*, vol. 1, Amsterdam and Cambridge: Cambridge University Press with the Baptist Historical Society, 1608/1915, pp. 269–320, pp. 278f.

6. See Whitley, 'Paul's Alley', p. 47.

7. Although the records refer to the minister going into the pulpit to preach, it is not clear whether the first part of the service was led by the minister from another position, or from a lower tier of a three-decker pulpit, or whether the early worship was led by someone else.

8. Crippen, 'Bury Street Church Records', p. 334.

9. Spurgeon, *Lectures*, p. 62. Charles Haddon Spurgeon (1834–92) was a dominant figure in nineteenth-century Nonconformity. Thousands gathered to hear his preaching each week at the New Park Street Church and later at the Metropolitan Tabernacle.

10. Brock, *Behaviour Becoming the House of God*, pp. 13f.

11. Brock, *Behaviour Becoming the House of God*, p. 22.

12. Brock, *Behaviour Becoming the House of God*, p. 23.

13. See, for example, Hugh Martin's suggestions for reform in Hugh Martin, 'The Conduct of Baptist Worship', *Baptist Quarterly*, 17, 1957, pp. 148–56: 'My second reform is the breaking up of the "long" prayer, which it is hard to defend. It is both too long and too miscellaneous, putting together as it does thanksgiving, petition, penitence and intercession', p. 155.

14. See Douglas McBain, *Fire over the Waters: Renewal among Baptists and Others from the 1960s to the 1990s*, London: Darton, Longman & Todd, 1997, pp. 177–82.

15. Ellis, *Baptist Worship Today*, p. 13.

16. Ellis, *Baptist Worship Today*, p. 32.

17. See, for example, the issues for 2 and 30 October 1868.

18. It was not only the hymns of Isaac Watts which were used in Particular Baptist circles in the eighteenth century. Other works of his were circulated and he was included in the recommended reading for those preparing for ministry at the Bristol Academy. See John Rippon, *The Baptist Annual Register*, London, 1790, vol. 1, p. 255.

19. Isaac Watts, 'A Guide to Prayer; or a Free and Rational Account of the Grace and Spirit of Prayer with Plain Directions how Every Christian may Attain Them' in J. Doddridge (ed.), *The Works of the Reverend and Learned Isaac Watts, D.D.*, London: J. Barfield, 1715, pp. 105–96, pp. 125ff.

20. See Ellis, *Baptist Worship Today*, pp. 13f. We must remember that these responses relate to free prayer, not all prayers. We also need to register a measure of caution as many of the responses will have been returned by people other than those actually leading the prayers and so may not always represent what is actually happening.

21. Arguably, 'ex tempore' refers to prayers specific to a particular occasion and could justifiably be used to refer to pre-composed prayers especially chosen for a service.

22. See for example, West Bridgeford, Nottingham, Tydale, Bristol, and Coats Memorial Paisley, Baptist churches.

23. See Spurr and Bonner, *Come Let Us Worship*. This was the fruit of local liturgical experiment by successive ministers and congregation of Hampstead Road Church, Birmingham, and was revised and published nationally by the Baptist Union publishing house. Spurr claims in the introduction (p. vii) that the material, in the form of complete services of worship with responsive prayers, had been in use in the Birmingham church for forty years. This places local use of liturgical services at the end of the nineteenth century. While we must see this as an exceptional situation, its wider publication in 1930 probably indicates a changing mood.

24. Melbourn E. Aubrey, *A Minister's Manual*, London: Kingsgate Press, 1927, p. v.

25. F. B. Meyer, *Free Church Service Manual*, London: National Free Church Council, 1911; Aubrey, *Minister's Manual*, 'containing orders of service for marriage, dedication of infants, baptism of believers, communion of the Lord's Supper, burial of the dead and other occasions'; Payne and Winward, *Orders and Prayers*; Alec Gilmore, Edward Smalley and Michael Walker, *Praise God: A Collection of Resource Material for Christian Worship*, London: Baptist Union of Great Britain and Ireland, 1980; and *Patterns and Prayers*.

26. While there is no statistical evidence available for the perception that *Praise God* was not widely accepted, that perception influenced the brief given to the group which was commissioned to compile *Patterns and Prayers for Christian Worship*.

27. In *Patterns and Prayers*, see for example, the Introduction (pp. 1–17), especially the third pattern for an 'Open Service' (p. 17) and the third pattern for the Lord's Supper (pp. 74–75).

28. Brock, *Behaviour Becoming the House of God*, pp. 13f.

29. Watts, 'Guide to Prayer', p.112.

30. Watts, 'Guide to Prayer', pp. 112 and 114.

31. While this adjective might strictly be regarded as anachronistic in regard of Watts, who predated the Evangelical Revival, it is a fair description of the tenor of his spirituality and the warmth of his affections expressed both in the 'Guide to Prayer' and in his hymns.

32. John Gill, *Two Discourses; the One on Prayer, the Other on Singing of Psalms*, London, 1751, pp. 13–21.

33. Wallin, *Gospel Requisites*, p. 4.

34. Alexander Maclaren (1826–1910) was renowned for his pulpit oratory, especially at the Union Chapel, Manchester, where he was minister for 45 years. He was the author of many expositional volumes which demonstrate both his commitment to higher criticism and his wide literary tastes. In 1905 he chaired the first Baptist World Congress.

35. See, for example, Hugh Martin, 'The Conduct of Baptist Worship', *Baptist Quarterly*, 17, 1957, pp. 148–56.

36. Bunyan, 'I will Pray with the Spirit', p. 235.

37. Watts was concerned to mediate between what he saw as the two extremes of a formal use of written prayers and a slovenly, unprepared worship.

38. Wallin, *Gospel Requisites*, p. 10.
39. Bunyan, 'I will Pray with the Spirit', p. 235.
40. Bunyan, 'I will Pray with the Spirit', p. 249.
41. This is not to limit the religious affections to the emotions, but to accept that there is some link between them.
42. Fawcett, *Holiness*, p. 27.
43. Following David Bebbington in his *Evangelicalism in Modern Britain*, David Gillett argues that the doctrine of assurance in John Wesley and subsequent Evangelicalism is based on an empirical approach to religious experience: 'The experimental, empiricist approach of Wesley, and, even more significantly, of Jonathan Edwards, is a thoroughgoing Enlightenment approach. It shows an acceptance of the fundamental principle of the Enlightenment that all knowledge derives from the enquiry of the senses; the Evangelicals merely included in their field of valid evidences the realm of the spirit.' Gillett, *Trust and Obey*, p. 47 n.
44. Bunyan, 'I will Pray with the Spirit', p. 252.
45. Brock, *Behaviour Becoming the House of God*, pp. 22f.
46. Alexander Maclaren, *Evangelical Mysticism*, London: Baptist Union of Great Britain and Ireland, 1901, p. 6.
47. With a reference to Leviticus 10.1–2, he suggests that prayer offered without the assistance of the Spirit is like the strange fire offered by the sons of Aaron which was rejected by God and consumed them. Bunyan, 'I will Pray with the Spirit', p. 243.
48. Bunyan, 'I will Pray with the Spirit', p. 246.
49. Burrage, *Early Dissenters*, vol. 2, p. 174.
50. However, here is also early evidence of what was to elicit one of the recurring criticisms of free prayer, namely, that it tends to over-long praying – 'we must strive in prayer with continuance'. Length is a consequence of the urgent and desperate need of a soul before God, resulting in an out-flowing of praise and petition which cannot readily be contained within the brief prayers and collects of a prayer book. The Bromheades conclude their argument for free prayer over and against written prayers with the Separatist belief that no good or true worship could be offered by a false church.
51. Davies, *Worship of the English Puritans*, p. 103.
52. Bunyan, 'I will Pray with the Spirit', p. 259.
53. Gill, however, is still keen to point out that such a belief in the necessity of inspiration does not mean that we only pray when we feel like it, as 'prayer may be considered as a natural duty'. Gill, *Two Discourses*, p. 29.
54. Spurgeon, *Lectures*, p. 43
55. Bunyan, 'I will Pray with the Spirit', pp. 236f.
56. Bunyan, 'I will Pray with the Spirit', p. 236.
57. Bunyan, 'I will Pray with the Spirit', pp. 237 and 248.
58. Bunyan, 'I will Pray with the Spirit', pp. 257f.
59. Bunyan, 'I will Pray with the Spirit', pp. 237–9. Cf. John Macquarrie's discussion of different kinds of knowledge. In particular, he likens the knowledge of God which becomes available through spirituality as being personal, rather than propositional. John Macquarrie, *In Search of Deity: An Essay in Dialectical Theism*, The Gifford Lectures for 1983–4, London: SCM Press, 1984, p. 188.
60. See, for example, Gill, *Two Discourses*, p. 30.
61. Spurgeon, *Lectures*, p. 70.

62. Wallin, *Gospel Requisites*, p. 12.

63. Bunyan, 'I will Pray with the Spirit', p. 247f.

64. Significantly, recent worship books of more liturgical traditions have tended to encourage some forms of free prayer and specially composed prayer in the contextualizing of the intercessions. See, for example, *The Alternative Service Book*, Oxford: Oxford University Press and A. R. Mowbray, 1980, p. 124; and *Common Worship: Services and Prayers for the Church of England*, London: Church House Publishing, 2000, p. 174.

65. His original German *Das Gebet* went through various editions as his views evolved. This development is not reflected in the single English translation and has led to some debate about the interpretation of his work. However, for the purposes of this study, the basic distinction which he makes between mystical and prophetic prayer will be used as of two types of prayer, different emphases within the various traditions of spirituality. See Heiler, *Prayer*; A. R. George, 'Prophetic Prayer' in G. S. Wakefield (ed.), *A Dictionary of Christian Spirituality*, London: SCM Press, 1983, pp. 317ff.; and 'Heiler', ibid., pp. 188–9.

66. The early editions of *Das Gebet* betray a Ritschlian suspicion of mysticism, but under the influence of Friedrich von Hügel, Heiler came to a more positive view of this tradition. See *Prayer*, p. 188. It does not distort his work to regard these two forms of prayer as complementary, and it need not be a matter of either/or.

67. Heiler, *Prayer*, pp. 265f.

68. See, for example, Claus Westermann, *Praise and Lament in the Psalms*, Atlanta GA: John Knox Press, 1981; and Walter Brueggemann, 'The Costly Loss of Lament', *Journal for the Study of the Old Testament*, 36, 1986, pp. 57–71.

69. Vavasor Powell, *Common Prayer Book No Divine Service or, XXVII Reasons against Forming and Imposing Human Liturgies or Common Prayer Books*, London: Livewel Chapman, 1661, p. 7.

70. See, for example, Pfatteicher, *Liturgical Spirituality*; and Susan J. White, *The Spirit of Worship: The Liturgical Tradition*, ed. P. Sheldrake, London: Darton, Longman & Todd, 1999.

71. While engagement can occur in worship without any outward sign, it will be argued in Chapter 8 that the need for greater active participation on the part of Baptist congregations has been one of the reasons for an increase in the proportion of congregational singing in Baptist services over the years.

72. Of course, this praying also leads to the developing of gifts, and the reading of prayers has been seen as a means of atrophying these gifts. Thus John Owen argued, 'we daily see men napkining their talents until they are taken from them'. John Owen, *A Discourse on the Work of the Holy Spirit in Prayer*, ed. Thomas Russell, London: Richard Baynes, 1826, p. 52.

73. Davies, *Worship of the English Puritans*, p. 105.

74. We can speculate that the domestic scale of much Baptist worship and its informality may well result in an immediacy between intention and action, lacking in more ceremonial liturgical environments. Over half the member churches of the Baptist Union of Great Britain have fewer than 50 members (see *Half the Denomination: The Report of the Working Group on the Care of Small Churches*, London: Baptist Union of Great Britain, 1983).

75. Ellis, *Baptist Worship Today*, p. 12.

76. John Skoglund, 'Free Prayer', *Studia Liturgica*, 4, 1974, pp. 151–66, p. 162.

77. Watts, 'Guide to Prayer', pp. 127f.

78. Indeed, we can see how the rubrics of late twentieth-century service books in the Anglican and Roman Catholic traditions now provide an opportunity for free intercessions and petitions for this same pastoral reason.

Chapter 7

1. Davies, *Worship of the English Puritans*, p. 182.

2. While the correlation is not exact, the distinction bears some comparison with the distinction between teaching and proclamation which we shall explore later in this chapter.

3. See, for example, Fawcett, *Holiness*, p. 25.

4. Quoted in Davies, *Worship of the English Puritans*, p. 185.

5. There are similarities between this distinction and the concern among some contemporary liturgists to distinguish between written liturgical texts and the event of worship. See, for example, Irwin, *Liturgical Theology*, pp. 68–72. Similarly, in the next chapter we shall not examine hymn texts, because of the difference between the written text and the event of performance.

6. Joseph Stennett, *The Work of the late Reverend and Learned Mr. Joseph Stennett*, London, 1732, vol. 1, p. 13. Though Stennett preached extempore, with only a few headings written down, the resulting transcripts are an example of polished rhetoric and reasoned argument, complete with classical as well as biblical allusions. For example, vol. 1 contains funeral sermons and a sermon on the occasion of the victory of the Duke of Marlborough at Blenheim in 1704.

7. John Rippon, *A Brief Memoir of the Life and Writings of the Reverend and Learned John Gill, D.D.*, London and Harrisonburg VA: Sprinkle Publications, 1838, p. 122.

8. Letter from Hughe and Anne Bromhead to Sir William Hammerson, probably 1609, reprinted in Burrage, *Early Dissenters*, vol. 2, p. 177.

9. Davies, *Worship of the English Puritans*, p. 95.

10. This is distinct from the earlier use of the word 'prophesying' to denote the weekday lectures of Zwingli in Zurich and the 'preaching class' meetings of local clergy, which were attempted and banned under Elizabeth. See Leonard J. Trinterud, 'The Origins of Puritanism', *Church History*, 21, 1952, p. 46.

11. Watts, *Dissenters*, p. 75; and Tolmie, *Triumph of the Saints*, p. 76.

12. Whitley, 'Paul's Alley', p. 47.

13. In Chapter 4 we noted that caution was needed in seeing the Barbican church as broadly representative of General Baptists.

14. Crippen, 'Bury Street Church Records', p. 334.

15. Davies, *From Watts and Wesley to Martineau*, vol. 1, p. 96.

16. J. H. Colligan, *Eighteenth Century Nonconformity*, London: Longmans, Green & Co., 1915, p.88.

17. Brown, *English Baptists*, p. 76.

18. Andrew Fuller (1754–1815) was a minister and theologian in Kettering. His moderate form of Calvinism (sometimes called 'Fullerism') reflected the devotional warmth and missionary zeal of the Evangelical Revival. This modified Calvinism, together with his zealous leadership, led to the establishing of what became the Baptist Missionary Society, with William Carey (1761–1834) as its first missionary.

19. Robert Hall, *Hearing the Word*, Kettering: Circular Letter of the Northamptonshire Baptist Association, 1814, p. 5. Robert Hall (1764–1831) was ministering in Leicester at the time, having previously served in Bristol (both the Broadmead church and the academy) and St Andrew's Street, Cambridge. He was later to return to Broadmead and was widely known for his polished rhetoric and radical views. See the opening section of this chapter.

20. Brock, *Behaviour Becoming the House of God*, pp. 19 and 15 respectively.

21. R. T. Jones, *Congregationalism in England, 1662–1962*, London: Independent Press, 1962, pp. 218–20.

22. *Sermons*, vol. 4, p. 108, quoted in Briggs, *English Baptists*, p. 32.

23. Ian Sellars, 'Other Times, Other Ministries: John Fawcett and Alexander Maclaren', *Baptist Quarterly*, 32, 1987, p. 188.

24. Ellis, *Baptist Worship Today*, pp. 10f.

25. See Judith W. Baker, 'The Use of *Kerygma* in the Early Church' in Robert E. Webber (ed.), *The Complete Library of Christian Worship*, vol. 3: *The Renewal of Sunday Worship*, Peabody MA: Hendrikson, 1993, pp. 288–9; and C. H. Dodd, *The Apostolic Preaching and its Developments*, London: Hodder & Stoughton, 1944, pp. 7–35.

26. For a discussion of this in relation to communication theory, see Duncan B. Forrester, J. I. H. McDonald and Gian Tellini, *Encounter with God: An Introduction to Christian Worship and Practice*, Edinburgh: T & T Clark, 1996, p. 79.

27. Raymond Brown argues that the teaching of Hyper-Calvinists like Brine and Gill was a departure from an earlier evangelical Calvinism epitomized in Keach. Brown, 'Baptist Preaching', p. 91. See also Keach, *Breach Repaired*; and Hayden, 'Evangelical Calvinism'.

28. Brown, *English Baptists*, p. 73.

29. From William Bagley's sermon at Gifford's funeral, as reported in Ivimey, *History*, vol. 3, p. 604.

30. While there was some ambiguity in the question to which the churches were responding, the accumulative effect of the words, 'evangelistic', 'challenging' and 'inspirational' suggest a form of preaching which is better understood as proclamatory, rather than didactic.

31. Spurgeon, *Lectures*, p. 72.

32. Collins was pastor of the Wapping church from 1677 until his death in 1702. He was concerned for the lack of ministers among the Particular Baptist churches at the opening of the eighteenth century and preached a sermon before church leaders in London which was subsequently amplified and published as Hercules Collins, *The Temple Repaired or, An Essay to Revive the Long-neglected Ordinances, of Exercising the Spiritual Gift of Prophecy for the Edification of the Churches; and of Ordaining Ministers Duly Qualified*, London: William & Joseph Marshall, 1702.

33. Collins, *Temple Repaired*, p. 18.

34. See White, *Protestant Worship*, p. 20: 'we must recognize that preaching takes a wide variety of forms and serves an assortment of functions'.

35. Wallin, *Gospel Requisites*, p. 22.

36. Spurgeon, *Lectures*, pp. 53–71.

37. See, for example, Hall, *Hearing the Word*.

38. *Five Disputations &c.*, p. 440, quoted in Davies, *Worship of the English Puritans*, p. 188.

39. In the USA, for example, the word 'preacher' is often synonymous with 'minister' or 'pastor'.

40. Thus the Midland Association of Particular Baptists, June 1656, Barrington R. White, *Association Records of the Particular Baptists of England, Wales and Ireland to 1660*, London: Baptist Historical Society, 1971, p. 25.

41. Stephen L. Copson, *Association Life of the Particular Baptists of Northern England 1699–1732*, Didcot: Baptist Historical Society, 1991, p. 98.

42. Copson, *Association Life*, p. 95.

43. See White, *Protestant Worship*, p. 20: 'For most Protestants, preaching is the most lengthy portion in the service . . . It is not a coincidence that most Protestant ordained ministers are referred to not as priest, presider, or prayer leader but as preacher.'

44. *Institutes*, IV. xvii. 39.

45. William Bradshaw, *Englishe Puritanisme, containing the maine opinions of the rigidest sort of those that are called Puritanes in the realm of England*, Oxford, 1646, p. 73.

46. Unlike Philip H. Pfatteicher, who has only one paragraph on preaching in the whole of his book. Pfatteicher, *Liturgical Spirituality*, p. 192.

47. For a discussion of preaching as an event in which God encounters the listeners, together with the other relationships which occur in the event of preaching, see Paul S. Wilson, *The Practice of Preaching*, Nashville: Abingdon, 1995, pp. 20–36.

48. For a discussion of the practical ways in which the preacher can communicate authoritatively through the 'ethos' and rhetoric, see Andre Resner, *Preacher and Cross: Person and Message in Theology and Rhetoric*, Grand Rapids MI and Cambridge: William B. Eerdmans, 1999.

49. H. W. Robinson, *The Christian Experience of the Holy Spirit*, London: Nisbet, 1928, pp. 181–3.

50. This is not to say that such participation is an ever-present reality, as is clear from the discussion below on the devotional exhortation to the hearers of the Word. In contrast, the 'dialogical preaching' of black majority churches offers a dynamic role for the hearers, who in fact become speakers in partnership with the preacher. See Joel Edwards, *Let's Praise Him Again*, Eastbourne: Kingsway, 1994, p. 53.

51. Copson, *Association Life*, pp. 98–101.

52. Benjamin Beddome, *Hymns adapted to Public Worship or Family Devotion*, ed. R. Hall, London 1818, pp. 3f. For the development of preaching in the biblical period, see Hughes O. Old, *The Reading and Preaching of the Scriptures in the Worship of the Christian Church*, vol. 1: *The Biblical Period*, Grand Rapids MI and Cambridge: William B. Eerdmans, 1998; H. G. Perelmuter, 'The Jewish Roots of the Christian Sermon' in Robert E. Webber (ed.), *The Complete Library of Christian Worship*, vol. 3: *The Renewal of Sunday Worship*, Peabody MA: Hendrikson, 1993, pp. 279–85; and Robert C. Worley, 'Teaching and Preaching in the Early Church' in Robert E. Webber (ed.), *The Complete Library of Christian Worship*, vol. 3: *The Renewal of Sunday Worship*, Peabody MA: Hendrikson, 1993, pp. 286–8; also Dodd, *Apostolic Preaching*.

53. However, the selection of the reading by the preacher and the use of topical or thematic preaching are among some of the ways in which this broad statement may need to be modified. In the 1996 survey, over 60 per cent of churches claimed that the reading was selected by the preacher. While the preacher may claim to be scriptural

in the content of the sermon, the selection of the text places the preacher in control over the reading. In addition, we may note the view that scriptural preaching is more about the presentation of a biblical proclamation than the development of a particular biblical text. See Edward Farley, 'Towards a New Paradigm for Preaching' in T. G. Long and Edward Farley (eds), *Preaching as a Theological Task: World, Gospel, Scripture*, Louisville KY: Westminster John Knox, 1996, pp. 165–75.

54. Spurgeon, *Lectures*, p. 76.

55. See Mark's account of the *Shema*: Mark 12.29–30; cf. Deuteronomy 6.4–5.

56. The title of John Gill's systematic theology. Certainly, the texts of published sermons from the eighteenth century often suggest a primarily didactic intent, but we must remember that their delivery might well have been more animated than the written script, transforming a didactic text into a challenging address.

57. Fawcett, *Holiness*, pp. 21f.

58. Spurgeon, *Lectures*, p. 78.

59. In 1656 the Midland messengers based their use of 1 Corinthians 14.3 on the belief that preaching was for edification. See White, *Association Records*, p. 28.

60. Collins, *Temple Repaired*, p. 16.

61. On the *Directory*, see Gordon S. Wakefield, *An Outline of Christian Worship*, Edinburgh: T & T Clark, 1998, pp. 107–10.

62. 'In raising doctrines from the text, his care ought to be, *First,* That the matter be the truth of God. *Secondly,* That it be a truth contained in or grounded on the text, that the hearers may discern how God teacheth it from thence. *Thirdly,* That he chiefly insist upon those doctrines which are principally intended, and make most for the edification of the hearers.' Carruthers, *Westminster Confession*, p. 379.

63. Collins, *Temple Repaired*, pp. 25f.

64. There are, or course, many sermon forms, though it is argued here that the division into heads is a form frequently used in many Baptist churches. On the variety of sermon forms in modern homiletical literature, see Fred B. Craddock, *Preaching*, Nashville TN: Abingdon, 1985, pp. 170–93, and David Buttrick, *Homiletics: Moves and Structures*, Philadelphia PA: Fortress Press, 1987, pp. 305–17.

65. Discussion has re-emerged in England in the post-war development of 'house groups'. These small gatherings carry obvious resonances of the small group which met in the Amsterdam bakehouse to worship and explore the Word.

66. Brock, *Behaviour Becoming the House of God*, p. 19.

67. In the modern period, when prospective ministers have gone to meet a local church with a view to being issued an invitation to become their minister, the whole visit has been colloquially called 'preaching with a view'.

68. Collins, *Temple Repaired*, p. 52.

69. White, *Association Records*, p. 57.

70. Collins, *Temple Repaired*, p.17.

71. See, for example, R. E. Cooper, *From Stepney to St. Giles: The Story of Regent's Park College 1810–1960*, London: Carey Kingsgate Press, 1960; Henry Foreman, 'The Early Separatists, the Baptists and Education 1580–1750 (With special reference to the education of the clergy)', unpublished PhD dissertation, University of Leeds, 1976; Norman S. Moon (ed.), *Education for Ministry: Bristol Baptist College 1679–1979*, Bristol: Bristol Baptist College, 1979; Hayden, 'Evangelical Calvinism'.

72. Spurgeon, *Lectures*, p. 54.

73. Hugh Evans and Caleb Evans, 'The Case for an Educated Ministry: Bristol Education Society 1770' in N. S. Moon (ed.), *Education for Ministry: Bristol Baptist College 1679–1979*, Bristol: Bristol Baptist College, 1979, pp. 129–34.

74. Caleb Evans, *Elisha's Exclamation: A Sermon Occasioned by the Death of Rev. Hugh Evans, preached at Broadmead, Bristol, April 8, 1781*, Bristol: W. Pine, 1781, p. 31.

75. Many writers who have been influenced by the Liturgical Movement have argued for a section of the service often described as 'The Response to the Word of God'. See, for example, Susan J. White, *Groundwork of Christian Worship*, London: Epworth, 1997, pp. 128f. and elsewhere. However, what is meant is that the very character of preaching should be such as to invoke a response and that it is 'bad preaching' which enables a congregation to avoid any kind of response. See Craddock, *Preaching*, p. 49.

76. The Scripture references they cited are all general statements about the importance of prayer, except Acts 6.4, which refers to the apostles agreeing that some of their duties should be delegated so that they might devote themselves 'to prayer and to serving the Word'. See White, *Association Records*, p. 101. The belief that preaching is a spiritual event is evident in the account of worship in the Amsterdam congregation which we have already examined.

77. Spurgeon, *Lectures*, pp. 40–52.

78. Spurgeon, *Lectures*, p. 89.

79. Spurgeon, *Lectures*, p. 90.

80. For an historical and contemporary discussion of character and preaching, see Resner, *Preacher and Cross*.

81. Collins, *Temple Repaired*, p. 54.

82. Copson, *Association Life*, p. 91.

83. Fawcett, *Holiness*, p. 26.

84. Hall, *Hearing the Word*, p. 14. For his reference to preaching as an ordinance, see page 2 of that letter.

85. Andrew Fuller, *On Reading the Word of God*, Kettering: Circular Letter of the Northamptonshire Baptist Association, 1813.

86. Hall, *Hearing the Word*, pp. 3f.

87. Brock, *Behaviour Becoming the House of God*, p. 18.

88. Brock, *Behaviour Becoming the House of God*, p. 20.

89. Hall, *Hearing the Word*, p. 7.

90. Hall, *Hearing the Word*, p. 9.

91. Hall, *Hearing the Word*, p. 10.

92. And, 'If you are not conscious of your need of religious instruction, why elect pastors or teachers for that purpose?', Hall, *Hearing the Word*, p. 12.

93. See, for example, Duncan D. Hair, 'From Meeting-House to Cathedral: The History of a Congregation 1795–1798–1894–1944' in *The Thomas Coats Memorial Church, Paisley: Jubilee Book, 1944*, Paisley: James Paton, 1945, pp. 13–156, and Binfield, 'Coats Family'.

94. Though there may be some verbal contributions, it is usually less than in black majority congregations, where the preaching has been described as 'dialogical'. Edwards, *Let's Praise Him Again*, pp. 53–5.

95. Brock, *Behaviour Becoming the House of God*, pp. 22f.

96. In 1996 most churches indicated that the readings were selected by the

preacher, usually for a series regarded as apposite for the congregation. Ellis, *Baptist Worship Today*, p. 8.

97.   Ion Bria, *The Liturgy After the Liturgy: Mission and Witness from an Orthodox Perspective*, Geneva: World Council of Churches, 1996. See also J. G. Davies, *Worship and Mission*, London: SCM Press, 1966.

98.   Hall, *Hearing the Word*, p. 10.

99.   See Payne, *Fellowship of Believers*, pp. 95–7.

100.   See Finney, *Revivals*, and his application to more recent 'seeker sensitive' evangelical worship in Lathrop, 'New Pentecost'.

Chapter 8

1. As altered and appearing as hymn 355 in *The Baptist Hymn Book*, 1962.

2. e.g. H. A. L. Jefferson, *Hymns in Christian Worship*, London: Rockliff, 1950; John Julian, *A Dictionary of Hymnology*, London: John Murray, 1892; and Louis F. Benson, *The English Hymn: Its Development and Use in Worship*, Richmond VA: John Knox Press, 1915.

3. e.g. Eric Routley, *Hymns and Human Life*, London: John Murray, 1952.

4. e.g. D. Davie, *The Eighteenth Century Hymn in England*, Cambridge: Cambridge University Press, 1993; and J. R. Watson, *The English Hymn: A Critical and Historical study*, Oxford: Clarendon Press, 1997.

5. Eric Routley, *Hymns and the Faith*, London: John Murray, 1955; and Frank Colquhoun, *Hymns that Live*, London: Hodder & Stoughton, 1980.

6. See A. S. Gregory, *Praises with Understanding: Illustrated from the Words and Music of the Methodist Hymnbook*, London: Epworth, 1936; and various hymnbook companions such as Hugh Martin and Ronald W. Thompson, *The Baptist Hymn Book Companion*, London: Psalms and Hymns Trust, 1962.

7. Julian, *Dictionary of Hymnology*.

8. Eric Routley, *Hymns Today and Tomorrow*, London: Darton, Longman & Todd, 1964.

9. The 1996 survey of contemporary Baptist worship indicated a variety of sung material. See Ellis, *Baptist Worship Today*, pp. 14–18. Thus the term 'hymn' refers to a text in which ideas are developed through a number of stanzas, where the repetition of the whole hymn would not make sense, and the term 'song' refers to a text which may consist of one or more stanzas but which can be repeated a number of times. No mention is made here of chants which have had very limited use in Baptist worship because they are primarily sung parts of a liturgical service. However, recent years have seen the use of some chants from Iona and Taizé and the publication of these in the 1991 *Baptist Praise and Worship*. These tend to be used in a way similar to worship songs, though their use as responses has subtly influenced the use of songs in a similar way. The chanting of prose psalms, while encouraged by official hymnbooks between 1900 and 1962, probably represents a minority taste of late Victorian 'upwardly mobile' congregations, and their successors, who sought to emulate Anglican worship. In *Baptist Praise and Worship* the psalms are set out for responsive congregational reading, but no chant tunes are offered.

10. Concerning the singing of a hymn as *event*, and a caution with regard to shared meaning, J. R. Watson argues, 'That [hymn] text exists in a book, in one form:

chameleon-like, it exists in the same shape, but in another, modified, sense in other books, because of the company it keeps; and it exists, too, and perhaps most "naturally", in the moments when it is sung by a congregation. Then it becomes once again speech, the sound made by the mouth and breath, the expression of the lungs and the body. It becomes, in Derrida's summary of Rousseau, "not grammatological but pneumatological". (Jacques Derrida, *Of Grammatology*, trans. Gayatri Chakravorty Spivak (Baltimore and London, 1976) It becomes, too, a congregational song made by individuals, each of whom may be interpreting the text in his or her own way; and that interpretation may vary from time to time, or with different circumstances.' Watson, *The English Hymn*, p. 24.

11. Bernard L. Manning, *The Hymns of Wesley and Watts*, London: Epworth, 1942, p. 133.

12. Cecil Northcott, *Hymns in Christian Worship: The Use of Hymns in the Life of the Church*, ed. J. G. Davies and A. R. George, London and Richmond VA: Lutterworth Press and John Knox Press, 1964, p. 21.

13. See especially John Wesley, *A Collection of Hymns for the Use of the People called Methodists*, London: J. Mason, 1780.

14. John Rippon, *A Selection of Hymns from the Best Authors, intended to be an appendix to Dr. Watts's Psalms and Hymns*, London, 1787, preface.

15. The opening words of the preface make clear that the new book was based on the two denominational predecessors, viz. *Psalms and Hymns* of the Particular Baptists and *The Baptist Hymnal* of the General Baptists. *The Baptist Church Hymnal*, London: Psalms and Hymns Trust, 1900, p. iv. See also Briggs, 'English Baptists and their Hymnody', p. 157.

16. Ellis, *Baptist Worship Today*, pp. 16f.

17. Edward Drapes, *Gospel-glory proclaimed before the sonnes of men in the Worship of God*, London, 1648, p. 133.

18. Grantham, *Christianismus Primitivus*, vol. 2, pp. 112–17.

19. Brown, *English Baptists*, p. 15.

20. *Minutes of the General Assembly of the General Baptist Churches in England, with Kindred Records*, ed. W. T. Whitley, London: Kingsgate Press with the Baptist Historical Society, 1910, p. 18.

21. Smyth, *Works*, vol. 1, p. 273.

22. Grantham, *Christianismus Primitivus*, vol. 2, p. 109.

23. Grantham, *Christianismus Primitivus*, vol. 2, p. 115. It is significant that George Fox gained some of his supporters from the General Baptists. See H. L. McBeth, *The Baptist Heritage*, Nashville TN: Broadman Press, 1987, p. 155. Horton Davies sees a kinship between Quaker and General Baptist worship; Davies, *From Cranmer to Baxter and Fox*, vol. 2, pp. 492–8. The intense dependence on the leading of the Spirit, a grave suspicion of pre-composed material leading to false worship and the setting aside of Scripture, are all features which resonate with early Quaker worship.

24. Samuel Deacon, *Barton Hymns: A New Composition of Hymns and Poems chiefly on Divine Subjects designed for the Amusement and Edification of Christians of all denominations: more particularly those of the General Baptist persuasion*, Coventry, 1785. A second, enlarged edition was published in 1797.

25. In time, *Barton Hymns* was developed into *The General Baptist Hymnbook* of 1830 and the later, official books, *The New Hymnbook* of 1851 and *The Baptist*

Hymnal of 1879. See Ernest A. Payne, 'Baptists and their Hymns' in H. Martin (ed.), *The Baptist Hymn Book Companion*, London: Psalms and Hymns Trust, 1962, p. 20.

26. Julian, *Dictionary of Hymnology*, p. 111. The turn of the century saw the old General Baptists and the New Connexion parting company over the former's inclination towards Unitarianism. Thus Stevenson may only have been referring to the New Connexion churches.

27. White, *Association Records*, p. 58. The instructions suggest that spontaneous solo singing needs to be sufficiently clear that the congregation can honestly respond with 'Amen', for praise is offered to God and is also for the building up of one another, following Colossians 3.16 and Ephesians 5.19. However, the record is not sufficiently clear as to whether this included conjoint singing.

28. Hayden, *Records*, p. 162.

29. Hayden, *Records*, pp. 160f.

30. Thomas Crosby, *History of the English Baptists*, London, 1738, vol. 4, p. 299.

31. The Westminster Assembly included within its definition of scriptural worship the 'singing of psalms with grace in the heart'. Carruthers, *Westminster Confession*, p. 92. Though the versions of the Psalter written by Rous and Barton respectively were presented to the Assembly, no one version was approved to replace the old Psalter. The English Psalter, commonly called 'Sternhold and Hopkins' or the 'Old Version' had been published in 1562. In fact, it also contained a number of hymns but it is questionable to what extent they were ever used in public worship. See Benson, *The English Hymn*, pp. 27–32.

32. Whitley, *History of British Baptists*, p. 186.

33. Apart from the devotional paraphrases attached for private use to the 'Old Version' of the psalms, and the devotional poems such as those by George Herbert in *The Temple*, William Barton is perhaps the most significant. He was disappointed that his Psalter did not become the approved version of the Westminster Assembly, but later he published *A Century of Select Hymns*. This collection increased in subsequent editions when he was a conforming clergyman in Leicester. In the preface he argued strongly for the use of hymns, though the climate within the Church of England after 1660 did not allow their regular use in worship. With the combined characteristics of scriptural paraphrases and hymns, Benson suggests, 'Barton's work thus occupies the very point of transition between the Metrical Psalm and the Hymn.' Benson, *The English Hymn*, p. 62.

34. Hugh Martin, 'The Baptist Contribution to Early English Hymnody', *Baptist Quarterly*, 19, 1962, pp. 195–208, p. 199.

35. Samuel Marlow, *A brief Discourse concerning Singing in the publick worship of God in the Gospel Church*, London, 1690.

36. Keach, *Breached Repaired*.

37. Hercules Collins had urged the duty of congregational singing in the appendix to his *Orthodox Christian* in 1680, as had Keach in his *Tropes and Figures* in 1682 and his *Treatise on Baptism* in 1689. John Bunyan had also spoken of congregational singing as a divine institution but, although his pilgrims were to break into song in *The Pilgrim's Progress*, his congregation was not to do so until the last decade of the century. By that time there were those at Bedford who were 'perswaded in their consciences that publick singing is an ordinance of God' and it was included in Sunday worship even though some continued to resist the practice. H. G. Tibbutt (ed.), *The*

Minutes of the First Independent Church (now Bunyan Meeting) at Bedford, Bedford: Bedfordshire Historical Record Society, 1976, p. 93.

38. See Crosby, *History of the English Baptists*, though its seems that the peace was less sudden and less untroubled than he suggests. See Benson, *English Hymn*, p. 99. Brown suggests that under the presenting issues of the hymn debate was the smouldering resentment which Marlow, a layman, felt for the ministerial dominance of Keach. The latter, in turn, was dismissive of what he perceived to be ignorant interference. See Brown, 'Baptist Preaching', pp. 46–8. Marlow and the other dissidents within the Horsleydown church left to join a neighbouring congregation, though in 1739 that congregation also adopted hymn singing.

39. Briggs, 'English Baptists and their Hymnody', p. 155.

40. For Watts see Harry Escott, *Isaac Watts, Hymnographer: A Study of the Beginnings, Development and Philosophy of the English Hymn*, London: Independent Press, 1962; and David G. Fountain, *Isaac Watts Remembered*, Harpenden, Herts: Gospel Standard Baptist Trust, 1974.

41. Isaac Watts, *Hymns and Spiritual Songs in Three Books: I Collected from the Scriptures. II Compos'd on Divine Subjects. III Prepar'd for the Lord's Supper*, ed. Selma L. Bishop, London: Faith Press, 1709, pp. li f.

42. This concern that not all the words of the psalms were appropriate for a Christian congregation and the need to provide a Christian gloss *within* the text of the psalms was not original to Watts. In 1679 John Patrick, 'Preacher to the Charter-House, London', had published *A Century of select Psalms and portions of the Psalms of David, especially those of praise*. Watts spoke appreciatively of this in the preface to *The Psalms of David imitated* (p. vi) and commented that it was used quite widely by Dissenters. Baxter had made a similar point about Patrick's *Psalms* in the preface to his *Poetical Fragments*; see Benson, *The English Hymn*, p. 53.

43. It was the main hymnbook, but others also were used. A number of authors published their own hymns for local or wider use and a number of supplements appeared in addition to Rippon's. A note by Robert Robinson in the church records of St Andrew's Street, Cambridge, indicates that Barton's version of the psalms was used on Sunday morning and Watts's hymns at other times. *Church Book: St Andrew's Street Baptist Church*, pp. 111f.

44. John Ash and Caleb Evans, *A Collection of Hymns adapted to Public Worship*, Bristol, 1769. An appendix with further hymns was published in 1771, and the book reached a tenth edition in 1827, long after the original compilers had died. See William T. Whitley, *Congregational Hymn-Singing*, London: J. M. Dent & Sons, 1933, p. 126.

45. The *Selection* was in use at the Metropolitan Tabernacle, for example, until Spurgeon produced his own *Our Own Hymn Book* in 1866.

46. Rippon, *Selection of Hymns*, p. v. These additions reflect both a concern for the *right* hymn for particular points in a service as well as the increased missionary concerns of the Baptist community in the intervening years.

47. Payne, 'Baptists and their Hymns', p. 19.

48. Ian Bradley, *Abide with Me: The World of Victorian Hymns*, London: SCM Press, 1997, p. 53.

49. See also *The Baptist Church Hymnal Revised* (1933), and *The Baptist Hymn Book* (1962).

50. See Ellis, *Baptist Worship Today*, pp. 16f.

51. The *Baptist Church Hymnary* was jointly sponsored by the Psalms and Hymns Trust, the trustees of *The Baptist Hymnal* and the Baptist Union.

52. Writing of the mid-nineteenth century, Bradley asserts, 'For non-Anglican churches the hymnbook came to take on something of the authority and status that the Prayer Book had in the Church of England and became an important bearer and symbol of denominational identity.' Bradley, *Abide with Me*, p. 59.

53. *Baptist Praise and Worship*, Oxford: Oxford University Press on behalf of the Psalms and Hymns Trust, 1991, p. v.

54. Perhaps this is not dissimilar to the use of Sankey's *Sacred Songs and Solos* in a previous generation, though the balance has shifted between the use of denominational and pan-Evangelical material.

55. Wesley, *Collection of Hymns*, Preface dated October 1779.

56. A comparatively recent example of this is Stephen F. Winward, 'How to Make the Best Use of the Hymn Book' in H. Martin and Ron W. Thomson (eds), *The Baptist Hymn Book Companion*, London: Psalms and Hymns Trust, 1962, p. 35.

57. Carruthers, *Westminster Confession*, p. 393.

58. Watts, *Hymns and Spiritual Songs*, p. liii.

59. Watts, *Psalms of David*, p. v.

60. Ash and Evans, *Collection of Hymns*, p. iii.

61. John Rippon, *A Selection of Psalm and Hymn Tunes from the best authors, in three and four parts: adapted principally to Dr. Watts's Hymns and Psalms and to Dr. Rippon's Selection of Hymns*, London, 1791, p. xii.

62. The minutes of the Methodist Conference outline a developing musical scene. Instruments began to be introduced after the fashion of the West End players in the parish churches, but there was reluctance to allow the introduction of organs until the process became unstoppable. See Benson, *The English Hymn*, pp. 242f.

63. Bradley argues that 'the first two decades of Queen Victoria's reign saw a burst of musical education and an expression of popular interest and involvement in choral singing unparalleled before or since'. Bradley, *Abide with Me*, p. 33.

64. J. S. Curwen, *Studies in Worship and Music, chiefly as regards Congregational Singing*, London: Curwen & Sons, 1880, pp. 429–30.

65. Briggs, *English Baptists*, p. 39.

66. Payne, *Fellowship of Believers*, p. 96.

67. For the wider claim 'that congregational singing as we know it is the end-product of a long process', see Eric Routley, *Christian Hymns Observed*, London and Oxford: Mowbray, 1982, p. 103.

68. In fact, we have seen that in the Bury Street church, this second psalm was placed earlier in the service, before Watts entered the pulpit, because of his nervous disposition. However, the records make clear that the customary place was following the sermon.

69. See Robert Hall's preface in Beddome, *Hymns*, p. ix. However, a word of caution must be expressed about the universal placing of a hymn after the sermon. Brock's account of Norfolk worship in 1845 includes two hymns, but does not mention one after the sermon. Brock, *Behaviour Becoming the House of God*, p. 15. Similarly, Curwen's account of worship at the Metropolitan Tabernacle in the 1870s records the use of three hymns, but he adds, 'The sermon was followed by the benediction; it is very rarely that a hymn is sung at this part of the service.' Curwen, *Studies in Worship and Music*, pp. 427f.

70. John Fawcett, *Hymns Adapted to the Circumstances of Public Worship and Private Devotion*, Leeds, 1782, p. iii.

71. Watson, *The English Hymn*, p. 76.

72. Payne and Winward offered some formal orders of service in 1960, with a suggested placing of hymns. See Payne and Winward, *Orders and Prayers*, pp. 31–48.

73. Ellis, *Baptist Worship Today*, p. 17. It is likely that some would have 'Prayer and Praise' services as alternatives to traditional worship, while others would regularly incorporate blocks of songs into relatively traditional services which also included interspersed hymns.

74. On the task of choosing hymns, see A. R. George, 'The Choosing of Hymns' in Charles Robertson (ed.), *Singing the Faith, Essays by Members of the Joint Liturgical Group on the Use of Hymns in Liturgy*, Norwich: Canterbury Press, 1990, pp. 70–88.

75. John Leach, *Liturgy and Liberty: Combining the Best of the Old with the Best of the New*, Tunbridge Wells: MARC with Monarch Publications, 1989, is a good example, from an Anglican quarter, of the attempt to improve Charismatic worship by giving guidance for the structuring of song sequences.

76. Payne points out that Particular Baptists were suspicious of Methodist Arminianism and that there was relatively little emphasis on the moment of conversion until the time of Moody and Sankey, when Baptist piety underwent significant modification. Payne, *Fellowship of Believers*, p. 97.

77. This concern for evangelism eventually came to characterize Sunday evening worship, with a consequent use of appropriately experiential material. See Briggs, *English Baptists*, pp. 39–42; and Payne, *Fellowship of Believers*, p. 97, for the use of *Sacred Songs and Solos* in evening worship.

78. The *CSSM* (Children's Special Service Mission) songbook for Scripture Union beach missions was a good example of this intermediate stage.

79. See early in this chapter Manning's comment on hymns as the Dissenters' equivalent of Anglican liturgy.

80. John L. Bell, *The Singing Thing: A Case for Congregational Song*, Glasgow: Wild Goose, 2000, pp. 17–20. See also Brian Wren, *Praying Twice: The Music and Words of Congregational Song*, Louisville KY: Westminster John Knox Press, 2000, p. 93.

81. For congregational song as 'corporeal', see Wren, *Praying Twice*, pp. 85–7.

82. This same dynamic may be seen in the sharing of personal testimonies in worship, though that represents an interaction of individuals with the community rather than the mutuality of joint singing.

83. Gill, *Two Discourses*, p. 61. This is a fascinating argument coming from the Baptist representative of High Calvinism in eighteenth-century London.

84. John Newton, *Baptist Praise and Worship*, 550.

85. Rippon, *Selection of Hymns*, preface.

86. Charles H. Spurgeon, *Our Own Hymn-book: A Collection of Psalms and Hymns for Public, Social and Private Worship*, Pasedena TX: Pilgrim Publications, 1866, p. iii.

87. Watts, *Hymns and Spiritual Songs*, p. li.

88. Rippon, *Selection of Psalm and Hymn Tunes*, p. iii.

89. Even though the words were prominently printed inside the back cover of *The*

Baptist Hymn Book and *Baptist Praise and Worship*.

90.   Rippon, *Selection of Psalm and Hymn Tunes*, p. iv.

91.   Patrick D. Miller, 'Enthroned on the Praises of Israel: The Praise of God in Old Testament Theology', *Interpretation*, 39, 1985, pp. 5–19, pp. 7 and 8 respectively.

92.   Walter Brueggemann, *Israel's Praise: Doxology against Idolatry and Ideology*, Philadelphia PA: Fortress Press, 1988, p. 27.

93.   So *The Baptist Church Hymnal* (1900); *The Baptist Church Hymnal* (*Revised Edition*, 1933); and *The Baptist Hymn Book* (1962) each included sub-sections entitled 'The Gospel Call' and 'Response in Repentance and Faith', while *Baptist Praise and Worship* had a major section entitled 'Celebrating the Gospel' which began with large sub-sections entitled 'Response in Faith' and 'Confessing the Faith'.

94.   Robert Steed was minister of the non-singing church at Broken Wharf which Marlow and the other malcontents joined on leaving Horsleydown.

95.   Briggs, 'English Baptists and their Hymnody', p. 155.

96.   See, for example, 'A Sexagenarian' in the issue of 2 October 1868.

97.   See Robert Steed, *An Epistle written to members of a Church in London concerning Singing, as it may or ought to be used in the worship of God in the Church; wherein briefly and plainly the nature of it is described, the primitive way presented and the common and popular way examined*, London, 1691, p. 8.

98.   Keach, *Breach Repaired*, pp. 170–2.

99.   Watts, 'Guide to Prayer', pp. 125–31. He even argues for the occasional use of forms of prayer for those whose spirits are at a low ebb through illness or other circumstances and asserts, 'Nor is it tying up the Spirit, but if consciably used, may be both attended with the Spirit's assistance, and find acceptance with God', p. 126.

100.   It may not be too fanciful to draw a parallel between the early development from free worship to congregational hymnody and the transition from the early, unstructured worship of the Charismatic Movement, with its exercising of the *charismata*, to a situation where Charismatic worship is more structured. Indeed, the meaning of that worship is often now expressed in terms of praise, and even 'spiritual warfare' is often presented as happening through the medium of praise such as in the 'praise marches' of the late 1980s.

101.   Cf. George Guiver's discussion of daily prayer as *opus dei*: 'The New Testament speaks not of coasting along in prayer, but of *persevering* in it', Guiver, *Company of Voices*, p. 30.

102.   Gill, *Two Discourses*, p. 49.

103.   Steed, *Epistle*, p. 8.

104.   However, there was some conservatism. John Gill, for example, thought that biblical psalms were adequate for most worship needs.

105.   The developing use of written prayers occurred much later than the use of hymns, but the 1996 survey showed that 54 per cent of churches at least sometimes used read prayers. It is not possible to speculate whether that figure will continue to increase, but it highlights not only a diversity of practice, but a recognition in prayer of what is already the case in singing: that the words of others can be assimilated and used with integrity in worship.

106.   Louis Bouyer, *Introduction to Spirituality*, London: Darton, Longman & Todd, 1961, p. 43.

107. Bradshaw, *Two Ways of Praying*, pp. 16f.

108. Samuel Crossman, *Baptist Praise and Worship*, 204.

109. See, for example, Martyn Percy's critique of *Vineyard* songs which he describes as being sung to 'smoochy, modern-romantic' music. Martyn Percy, *Words, Wonders and Power: Understanding Contemporary Christian Fundamentalism and Revivalism*, London: SPCK, 1996.

110. A member of the Broughton church in Hampshire, Anne Steele's hymns were included in both the Bristol hymnbook and Rippon's *Selection* under the name 'Theodosia'.

111. Lumpkin, *Baptist Confessions*, p. 281.

112. Keach, *Breach Repaired*, p. 21. Cf. the *Westminster Directory*, Carruthers, *Westminster Confession*, p. 393.

113. Gill, *Two Discourses*, p. 35. That he should pay such attention to arguing that praise singing was a divine ordinance still in effect in the Christian dispensation, suggests that the debate for and against singing continued well into the eighteenth century – though such an assumption cannot specify that his opponents were Particular Baptists, but simply Dissenters against whom he needed to take a stand.

114. For a discussion of the use of Scripture in Christian worship, see Paul F. Bradshaw, 'The Use of the Bible in Liturgy: Some Historical Perspectives', *Studia Liturgica*, 22, 1992, pp. 35–52.

Chapter 9

1. Ed. L. E. Addicott and L. G. Champion, *Church Book: St. Andrew's Street Baptist Church, Cambridge 1720–1832*, English Baptist Records, Didcot: Baptist Historical Society, 1991, p. 27.

2. E. P. Winter, 'Calvinist and Zwinglian Views of the Lord's Supper among the Baptists of the Seventeenth Century', *Baptist Quarterly*, 15, 2003, pp. 323–9.

3. Extracts from the confession drafted by Smyth and published by his congregation after his death. Lumpkin, *Baptist Confessions*, pp. 137f.

4. Benjamin Keach, *Tropologia: A Key to Open Scripture Metaphors*, London: Collingridge, 1683/1855, Book IV, pp. 623–5.

5. Paragraph 96.

6. Hercules Collins, *An Orthodox Catechism*, quoted in 'Calvinist and Zwinglian Views', Winter, p. 327.

7. Question XCIII, quoted in Payne, *Fellowship of Believers*, p. 70.

8. Andrew Fuller, *The Practical Uses of Christian Baptism*, Northampton: The Circular Letter of the Northamptonshire Association, 1802, p. 5.

9. Robert Hall, *Works*, 7th edn, London, 1841, vol. 3, pp, 10, 45 and 61 respectively.

10. This seems to be how the Particular Baptists understood the term when they used it to replace the word 'sacrament' in their revision of the *Westminster Confession* in their *Second London Confession*.

11. For an account of nineteenth-century debates concerning the Lord's Supper, see Walker, *Baptists at the Table*.

12. Walker, *Baptists at the Table*, pp. 164–94.

13. Charles H. Spurgeon, *Till He Come: Communion Meditations and Addresses*, London: Passmore & Alabaster, 1894, p. 17.

14. Robinson, *Life and Faith*, pp. 144–6.

15. See Payne, *Fellowship of Believers*, p. 88.

16. The contribution of the evangelical New Testament scholar George Beasley-Murray is particularly significant. See especially George R. Beasley-Murray, *Baptism in the New Testament*, London: Macmillan, 1962.

17. Neville Clark, *An Approach to the Theology of the Sacraments*, London: SCM Press, 1956, p. 71.

18. Edward Schillebeeckx, *Christ the Sacrament of the Encounter with God*, London: Sheed & Ward, 1963/1989, p. 15.

19. Schillebeeckx, *Christ the Sacrament*, pp. 43–5.

20. Empereur, *Models*, p. 23.

21. Wainwright, *Doxology*, p. 70.

22. Forrester, McDonald, and Tellini, *Encounter*, p. 72.

23. Matthew 28.18–20; 1 Corinthians 11.23–6 and the Gospel parallels.

24. The notion of 'a dominical ordinance' is, of course, narrower than its general use by the Puritans and Separatists, who used precedent as well as injunction as ordinances for the general ordering of worship. See, for example, the Beddome catechism above, where 'ordinance' includes Scripture and prayer as well as the sacraments.

25. In the 1997 survey, is was noted that those churches which celebrate the Lord's Supper once in the morning and once in the evening each month are partly offering a monthly eucharistic opportunity to people who only come to one service each week. This applied in sixty-five per cent of churches, with a further twenty-three per cent having only one communion service each month. Ellis, *Baptist Worship Today*, p. 20.

26. By contrast, note: 'The Eucharist is *the* Sacrament of the Church, i.e. her eternal actualization as the Body of Christ, united in Christ by the Holy Spirit . . . it is also source and goal of the entire liturgical life of the Church. Any liturgical theology not having the Eucharist as the foundation of its whole structure is basically defective.' Schmemann, *Introduction to Liturgical Theology*, p. 24.

27. See W. M. S. West, *Baptist Principles*, London: Baptist Union of Great Britain and Ireland, 1967, p. 26.

28. For a study of Anglican eucharistic theology in the seventeenth century, see Kenneth Stevenson, *Covenant of Grace Renewed: A Vision of the Eucharist in the Seventeenth Century*, London: Darton, Longman & Todd, 1994.

29. Henry Wheeler Robinson, *The Life and Faith of the Baptists*, London: Kingsgate Press, 1946, p. 97.

30. From Thomas Grantham, *Hear the Church: or, an appeal to the mother of us all. Being an epistle to all baptized believers in England; exhorting them to stedfastness in the truth, according to the scriptures, &c.*, London, 1687, quoted in 'Administration of the Lord's Supper', Winter, p. 196.

31. Whitley, 'Paul's Alley', p. 47.

32. Hayden, *Records*, p. 54.

33. Again, Watts's congregation can give us some indication of Particular Baptist worship of the early eighteenth century.

34. Crippen, 'Bury Street Church Records', pp. 334f. The full account is reprinted at the beginning of this chapter.

35. *Baptist Praise and Worship*, 438.

36. Payne, *Fellowship of Believers*, p. 57. However, the issue is more to do with

theologies of ministry than sacramental theology and cannot be addressed in detail here.

37. See Briggs, *English Baptists*, p. 67.

38. Especially the *Book of Common Prayer*, the *Prayer Book as Proposed in 1928*, and the Church of Scotland's *Book of Common Order*. See Payne and Winward, *Orders and Prayers*, p. xxiii.

39. Gregory Dix, *The Shape of the Liturgy*, London: Dacre Press, 1945.

40. See Walker, *Baptists at the Table*, pp. 32–83.

41. *Patterns and Prayers*, pp. 71–3.

42. *Patterns and Prayers*, pp. 73f.

43. Only 5 per cent of Baptist churches in 1997 celebrated the Lord's Supper weekly, while 88 per cent celebrated the Supper monthly or once each month in the morning and evening respectively. See Ellis, *Baptist Worship Today*, pp. 19f.

44. In the early period of Baptist history, the communion table would often be placed in the centre of the meeting house, with its head towards the pulpit, accentuating the communal nature of the meal.

45. McClendon, *Ethics*, p. 31.

46. Dodd, *Apostolic Preaching*, p. 94.

47. This is not to say that the absence of celebration *causes* the devotional mood, rather, the concern for devotion, together with the concern for re-enactment, leads to an emphasis on spiritual reflection and so to a diminution of public rhetoric. The absence of celebration is best seen, therefore, as evidence of this devotional emphasis rather than its cause.

48. William Kiffin, *A Sober Discourse of Right to Church Communion*, London: Enoch Prosser, 1681, quoted in B. A. Ramsbottom, *Stranger than Fiction: The Life of William Kiffin*, Harpenden, Herts: Gospel Standard Trust Publications, 1989, p. 72.

49. See Wheeler Robinson, *Life and Faith*, p. 99; and Payne, *Fellowship of Believers*, pp. 59–60. Also Walker, *Baptists at the Table*, pp. 1–31.

50. Alexander Maclaren, *St. Paul's Epistles to the Corinthians (To 2 Corinthians, Chapter 5)*, London: Hodder & Stoughton, 1909, p. 173. However, such strong language assumes a debate in which there are contrary views. See Keith G. Jones, *A Shared Meal and A Common Table: Some Reflections on the Lord's Supper and Baptists*, Oxford: Whitley Publications, 1999, especially pp. 8–14.

51. Wheeler Robinson, *Life and Faith*, p. 99.

52. From the hymn 'To Jesus our exalted Lord', which was included in Rippon, *Selection of Hymns*, 487, reprinted in *Hymns by Anne Steele*, ed. D. Sedgewick, London: Gospel Standard Baptist Trust, 1863, p. 109.

53. John Sutcliffe, *The Ordinance of the Lord's Supper Considered*, Northampton: The Circular Letter from the Ministers and Messengers of the Several Baptist Churches of the Northamptonshire Association, 1803, p. 7. John Sutcliffe (1752–1814) was minister at Olney and an influential partner with Fuller and Carey in the beginnings of the Baptist Missionary Society, as well as receiving students for ministerial training.

54. Though some churches have discontinued this practice and incorporated the fund into their general finances.

55. See Sutcliffe, *Ordinance of the Lord's Supper*, p. 6.

56. In the seventeenth and eighteenth centuries the congregation would often gather around the table in a way which highlighted this communal dimension. See,

for example, *Church Book: St Andrew's Street Baptist Church*, p. 27.

57. Ellis, *Baptist Worship Today*, p. 21.

58. Consequently, its inclusion in the second pattern for the Lord's Supper in 1991 was linked to those other elements which expressed this communal dimension. See *Patterns and Prayers*, p. 72.

59. It has not been a Baptist custom to say the Lord's Prayer at the Lord's table. However, to use the 'Kingdom Prayer' would sharpen this declaration of Kingdom concern and Kingdom living.

60. Walker, *Baptists at the Table*; and Payne, *Fellowship of Believers*.

61. Wheeler Robinson, *Life and Faith*, p. 101.

Chapter 10

1. *Church Book: St Andrew's Street Baptist Church*, pp. 41f.

2. For a good example of such ecumenical exploration through the mutual recognition of the processes of initiation, rather than mutual recognition of baptism, see Paul S. Fiddes, 'Baptism and the Process of Christian Initiation' in S. E. Porter and A. R. Cross (eds), *Dimensions of Baptism: Biblical and Theological Studies*, Sheffield: Sheffield Academic Press, 2002, pp. 280–303.

3. *Baptism, Eucharist and Ministry*, Faith and Order Paper No. 111, Geneva: World Council of Churches, 1982.

4. See, for example, Best and Heller, *Becoming a Christian*, and a reflection on this in Christopher J. Ellis, 'A View from the Pool: Baptists, Sacraments and the Basis of Unity', *Baptist Quarterly*, 39, 2001, pp. 107–20.

5. See White, *English Separatist Tradition*, pp. 28–30 and 60–61.

6. Wheeler Robinson, *Life and Faith*, p. 73.

7. Wheeler Robinson, *Life and Faith*, p. 73.

8. *A Declaration of Faith of English People remaining at Amsterdam in Holland*, 13 and 14 in Lumpkin, *Baptist Confessions*, p. 120.

9. For a modern discussion of 're-baptism' and its ecumenical implications, see *Believing and Being Baptized: Baptism, so-called Rebaptism and Children in the Church*, Didcot: Baptist Union of Great Britain, 1996.

10. Daniel Featley in *The Dippers Dipt* declared there would be no objection to this clause if the word *only* were omitted.

11. Chapter 39. Later editions added 'and after to partake of the Lord's Supper', Lumpkin, *Baptist Confessions*, p. 167.

12. Chapter 24. Lumpkin, *Baptist Confessions*, p. 209.

13. In fact, there is an allusion to Matthew 28.18–20 in clause XXIV of the 1656 confession: Lumpkin, *Baptist Confessions*, p. 209.

14. Chapter 29. Lumpkin, *Baptist Confessions*, pp. 290f.

15. Chapter 28. Carruthers, *Westminster Confession*, pp. 112–15.

16. Chapter 26 6. Lumpkin, *Baptist Confessions*, p. 286.

17. The *Second London Confession* cites Matthew 3.16 and John 3.23 at this point. The former refers to Jesus coming up out of the water and the latter refers to baptisms at Ainon because of the local abundance of water.

18. Chapter 29 1. Lumpkin, *Baptist Confessions*, p. 291.

19. For a small anthology of descriptions of baptisms at different times and in various places, see Roger Hayden, 'Believers Baptized: An Anthology' in Paul S.

Fiddes (ed.), *Reflections on the Water: Understanding God and the World through the Baptism of Believers*, Oxford with Macon GA: Regent's Park College with Smyth & Helwys, 1996, pp. 9–21.

20. See William T. Whitley, *The Baptists of London 1612–1928: Their Fellowship, their Expansion, with notes on their 850 churches*, London: Kingsgate Press, 1928, pp. 15–17.

21. In the USA some church buildings have a baptistery located in a gallery behind the pulpit in full view of the congregation.

22. This concern to be obedient explains some of the strong convictions which are present when a person asks to be baptized as a believer having previously been baptized as an infant. Rites for the renewal of baptismal vows are often considered not sufficient by a person who sees obedience as a matter of discipleship.

23. See Ellis, *Baptist Worship Today*, pp. 21f.

24. See, for example, the second baptismal pattern in *Patterns and Prayers*, p. 95.

25. This order broadly follows the first baptismal pattern in *Patterns and Prayers*, p. 94.

26. Payne and Winward, *Orders and Prayers*, pp. 176–8.

27. Ellis, *Baptist Worship Today*, p. 23.

28. Benjamin Keach was a particular proponent of the necessity of the imposition of hands. This was a position he maintained long after his move from the General Baptists to the Particular Baptists. See Brown, *English Baptists*, pp. 44f.

29. He expounded baptism as (1) a representation of the sufferings, burial and resurrection of Christ; (2) for the remission of sins – 'not that that is a procuring of meritorious cause of it, which only is the blood of Christ; but they who submit unto it may, by means of it, be led, directed and encouraged to expect it from Christ'; (3) a directing towards Christ for the cleansing from sin; (4) for a leading of the one baptized in faith to Christ; (5) for a clear conscience through being obedient to the command of Christ; and (6) a means of expressing love to God through submission to the ordinance. John Gill, *A Body of Practical Divinity: or, A System of Practical Truths*, London: George Keith, 1770, pp. 339f. See also Payne, *Fellowship of Believers*, p. 85.

30. Gill, *Body of Practical Divinity*, p. 331. See also Payne, *Fellowship of Believers*, pp. 84f.

31. Payne, *Fellowship of Believers*, p. 84.

32. See Anthony R. Cross, *Baptism and the Baptists: Theology and Practice in Twentieth Century Britain*, Carlisle: Paternoster Press, 2000.

33. For a discussion of these concerns and a proposed sacramental interpretation which addresses them, see Christopher J. Ellis, 'Believer's Baptism and the Sacramental Freedom of God' in Paul S. Fiddes (ed.), *Reflections on the Water: Understanding God and the World through the Baptism of Believers*, Oxford and Macon GA: Regent's Park College with Smyth & Helwys, 1996, pp. 23–45.

34. See Beasley-Murray, *Baptism*, pp. 263–305.

35. So, for example, 'the Church is inseparable from the "Body of Christ" into which the person has been baptized (1 Cor. 12.12f.). *There should thus be no baptism without membership in a church which is a local manifestation of the universal Body of Christ.*' *Believing and Being Baptized*, p. 12 (original emphasis).

36. It is not the intention to make critical comments upon the practice of paedo-baptism. The purpose here is rather to offer an exposition of the baptism of believers

which is *different* from the baptism of infants, despite the attempts of the Lima document to seek a theological convergence separate from the divergent practices of the churches involved. See *Baptism, Eucharist and Ministry*; J. Crawford, 'Becoming a Christian: The Ecumenical Challenge of our Common Baptism' in T. F. Best and D. Heller (eds), *Becoming a Christian: The Ecumenical Implications of Our Common Baptism*, Geneva: World Council of Churches, 1999, pp. 8–12; Christopher J. Ellis, 'The Difficulties of Baptism as the Basis for Unity', unpublished paper for the Doctrine and Worship Committee of the Baptist Union of Great Britain, 1993; and Christopher J. Ellis, 'The Baptism of Disciples and the Nature of the Church' in Stanley E. Porter and Anthony R. Cross (eds), *Dimensions of Baptism: Biblical and Theological Studies*, Sheffield: Sheffield Academic Press, 2002.

37. The word 'ordinance' primarily operated in its root mean of a divine command, rather than its secondary meaning as an alternative to 'sacrament'.

38. Thus Jesus instructing his disciples, 'Do this in memory of me' (Luke 22.19 and 1 Corinthians 11.24f.) at the Last Supper gave a continuing authority to the Lord's Supper in a way which was different from his comment after the foot washing, 'For I have set you an example, that you also should do as I have done to you' (John 13.15) or his instruction on prayer, 'Pray then in this way: Our Father . . .' (Matthew 9.9). Interestingly, General Baptists in the seventeenth century practised foot washing as an ordinance instituted by Christ, and various writers on prayer refer to prayer as an ordinance which continues to be binding for faithful Christian practice.

39. Baptists have not often recognized that there are a number of logical steps between the practice of the early Church and the claim that this practice is binding on future generations. They have been on stronger ground when they have argued from theological arguments in Scripture rather than from narrative precedent. See Christopher J. Ellis, 'Relativity, Ecumenism and the Liberation of the Church', *Baptist Quarterly*, 29, 1981, pp. 81–91.

40. For a study of the biblical models which were influential in the various liturgies of the early Church, see Kilian McDonnell and George T. Montague, *Christian Initiation and Baptism in the Holy Spirit: Evidence from the First Eight Centuries*, Collegeville MN: Liturgical Press, 1991.

41. Mark 1.9–11 and parallels; Matthew 28.18–20; Acts 2.37–42; and Romans 6.3–4.

42. See Payne and Winward, *Orders and Prayers*, pp. 168–72; and *Patterns and Prayers*, pp. 96–9.

43. For an expansion of this argument see Ellis, 'Baptism of Disciples'.

44. Chapter 25 21. Lumpkin, *Baptist Confessions*, p. 211. We should note that there were some General Baptist churches represented in a predominantly Calvinistic association and Lumpkin suggests (p. 202) that their statements in the 1650s show some evidence of trying to comprehend the inevitable theological breadth.

45. White, *Association Records*, p. 56.

46. Lumpkin, *Baptist Confessions*, p. 163.

47. For the work of grace as expounded by General Baptists, see, for example, clause 20 in 'The Orthodox Creed' of 1678, though Lumpkin suggests it represents an attempt at convergence with the Particular Baptists. Lumpkin, *Baptist Confessions*, pp. 312 and 296.

48. For a survey of twentieth-century Baptist baptismal theology and practices, see Cross, *Baptism and the Baptists*. While, in the modern era, baptism has sometimes

been separated from reception into membership of the Church, theological commentators and those entrusted with providing resources for worship have sought to call the churches back to the integrity of baptism and covenanted membership of a local community. See, for example, *Believing and Being Baptized*, pp. 11–12; and *Patterns and Prayers*, pp. 93–107.

49. This represents the majority practice in churches and is the practice advocated by those who, in a representative capacity, have written in recent years about the theology and practice of baptism.

50. The role of the church meeting is significant. It is not the minister who decides the readiness of a person for baptism, but the community, for they are a covenant community of disciples.

51. See Payne and Winward, *Orders and Prayers*, p. 168; and *Patterns and Prayers*, pp. 93–107.

52. Ellis, *Baptist Worship Today*, pp. 21f.

53. Payne identifies John Bunyan as the most famous exponent of this view, and then traces the practice through the intervening Baptist history. Payne, *Fellowship of Believers*, pp. 77–83.

54. *Believing and Being Baptized*, p. 12, the emphasis is original. See also West, *Baptist Principles*, pp. 31f. and Payne and Winward, *Orders and Prayers*, p. 168. Although, logically, baptism is a prerequisite for membership, nearly a quarter of churches in 1996 did not act on the converse principle, and did not necessarily follow baptism with reception into membership. As part of the reaction to the nineteenth-century debate on sacramentalism, these churches have seen baptism as a stand-alone ordinance, rather than a rite of initiation. This view implies that the Christian life is primarily an individual calling and that being baptized 'into Christ' is not to be interpreted in a communal or ecclesial way. It is likely that emphasis on the word 'ordinance' in such churches will carry the meaning that Christians should be baptized because they are commanded so to be. Accordingly, baptism is presented as an act of witness and obedience, often with a strong evangelistic concern.

55. Ellis, *Baptist Worship Today*, pp. 21–3.

56. See R. E. O. White, *The Biblical Doctrine of Initiation*, London: Hodder & Stoughton, 1960 and Beasley-Murray, *Baptism*, among others.

57. See Walton, *Gathered Community*, p. 163.

58. West, *Baptist Principles*, p. 31. Compare Brian Haymes: 'Those Baptists who are prepared to baptize people without the privileges and responsibilities of church membership being straightforwardly implied do not seem to me to have grasped the full significance of baptism, of the Church, or of the fellowship of Christ.' Haymes, *Question of Identity*, p. 10.

59. Wheeler Robinson, *Life and Faith*, p, 16.

60. Gordon W. Lathrop, 'The Water that Speaks: The Ordo of Baptism and its Ecumenical Implications' in Thomas F. Best and Dagmar Heller (eds), *Becoming a Christian: The Ecumenical Implications of our Common Baptism*, Geneva: World Council of Churches, 1999, pp. 13–29, especially pp. 17f.; and Brian Haymes, 'Baptism as a Political Act' in P. S. Fiddes (ed.), *Reflections on the Water: Understanding God and the World through the Baptism of Believers*, Oxford and Macon GA: Regent's Park College with Smyth & Helwys, 1996, pp. 69–83.

61. Haymes, 'Baptism as a Political Act', p. 72.

62. Chapter 40. Lumpkin, *Baptist Confessions*, p. 167.

63. See *Believing and Being Baptized*, p. 19; and Ellis, 'Believer's Baptism' p. 37.

Chapter 11

1. Fawcett, *Holiness*, pp. 6f.

2. For a discussion of worship as text, see Aidan Kavanagh, 'Textuality and Deritualization: The Case for Western Usage', *Studia Liturgica*, 23, 1993, pp. 70–7 and Irwin, *Context and Text*, pp. 52–74.

3. Arguably, the study of Baptist commentaries on worship is not hugely different from Schmemann's use of the *typica,* as those Orthodox rubrics provide an interpretation of worship through its ordering.

4. Irwin, *Context and Text*, pp. 46–9. He says of this theology of liturgy that it 'describes what Christian liturgy is and what it does in terms of actualizing the reality of Christ's paschal mystery for the Church, gathered and enlivened by the power of the Holy Spirit'.

5. While implied by Irwin, it is explicit in his exposition of the epicletic dimension of worship: 'What really matters . . . in every act of liturgy is what God accomplishes among us through Christ in the power of the Spirit.' Irwin, *Context and Text*, p. 48.

6. See Alexander Schmemann, 'Liturgy and Eschatology' in Thomas Fisch (ed.), *Liturgy and Tradition: Theological Reflections of Alexander Schmemann*, Crestwood NY: St Vladimir's Seminary Press, 1990, pp. 89–100; and Alexander Schmemann, *The Eucharist: Sacrament of the Kingdom*, Crestwood NY: St Vladimir's Seminary Press, 1988, especially pp. 27–48. See also Dix, *Shape of the Liturgy*, pp. 263–6; and Dodd, *Apostolic Preaching*, pp. 93f.

7. For example, the eighteenth-century Salisbury Church Covenant stated that love for one another was 'manifested by praying for one another'. Quoted in Karen E. Smith, 'The Community and the Believer: A Study of Calvinistic Baptist Spirituality in some Towns and Villages of Hampshire and the Borders of Wiltshire, 1730–1830', D. Phil. dissertation, University of Oxford, 1986, p. 259.

8. See Acts 2 for a presentation of the Spirit as an eschatological reality.

9. For the application of the missiological category to Baptist churches, see Anthony A. Peck, *An Introduction to Missionary Congregations*, Leeds: Yorkshire Baptist Association, 1997.

10. Karl Barth, *Church Dogmatics*, I/1: *The Doctrine of the Word of God*, Edinburgh: T & T Clark, 1936, p. 361.

11. Barth, *Church Dogmatics*, I/1, pp. 357f.

12. See, for example, Christopher Cocksworth, *Holy, Holy, Holy: Worshipping the Trinitarian God*, London: Darton, Longman & Todd, 1997.

13. However, there are aspects of the way they express this Lordship which may be regarded as distinctively Baptist. Brian Haymes argues, for example, 'I hold that there is none the less a Baptist wisdom in the tradition that says it is the whole church listening, praying, deciding together that determines that congregation's life under Christ.' Haymes, *Question of Identity*, p. 18.

14. Karl Barth, *Church Dogmatics*, IV/1: *The Doctrine of Reconciliation*, Edinburgh: T & T Clark, 1956, p. 20.

15. See, however, Wainwright, *Doxology*, for an attempt to do this in an ecumenical way.

16. F. Schleiermacher, *The Christian Faith*, Edinburgh: T & T Clark, 1928, p. 88.

17. McClendon, *Ethics*, p. 23.

18. They define a conviction as, 'A persistent belief that if X (a person or a community) has a conviction, it will not easily be relinquished, and it cannot be relinquished without making X a significantly different person (or community) than before.' James W. McClendon, Jr. and James M. Smith, *Convictions: Defusing Religious Relativism*, Valley Forge PA: Trinity Press International, 1975, p. 5.

19. McClendon and Smith, *Convictions*, p. 99.

20. Although McClendon and Smith suggest that a presiding conviction will rarely be uttered, the Lordship of Jesus Christ is indeed frequently articulated as a central theme of Christian worship.

21. James W. McClendon, Jr, *Systematic Theology*, vol. 2: *Doctrine*, Nashville TN: Abingdon Press, 1994, p. 64.

22. Lumpkin, *Baptist Confessions*, pp.153f. Ernest Payne points out that the term 'Baptist' originated as a contraction of 'Anabaptist', a nickname which the early Baptists sought to resist. For example, the Confession is entitled, 'The Confession of Faith of those churches which are commonly (though falsely) called Anabaptists'. See Payne, *Fellowship of Believers*, pp. 71f.

23. Lumpkin, *Baptist Confessions*, p. 158.

24. Lumpkin, *Baptist Confessions*, p. 170.

25. He cites Thomas Helwys, William Knibb and Martin Luther King. Haymes, *Question of Identity*, p. 20.

26. Payne, 'Elegy'.

27. Leonard G. Champion, *The Living Christ in His Church*, London: Carey Kingsgate Press, 1964, pp. 14f.

28. *Baptist Union Directory 2002–03*, p. 9.

29. However, it was recently printed for discretionary use in one of the ordination services published by the Union. *Patterns and Prayers*, pp. 188 and 204.

30. Kidd, *Something to Declare*, p. 28.

31. Barth, *Church Dogmatics* I/1, pp. 98–140.

32. See the survey in Cross, *Baptism and the Baptists*, pp. 348–57; also Ellis, 'Believer's Baptism', pp. 33f.; and a Charismatic Roman Catholic discussion in McDonnell and Montague, *Christian Initiation*.

33. It is significant that the authors of *Something to Declare* use this passage as a hermeneutical key for the whole of the *Declaration of Principle* where the second and third clauses refer to baptism and evangelism.

34. Compare Matthew 10.16–20, where Jesus warns of persecution because of faithful discipleship.

35. See Haymes, 'Baptism as a Political Act', with regard to the political implications.

36. See, for example, Matthew 28.18–20; Philippians 2.9–11; and Colossians 1.15–20. For an ecumenical statement which illustrates some of this, see the ARCIC report of 1976, which opens with the words, 'The confession of Christ as Lord is the heart of the Christian faith. To him God has given all authority in heaven and on earth. As Lord of the Church he bestows the Holy Spirit to create a communion of men with God and with one another.' Anglican–Roman Catholic International Commission, *The Final Report*, London: SPCK and the Catholic Truth Society, 1982, p. 52.

37. Lathrop, *Holy Things*, p. 9.

38. The *Constitution of the Sacred Liturgy* affirms the principle that liturgy is an ecclesial action. (*Documents of the Liturgy, 1963–1979: Conciliar, Papal and Curial Texts*, Collegeville MN: Liturgical Press, 1982, nos. 2, 7, 26, 41, 42.) See also M. M. Kelleher, 'Liturgy: An Ecclesial Act of Meaning', *Worship*, 59, 1985, pp. 482–497, especially p. 482, who also quotes Yves Congar's claim that this was 'a retrieval of the ancient tradition that the *ecclesia*, the Christian community, is the subject of the liturgical action'.

39. Kelleher, 'Liturgy', pp. 491 and 492.

40. So Kelleher explains, 'Both individual and collective subjects, communities, mediate themselves by their living. In other words, in their choices, decisions, and actions they both manifest and create a self. This means that every assembly engaged in liturgical action is also involved in the process of mediating itself. Since liturgical assemblies are particular realizations of the church, the church itself is being mediated' (p. 493).

41. See Chapter 1 above. Allmen, *Worship*, p. 42.

42. For a discussion of the eschatological nature of worship, see, Dix, *Shape of the Liturgy*, especially pp. 129f., 156–9 and 621–5; Schmemann, *Introduction to Liturgical Theology*, pp. 64–80; Brunner, *Worship*, pp. 72–83; and Don E. Saliers, *Worship as Theology: Foretaste of Divine Glory*, Nashville TN: Abingdon Press, 1994, pp. 49–68 and 217–30.

43. Wainwright, *Doxology*, p. 121.

44. This also made it easier to clarify those aspects of Baptist thought and practice which were genuinely distinctive, such as ecclesiology and, of course, baptism. So the 1644 *London Confession* was for 'the cleering of the truth we professe' in response to lies that had been spread, with the result that 'many that feare God are discouraged and forestalled in harbouring a good thought, either of us or what wee professe; and many that know not God incouraged, if they can find the place of our meeting, to get together in Clusters to stone us, as looking upon us as a people holding such things, as wee are not worthy to live . . . ' Lumpkin, *Baptist Confessions*, p. 155. Despite a general suspicion of creeds, Baptists have from time to time, as we have seen, used confessions of faith, albeit viewing these as more provisional than other Christians have viewed the historic creeds. Lumpkin, *Baptist Confessions*, p. 16; and McClendon, *Doctrine*, pp. 470f. However, they have sometimes even affirmed their place within the wider Church through their affirmation of those historic creeds. For example, the General Baptist *Orthodox Creed* of 1678 sought to 'unite all true protestants in the fundamental articles of the Christian religion' and article 38 states, 'The three creeds, viz. Nicene creed, Athanasius's creed, and the Apostles' creed, as they are commonly called, ought thoroughly to be received and believed. For we believe, they may be proved, by most undoubted authority of holy Scripture, and are necessary to be understood of all christians'; Lumpkin, *Baptist Confessions*, pp. 295 and 326. Thomas Grantham, the messenger among the General Baptists also published an account of Christianity which commended the Apostles' and Nicene Creeds, suggesting that they 'might be a good means to bring to a greater degree of unity many of the divided parties professing Christianity'. Grantham, *Christianismus Primitivus*, vol. 2, p. 61. At the inaugural Congress of the Baptist World Alliance in London in 1905, Alexander Maclaren invited the gathering to say together the Apostles' Creed, and the resource material for covenant services in 2001 included that creed, with a credal selection of Scripture verses and the Nicene Creed as alternatives. *Covenant 21*.

45. Ernest A. Payne, *The Baptist Union: A Short History*, London: Carey Kingsgate Press, 1959, pp. 218f.

46. R. Hayden, *Baptist Union Documents*, London: Baptist Historical Society, 1980, p. 5.

47. Indeed, he added a new chapter with that title: A. Dulles, *Models of the Church*, Dublin: Gill & Macmillan, 1976/1987.

48. McClendon, *Ethics*, p. 31.

49. Ernest Best, *Following Jesus: Discipleship in the Gospel of Mark*, Journal for the Study of the New Testament, Supplement Series, Sheffield: JSOT Press, 1981, p. 12.

50. Wolfhart Pannenberg, *Jesus – God and Man*, London: SCM Press, 1968, p. 64.

51. Pannenberg, *Jesus*, p. 67.

52. Acts 2.36. Cf. Romans 10.9 and Matthew 28.18 for a link between Lordship and the resurrection.

53. Romans 10.9; 1 Corinthians 12.3; and Philippians 2.11. For a discussion of *Kyrios* in relation to the historical Jesus, see W. Foerster and G. Friedrich, '*Kyrios*' in G. Kittel (ed.), *Theological Dictionary of the New Testament*, Grand Rapids MI: Eerdmans, 1965, pp. 1081–98, especially pp. 1092–4, and Vincent Taylor, *The Names of Jesus*, London: Macmillan, 1953, pp. 38–51.

54. Best points out that the relationship of Jesus to his followers is analogous to but distinct from that of a rabbi or teacher/philosopher because Jesus is unique and the one learning from him never replaces him. Best, *Following Jesus*, pp. 248f. See also J. L. Houlden, 'Why were the Disciples ever called Disciples?', *Theology*, 105, 2002, pp. 411–17.

55. See Alan Richardson, *An Introduction to the Theology of the New Testament*, London: SCM Press, 1958, pp. 153f. for the breadth of usage in the apostolic Church.

56. Haymes, *Question of Identity*, p. 5.

57. McClendon, *Doctrine*, pp. 64ff.

58. See Schmemann, *Introduction to Liturgical Theology*, pp. 75–80; and Frank C. Senn, *New Creation: A Liturgical Worldview*, Minneapolis MN: Fortress Press, 2000, pp. 25 and 31.

59. Perhaps the most influential modern discussion of the relationship of the Scriptures to God's revelation in Christ is that found in the opening volume of Karl Barth's *Church Dogmatics*, I/1 (1936), pp. 98–140, but see also Paul Tillich, *Systematic Theology*, Chicago: University of Chicago Press, 1953, p. 176, who prefers not to use the phrase 'word of God' in relation to Scripture because of the confusion which he believes results. See also Michael Ramsey, 'The Authority of the Bible' in M. Black (ed.), *Peake's Commentary on the Bible*, London: Nelson, 1962, pp. 1–7; John Barton, 'Authority of Scripture' in R. J. Coggins and J. L. Houlden (eds), *A Dictionary of Biblical Interpretation*, London and Philadelphia: SCM Press and Trinity Press International, 1990, pp. 69–72; and 'Scripture: Theology's "Norming Norm"' in Stanley J. Grenz and John R. Franke, *Beyond Foundationalism: Shaping Theology in a Postmodern Context*, Louisville KY: Westminster John Knox Press, 2001, pp. 57–92.

60. McClendon, *Doctrine*, p. 463. Cf. The Declaration of Principle of the Baptist Union in *Baptist Union Directory 2002–03*, p. 9.

61. Note how Isaac Watts imitated rather than paraphrased the psalms, 'in order to accommodate the book of psalms to Christian worship'. See the preface in Watts, *Psalms of David*.

62. Maxwell, *Outline of Christian Worship*, p. 114.

63. For types of prayer in contemporary Baptist services, see Ellis, *Baptist Worship Today*, pp. 12f.

64. For an example of penitential language in a prayer of Watts, see Chapter six above.

65. See Bouyer, *Introduction to Spirituality*, p. 59.

66. See 'The Baptist Doctrine of the Church: A Statement Approved by the Council of the Baptist Union of Great Britain and Ireland, March 1948' in R. Hayden (ed.), *Baptist Union Documents 1948–1977*, London: Baptist Historical Society, 1980; and Lathrop, *Holy Things* p. 9: 'From the viewpoint of liturgical theology, the most basic and constitutive sense of the word "church" refers to the communal gathering around washing, texts, and meal, as these are interpreted as having to do with Jesus Christ. The "catholic church" is best perceived as the deep, biblically grounded structure that links these churches and comes to expression in their gatherings. To be part of the assembly, then, is to be part of the church. To interpret the meaning of the assembly is to interpret the meaning of "church" and the church's faith.'

67. Matthew 6.9–13; and Luke 11.2–4. See George R. Beasley-Murray, *Jesus and the Kingdom of God*, Grand Rapids MI and Carlisle: Eerdmans and Paternoster, 1986, pp. 147–57; and Oscar Cullmann, *Prayer in the New Testament*, London: SCM Press, 1995, pp. 37–69, especially pp. 45–7.

68. See Walter Brueggemann, 'Praise and the Psalms: A Politics of Glad Abandonment' in P. D. Miller (ed.), *The Psalms and the Life of Faith*, Minneapolis MN: Fortress Press, 1992, pp. 112–32.

69. Jürgen Moltmann, *The Church in the Power of the Spirit: A Contribution to Messianic Ecclesiology*, London: SCM Press, 1977, p. 262. Interestingly, the 1948 report on the nature of the Church referred to it as the 'Messianic community'. See 'Baptist Doctrine of the Church', p. 6.

70. Keith G. Jones, *A Believing Church: Learning from some Contemporary Anabaptist and Baptist Perspectives*, Didcot: Baptist Union of Great Britain, 1998, pp. 38f. and p. 64.

71. See Philippians 2.9–11 for an expressing of the coming Kingdom in terms of the Lordship of Jesus Christ.

Chapter 12

1. Spurgeon, *Lectures*, pp. 53f.

2. The complementary nature of these two forms of theological expression – the explanatory language of academic theology and the embodied and symbolic language of worship – may be designated as 'secondary theology' and 'primary theology' respectively. See Chapter 2.

3. For example, in the official 'century' histories of English Baptists published by the Baptist Historical Society, we have to wait until the nineteenth century to find any sustained account of Baptist worship. See Briggs, *English Baptists*.

4. It is true that most Free Churches have a national decision-making body, such

Notes 301

as the Baptist Assembly or the United Reformed Church Assembly. However, the control such a body has over local church life varies between denominations and in most cases its influence is moral rather than juridical. Certainly, a recognition of local variety tends to mean that developments in worship happen through the encouragement of good practice rather than through legislation. Compare this with the speed with which liturgical revision and reform occurred within the Roman Catholic Church following the Second Vatican Council or the influence which is possible through the introduction of new service books in those denominations which require central authorization of liturgical rites.

5. Quite apart from the challenges of local liturgical situations, and the provision of educational opportunities for liturgical practitioners, further work could address the perceived weaknesses in Baptist worship such as those identified in the so-called Berlin Declaration. See 'The Berlin Worship Declaration' in T. Cupit (ed.), *Baptists in Worship: Report of an International Baptist Conference in Berlin, Germany*, McClean VA: Baptist World Alliance, 1998, pp. 240–3.

6. The work of Paul Bradshaw, who has used the models of 'cathedral worship' and 'monastic worship' as a way of analysing the dynamics of corporate worship, could well be applied to the worship of Baptists. The intersection of the one and the many remains a crucial challenge both for those who dare to lead others in worship and for those who seek to understand that worship. See Bradshaw, *Two Ways of Praying*.

7. In fact, Schmemann used the term 'theology of liturgy'. See Schmemann, 'Liturgical Theology: Remarks on Method', especially pp. 137f.

8. Johnson, 'Liturgy and Theology', p. 206.

9. Schmemann, 'Liturgical Theology, Theology of Liturgy, and Liturgical Reform', p. 42.

10. Schmemann, *Introduction to Liturgical Theology*, p. 39.

11. Schmemann, *Introduction to Liturgical Theology*, p. 21.

12. Johnson, 'Liturgy and Theology', p. 208.

13. The 'normally' in this statement must be qualified as social and intellectual trends have inevitably influenced changes in this. For example, among Baptists, both General and Particular Baptists lived by the Genevan principle that worship practices should be ordered by the command or example of Scripture. However, the nineteenth and twentieth centuries have seen a process of liberalization in which Scripture offers guidelines, rather than injunctions, for worship and in which ecumenical borrowings and evangelistic imperatives have led to a more pragmatic approach to what is permissible in worship. Nonetheless, Scripture remains an important aspect of any theology of worship.

14. Wainwright, *Doxology*, p. 251.

15. Lossky, 'Tradition and Traditions', p. 15.

16. For discussion by a Baptist of the dynamic relationship between Scripture and Tradition see Grenz, *Theology*, pp. 14–20; and the chapter 'Tradition: Theology's Hermeneutical Trajectory' in Grenz and Franke, *Beyond Foundationalism*, pp. 93–129.

17. See Winward, *Reformation of Our Worship*, pp 1f.; and Martin, *The Worship of God*, p. 4. Cf. James F. White, *Introduction to Christian Worship*, Nashville TN: Abingdon, 1980, p. 33; and Forrester, McDonald and Tellini, *Encounter*, pp. 2–6.

18. Lathrop, *Holy Things*, pp. 33–53.

19. Schmemann, *Introduction to Liturgical Theology*, pp. 49–89.

20. James F. White, 'How Do We Know it is Us?' in E. Byron Anderson and Bruce T. Morrill (eds), *Liturgy and the Moral Self: Humanity at Full Stretch Before God. Essays in Honour of Don E. Saliers*, Collegeville MN: Liturgical Press, 1998, pp. 55–65, p. 57.

21. Lathrop, *Holy Things*, pp. 15–20.

22. See Kallistos Ware, *The Orthodox Church*, Harmondsworth: Penguin Books, 1963/1969, p. 41; and Leonide Ouspensky, *Theology of the Icon*, Crestwood NY: St Vladimir's Seminary Press, 1978, pp. 55–8.

23. Of course, contemporary Western culture is becoming increasingly visual, and changes in avant-garde Protestant worship are beginning to reflect that. See, for example, Len Wilson and Jason Moore, *Digital Storytellers: The Art of Communicating the Gospel in Worship*, Nashville TN: Abingdon, 2002.

24. For a Roman Catholic treatment of liturgical sources that argues something similar in relation to initiation rites, see McDonnell and Montague, *Christian Initiation*.

25. Maxwell E. Johnson, 'Can We Avoid Relativism in Worship? Liturgical Norms in the Light of Contemporary Liturgical Scholarship', *Worship*, 74, 2000, pp. 135–55, pp. 150f.

26. See Schillebeeckx, *Christ the Sacrament*.

27. For the first two and a half centuries of Baptist life, congregations often held mid-week prayer meetings in preparation for the monthly celebration of the Lord's Supper. In addition, a Bristol congregation in the late seventeenth century abstained from gathering for the Supper for eighteen months because their pastor was in prison. This eucharistic abstinence was not because they required a minister to preside, as other local ministers were available, but because the body was broken by that imprisonment. This is a high view of the sacrament which has been much eroded by nineteenth-century reaction to the Oxford Movement.

28. Lathrop, *Holy Things*, p. 47.

29. For example, we have seen how three of our core convictions are closely related to Irwin's proposed characteristics of Christian worship as anamnetic, epicletic and ecclesial. Interestingly, from an Anglican perspective, Stephen Sykes also speaks of three 'vital conditions' for worship – anamnesis, prayer and praise (cf. epiclesis) and worship as corporate. Stephen Sykes, *The Identity of Christianity: Theologians and the Essence of Christianity from Schleiermacher to Barth*, London: SPCK, 1984, p. 265.

30. See Empereur, *Models*; and *Worship*; and his 'Models of Liturgical Theology' in R. E. Webber (ed.), *Twenty Centuries of Christian Worship*, The Complete Library of Christian Worship, Nashville TN: Star Song, 1994, pp. 263–6.

31. We have already noted that Avery Dulles revised his study on ecclesiology by adding a significant chapter on the Church as 'the community of disciples'.

32. Empereur, *Models*, p. 44.

33. Empereur, *Models*, p. 9.

Bibliography

2003 Yearbook of the Baptist World Alliance, Falls Church VA: Baptist World Alliance, 2003

Abba, Raymond, *Principles of Christian Worship with Special Reference to the Free Churches*, Oxford: Oxford University Press, 1957

Allmen, Jean-Jacques von, *Worship: Its Theology and Practice*, London: Lutterworth Press, 1965

Alternative Service Book, Oxford: Oxford University Press and A. R. Mowbray, 1980

Anglican–Roman Catholic International Commission, *The Final Report*, London: SPCK and the Catholic Truth Society, 1982

Ash, John and Evans, Caleb, *A Collection of Hymns adapted to Public Worship*, Bristol, 1769

Aubrey, Melbourn E., *A Minister's Manual*, London: Kingsgate Press, 1927

Baker, Judith W., 'The Use of *Kerygma* in the Early Church' in Robert E. Webber (ed.), *The Complete Library of Christian Worship*, vol. 3: *The Renewal of Sunday Worship*, Peabody MA: Hendrikson, 1993

Ballard, Paul and Pritchard, John, *Practical Theology in Action: Christian Thinking in the Service of Church and Society*, London: SPCK, 1996

Baptism, Eucharist and Ministry, Faith and Order Paper No. 111, Geneva: World Council of Churches, 1982

Baptist Church Hymnal, London: Psalms and Hymns Trust, 1900

Baptist Praise and Worship, Oxford: Oxford University Press on behalf of the Psalms and Hymns Trust, 1991

Baptist Union Directory 2002–2003, Didcot: Baptist Union of Great Britain, 2002

Barth, Karl, *Church Dogmatics*, Edinburgh: T & T Clark, 1936

Barton, John, 'Authority of Scripture' in R. J. Coggins and J. L. Houlden (eds), *A Dictionary of Biblical Interpretations*, London and Philadelphia: SCM Press and Trinity Press International, 1990

Baumstark, Anton, *Comparative Liturgy*, Oxford: Mowbray, 1958

Beasley-Murray, George R., *Baptism in the New Testament*, London: Macmillan, 1962

Beasley-Murray, George R., *Jesus and the Kingdom of God*, Grand Rapids MI and Carlisle: Eerdmans and Paternoster, 1986

Bebbington, David W., *Evangelicalism in Modern Britain: A History from the 1730s to the 1980s*, London: Unwin Hyman, 1989

Beddome, Benjamin, *Hymns adapted to Public Worship or Family Devotion*, ed. R. Hall, London, 1818

Believing and Being Baptized: Baptism, so-called Rebaptism and Children in the Church, Didcot: Baptist Union of Great Britain, 1996

Bell, John L., *The Singing Thing: A Case for Congregational Song*, Glasgow: Wild Goose, 2000

Benson, Louis F., *The English Hymn: Its development and Use in Worship*, Richmond VA: John Knox Press, 1915

Best, Ernest, *Following Jesus: Discipleship in the Gospel of Mark*, Journal for the Study of the New Testament Supplement Series, Sheffield: JSOT Press, 1981

Best, Thomas F. and Heller, Dagmar (eds), *Becoming a Christian: The Ecumenical Implications of our Common Baptism*, Geneva: World Council of Churches, 1999

Binfield, Clyde, 'The Coats Family and Paisley Baptists', *Baptist Quarterly*, 36, 1995, pp. 29–42

Birrell, Charles M., *Life of William Brock D.D.*, London: James Nisbet, 1878

Bloomsbury Chapel Year Book, London, 1850

Bloomsbury Chapel Year Book, London, 1862

Bonhoeffer, Dietrich, *Ethics*, London: SCM Press, 1955

Booth, Charles, *Life and Labour of the People of London*, London: Macmillan, 1903

Bouyer, Louis, *Liturgical Piety*, Notre Dame IN: University of Notre Dame Press, 1955

Bouyer, Louis, *Introduction to Spirituality*, London: Darton, Longman & Todd, 1961

Bradley, Ian, *Abide with Me: The World of Victorian Hymns*, London: SCM Press, 1997

Bradshaw, Paul F., *Daily Prayer in the Early Church*, London: Alcuin Club and SPCK, 1981

Bradshaw, Paul F., 'The Reshaping of Liturgical Studies', *Anglican Theological Review*, 72, 1990, pp. 481–7

Bradshaw, Paul F., *The Search for the Origins of Christian Worship: Sources and Methods for the Study of Early Liturgy*, London: SPCK, 1992

Bradshaw, Paul F., 'The Use of the Bible in Liturgy: Some Historical Perspectives', *Studia Liturgica*, 22, 1992, pp. 33–52

Bradshaw, Paul F., *Two Ways of Praying: Introducing Liturgical Spirituality*, London: SPCK, 1995

Bradshaw, William, *Englishe Puritanisme, containing the maine opinions of the rigidest sort of those that are called Puritanes in the realm of England*, Oxford, 1646

Bria, Ion, *The Liturgy After the Liturgy: Mission and Witness from an Orthodox Perspective*, Geneva: World Council of Churches, 1996

Briggs, John H. Y., *The English Baptists of the Nineteenth Century*, Didcot: Baptist Historical Society, 1994

Briggs, John H. Y., 'English Baptists and their Hymnody: An Introduction' in W. H. Brackney (ed.), *Baptist Faith and Witness: The Papers of the Study and Research Division of the Baptist World Alliance, 1990–1995*, Birmingham AL and McClean VA: Samford University Press and the Baptist World Alliance, 1995

Brock, William, *The Behaviour Becoming the House of God*, Norwich: Norfolk and Norwich Association of Baptist Churches, 1845

Brown, Raymond, 'Baptist Preaching in Early Eighteenth Century England', *Baptist Quarterly*, 31, 1985, pp. 4–22

Brown, Raymond, *The English Baptists of the Eighteenth Century*, London: Baptist Historical Society, 1986

Brueggemann, Walter, 'The Costly Loss of Lament', *Journal for the Study of the Old Testament*, 36, 1986, pp. 57–71

Brueggemann, Walter, *Israel's Praise: Doxology against Idolatry and Ideology*, Philadelphia PA: Fortress Press, 1988

Brueggemann, Walter, 'Praise and the Psalms: A Politics of Glad Abandonment' in P. D. Miller (ed.), *The Psalms and the Life of Faith*, Minneapolis MN: Fortress Press, 1992

Brunner, Peter, *Worship in the Name of Jesus*, St Louis MO and London: Concordia, 1968

Bunyan, John, 'I will Pray with the Spirit' (1663) in *The Doctrine of the Law and Grace Unfolded: The miscellaneous works of John Bunyan series*, vol. 2, ed. Richard L. Greaves, Oxford University Press, 1976

Bunyan, John, *Grace Abounding to the Chief of Sinners* (1666), ed. R. Sharrock, Oxford: Clarendon Press, 1962

Burrage, Champlin, *The Early Dissenters in the Light of Recent Research (1550–1641)*, Cambridge: Cambridge University Press, 1912

Buttrick, David, *Homiletics: Moves and Structures*, Philadelphia PA: Fortress Press, 1987

Calvin, John, *Institutes of the Christian Religion*, London: James Clarke, 1957

Carey, William, *An Enquiry into the Obligations of Christians to use Means for the Conversion of the Heathen*, Leicester, 1792

Carlson, Leland H. (ed.), *The Writings of John Greenwood 1587–1590, Together with the Joint Writings of Henry Barrow and John Greenwood 1587–1590*, London: George Allen & Unwin and the Sir Halley Stewart Trust, 1962

Carruthers, S. W., *Westminster Confession of Faith*, Glasgow: Free Presbyterian Publications, 1646/1994

Champion, Leonard G., *The Living Christ in His Church*, London: Carey Kingsgate Press, 1964

Chandlee, H. Ellsworth, 'The Liturgical Movement' in J. G. Davies (ed.), *A Dictionary of Liturgy and Worship*, London: SCM Press, 1972

Church Book: St. Andrew's Street Baptist Church, Cambridge 1720–1832, ed. L. E. Addicott, L. G. Champion and K. A. Parsons, English Baptist Records, Didcot: Baptist Historical Society, 1991

Clark, Neville, *An Approach to the Theology of the Sacraments*, London: SCM Press, 1956

Clark, Neville, *Call to Worship*, London: SCM Press, 1960

Cocksworth, Christopher, *Holy, Holy, Holy: Worshipping the Trinitarian God*, London: Darton, Longman & Todd, 1997

Cohen, Charles L., *God's Caress: The Psychology of Puritan Religious Experience*, New York: Oxford University Press, 1986

Colligan, J. H., *Eighteenth Century Nonconformity*, London: Longmans, Green & Co., 1915

Collins, Hercules, *The Temple Repaired or, An Essay to Revive the Long-neglected Ordinances, of Exercising the Spiritual Gift of Prophecy for the Edification of the Churches; and of Ordaining Ministers Duly Qualified*, London: William & Joseph Marshall, 1702

Collins, Mary and Power, David (eds), *Liturgy: A Creative Tradition*, Concilium, Edinburgh: T & T Clark, 1983

Colquhoun, Frank, *Hymns that Live*, London: Hodder & Stoughton, 1980

Common Worship: Services and Prayers for the Church of England, London: Church House Publishing, 2000

Cooper, R. E., *From Stepney to St. Giles: The Story of Regent's Park College 1810–1960*, London: Carey Kingsgate Press, 1960

Copson, Stephen L., *Association Life of the Particular Baptists of Northern England 1699–1732*, Didcot: Baptist Historical Society, 1991

Covenant 21, Didcot: Baptist Union of Great Britain, 2000

Craddock, Fred B., *Preaching*, Nashville TN: Abingdon, 1985

Crawford, J., 'Becoming a Christian: The Ecumenical Challenge of our Common Baptism' in T. F. Best and D. Heller (eds), *Becoming a Christian: The Ecumenical Implications of our Common Baptism*, Geneva: World Council of Churches, 1999

Crippen, T. G., 'From the Bury Street Church Records', *Transactions of the Congregational Historical Society*, 6, 1913, pp. 334–42

Crosby, Thomas, *History of the English Baptists*, London, 1738

Cross, Anthony R., *Baptism and the Baptists: Theology and Practice in Twentieth Century Britain*, Carlisle: Paternoster Press, 2000

Cullmann, Oscar, *Prayer in the New Testament*, London: SCM Press, 1995

Curwen, J. S., *Studies in Worship and Music, chiefly as regards Congregational Singing*, London: Curwen & Sons, 1880

Davie, D., *The Eighteenth Century Hymn in England*, Cambridge: Cambridge University Press, 1993

Davies, Horton, *The Worship of the English Puritans*, London: Dacre Press, 1948

Davies, Horton, *Worship and Theology in England: From Watts and Wesley to Martineau, 1690–1900*, Grand Rapids MI and Cambridge: Eerdmans, 1961/1996

Davies, Horton, *Worship and Theology in England: The Ecumenical Century, 1900 to the Present*, Grand Rapids MI & Cambridge: Eerdmans, 1965/1996

Davies, Horton, *Worship and Theology in England: From Cranmer to Baxter and Fox, 1534–1690*, Grand Rapids MI and Cambridge: Eerdmans, 1970/1996

Davies, J. G., *Worship and Mission*, London: SCM Press, 1966

Deacon, Samuel, *Barton Hymns: A New Composition of Hymns and Poems chiefly on Divine Subjects designed for the Amusement and Edification of Christians of all denominations: more particularly those of the General Baptist persuasion*, Coventry, 1785

Dix, Gregory, *The Shape of the Liturgy*, London: Dacre Press, 1945

Documents on the Liturgy, 1963–1979: Conciliar, Papal and Curial Texts, Collegeville MN: Liturgical Press, 1982

Dodd, C. H., *The Apostolic Preaching and its Developments*, London: Hodder & Stoughton, 1944

Drapes, Edward, *Gospel-glory proclaimed before the sonnes of men in the Worship of God*, London, 1649

Dulles, A., *Models of the Church*, Dublin: Gill & Macmillan, 1976/198

Durnbaugh, Donald F., *The Believers' Church: The History and Character of Radical Protestantism*, Scottdale PA: Herald Press, 1968/1985

Edwards, A. R., *The Church's Worship*, Annual Report of the Western Baptist Association, 1911

Edwards, Joel, *Let's Praise Him Again*, Eastbourne: Kingsway, 1994

Ellis, Christopher J., 'Relativity, Ecumenism and the Liberation of the Church', *Baptist Quarterly*, 29, 1981, pp. 81–91

Ellis, Christopher J., 'The Difficulties of Baptism as the Basis for Unity', unpublished paper for the Doctrine and Worship Committee of the Baptist Union of Great Britain, 1993

Ellis, Christopher J., 'Believer's Baptism and the Sacramental Freedom of God' in Paul S. Fiddes (ed.), *Reflections on the Water: Understanding God and the World through the Baptism of Believers*, Oxford and Macon GA: Regent's Park College with Smyth & Helwys, 1996

Ellis, Christopher J., *Baptist Worship Today*, Didcot: Baptist Union of Great Britain, 1999

Ellis, Christopher J., 'A View from the Pool: Baptists, Sacraments and the Basis of Unity', *Baptist Quarterly*, 39, 2001, pp. 107–20

Ellis, Christopher J., 'The Baptism of Disciples and the Nature of the Church' in Stanley E. Porter and Anthony R. Cross (eds) *Dimensions of Baptism: Biblical and Theological Studies*, Sheffield: Sheffield Academic Press, 2002

Empereur, James L., *Models of Liturgical Theology*, Bramcote, Nottingham: Grove Books, 1987

Empereur, James L., *Worship: Exploring the Sacred*, Washington DC: Pastoral Press, 1987

Empereur, James L., 'Models of Liturgical Theology' in R. E. Webber (ed.), *Twenty Centuries of Christian Worship*, The Complete Library of Christian Worship, Nashville TN: Star Song, 1994

Escott, Harry, *Isaac Watts, Hymnographer: A Study of the Beginnings, Development and Philosophy of the English Hymn*, London: Independent Press, 1962

Evans, Caleb, *Elisha's Exclamation: A Sermon Occasioned by the Death of Rev. Hugh Evans, preached at Broadmead, Bristol, April 8, 1781*, Bristol: W. Pine, 1781

Evans, Hugh and Evans, Caleb, 'The Case for an Educated Ministry: Bristol Education Society 1770' in N. S. Moon (ed.), *Education for Ministry: Bristol Baptist College 1679–1979*, Bristol: Bristol Baptist College, 1979

Fagerberg, David W., *What is Liturgical Theology? A Study in Methodology*, Collegeville MN: Liturgical Press, 1992

Farley, Edward, 'Towards a New Paradigm for Preaching' in T. G. Long and Edward Farley (eds), *Preaching as a Theological Task: World, Gospel, Scripture*, Louisville KY: Westminster John Knox, 1996

Fawcett, John, *Hymns Adapted to the Circumstances of Public Worship and Private Devotion*, Leeds, 1782

Fawcett, John, *The Holiness which Becometh the House of the Lord*, Halifax, 1808

Fenstanton, Warboys and Hexham Records, ed. E. B. Underhill, 1847

Fenwick, John and Spinks, Bryan, *Worship in Transition: The Twentieth Century Liturgical Movement*, Edinburgh: T & T Clark, 1995

Fiddes, Paul S., 'Theology and a Baptist Way of Community' in Paul S. Fiddes (ed.), *Doing Theology in a Baptist Way*, Oxford: Whitley Publications, 2000

Fiddes, Paul S., 'Baptism and the Process of Christian Initiation' in S. E. Porter and A. R. Cross (eds), *Dimensions of Baptism: Biblical and Theological Studies*, Sheffield: Sheffield Academic Press, 2002

Fiddes, Paul S., Hayden, Roger, Kidd, Richard L., Clements, Keith W., and Haymes, Brian, *Bound to Love: The Covenant Basis of Baptist Life and Mission*, London: Baptist Union of Great Britain, 1985

Finney, Charles G., *Revivals of Religion*, ed. W. H. Harding, London: Morgan & Scott, 1835

Fisch, Thomas, 'Schmemann's Theological Contribution to the Liturgical Renewal of the Churches' in Thomas Fisch (ed.), *Liturgy and Tradition: Theological Reflections of Alexander Schmemann*, Crestwood NY: St Vladimir's Seminary Press, 1990

Foerster, W. and Friedrich, G., '*Kyrios*' in G. Kittel (ed.), *Theological Dictionary of the New Testament*, Grand Rapids MI: Eerdmans, 1965

Foreman, Henry, 'The Early Separatists, the Baptists and Education 1580–1750 (With special reference to the education of the clergy)', PhD, University of Leeds, 1976

Forrester, Duncan B., McDonald, J. Ian H., and Tellini, Gian, *Encounter with God: An Introduction to Christian Worship and Practice*, Edinburgh: T & T Clark, 1996

Fountain, David G., *Isaac Watts Remembered*, Harpenden, Herts: Gospel Standard Baptist Trust, 1974

Fuller, Andrew, *The Practical Uses of Christian Baptism*, Northampton: Circular Letter of the Northamptonshire Association, 1802

Fuller, Andrew, *On Reading the Word of God*, Kettering: Circular Letter of the Northamptonshire Baptist Association, 1813

Gennep, Arnold van, *The Rites of Passage*, London: Routledge & Kegan Paul, 1960

George, A. Raymond, 'Heiler' in G. S. Wakefield (ed.), *A Dictionary of Christian Spirituality*, London: SCM Press, 1983

George, A. Raymond, 'Prophetic Prayer' in G. S. Wakefield (ed.), *A Dictionary of Christian Spirituality*, London: SCM Press, 1983

George, A. Raymond, 'The Choosing of Hymns' in Charles Robertson (ed.), *Sing the Faith: Essays by Members of the Joint Liturgical Group on the Use of Hymns in the Liturgy*, Norwich: Canterbury Press, 1990

Gerhards, Albert, 'Koinonia and the Development of the Liturgy: A Response to Gordon Lathrop', *Studia Liturgica*, 26, 1996, pp. 82–90

Gill, John, *Two Discourses; the One on Prayer, the Other on Singing of Psalms*, London, 1751

Gill, John, *A Body of Practical Divinity: or, A System of Practical Truths*, London: George Keith, 1770

Gillett, David K., *Trust and Obey: Explorations in Evangelical Spirituality*, London: Darton, Longman & Todd, 1993

Gilmore, Alec, *The Pattern of the Church: A Baptist View*, London: Lutterworth Press, 1963

Gilmore, Alec, Smalley, Edward, and Walker, Michael, *Praise God: A Collection of Resource Material for Christian Worship*, London: Baptist Union of Great Britain and Ireland, 1980

Gordon, James M., *Evangelical Spirituality from the Wesleys to John Stott*, London: SPCK, 1991

Gough, Thomas T., *Christian Worship*, The Circular Letter from the Ministers and Messengers of the several Baptist Churches in the Northamptonshire Association assembled at Olney, 1845

Grantham, Thomas, *Christianismus Primitivus: or, The Ancient Christian Religion, in its nature, certainty, excellency, and beauty, (internal and external) particularly considered, asserted, and vindicated &c*, London: Francis Smith, 1678

Green, Laurie, *Let's Do Theology*, London: Mowbray, 1990

Gregory, A. S., *Praises with Understanding: Illustrated from the Words and Music of the Methodist Hymnbook*, London: Epworth, 1936

Grenz, Stanley J., *Theology for the Community of God*, Grand Rapids MI and Vancouver BC: Eerdmans with Regent College Publishing, 1994

Grenz, Stanley J. and Franke, John R., *Beyond Foundationalism: Shaping Theology in a Postmodern Context*, Louisville KY: Westminster John Knox Press, 2001

Guiver, George, *Company of Voices: Daily Prayer and the People of God*, London: SPCK, 1988

Hair, Duncan D., 'From Meeting-House to Cathedral: The History of a Congregation 1795–1798–1894–1944' in *The Thomas Coats Memorial Church, Paisley: Jubilee Book, 1944*, Paisley: James Paton, 1945

Hall, Robert, *Hearing the Word*, Kettering: Circular Letter of the Northamptonshire Baptist Association, 1814

Hayden, Philip, 'Nonconformist Meeting-Houses and Chapels', unpublished address to the Canterbury Archaeological Society, 1978

Hayden, R., *Baptist Union Documents*, London: Baptist Historical Society, 1980

Hayden, Roger, *The Records of a Church of Christ in Bristol, 1640–1687*, Bristol: Bristol Record Society, 1974

Hayden, Roger, 'Evangelical Calvinism among British Baptists with particular reference to Bernard Foskett, Hugh and Caleb Evans and the Bristol Academy, 1690–1791', PhD, University of Keele, 1991

Hayden, Roger, 'Believers Baptized: An Anthology' in Paul S. Fiddes (ed.), *Reflections on the Water: Understanding God and the World through the Baptism of Believers*, Oxford and Macon GA: Regent's Park College with Smyth & Helwys, 1996

Haymes, Brian, *A Question of Identity: Reflections on Baptist Principles and Practice*, Leeds: Yorkshire Baptist Association, 1986

Haymes, Brian, 'Baptism as a Political Act' in Paul S. Fiddes (ed.), *Reflections on the Water: Understanding God and the World through the Baptism of Believers*, Oxford & Macon GA: Regent's Park College with Smyth & Helwys, 1996

Heiler, Friedrich, *Prayer: A Study in the History and Psychology of Religion*, London: Oxford University Press, 1932

Hill, Christopher, *The Century of Revolution: 1603–1741*, London: Nelson, 1961

Hill, Christopher, *A Turbulent, Seditious, and Factious People: John Bunyan and his Church*, Oxford: Oxford University Press, 1988

Houlden, J. Leslie., 'Why Were the Disciples Ever Called Disciples?', *Theology*, 105, 2002, pp. 411–17

Hymns by Anne Steele, ed. D. Sedgewick, London: Gospel Standard Baptist Trust, 1863

Irwin, Kevin, *Liturgical Theology: A Primer*, Collegeville MN: Liturgical Press, 1990

Irwin, Kevin, *Context and Text: Method in Liturgical Theology*, Collegeville MN: Liturgical Press, 1994

Ivimey, Joseph, *A History of the English Baptists*, London, 1811

Jefferson, H. A. L., *Hymns in Christian Worship*, London: Rockliff, 1950

Johnson, Maxwell E., 'Liturgy and Theology' in P. Bradshaw and B. Spinks (eds), *Liturgy in Dialogue: Essays in Memory of Ronald Jasper*, London: SPCK, 1993

Johnson, Maxwell E., 'Can We Avoid Relativism in Worship? Liturgical Norms in the Light of Contemporary Liturgical Scholarship', *Worship*, 74, 2000, pp. 135–55

Johnson, Maxwell E., 'Mystagogical Catechesis' in Paul Bradshaw (ed.), *The New SCM Dictionary of Liturgy and Worship*, London: SCM Press, 2002

Jones, Keith G., *A Believing Church: Learning from some Contemporary Anabaptist and Baptist Perspectives*, Didcot: Baptist Union of Great Britain, 1998

Jones, Keith G., *A Shared Meal and A Common Table: Some Reflections on the Lord's Supper and Baptists*, Oxford: Whitley Publications, 1999

Jones, R. Tudur, *Congregationalism in England, 1662–1962*, London: Independent Press, 1962

Julian, John, *A Dictionary of Hymnology*, London: John Murray, 1892

Kavanagh, Aidan, 'Response: Primary Theology and Liturgical Act', *Worship*, 57, 1983, pp. 321–4

Kavanagh, Aidan, *On Liturgical Theology*, Collegeville MN: Liturgical Press, 1984

Kavanagh, Aidan, 'Textuality and Deritualization: The Case for Western Usage', *Studia Liturgica*, 23, 1993, pp. 70–7

Keach, Benjamin, *The Breach Repaired in God's Worship: or singing psalms and hymns, and spiritual songs, proved to be an holy ordinance of Jesus Christ*, London, 1691/1700

Keach, Benjamin, *The Display of Glorious Grace: or the Covenant of Peace*, London, 1698

Kelleher, M. M., 'Liturgy: An Ecclesial Act of Meaning', *Worship*, 59, 1985, pp. 482–97

Kidd, Richard, *Something to Declare: A Study of the Declaration of Principle*, Oxford: Whitley Publications, 1996

Kiffin, William, *A Sober Discourse of Right to Church Communion*, London: Enoch Prosser, 1681

Kilmartin, Edward J., *Christian Liturgy: Theology and Practice*, 1: *Systematic Theology of Liturgy*, Kansas City: Sheed & Ward, 1988

Ladd, George E., *The New Testament and Criticism*, London: Hodder & Stoughton, 1967

Lathrop, Gordon W., *Holy Things: A Liturgical Theology*, Minneapolis MN: Fortress Press, 1993

Lathrop, Gordon W., 'Koinonia and the Shape of the Liturgy', *Studia Liturgica*, 26, 1996, pp. 65–81, 1996

Lathrop, Gordon W., 'New Pentecost or Joseph's Britches? Reflections on the History and Meaning of the Worship Ordo in the Megachurches', *Worship*, 72, 1998, pp. 521–38

Lathrop, Gordon W., 'The Water that Speaks: The Ordo of Baptism and its Ecumenical Implications' in Thomas F. Best and Dagmar Heller (eds), *Becoming a Christian: The Ecumenical Implications of our Common Baptism*, Geneva: World Council of Churches, 1999

Leach, John, *Liturgy and Liberty: Combining the Best of the Old with the Best of the New*, Tunbridge Wells: MARC with Monarch Publications, 1989

Lossky, Vladimir, 'Tradition and Traditions' in Leonid Ouspensky and Vladimir Lossky (eds), *The Meaning of Icons*, Crestwood NY: St. Vladimir's Seminary Press, 1952

Lumpkin, William L., *Baptist Confessions of Faith*, Valley Forge PA: Judson Press, 1969

Maclaren, Alexander, *Evangelical Mysticism*, London: Baptist Union of Great Britain and Ireland, 1901

Maclaren, Alexander, *Pulpit Prayers*, London: Hodder & Stoughton, 1907

Maclaren, Alexander, *St. Paul's Epistles to the Corinthians (To 2 Corinthians, Chapter 5)*, London: Hodder & Stoughton, 1909

Maclaren, Alexander, *Pulpit Prayers (Second Series)*, London: Hodder & Stoughton, 1911

Macquarrie, John, *In Search of Deity: An Essay in Dialectical Theism, The Gifford Lectures for 1983–4*, London: SCM Press, 1984

Manley, Kenneth R., 'Origins of the Baptists: The Case for Development from Puritanism-Separatism' in William H. Brackney and Ruby J. Burke (eds), *Faith, Life and Witness: The Papers of the Study and Research Division of the Baptist World Alliance, 1986–1990*, Birmingham AL: Samford University Press, 1990

Manning, Bernard L., *The Hymns of Wesley and Watts*, London: Epworth, 1942

Marlow, Samuel, *A brief Discourse concerning Singing in the publick worship of God in the Gospel Church*, London, 1690

Marshall, Paul V., 'Reconsidering "Liturgical Theology": Is there a Lex Orandi for all Christians?', *Studia Liturgica*, 25, 1995, pp. 129–51

Martin, Hugh, 'The Conduct of Baptist Worship', *Baptist Quarterly*, 17, 1957, pp. 148–56

Martin, Hugh, 'The Baptist Contribution to Early English Hymnody', *Baptist Quarterly*, 19, 1962, pp. 195–208

Martin, Hugh and Thompson, Ronald W. (eds), *The Baptist Hymn Book Companion*, London: Psalms and Hymns Trust, 1962

Martin, Ralph P., *The Worship of God: Some Theological, Pastoral and Practical Reflections*, Grand Rapids MI: Eerdmans, 1982

Maxwell, William D., *The Liturgical Portions of the Genevan Service Book used by John Knox while a Minister of the English Congregation of Marian Exiles at Geneva, 1556–1559*, Edinburgh and London: Oliver & Boyd, 1931

Maxwell, William D., *An Outline of Christian Worship: Its Developments and Forms*, London: Oxford University Press, 1936

McBain, Douglas, *Fire over the Waters: Renewal among Baptists and Others from the 1960s to the 1990s*, London: Darton, Longman & Todd, 1997

McBeth, H. Leon, *The Baptist Heritage*, Nashville TN: Broadman Press, 1987

McClendon, James W., Jr, *Ethics*, vol. 1 of *Systematic Theology*, Nashville TN: Abingdon Press, 1986

McClendon, James W., Jr, *Doctrine*, vol. 2 of *Systematic Theology*, Nashville TN: Abingdon Press, 1994

McClendon, James W., Jr, and Smith, James M., *Convictions: Defusing Religious Relativism*, Valley Forge PA: Trinity Press International, 1975

McDonnell, Kilian and Montague, George T., *Christian Initiation and Baptism in the Holy Spirit: Evidence from the First Eight Centuries*, Collegeville MN: Liturgical Press, 1991

McFague, Sally, *Metaphorical Theology: Models of God in Religious Language*, Philadelphia PA: Fortress Press, 1982

McGrath, Alister E., *The Intellectual Origins of the European Reformation*, Oxford: Basil Blackwell, 1987

McGrath, Alister E., *Roots that Refresh: A Celebration of Reformation Spirituality*, London: Hodder & Stoughton, 1991

McKibben, Thomas R., Jr, 'Our Baptist Heritage in Worship', *Review and Expositor*, 80, 1983, pp. 53–69

Meyer, F. B., *Free Church Service Manual*, London: National Free Church Council, 1911

Micklem, Nathaniel (ed.), *Christian Worship: Studies in its Meaning by Members of Mansfield College*, London: Oxford University Press, 1936

Miller, Patrick D., 'Enthroned on the Praises of Israel: The Praise of God in Old Testament Theology', *Interpretation*, 39, 1985, pp. 5–19

Moltmann, Jürgen, *The Church in the Power of the Spirit: A Contribution to Messianic Ecclesiology*, London: SCM Press, 1977

Moon, Norman S. (ed.), *Education for Ministry: Bristol Baptist College 1679–1979*, Bristol: Bristol Baptist College, 1979

Morgenthaler, Sally, *Worship Evangelism: Inviting Unbelievers into the Presence of God*, Grand Rapids MI: Zondervan, 1995

Northcott, Cecil, *Hymns in Christian Worship: The Use of Hymns in the Life of the Church*, ed. J. G. Davies and A. Raymond George, London and Richmond VA: Lutterworth Press and John Knox Press, 1964

Old, Hughes Oliphant, *The Reading and Preaching of the Scriptures in the Worship of the Christian Church*, vol. 1: *The Biblical Period*, Grand Rapids MI and Cambridge: William B. Eerdmans, 1998

Ouspensky, Leonide, *Theology of the Icon*, Crestwood NY: St. Vladimir's Seminary Press, 1978

Owen, John, *A Discourse on the Work of the Holy Spirit in Prayer*, ed. Thomas Russell, London: Richard Baynes, 1826

Pannenberg, Wolfhart, *Jesus – God and Man*, London: SCM Press, 1968

Patterns and Prayers for Christian Worship, Oxford University Press on behalf of the Baptist Union of Great Britain, 1991

Payne, Ernest A., 'An Elegy on Andrew Gifford', *Baptist Quarterly*, 9, 1938, pp. 54–7

Payne, Ernest A., *The Fellowship of Believers: Baptist Thought and Practice Yesterday and Today*, London: Carey Kingsgate Press, 1952

Payne, Ernest A., *The Baptist Union: A Short History*, London: Carey Kingsgate Press, 1959

Payne, Ernest A., 'Baptists and their Hymns' in H. Martin (ed.), *The Baptist Hymn Book Companion*, London: Psalms and Hymns Trust, 1962

Payne, Ernest A., *Free Churchmen, Unrepentant and Repentant and Other Papers*, London: Carey Kingsgate Press, 1965

Payne, Ernest A., 'The Baptist Church near the Barbican', *Baptist Quarterly*, 39, 2001, pp. 132–45

Payne, Ernest A. and Winward, Stephen F., *Orders and Prayers for Church Worship: A Manual for Ministers*, London: Baptist Union of Great Britain and Ireland, 1960

Peaston, A. Elliott, *The Prayer Book Tradition in the Free Churches*, London: James Clarke, 1964

Peck, Anthony A., *An Introduction to Missionary Congregations*, Leeds: Yorkshire Baptist Association, 1997

Percy, Martyn, *Words, Wonders and Power: Understanding Contemporary Christian Fundamentalism and Revivalism*, London: SPCK, 1996

Perelmuter, H. G., 'The Jewish Roots of the Christian Sermon' in Robert E. Webber (ed.), *The Complete Library of Christian Worship*, vol. 3: *The Renewal of Sunday Worship*, Peabody MA: Hendrikson, 1993

Pfatteicher, Philip H., *Liturgical Spirituality*, Valley Forge PA: Trinity Press International, 1997

Powell, Vavasor, *Common Prayer Book No Divine Service or, XXVII Reasons against Forming and Imposing Human Liturgies or Common Prayer Books*, London: Livewel Chapman, 1661

Power, David, 'Two Expressions of Faith: Worship and Theology', *Concilium*, 82, 1973, pp. 95–103

Ramsbottom, B. A., *Stranger than Fiction: The Life of William Kiffin*, Harpenden, Herts: Gospel Standard Trust Publications, 1989

Ramsey, Michael, 'The Authority of the Bible' in M. Black (ed.), *Peake's Commentary on the Bible*, London: Nelson, 1962

Read, Hubert, *The Cult of Sincerity*, London: Faber & Faber, 1968

Regan, David, *Experience the Mystery: Pastoral Possibilities for Christian Mystagogy*, London: Geoffrey Chapman, 1994

Resner, Andre, *Preacher and Cross: Person and Message in Theology and Rhetoric*, Grand Rapids MI and Cambridge: William B. Eerdmans, 1999

Richardson, Alan, *An Introduction to the Theology of the New Testament*, London: SCM Press, 1958

Rippon, John, *A Selection of Hymns from the Best Authors, intended to be an appendix to Dr. Watts's Psalms and Hymns*, London, 1787

Rippon, John, *The Baptist Annual Register*, London, 1790

Rippon, John, *A Selection of Psalm and Hymn Tunes from the best authors, in three and four parts: adapted principally to Dr. Watts's Hymns and Psalms and to Dr. Rippon's Selection of Hymns*, London, 1791

Rippon, John, *A Brief Memoir of the Life and Writings of the Reverend and Learned John Gill, D.D.*, London and Harrisonburg VA: Sprinkle Publications, 1838

Robinson, H. W., *The Christian Experience of the Holy Spirit*, London: Nisbet, 1928

Robinson, Henry Wheeler, *The Life and Faith of the Baptists*, London: Kingsgate Press, 1946

Routley, Eric, *Hymns and Human Life*, London: John Murray, 1952

Routley, Eric, *Hymns and the Faith*, London: John Murray, 1955

Routley, Eric, *Hymns Today and Tomorrow*, London: Darton, Longman & Todd, 1964

Routley, Eric, *Christian Hymns Observed*, London and Oxford: Mowbray, 1982

Ryland, John, *The Beauty of Social Religion or the Nature and Glory of a Gospel Church*, Circular Letter of the Northamptonshire Association, 1777

Saliers, Don E., *Worship as Theology: Foretaste of Divine Glory*, Nashville TN: Abingdon Press, 1994

Schillebeeckx, Edward, *Christ the Sacrament of the Encounter with God*, London: Sheed & Ward, 1963/1989

Schleiermacher, F., *The Christian Faith*, Edinburgh: T & T Clark, 1928

Schlink, Edmund, *The Coming Christ and the Coming Church*, Philadelphia PA: Fortress Press, 1968

Schmemann, Alexander, 'Theology and Liturgical Tradition' in T. Fisch (ed.), *Liturgy and Tradition: Theological Reflections of Alexander Schmemann*, Crestwood NY: St Vladimir's Seminary Press, 1963

Schmemann, Alexander, *Introduction to Liturgical Theology*, Crestwood NY: St Vladimir's Seminary Press, 1966/1996

Schmemann, Alexander, 'Liturgical Theology, Theology of Liturgy, and Liturgical Reform' in T. Fisch (ed.), *Liturgy and Tradition: Theological Reflections of Alexander Schmemann*, Crestwood NY: St Vladimir's Seminary Press, 1969

Schmemann, Alexander, 'Liturgy and Theology' in T. Fisch (ed.), *Liturgy and Tradition: Theological Reflections of Alexander Schmemann*, Crestwood NY: St Vladimir's Seminary Press, 1972

Schmemann, Alexander, 'Liturgical Theology: Remarks on Method' in T. Fisch (ed.), *Liturgy and Tradition: Theological Reflections of Alexander Schmemann*, Crestwood NY: St Vladimir's Seminary Press, 1982

Schmemann, Alexander, *The Eucharist: Sacrament of the Kingdom*, Crestwood NY: St Vladimir's Seminary Press, 1988

Schmemann, Alexander, 'Liturgy and Eschatology' in T. Fisch (ed.), *Liturgy and Tradition: Theological Reflections of Alexander Schmemann*, Crestwood NY: St Vladimir's Seminary Press, 1990

Sellars, Ian, 'Other Times, Other Ministries: John Fawcett and Alexander Maclaren', *Baptist Quarterly*, 32, 1987, pp. 181–99

Senn, Frank C., *Christian Liturgy: Catholic and Evangelical*, Minneapolis MN: Fortress Press, 1997

Senn, Frank C., *New Creation: A Liturgical Worldview*, Minneapolis MN: Fortress Press, 2000

Sheldrake, Philip, *Spirituality and History: Questions of Interpretation and Method*, London: SPCK, 1995

Sheldrake, Philip, *Spirituality and Theology: Christian Living and the Doctrine of God*, ed. S. Sykes, London: Darton, Longman & Todd, 1998

Skoglund, John, 'Free Prayer', *Studia Liturgica*, 4, 1974, pp. 151–66

Smith, Karen E., 'The Community and the Believer: A Study of Calvinistic Baptist Spirituality in some Towns and Villages of Hampshire and the Borders of Wiltshire, 1730–1830', *The Community and the Believer*, University of Oxford, 1986

Smyth, John, *The Works of John Smyth, Fellow of Christ's College, 1594–8*, ed. W. T. Whitley, Cambridge: Cambridge University Press, 1915

Smyth, John, 'The Differences of the Churches of the Seperation: containing a description of the Leitovrgie and Ministries of the visible Church' (1608) in W. T. Whitley (ed.), *The Works of John Smyth*, vol. 1, Amsterdam and Cambridge: Cambridge University Press with the Baptist Historical Society, 1915

So We Believe, So We Pray: Towards Koinonia in Worship, ed. Thomas F. Best and Dagmar Heller, Geneva: World Council of Churches, 1995

Spurgeon, Charles Haddon, *Our Own Hymn-book: A Collection of Psalms and Hymns for Public, Social and Private Worship*, Pasedena TX: Pilgrim Publications, 1866

Spurgeon, Charles Haddon, *Till He Come: Communion Meditations and Addresses*, London: Passmore & Alabaster, 1894

Spurgeon, Charles Haddon, *Lectures to my Students: A Selection of Addresses delivered to the Students of the Pastors' College, Metropolitan Tabernacle*, London: Passmore & Alabaster, 1906

Spurgeon, Charles Haddon, *Spurgeon's Prayers*, Fearn, Ross-shire: Christian Focus, 1993

Spurr, Frederic C. and Bonner, Henry, *Come Let Us Worship: A Book of Common Worship for use in Free Churches*, London: Kingsgate Press, 1930

Steed, Robert, *An Epistle written to members of a Church in London concerning Singing, as it may or ought to be used in the worship of God in the Church; wherein briefly and plainly the nature of it is described, the primitive way presented and the common and popular way examined*, London, 1691

Stennett, Joseph, *The Work of the late Reverend and Learned Mr. Joseph Stennett*, London, 1732

Stevenson, Kenneth, *Covenant of Grace Renewed: A Vision of the Eucharist in the Seventeenth Century*, London: Darton, Longman & Todd, 1994

Stringer, Martin D., *On the Perception of Worship: The Ethnography of Worship in Four Christian Congregations in Manchester*, Birmingham: University of Birmingham Press, 1999

Sutcliffe, John, *The Ordinance of the Lord's Supper Considered*, Northampton: Circular Letter from the Ministers and Messengers of the Several Baptist Churches of the Northamptonshire Association, 1803

Sykes, Stephen, *The Identity of Christianity: Theologians and the Essence of Christianity from Schleiermacher to Barth*, London: SPCK, 1984

Taft, Robert, 'The Structural Analysis of Liturgical Units: An Essay in Methodology' in *Beyond East and West: Problems in Liturgical Understanding*, Washington DC: Pastoral Press, 1984

Taft, Robert, *The Liturgy of the Hours in East and West: The Origins of the Divine Office and its Meaning for Today*, Collegeville MN: Liturgical Press, 1986

Taylor, Michael H., *Variations on a Theme: Some Guidelines for Everyday Christians who Want to Reform the Liturgy*, London: Galliard; Stainer & Bell, 1973

Taylor, Vincent, *The Names of Jesus*, London: Macmillan, 1953

'The Baptist Doctrine of the Church: A Statement Approved by the Council of the Baptist Union of Great Britain and Ireland, March 1948' in R. Hayden (ed.), *Baptist Union Documents 1948–1977*, London: Baptist Historical Society, 1980

'The Berlin Worship Declaration' in T. Cupit (ed.), *Baptists in Worship: Report of an International Baptist Conference in Berlin, Germany*, McClean VA: Baptist World Alliance, 1998

The Nature of the Assembly and the Council of the Baptist Union of Great Britain, Didcot: Baptist Union of Great Britain, 1994

Tibbutt, H. Gordon (ed.), *The Minutes of the First Independent Church (now Bunyan Meeting) at Bedford, Bedford Minutes*, Bedford: Bedfordshire Historical Record Society, 1976

Tillich, Paul, *Systematic Theology*, Chicago: University of Chicago Press, 1953

Tolmie, Murray, *The Triumph of the Saints: The Separate Churches of London 1616–1649*, Cambridge: Cambridge University Press, 1977

Trilling, Lionel, *Sincerity and Authenticity*, London: Oxford University Press, 1972

Trinterud, Leonard J., 'The Origins of Puritanism', *Church History*, 21, 1952

Ulanov, Ann and Ulanov, Barry, *Primary Speech: A Psychology of Prayer*, London: SCM Press, 1985

Wainwright, Geoffrey, *Doxology: The Praise of God in Worship, Doctrine and Life*, London: Epworth, 1980

Wakefield, Gordon S., *An Outline of Christian Worship*, Edinburgh: T & T Clark, 1998

Walker, Michael J., *Baptists at the Table*, Didcot: Baptist Historical Society, 1992

Wallace, Jamie, *What Happens in Worship*, London: Baptist Union of Great Britain and Ireland, 1982

Wallin, Benjamin, *Gospel Requisites to Acceptable Prayer*, London, 1770

Walton, Robert C., *The Gathered Community*, London: Carey Press, 1946

Ware, Kallistos, *The Orthodox Church*, Harmondsworth: Penguin Books, 1963/1969

Watkins, Owen C., *The Puritan Experience*, London: Routledge & Kegan Paul, 1972

Watson, J. Richard, *The English Hymn: A Critical and Historical study*, Oxford: Clarendon Press, 1997

Watts, Isaac, *Hymns and Spiritual Songs in Three Books: I Collected from the Scriptures. II Compos'd on Divine Subjects. III Prepar'd for the Lord's Supper*, ed. Selma L. Bishop, London: Faith Press, 1709

Watts, Isaac, 'A Guide to Prayer; or a Free and Rational Account of the Grace and Spirit of Prayer with Plain Directions how Every Christian may Attain Them' in J. Doddridge (ed.), *The Works of the Reverend and Learned Isaac Watts, D.D.*, London: J. Barfield, 1715

Watts, Isaac, *The Psalms of David, imitated in the Language of the New Testament, And apply'd to the Christian State and Worship*, London, 1719

Watts, Michael, *The Dissenters: From the Reformation to the French Revolution*, Oxford: Clarendon Press, 1978

We Baptists, Franklin TN: Baptist World Alliance, 1999

Wesley, John (ed.), *A Collection of Hymns for the Use of the People called Methodists*, London: J. Mason, 1780

West, W. Morris S., *Baptist Principles*, London: Baptist Union of Great Britain and Ireland, 1967

Westermann, Claus, *Praise and Lament in the Psalms*, Atlanta GA: John Knox Press, 1981

Wheeler Robinson, Henry, *The Life and Faith of the Baptists*, London: Kingsgate Press, 1946

Whitby, F. F., *Our Worship in the Light of our Principles*, Annual Report of the Western Baptist Association, 1903

White, Barrington R., *Association Records of the Particular Baptists of England, Wales and Ireland to 1660*, London: Baptist Historical Society, 1971

White, Barrington R., *The English Separatist Tradition: From the Marian Martyrs to the Pilgrim Fathers*, London: Oxford University Press, 1971

White, Barrington R., *The English Baptists of the Seventeenth Century*, Didcot: Baptist Historical Society, 1983/1996

White, James F., *Introduction to Christian Worship*, Nashville TN: Abingdon, 1980

White, James F., *Protestant Worship: Traditions in Transition*, Louisville KY: Westminster John Knox Press, 1989

White, James F., *A Brief History of Christian Worship*, Nashville TN: Abingdon, 1993

White, James F., 'How Do We Know it is Us?' in E. Byron Anderson and Bruce T. Morrill (eds), *Liturgy and the Moral Self: Humanity at Full Stretch Before God, Essays in Honour of Don E. Saliers*, Collegeville MN: Liturgical Press, 1998

White, R. E. O., *The Biblical Doctrine of Initiation*, London: Hodder & Stoughton, 1960

White, Susan J., *Groundwork of Christian Worship*, London: Epworth, 1997

White, Susan J., *The Spirit of Worship: The Liturgical Tradition*, ed. P. Sheldrake, London: Darton, Longman & Todd, 1999

Whitley, W. T. (ed.), *Minutes of the General Assembly of the General Baptist Churches in England, with Kindred Records*, London: Kingsgate Press with the Baptist Historical Society, 1910

Whitley, William T., 'Paul's Alley, Barbican, 1695–1768', *Transactions of the Baptist Historical Society*, 4, 1914, pp. 46–54

Whitley, William T., *A History of British Baptists*, London: Kingsgate Press, 1923

Whitley, William T., *The Baptists of London 1612–1928: Their Fellowship, their Expansion, with notes on their 850 churches*, London: Kingsgate Press, 1928

Whitley, William T., *Congregational Hymn-Singing*, London: J. M. Dent & Sons, 1933

Williams, George H., *The Radical Reformation*, London: Weidenfeld & Nicolson, 1962

Wilson, Len and Moore, Jason, *Digital Storytellers: The Art of Communicating the Gospel in Worship*, Nashville TN: Abingdon, 2002

Wilson, Paul S., *The Practice of Preaching*, Nashville TN: Abingdon, 1995

Winter, E. P., 'The Administration of the Lord's Supper among the Baptists of the Seventeenth Century', *Baptist Quarterly*, 18, 1952, pp. 196–204

Winter, E. P., 'Calvinist and Zwinglian Views of the Lord's Supper among the Baptists of the Seventeenth Century', *Baptist Quarterly*, 15, 2003, pp. 323–9

Winward, Stephen F., 'How to Make the Best Use of the Hymn Book' in H. Martin and Ron W. Thomson (eds), *The Baptist Hymn Book Companion*, London: Psalms & Hymns Trust, 1962

Winward, Stephen F., *The Reformation of our Worship*, London: Carey Kingsgate Press, 1964

Worley, Robert C., *Teaching and Preaching in the Early Church*, Peabody MA: Hendrikson, 1993

Wren, Brian, *Praying Twice: The Music and Words of Congregational Song*, Louisville KY: Westminster John Knox Press, 2000

Acknowledgements

The author acknowledges permission to quote from the following works.

Introduction to Liturgical Theology, Alexander Schmemann, Crestwood NY: St Vladimir's Seminary Press, 1966/1996.

Liturgy and Tradition: Theological Reflections of Alexander Schmemann, edited by Thomas Fisch, Crestwood NY: St Vladimir's Seminary Press, 1990.

The Doctrine of the Law and Grace Unfolded: The miscellaneous works of John Bunyan Series, Vol. 2, John Bunyan, edited by Richard L. Greaves, 1976. Extracts from pages 235–7, 248, 252 and 257. Reprinted by permission of Oxford University Press.

Baptist Confessions of Faith, William L. Lumpkin, Valley Forge PA: Judson Press, 1959. Extracts from pages 119f., 137f., 153–5, 167, 209, 211–13, 280, 295 and 326. Reprinted by permission of the publisher, 1-800-4-JUDSON.

Unless stated otherwise, all scriptural quotations are from the *New Revised Standard Version*, copyright 1989 by The Division of Christian Education of the National Council of the Churches of Christ in the USA. Used by permission. All rights reserved.

Index of Names and Subjects

Index of Biblical References